ALSO BY ROBERT D. KAPLAN

Monsoon: The Indian Ocean and the
Future of American Power

Hog Pilots, Blue Water Grunts: The American Military
in the Air, at Sea, and on the Ground

Imperial Grunts: The American Military on the Ground

Mediterranean Winter: The Pleasures of History and Landscape
in Tunisia, Sicily, Dalmatia, and the Peloponnese

Warrior Politics: Why Leadership Demands a Pagan Ethos

Eastward to Tartary: Travels in the Balkans,
the Middle East, and the Caucasus

The Coming Anarchy: Shattering the Dreams
of the Post Cold War

An Empire Wilderness: Travels into America's Future

The Ends of the Earth: From Togo to Turkmenistan,
from Iran to Cambodia

The Arabists: The Romance of an American Elite

Balkan Ghosts: A Journey Through History

Soldiers of God: With Islamic Warriors
in Afghanistan and Pakistan

Surrender or Starve: Travels in Ethiopia,
Sudan, Somalia, and Eritrea

THE REVENGE OF GEOGRAPHY

THE REVENGE OF GEOGRAPHY

WHAT THE MAP TELLS US ABOUT COMING CONFLICTS

AND THE BATTLE AGAINST FATE

Robert D. Kaplan

RANDOM HOUSE

NEW YORK

Copyright © 2012 by Robert D. Kaplan
Maps copyright © 2012 by David Lindroth, Inc.

Published in the United States by Random House,
an imprint of The Random House Publishing Group,
a division of Random House, Inc., New York.

RANDOM HOUSE and colophon are registered
trademarks of Random House, Inc.

The preface contains material from four earlier titles by Robert D. Kaplan:
Soldiers of God (New York: Houghton Mifflin Harcourt Publishing Company,
1990), *An Empire Wilderness* (New York: Random House, Inc., 1998),
Eastward to Tartary (New York: Random House, Inc., 2000), and
Hog Pilots, Blue Water Grunts (New York: Random House, Inc., 2007).

LIBRARY OF CONGRESS CATALOGING-IN-PUBLICATION DATA
Kaplan, Robert D.
The revenge of geography : what the map tells us about coming conflicts
and the battle against fate / by Robert D. Kaplan.
p. cm.
Includes bibliographical references and index.
ISBN 978-1-4000-6983-5
eBook ISBN 978-0-679-60483-9
1. Political geography. I. Title.
JC319.K335   2012
320.1'2—dc23   2012000655

Printed in the United States of America on acid-free paper

www.atrandom.com

2 4 6 8 9 7 5 3 1

FIRST EDITION

Book design by Dana Leigh Blanchette
Title-spread image: © iStockphoto

TO THE MEMORY OF

HARVEY SICHERMAN

1945–2010

PRESIDENT,

FOREIGN POLICY RESEARCH INSTITUTE,

PHILADELPHIA

But precisely because I expect little of the human condition, man's periods of felicity, his partial progress, his efforts to begin over again and to continue, all seem to me like so many prodigies which nearly compensate for the monstrous mass of ills and defeats, of indifference and error. Catastrophe and ruin will come; disorder will triumph, but order will too, from time to time.

—Marguerite Yourcenar
Memoirs of Hadrian (1951)

Contents

Part II

THE EARLY-TWENTY-FIRST-CENTURY MAP

Part III

AMERICA'S DESTINY

Preface

FRONTIERS

A good place to understand the present, and to ask questions about the future, is on the ground, traveling as slowly as possible.

As the first rank of domed hills appeared on the horizon, rippling upward from the desert floor in northern Iraq, to culminate in ten-thousand-foot massifs clothed in oak and mountain ash, my Kurdish driver glanced back at the vast piecrust plain, sucked his tongue in contempt, and said, "Arabistan." Then, looking toward the hills, he murmured, "Kurdistan," and his face lit up. It was 1986, the pinnacle of Saddam Hussein's suffocating reign, and yet as soon as we penetrated further into prisonlike valleys and forbidding chasms, the ubiquitous billboard pictures of Saddam suddenly vanished. So did Iraqi soldiers. Replacing them were Kurdish peshmergas with bandoliers, wearing turbans, baggy trousers, and cummerbunds. According to the political map, we had never left Iraq. But the mountains had declared a limit to Saddam's rule—a limit overcome by the most extreme of measures.

In the late 1980s, enraged at the freedom that these mountains had over the decades and centuries ultimately granted the Kurds, Saddam launched a full-scale assault on Iraqi Kurdistan—the infamous Al-Anfal campaign—that killed an estimated 100,000 civilians. The mountains were clearly not determinative. But they did serve as the backdrop—the original fact—to this tragic drama. It is because of the mountains that Kurdistan has to a significant extent now effectively seceded from the Iraqi state.

Mountains are a conservative force, often protecting within their defiles indigenous cultures against the fierce modernizing ideologies that have too often plagued the flatlands, even as they have provided refuge for Marxist guerrillas and drug cartels in our own era.[1] The Yale anthropologist James C. Scott writes that "hill peoples are best understood as runaway, fugitive, maroon communities who have, over the course of two millennia, been fleeing the oppressions of state-making projects in the valleys."[2] For it was on the plain where the Stalinist regime of Nicolae Ceaușescu really sank its teeth into the population. Ascending the Carpathians several times in the 1980s, I saw few signs of collectivization. These mountains that declare Central Europe's rear door were defined more by wood and natural stone dwellings than by concrete and scrap iron, favorite material elements of Romanian communism.

The Carpathians that girdle Romania are no less a border than the mountains of Kurdistan. Entering the Carpathians from the west, from the threadbare and majestically vacant Hungarian Puszta, marked by coal-black soil and oceans of lemon-green grass, I began to leave the European world of the former Austro-Hungarian Empire and to gradually make my way into the economically more deprived terrain of the former Ottoman Turkish Empire. Ceaușescu's oriental despotism, so much more oppressive than Hungary's haphazard goulash communism, was, ultimately, made possible by the ramparts of the Carpathians.

And yet the Carpathians were not impenetrable. For centuries traders had thrived in their many passes, the bearers of goods and high culture so that a poignant semblance of Central Europe could take root well beyond them, in cities and towns like Bucharest and Ruse. But the mountains did constitute an undeniable gradation, the first in a series in an easterly direction, that would conclude finally in the Arabian and Kara Kum deserts.

In 1999, I took a freighter overnight from the Azerbaijani capital of Baku, on the western shore of the Caspian Sea, to Krasnovodsk in Turkmenistan, on the eastern shore, the beginning of what the Sassanid Persians in the third century A.D. called Turkestan. I awoke to a spare, abstract shoreline: whitish hutments against cliffs the clay color of death. All the passengers were ordered to line up in single file in the 100-degree temperature before a peeling gate where a lone policeman checked our passports. We then passed into a bare, broiling shed, where another policeman, finding my Pepto-Bismol tablets, accused me of smuggling narcotics. He took my flashlight and emptied the 1.5-volt batteries onto the dirt floor. His expression was as bleak and untamed as the landscape. The town that beckoned beyond the shed was shadeless and depressingly horizontal, with little architectural hint of a material culture. I suddenly felt nostalgia for Baku, with its twelfth-century Persian walls and dream palaces built by the first oil barons, embellished with friezes and gargoyles, a veneer of the West that despite the Carpathians, the Black Sea, and the high Caucasus, refused to completely die out. Traveling eastward, Europe had evaporated in stages before my eyes, and the natural border of the Caspian Sea had indicated the last stage, heralding the Kara Kum Desert.

Of course, geography does not demonstrate Turkmenistan's hopelessness. Rather, it signifies only the beginning of wisdom in the search for a historical pattern: one of repeated invasions by Parthians,

Mongols, Persians, czarist Russians, Soviets, and a plethora of Turkic tribes against a naked and unprotected landscape. There was the barest existence of a civilization because none was allowed to permanently sink deep roots, and this helps explain my first impressions of the place.

The earth heaved upward, and what had moments before seemed like a unitary sandstone mass disintegrated into a labyrinth of scooped-out riverbeds and folds reflecting gray and khaki hues. Topping each hill was a slash of red or ocher as the sun caught a higher, steeper slope at a different angle. Lifts of cooler air penetrated the bus—my first fresh taste of the mountains after the gauzy heat film of Peshawar in Pakistan's North-West Frontier Province.[3] By themselves, the dimensions of the Khyber Pass are not impressive. The highest peak is under seven thousand feet and the rise is rarely steep. Nevertheless, in under an hour in 1987, I was transported through a confined, volcanic netherworld of crags and winding canyons; from the lush, tropical floor of the Indian Subcontinent to the cool, tonsured wastes of middle Asia; from a world of black soil, bold fabrics, and rich, spicy cuisine to one of sand, coarse wool, and goat meat.

But like the Carpathians, whose passes were penetrated by traders, geography on the Afghanistan-Pakistan border has different lessons to offer: for what the British were the first to call the "North-West Frontier" was "historically no frontier at all," according to Harvard professor Sugata Bose, "but the 'heart'" of an "Indo-Persian" and "Indo-Islamic" continuum, the reason why Afghanistan and Pakistan form an organic whole, contributing to their geographical incoherence as separate states.[4]

Then there were borders more artificial still:

I crossed the Berlin Wall into East Berlin twice, in 1973 and in 1981. The twelve-foot-high concrete curtain, topped by a broad pipe, cut through a filmy black-and-white landscape of poor Turkish and

Yugoslav immigrant neighborhoods on the West German side, and deserted and World War II–scarred buildings on the East German one. You could walk up and touch the Wall almost anywhere on the western side, where the graffiti was; the minefields and guard towers all lay to the east.

As surreal as this prison yard of an urban terrain appeared at the time, one didn't question it except in moral terms, for the paramount assumption of the age was that the Cold War had no end. Particularly for those like myself, who had grown up during the Cold War but had no memory whatsoever of World War II, the Wall, however brutal and arbitrary, seemed as permanent as a mountain range. The truth only emerged from books and historical maps of Germany that I had, entirely by coincidence, begun to consult during the first months of 1989, while in Bonn on a magazine assignment. The books and maps told a story:

Occupying the heart of Europe between the North and Baltic seas and the Alps, the Germans, according to the historian Golo Mann, have always been a dynamic force locked up in a "big prison," wanting to break out. But with the north and south blocked by water and mountains, outward meant east and west, where there was no geographical impediment. "What has characterized the German nature for a hundred years is its lack of form, its unreliability," writes Mann, referring to the turbulent period from the 1860s to the 1960s, marked by Otto von Bismarck's expansion and the two world wars.[5] But the same could also be said for Germany's size and shape on the map throughout its history.

Indeed, the First Reich, founded by Charlemagne in 800, was a great shifting blob of territory that, at one time or another, encompassed Austria and parts of Switzerland, France, Belgium, the Netherlands, Poland, Italy, and Yugoslavia. Europe seemed destined to be ruled from what now corresponds with Germany. But then came Martin Luther, who split Western Christianity with the Reformation, which, in turn, ignited the Thirty Years' War, fought primarily on German soil. Hence, Central Europe was ravished. The more I read— about the eighteenth-century dualism between Prussia and Habsburg

Austria, about the early-nineteenth-century tariff union between the various German states, and Bismarck's late-nineteenth-century Prussian-based unification—the more it became apparent that the Berlin Wall was just another stage in this continuing process of territorial transformation.

The regimes that had fallen soon after the Berlin Wall did—in Czechoslovakia, Hungary, Romania, Bulgaria, and elsewhere—were ones I had known intimately through work and travel. Up close they had seemed so impregnable, so fear-inducing. Their abrupt unraveling was a signal lesson for me, not only about the underlying instability of all dictatorships, but about how the present, as permanent and overwhelming as it can seem, is fleeting. The only thing enduring is a people's position on the map. Thus, in times of upheaval maps rise in importance. With the political ground shifting rapidly under one's feet, the map, though not determinitive, is the beginning of discerning a historical logic about what might come next.

Violence was the reigning impression of the demilitarized zone (DMZ) between the two Koreas. In 2006, I saw South Korean soldiers standing frozen in tae kwon do–ready positions, their fists and forearms clenched, staring into the faces of their North Korean counterparts. Each side picked its tallest, most intimidating soldiers for the task. But the formalized hatred on display in the midst of barbed wire and minefields will probably be consigned to history on some foreseeable morrow. When you look at other divided-country scenarios in the twentieth century—Germany, Vietnam, Yemen—it is apparent that however long the division persisted, the forces of unity ultimately triumph, in an unplanned, sometimes violent and fast-moving fashion. The DMZ, like the Berlin Wall, is an arbitrary border of no geographical logic that divides an ethnic nation at the spot where two opposing armies happened to come to rest. Just as Germany was reunited, we might expect, or at least should plan for, a united Greater

Korea. Again, the forces of culture and geography are likely to prevail at some point. A man-made border that does not match a natural frontier zone is particularly vulnerable.

I crossed, too, the land borders from Jordan to Israel and from Mexico to the United States: more on those borders and others later. For I now wish to take another journey—of a radically different sort—through selected pages of history and political science that have survived across the chasm of the decades and, in some cases, the centuries, and on account of their emphasis on geography allow us to read the relief map better, and with that, help us glimpse, however vaguely, the contours of future politics. For it was the very act of crossing so many frontiers that made me intensely curious about the fate of the places through which I had passed.

My reporting over three decades has convinced me that we all need to recover a sensibility about time and space that has been lost in the jet and information ages, when elite molders of public opinion dash across oceans and continents in hours, something which allows them to talk glibly about what the distinguished *New York Times* columnist Thomas L. Friedman has labeled a *flat world*. Instead, I will introduce readers to a group of decidedly unfashionable thinkers, who push up hard against the notion that *geography no longer matters*. I will lay out their thinking in some depth in the first half of this journey in order to apply their wisdom in the second half, as to what has happened and is likely to happen across Eurasia—from Europe to China, including the Greater Middle East and the Indian Subcontinent. To find out what it is exactly that has been lost in our view of physical reality, to discover how we lost it, and then to restore it by slowing down our pace of travel and of observation itself—by way of the rich erudition of now deceased scholars: that is the goal of this journey.

Geography, from a Greek word that means essentially a "description of the earth," has often been associated with fatalism and therefore stigmatized: for to think geographically is to limit human choice, it is said. But in engaging with such tools as relief maps and population studies I merely want to add another layer of complexity to conventional foreign policy analyses, and thus find a deeper and more powerful way to look at the world. You do not have to be a geographical determinist to realize that geography is vitally important. The more we remain preoccupied with current events, the more that individuals and their choices matter; but the more we look out over the span of the centuries, the more that geography plays a role.

The Middle East is a case in point.

As I write, the region from Morocco to Afghanistan is in the midst of a crisis of central authority. The old order of autocracies has become untenable, even as the path toward stable democratization is tortuous. The first phase of this great upheaval has featured the defeat of geography through the power of new communications technologies. Satellite television and social networking Internet sites have created a single community of protesters throughout the Arab world: so that democracy advocates in such disparate places as Egypt and Yemen and Bahrain are inspired by what has begun in Tunisia. Thus, there exists a commonality in the political situations of all these countries. But as the revolt has gone on, it has become clear that each country has developed its own narrative, which, in turn, is influenced by its own deep history and geography. The more one knows about the history and geography of any particular Middle Eastern country, therefore, the less surprised one will be about events there.

For it may be only partly accidental that the upheaval started in Tunisia. A map of classical antiquity shows a concentration of settlements where Tunisia is today, juxtaposed with the relative emptiness that characterizes modern-day Algeria and Libya. Jutting out into the Mediterranean close to Sicily, Tunisia was the demographic hub of North Africa not only under the Carthaginians and Romans, but under the Vandals, Byzantines, medieval Arabs, and Turks. Whereas Algeria to the west and Libya to the east were but vague geographical expressions, Tunisia is an age-old cluster of civilization. (As for Libya, its western region of Tripolitania was throughout history oriented toward Tunisia, while its eastern region of Cyrenaica—Benghazi—was always oriented toward Egypt.)

For two thousand years, the closer to Carthage (roughly the site of modern-day Tunis) the greater the level of development. Because urbanization in Tunisia started two millennia ago, tribal identity based on nomadism—which the medieval historian Ibn Khaldun said disrupted political stability—is correspondingly weak. Indeed, after the Roman general Scipio defeated Hannibal in 202 B.C. outside Tunis, he dug a demarcation ditch, or *fossa regia*, that marked the extent of civilized territory. The *fossa regia* remains relevant to the current Middle East crisis. Still visible in places, it runs from Tabarka on Tunisia's northwestern coast southward, and turns directly eastward to Sfax, another Mediterranean port. The towns beyond that line have fewer Roman remains, and today tend to be poorer and less developed, with historically higher rates of unemployment. The town of Sidi Bouzid, where the Arab revolt started in December 2010, when a vendor of fruit and vegetables set himself on fire as an act of protest, lies just beyond Scipio's line.

This is not fatalism. I am merely providing geographical and historical context to current events: the Arab revolt for democracy began in what in historical terms was the most advanced society in the Arab world—the one physically closest to Europe—yet it also began specifically in a part of that country which since antiquity had been ignored and suffered consequent underdevelopment.

Such knowledge can add depth to what has been transpiring elsewhere: whether it be in Egypt, another age-old cluster of civilization with a long history as a state just like Tunisia; or Yemen, the demographic core of the Arabian Peninsula, whose attempts at unity have been bedeviled by a sprawling and mountainous topography that has worked to weaken central government and consequently raise the importance of tribal structures and separatist groups; or Syria, whose truncated shape on the map harbors divisions within it based on ethnicity and sectarian identity. Geography testifies that Tunisia and Egypt are naturally cohesive; Libya, Yemen, and Syria less so. It

follows, therefore, that Tunisia and Egypt required relatively moderate forms of autocracy to hold them together, while Libya and Syria
required more extreme varieties. Meanwhile, geography has always
made Yemen hard to govern at all. Yemen has been what the twentieth-
century European scholars Ernest Gellner and Robert Montagne call
a "segmentary" society, the upshot of a Middle Eastern landscape
riven by mountains and desert. Hovering between centralization and
anarchy, such a society in Montagne's words is typified by a regime
that "drains the life from a region," even though "because of its own
fragility," it fails to establish lasting institutions. Here tribes are
strong and the central government comparatively weak.[6] The struggle
to construct liberal orders in such places cannot be divorced from
such realities.

As political upheavals accumulate and the world becomes seemingly
more unmanageable, with incessant questions as to how the United
States and its allies should respond, geography offers a way to make
at least some sense of it all. By engaging with old maps, and with
geographers and geopolitical thinkers from earlier eras, I want to
ground-truth the globe in the twenty-first century much as I did at
these frontiers beginning in the late twentieth. For even if we can send
satellites into the outer solar system—and even as financial markets
and cyberspace know no boundaries—the Hindu Kush still constitutes a formidable barrier.

Part I

VISIONARIES

Chapter I

FROM BOSNIA TO BAGHDAD

To recover our sense of geography, we first must fix the moment in recent history when we most profoundly lost it, explain why we lost it, and elucidate how that affected our assumptions about the world. Of course, such a loss is gradual. But the moment I have isolated, when that loss seemed most acute, was immediately after the collapse of the Berlin Wall. Though an artificial border whose crumbling should have enhanced our respect for geography and the relief map—and what that map might have foreshadowed in the adjacent Balkans and the Middle East—the Berlin Wall's erasure made us blind to the real geographical impediments that still divided us, and still awaited us.

For suddenly we were in a world in which the dismantling of a man-made boundary in Germany had led to the assumption that all human divisions were surmountable; that democracy would conquer Africa and the Middle East as easily as it had Eastern Europe; that globalization—soon to become a buzzword—was nothing less than a moral direction of history and a system of international security, rather than what it actually was, merely an economic and cultural stage of development. Consider: a totalitarian ideology had just been vanquished, even as domestic security in the United States and Western Europe was being taken for granted. The semblance of peace reigned generally. Presciently capturing the zeitgeist, a former deputy director of the U.S. State Department's Policy Planning Staff, Francis Fukuyama, published an article a few months before the fall of the Berlin Wall, "The End of History," proclaiming that while wars and rebellions would continue, history in a Hegelian sense was over now, since the success of capitalist liberal democracies had ended the argument over which system of government was best for humankind.[1] Thus, it was just a matter of shaping the world more in our own image, sometimes through the deployment of American troops; deployments that in the 1990s would exact relatively little penalty. This, the first intellectual cycle of the Post Cold War, was an era of illusions. It was a time when the words "realist" and "pragmatist" were considered pejoratives, signifying an aversion to humanitarian intervention in places where the national interest, as conventionally and narrowly defined, seemed elusive. Better in those days to be a neoconservative or liberal internationalist, who were thought of as good, smart people who simply wanted to stop genocide in the Balkans.

Such a burst of idealism in the United States was not unprecedented. Victory in World War I had unfurled the banner of "Wilsonianism," a notion associated with President Woodrow Wilson that, as it would turn out, took little account of the real goals of America's European allies and even less account of the realities of the Balkans and the Near East, where, as events in the 1920s would show, democracy and freedom from the imperial overlordship of the Ottoman Turks meant mainly heightened ethnic awareness of a narrow sort in the individual parts of the old sultanate. It was a similar phenomenon that followed the West's victory in the Cold War, which many believed would simply bring freedom and prosperity under the banners of "democracy" and "free markets." Many suggested that even Africa, the poorest and least stable continent, further burdened with the world's most artificial and illogical borders, might also be on the brink of a democratic revolution; as if the collapse of the Soviet Empire in the heart of Europe held supreme meaning for the world's least developed nations, separated by sea and desert thousands of miles away, but connected by television.[2] Yet, just as after World War I and World War II, our victory in the Cold War would usher in less democracy and global peace than the next struggle for survival, in which evil would wear new masks.

Democracy and better government would, in fact, begin to emerge in Africa of all places. But it would be a long and difficult struggle, with anarchy (in the cases of several West African countries), insurrection, and outright wickedness (in the case of Rwanda) rearing their heads for considerable periods in between. Africa would go a long way toward defining the long decade between November 9, 1989, and September 11, 2001—between the collapse of the Berlin Wall and the al Qaeda attacks on the Pentagon and World Trade Center: a twelve-year period that saw mass murder and belated humanitarian interventions frustrate idealist intellectuals, even as the ultimate success of those interventions raised idealist triumphalism to heights that were to prove catastrophic in the decade that began after 9/11.

In that new decade following 9/11, geography, a factor certainly in the Balkans and Africa in the 1990s, would go on to wreak unmitigated havoc on America's good intentions in the Near East. The journey from Bosnia to Baghdad, from a limited air and land campaign in the western, most developed part of the former Turkish Empire in the Balkans to a mass infantry invasion in the eastern, least developed part in Mesopotamia, would expose the limits of liberal universalism, and in the process concede new respect to the relief map.

The Post Cold War actually began in the 1980s, before the collapse of the Berlin Wall, with the revival of the term "Central Europe," later defined by the journalist and Oxford scholar Timothy Garton Ash as "a political-cultural distinction against the Soviet 'East.' "[3] Central Europe, *Mitteleuropa,* was more of an idea than a fact of geography. It constituted a declaration of memory: that of an intense, deliciously cluttered, and romantic European civilization, suggestive of cobblestone streets and gabled roofs, of rich wine, Viennese cafés, and classical music, of a gentle, humanist tradition infused with edgy and disturbing modernist art and thought. It conjured up the Austro-Hungarian Empire and such names as Gustav Mahler, Gustav Klimt, and Sigmund Freud, leavened with a deep appreciation of the likes of Immanuel Kant and the Dutch-Jewish philosopher Baruch Spinoza. Indeed, "Central Europe," among so many other things, meant the endangered intellectual world of Jewry before the ravages of Nazism and communism; it meant economic development, with a sturdy recall of Bohemia, prior to World War II, as having enjoyed a higher level of industrialization than Belgium. It meant, with all of its decadence and moral imperfections, a zone of relative multiethnic tolerance under the umbrella of a benign if increasingly dysfunctional Habsburg Empire. In the last phase of the Cold War, Central Europe was succinctly captured by Princeton professor Carl E. Schorske in his troubling, icy-eyed classic *Fin-de-Siècle Vienna: Politics and Culture,* and by the Italian writer Claudio Magris in his sumptuous travelogue *Danube.* For Magris, *Mitteleuropa* is a sensibility that "means the defence of the particular against any totalitarian programme." For the Hungarian writer György Konrád and the Czech writer Milan Kundera, *Mitteleuropa* is something "noble," a "master-key" for liberalizing political aspirations.[4]

To speak of "Central Europe" in the 1980s and 1990s was to say that a culture in and of itself comprised a geography every bit as much as a mountain range did, or every bit as much as Soviet tanks did. For the idea of Central Europe was a rebuke to the geography of the Cold War, which had thrown up the term "Eastern Europe" to denote the half of Europe that was communist and controlled from Moscow. East Germany, Czechoslovakia, Poland, and Hungary had all been part of Central Europe, it was rightly argued, and therefore should not have been consigned to the prison of nations that was communism and the Warsaw Pact. A few years later, ironically, when ethnic war broke out in Yugoslavia, "Central Europe," rather than a term of unification, would also become one of division; with "the Balkans" dismembered in people's minds from Central Europe, and becoming, in effect, part of the new/old Near East.

The Balkans were synonymous with the old Turkish and Byzantine empires, with unruly mountain ranges that had hindered development, and with a generally lower standard of living going back decades and centuries compared to the lands of the former Habsburg and Prussian empires in the heart of Europe. During the monochrome decades of communist domination, Balkan countries such as Romania and Bulgaria did, in fact, suffer a degree of poverty and repression unknown to the northern, "Central European" half of the Soviet Empire. The situation was complicated, of course. East Germany was the most truly occupied of the satellite states, and consequently its communist system was among the most rigid, even as Yugoslavia—not formally a member of the Warsaw Pact—allowed a degree of freedom, particularly in its cities, that was unknown in Czechoslovakia, for example. And yet, overall, the nations of former Turkish and Byzantine southeastern Europe suffered in their communist regimes nothing less than a version of oriental despotism, as though a second Mongol invasion, whereas those nations of former Catholic Habsburg Europe mainly suffered something less malignant: a dreary mix in varying degrees of radical socialist populism. In this regard traveling from relatively liberal, albeit communist, Hungary under János Kádár to Romania under the totalitarianism of Nicolae Ceauşescu was typical in this regard. I made the trip often in the 1980s: as my train passed into Romania from Hungary, the quality of the building materials suddenly worsened; officials ravaged my luggage and made me pay a bribe for my typewriter; the toilet paper in the lavatory disappeared and lights went dim. True, the Balkans were deeply influenced by Central Europe, but they were just as influenced by the equally proximate Middle East. The dusty steppe with its bleak public spaces—imports both from Anatolia—were a feature of life in Kosovo and Macedonia, where the cultured conviviality of Prague and Budapest was harder to find. Thus, it was not altogether an accident, or completely the work of evil individuals, that violence broke out in the ethnic mélange of Yugoslavia rather than, say, in the uniethnic Central European states of Hungary and Poland. History and geography also had something to do with it.

Yet by holding up Central Europe as a moral and political cynosure, rather than as a geographical one, liberal intellectuals like Garton Ash—one of the most eloquent voices of the decade—propounded a vision not only of Europe, but of the world that was inclusive rather than discriminatory. In this view, not only should the Balkans not be consigned to underdevelopment and barbarism, but neither should any place: Africa, for example. The fall of the Berlin Wall should affect not only Germany, but, rather, should unleash the dream of Central Europe writ large across the globe. This humanist approach was the essence of a cosmopolitanism that liberal internationalists and neoconservatives both subscribed to in the 1990s. Recall that before he became known for his support of the Iraq War, Paul Wolfowitz was a proponent of military intervention in Bosnia and Kosovo, in effect, joining hands with liberals like Garton Ash at the left-leaning *New York Review of Books*. The road to Baghdad had roots in the Balkan interventions of the 1990s, which were opposed by realists and pragmatists, even as these military deployments in the former Yugoslavia were to prove undeniably successful.

The yearning to save the Muslims of Bosnia and Kosovo cannot be divorced from the yearning for the restoration of Central Europe, both as a real and poignantly imagined place, that would demonstrate how, ultimately, it is morality and humanism that sanctify beauty. (Though Garton Ash himself was skeptical of the effort to idealize Central Europe, he did see the positive moral use to which such an idealization might be applied.)

The humanist writings of Isaiah Berlin captured the intellectual spirit of the 1990s. " '*Ich bin ein Berliner,*' I used to say, meaning an Isaiah Berliner," Garton Ash wrote in a haunting memoir of his time in East Germany.[5] Now that communism had been routed and Marxist utopias exposed as false, Isaiah Berlin was the perfect antidote to the trendy monistic theories that had ravished academic life for the previous four decades. Berlin, who taught at Oxford and whose life was coeval with the twentieth century, had always defended bourgeois pragmatism and "temporizing compromises" over political experimentation.[6] He loathed geographical, cultural, and all other forms of determinism, refusing to consign anyone and anybody to their fate. His views, articulated in articles and lectures over a lifetime, often as a lone academic voice in the wilderness, comprised the perfect synthesis of a measured idealism that was employed both against communism and the notion that freedom and security were only for some peoples and not for others. His philosophy and the ideal of Central Europe were perfect fits.

But though Central Europe writ large, as expounded by these wise and eloquent intellectuals, was indeed a noble cause, one which should perennially play a role in the foreign policies of all Western nations as I will demonstrate, it does face a hurdle with which I am also forced to deal.

For there remains a problem with this exalted vision, an ugly fact that throughout history has often turned the concept of Central Europe into something tragic. Central Europe simply has no reality on the relief map. (Garton Ash intuited this with the title of his own article, "Does Central Europe Exist?")[7] Enter the geographical determinists, so harsh and lowering compared to the gentle voice of Isaiah Berlin: particularly the Edwardian era voice of Sir Halford J. Mackinder and his disciple James Fairgrieve, for whom the idea of Central Europe has a "fatal geographical flaw." Central Europe, Mackinder and Fairgrieve tell us, belongs to the "crush zone" that lays athwart Maritime Europe, with its "oceanic interests," and the "Eurasian Heartland with its continental outlook." In short, strategically speaking, there is "no space" for Central Europe in the view of Mackinder and Fairgrieve.[8] The celebration of Central Europe, the justifiable indulgence of it by the liberal intellectuals, the writings of Mackinder and Fairgrieve suggest, indicates a respite from geopolitics—or at least the desire for one. Yet the fall of the Berlin Wall did not—could not—end geopolitics, but merely brought it into a new phase. You cannot simply wish away the struggle of states and empires across the map.

I will explore Mackinder's work, particularly his "Heartland" thesis, later at great length. Suffice it to say now that, expounded well over a hundred years ago, it proved remarkably relevant to the dynamics of World War I, World War II, and the Cold War. Stripped down to their most austere logic, the two world wars were about whether or not Germany would dominate the Heartland of Eurasia that lay to its east, while the Cold War centered on the Soviet Union's domination of Eastern Europe—the western edge of Mackinder's Heartland. This Soviet Eastern Europe, by the way, included in its domain East Germany, historic Prussia that is, which had traditionally been territorially motivated with an eastward, Heartland orientation; while inside NATO's oceanic alliance was West Germany, historically Catholic, and industrially and commercially minded, oriented toward the North Sea and the Atlantic. A renowned American geographer of the Cold War period, Saul B. Cohen, argues that "the boundary zone that divides the East from West Germany . . . is one of the oldest in history," the one which separated Frankish and Slavonic tribes in the Middle Ages. In other words, there was little artificial about the frontier between West and East Germany. West Germany, according to Cohen, was a "remarkable reflection of Maritime Europe," whereas East Germany belonged to the "Continental Land-power Realm." Cohen supported a divided Germany as "geopolitically sound and strategically necessary," because it stabilized the perennial battle between Maritime and Heartland Europe.[9] Mackinder, too, wrote presciently in 1919 that "the line through Germany . . . is the very line which we have on other grounds taken as demarking the Heartland in a strategical sense from the Coastland."[10] So while the division of Berlin itself was artificial, the division of Germany was less so.

Cohen called Central Europe a "mere geographical expression that lacks geopolitical substance."[11] The reunification of Germany, according to this logic, rather than lead to the rebirth of Central Europe, would simply lead to a renewed battle for Europe and, by inference, for the Heartland of Eurasia: Which way, in other words, would Germany swing, to the east and toward Russia, with great consequences for Poland, Hungary, and the other former satellite countries; or to the west and toward the United Kingdom and the United States, providing a victory for the Maritime realm? We still do not know the answer to this because the Post Cold War is still in its early stages. Cohen and others could not have foreseen accurately the "debellicized" nature of today's united Germany, with its "aversion to military solutions" existing at a deep cultural level, something which in the future may help stabilize or destabilize the continent, depending upon the circumstances.[12] Precisely because they have occupied the center of Europe as a land power, Germans have always demonstrated a keen awareness of geography and strategy as a survival mechanism. This is something which Germans may yet recover, allowing them to move beyond the quasi-pacifism of the moment. Indeed, might a reunited and liberal Germany become a balancing power in its own right—between the Atlantic Ocean and the Eurasian Heartland—permitting a new and daring interpretation of Central European culture to take root, and thus providing the concept of Central Europe with geopolitical ballast? That would give those like Garton Ash credence over Mackinder and Cohen.

In sum, will Central Europe, as an ideal of tolerance and high civilization, survive the onslaught of new great power struggles? For such struggles in the heart of Europe there will be. The vibrant culture of late-nineteenth-century Central Europe that looked so inviting from the vantage point of the late twentieth century was itself the upshot of an unsentimental and specific imperial and geopolitical reality, namely Habsburg Austria. Liberalism ultimately rests on power: a benign power, perhaps, but power nevertheless.

But humanitarian interventionists in the 1990s were not blind to power struggles; nor in their eyes did Central Europe constitute a utopian vision. Rather, the restoration of Central Europe through the stoppage of mass killing in the Balkans was a quiet and erudite rallying cry for the proper employment of Western military force, in order to safeguard the meaning of victory in the Cold War. After all, what was the Cold War ultimately about, except to make the world safe for individual freedom? "For liberal internationalists Bosnia has become the Spanish Civil War of our era," wrote Michael Ignatieff, the intellectual historian and biographer of Isaiah Berlin, referring to the passion with which intellectuals like himself approached the Balkans.[13]

The call for human agency—and the defeat of determinism—was urgent in their minds. One recalls the passage from Joyce's *Ulysses,* when Leopold Bloom laments the "generic conditions imposed by natural" law: the "decimating epidemics," the "catastrophic cataclysms," and "seismic upheavals." To which Stephen Dedalus responds by simply, poignantly affirming "his significance as a conscious rational animal."[14] Yes, atrocities happen, it is the way of the world. But it doesn't have to be accepted thus. Because man is rational, he ultimately has the ability to struggle against suffering and injustice.

And so, with Central Europe as the lodestar, the road led southeastward, first to Bosnia, then to Kosovo, and onward to Baghdad. Of course, many of the intellectuals who supported intervention in Bosnia would oppose it in Iraq—or at least be skeptical of it; but neoconservatives and others would not be deterred. For as we shall see, the Balkans showed us a vision of interventionism, delayed though it was, that cost little in soldiers' lives, leaving many with the illusion that painless victory was now the future of war. The 1990s, with their belated interventions were, as Garton Ash wrote searingly, reminiscent of W. H. Auden's "low, dishonest decade" of the 1930s.[15] True, but in another sense they were much too easy.

At the time, in the 1990s, it did seem that history and geography had indeed reared their implacable heads. Less than two years after the fall of the Berlin Wall, with all of the ahistorical and universalist stirrings that had followed that event, the world media suddenly found themselves immersed in the smoky ruins, mountains of rubble, and twisted metal of towns with difficult to pronounce names, in frontier regions of the old Austrian and Turkish empires, namely Slavonia and Krajina, which had just witnessed atrocities not experienced in Europe since the Nazis. From airy contemplations of global unity, the conversation among elites now turned to unraveling complex local histories only a few hours' drive across the Pannonian Plain from Vienna, very much inside Central Europe. The relief map showed southern and eastern Croatia, close to the Sava River, as the southern terminus of the broad European flatland, which here heralded, beyond the Sava's banks, the tangle of mountain ranges collectively known as the Balkans: the relief map, which shows a vast and flat green splash from France all the way to Russia (from the Pyrenees to the Urals), abruptly, on the southern bank of the Sava, turns to yellow and then to brown, signifying higher, more rugged terrain that will continue thus southeastward into Asia Minor. This region, near to where the mountains begin, was the overlapping, back-and-forth marchlands of the Habsburg Austrian and Ottoman Turkish armies: here Western Christianity ends and the world of Eastern Orthodoxy and Islam begins; here Croatia jams up against Serbia.

The Krajina, which means "frontier" in Serbo-Croatian, was a military zone that the Austrians in the late sixteenth century established against Turkish expansion, luring to their side of the frontier both Croats and Serbs as refugees from the despotism of the Ottoman Sultanate. Consequently, this became a mixed-ethnic region that, once the imperial embrace of Austria vanished following World War I, experienced the further evolution of uniethnic identities. Though Serbs and Croats were united in the interwar years under the Kingdom of the Serbs, Croats, and Slovenes, they were divided and at each other's throats during the Nazi occupation, when a fascist Croatian puppet state of the Nazis murdered tens of thousands of Serbs in death camps. United once more under the carapace of Tito's authoritarian communist rule, Yugoslavia's collapse in 1991 saw Serb troops storm just over the Serbian border into Slavonia and Krajina, ethnically cleansing the region of Croats. Later, when the Croats retook the region, the ethnic Serbs here would take flight back to Serbia. From Croatia's borderlands with Serbia, the war would next spread to Bosnia, where hundreds of thousands would perish in grisly fashion.

There was history and geography aplenty here, but committed journalists and intellectuals would have relatively little of it. And they certainly had a point, much more than a point. First came the sheer horror and revulsion. Again, there was Garton Ash:

What have we learned from this terrible decade in former Yugoslavia? . . . We have learned that human nature has not changed. That Europe at the end of the twentieth century is quite as capable of barbarism as it was in the Holocaust of mid-century. . . . Our Western political mantras at the end of the twentieth century have been "integration," "multicultural-ism," or, if we are a little more old-fashioned, "the melting pot." Former Yugoslavia has been the opposite. It has been like a giant version of the machine called a "separator": a sort of spinning tub which separates out cream and butter. . . . Here it is peoples who were separated out as the giant tub spun furi-ously round . . . while blood dripped steadily from a filter at the bottom.[16]

Following from this revulsion came charges of "appeasement" by the West, appeasement of Slobodan Milosevic: an evil communist politician who, in order for himself and his party to survive politically following the collapse of the Berlin Wall, and retain their villas and and hunting lodges and other perks of office, rebranded himself as a rabid Serbian nationalist, igniting a second Holocaust of sorts. The appeasement of Hitler at Munich in 1938 quickly became the reign-ing analogy of the 1990s.

In fact, the fear of another Munich was not altogether new. It had been an underlying element in the decision to liberate Kuwait from Saddam Hussein's aggression in 1991. If we didn't stop Saddam in Kuwait, he would have next invaded Saudi Arabia, thereby control-ling the world's oil supply and taking human rights in the region to an unutterable level of darkness. But it was the Serb onslaught on Croatia and then Bosnia, between 1991 and 1993—and the West's failure to respond—that really made Munich a charged word in the international vocabulary.

The Munich analogy tends to flourish after a lengthy and prosperous peace, when the burdens of war are far enough removed to appear abstract: the case in the 1990s, by which time America's memories of a dirty land war in Asia, then more than two decades old, had sufficiently dimmed. Munich is about universalism, about taking care of the world and the lives of others. It would be heard often in reaction to the failure to stop genocide in Rwanda in 1994. But Munich reached a fever pitch in the buildup to NATO's tardy yet effective military interventions in Bosnia in 1995 and in Kosovo in 1999. Those opposed to our Balkan interventions tried to raise the competing Vietnam analogy, but because quagmire never resulted, it was in the Balkans in the 1990s where the phantoms of Vietnam were once and for all exorcised—or so it was thought and written at the time.[17]

Military force, so hated during the Vietnam years, now became synonymous with humanitarianism itself. "A war against genocide must be fought with a fury, because a fury is what it is fighting," wrote Leon Wieseltier, literary editor of *The New Republic*. "For the purpose of stopping genocide, the use of force is not a last resort: it is a first resort." Wieseltier went on to rail against the need for exit strategies in humanitarian interventions:

In 1996, Anthony Lake, his [President Bill Clinton's] tortured and timid national security adviser, went so far as to codify an "exit strategy doctrine": "Before we send our troops into a foreign country, we should know how and when we're going to get them out." Lake was making omniscience into a condition of the use of American force. The doctrine of "exit strategy" fundamentally misunderstands the nature of war and, more generally, the nature of historical action. In the name of caution, it denies the contingency of human affairs. For the knowledge of the end is not given to us at the beginning.[18]

As an example, Wieseltier cited Rwanda, where a million Tutsis perished in a holocaust in 1994: a Western military quagmire, had we intervened to stop the killing, he wrote, would surely have been preferable to what happened. Wieseltier, who, like Garton Ash, was one of the most formidable and morally persuasive voices of the decade, was writing in regards to the frustration he felt over the limited and belated NATO air war to liberate Muslim Albanians in Kosovo from Milosevic's policies of expulsion and extermination. The air war targeted Serbian towns and cities, where what was required, according to humanitarian interventionists, was to liberate Kosovar towns with ground troops. Clinton's hesitant way of waging war was complicit in large-scale suffering. "The work of idealism," Wieseltier wrote, "has been reduced to relief and rescue, to the aftermath of catastrophe. Where we should have rushed bullets we are now rushing blankets." Clinton, he said, had discovered a kind of warfare "in which Americans do not die, a . . . cowardly war with precision technology that leaves polls and consciences unperturbed." He predicted that "this age of immunity will not last forever. Sooner or later the United States will have to send its soldiers to . . . a place where they will suffer injury or death. What will matter is whether the cause is just, not whether the cause is dangerous."[19]

Indeed, an invasion of Iraq began to emerge as a cause in the 1990s, when the U.S. military was seen as invincible against the forces of history and geography, if only it would be unleashed in time, and to its full extent, which meant boots on the ground. It was idealists who loudly and passionately urged military force in Somalia, Haiti, Rwanda, Bosnia, and Kosovo, even as realists like Brent Scowcroft and Henry Kissinger, increasingly pilloried as heartless, urged restraint.

Yet, in fact, the 1990s was less a decade of military power overall than it was specifically a decade of air power. Air power had been crucial to ousting Iraqi forces from Kuwait in 1991: though geography, in this case, made high-tech war easy, as operations were conducted over a featureless desert where it rarely rained. Air power was also a factor in ending the war in Bosnia four years later, and with all

its demonstrated limitations, carried the day against Milosevic in
Kosovo four years after that. The ethnic Albanian refugees ultimately
returned to their homes, even as Milosevic was weakened to the extent that he fell from power the following year in 2000. *We Don't Do
Mountains,* went the phrase summarizing the U.S. Army's initial resistance to sending troops to Bosnia and Kosovo. But it turned out
that as long as we owned the air, the Army *did mountains* rather well.
Geography had reared its head all right in the Balkans, but air power
quickly overcame it. Then there were the Air Force and Navy fighter
jets patrolling the Iraqi no-fly zones, keeping Saddam in his box
throughout the decade and beyond. Consequently, segments of the
elite, awestruck at the American military's might, became infused
with a sense of moral indignation against the George H. W. Bush and
Clinton administrations for not using the military in time to save a
quarter of a million people from genocide in the Balkans (not to mention the million in Rwanda). It was a mind-set that at least for some
could lead to adventurism, which it did. That, in turn, would lead in
the next decade to the partial undoing of the Munich analogy, and
restore to geography some of the respect that it had lost in the 1990s.
The 1990s saw the map reduced to two dimensions because of air
power. But soon after the three-dimensional map would be restored:
in the mountains of Afghanistan and in the treacherous alleyways of
Iraq.

In 1999, articulating a sentiment increasingly common among liberal
intellectuals, Wieseltier wrote:

> The really remarkable thing about Clinton's refusal to include
> the removal of this villain [Slobodan Milosevic] among his war
> aims is that he himself inherited the consequences of his prede-
> cessor's refusal to include the removal of another villain among
> his war aims. In 1991, half a million American soldiers were a
> few hundred kilometers away from Saddam Hussein, and
> George Bush did not order them to Baghdad. His generals

feared casualties, and they had just concluded a zero-defects war of their own. They, too, adverted to the "territorial integrity" of Iraq, as if the misery that would result from the collapse of the state would be commensurate with the misery that had already resulted, to the Kurds in the north and to the Shia in the south, from the survival of the state.[20]

It was as if the imaginary borders of Central Europe were limitless, extending unto Mesopotamia. Things would turn out differently, of course. But in 2006, during the worst of Iraq's sectarian carnage, following the collapse of the state, which may have rivaled the violence that Saddam had inflicted on the country, Wieseltier had the grace to confess an "anxiety about arrogance." He admitted to having nothing useful to say despite his support of the war. He would not be among those supporters of the invasion who were toiling strenuously in print to vindicate themselves.[21]

I, too, supported the Iraq War, in print and as part of a group that urged the Bush administration to invade.[22] I had been impressed by the power of the American military in the Balkans, and given that Saddam had murdered directly or indirectly more people than had Milosevic, and was a strategic menace believed to possess weapons of mass destruction, it seemed to me at the time that intervention was warranted. I was also a journalist who had gotten too close to my story: reporting from Iraq in the 1980s, observing how much more oppressive Saddam's Iraq was than Hafez al-Assad's Syria, I became intent on Saddam's removal. It would later be alleged that a concern for Israel and a championing of its territorial aggrandizement had motivated many of those in support of the war.[23] But my experience in dealing with neoconservatives and some liberals, too, during this time period was that Bosnia and Kosovo mattered more than Israel did in their thinking.[24] The Balkan interventions, because they paid strategic dividends, appeared to justify the idealistic approach to foreign policy. The 1995 intervention in Bosnia changed the debate from "Should NATO Exist?" to "Should NATO Expand?" The 1999 war in Kosovo, as much as 9/11, allowed for the eventual expansion of NATO to the Black Sea.

For quite a few idealists, Iraq was a continuation of the passions of the 1990s. It represented, however subconsciously, either the defeat of geography or the utter disregard of it, dazzled as so many were with the power of the American military. The 1990s was a time when West African countries such as Liberia and Sierra Leone, despite their violence, and despite being institutionally far less developed than Iraq, were considered credible candidates for democracy. But it was the power of the military, and in particular that of the Air Force, which was the hidden hand that allowed universalist ideas to matter so much more than terrain and the historical experience of people living on it.

Munich, too, was at work in approaching the dilemma of Saddam Hussein after 9/11. Though the United States had just suffered an attack on its soil comparable to Pearl Harbor, the country's experience with ground war had been, for a quarter-century, minimal, or at least not unpleasant. Moreover, Saddam was not just another dictator, but a tyrant straight out of Mesopotamian antiquity, comparable in many eyes to Hitler or Stalin, who harbored, so it was believed, weapons of mass destruction. In light of 9/11—in light of Munich—history would never forgive us if we did not take action.

When Munich led to overreach, the upshot was that other analogy, thought earlier to have been vanquished: Vietnam. Thus began the next intellectual cycle of the Post Cold War.

In this next cycle, which roughly corresponded with the first decade of the twenty-first century and the difficult wars in Iraq and Afghanistan, the terms "realist" and "pragmatist" became marks of respect, signifying those who were skeptical from the start of America's adventure in Mesopotamia, while "neoconservative" became a mark of derision. Whereas in the 1990s, ethnic and sectarian differences in far-off corners of the world were seen as obstacles that good men should strive to overcome—or risk being branded as "fatalists" or "determinists"—in the following decade such hatreds were seen as factors that might have warned us away from military action; or should have. If one had to pick a moment when it became undeniable that the Vietnam analogy had superseded the one of Munich, it was February 22, 2006, when the Shiite al-Askariyah Mosque at Samarra was blown up by Sunni al Qaeda extremists, unleashing a fury of inter-communal atrocities in Iraq, which the American military was unable to stop. Suddenly, our land forces were seen to be powerless amid the forces of primordial hatreds and chaos. The myth of the omnipotent new United States military, born in Panama and the First Gulf War, battered a bit in Somalia, then repaired and burnished in Haiti, Bosnia, and Kosovo, was for a time shattered, along with the idealism that went with it.

While Munich is about universalism, about taking care of the world and the lives of distant others, Vietnam is domestic in spirit. It is about taking care of one's own, following the 58,000 dead from that war. Vietnam counsels that tragedy is avoided by thinking tragically. It decries incessant fervor, for it suggests how wrong things can go. Indeed, it was an idealistic sense of mission that had embroiled the United States in that conflict in Southeast Asia in the first place. The nation had been at peace, at the apex of its post–World War II prosperity, even as the Vietnamese communists—as ruthless and determined a group of people as the twentieth century produced—had murdered more than ten thousand of their own citizens before the arrival of the first regular American troops. What war could be more just? Geography, distance, our own horrendous experience in the jungles of the Philippines in another irregular war six decades previously at the turn of the twentieth century were the last things in people's minds when we entered Vietnam.

Vietnam is an analogy that thrives following national trauma. For realism is not exciting. It is respected only after the seeming lack of it has made a situation demonstrably worse. Indeed, just look at Iraq, with almost five thousand American dead (and with over thirty thousand seriously wounded) and perhaps hundreds of thousands of

Iraqis killed, at a cost of over a trillion dollars. Even were Iraq to evolve into a semi-stable democracy and an implicit ally of the United States, the cost has been so excessive that, as others have noted, it is candidly difficult to see the ethical value in the achievement. Iraq undermined a key element in the mind-set of some: that the projection of American power always had a moral result. But others understood that the untamed use of power by any state, even a freedom-loving democratic one like America, was not necessarily virtuous.

Concomitant with a new respect for realism came renewed interest in the seventeenth-century philosopher Thomas Hobbes, who extols the moral benefits of fear and sees violent anarchy as the chief threat to society. For Hobbes, fear of violent death is the cornerstone of enlightened self-interest. By establishing a state, men replace the fear of violent death—an all-encompassing, mutual fear—with the fear that only those who break the law need face. Such concepts are difficult to grasp for the urban middle class, who have long since lost any contact with man's natural condition.[25] But the horrific violence of a disintegrating Iraq, which, unlike Rwanda and Bosnia in some respects, was not the result of a singularly organized death machine, but of the very breakdown of order, allowed many of us to imagine man's original state. Hobbes thus became the philosopher of this second cycle of the Post Cold War, just as Berlin had been of the first.[26]

And so this is where the Post Cold War has brought us: to the recognition that the very totalitarianism that we fought against in the decades following World War II might, in quite a few circumstances, be preferable to a situation where nobody is in charge. There are things worse than communism, it turned out, and in Iraq we brought them about ourselves. I say this as someone who supported regime change.

In March 2004, I found myself in Camp Udari in the midst of the Kuwait desert. I had embedded with a Marine battalion that, along with the rest of the 1st Marine Division, was about to begin the overland journey to Baghdad and western Iraq, replacing the Army's 82nd

Airborne Division there. It was a world of tents, pallets, shipping containers, and chow halls. Vast lines of seven-ton trucks and Humvees stretched across the horizon, all headed north. The epic scale of America's involvement in Iraq quickly became apparent. A sandstorm had erupted. There was an icy wind. Rain threatened. Vehicles broke down. And we hadn't even begun the several-hundred-kilometer journey to Baghdad that a few short years before, those who thought of toppling Saddam Hussein as merely an extension of toppling Slobodan Milosevic, had dismissed as easily done. Vast gravel mazes that smelled of oil and gasoline heralded the first contractor-built truck stop, one of several constructed along the way to service the many hundreds of vehicles headed north, and to feed the thousands of Marines. Engines and generators whined in the dark. It took days of the most complex logistics—storing and transporting everything from mineral water bottles to Meals Ready to Eat to tool kits—to cross the hostile desert till we arrived in Fallujah west of Baghdad. *A mere several hundred kilometers.*[27] And this was the easy, nonviolent part of an American military occupation across the whole country. It was surely wrong to suggest that physical terrain no longer mattered.

Chapter II

THE REVENGE OF GEOGRAPHY

The debacle of the early years in Iraq has reinforced the realist dictum, disparaged by idealists in the 1990s, that the legacies of geography, history, and culture really do set limits on what can be accomplished in any given place. Yet those who were opposed to Iraq should be careful about taking the Vietnam analogy too far. For that analogy can be an invitation to isolationism, just as it is to appeasement and, in the words of the Middle East scholar Fouad Ajami, to the easy prejudice of low expectations. Remember that the Munich conference occurred only twenty years after the mass death of World War I, making realist politicians like Neville Chamberlain understandably hell-bent on avoiding another conflict. Such situations are perfectly suited for the machinations of a tyrannical state that knows no such fears: Nazi Germany and Imperial Japan.

Vietnam is about limits; Munich about overcoming them. Each analogy on its own can be dangerous. It is only when both are given equal measure that the right policy has the best chance to emerge. For wise policymakers, while aware of their nation's limitations, know that the art of statesmanship is about working as close to the edge as possible, without stepping over the brink.[1]

In other words, true realism is an art more than a science, in which the temperament of a statesman plays as much of a role as his intellect. While the roots of realism hark back 2,400 years to Thucydides' illusion-free insights about human behavior in *The Peloponnesian War,* modern realism was perhaps most comprehensively summed up in 1948 by Hans J. Morgenthau in *Politics Among Nations: The Struggle for Power and Peace.* Let me pause awhile with this book, the effort of a German refugee who taught at the University of Chicago, in order to set the stage for my larger discussion about geography: for realism is crucial to a proper appreciation of the map, and in fact leads us directly to it.

Morgenthau begins his argument by noting that the world "is the result of forces inherent in human nature." And, human nature, as Thucydides pointed out, is motivated by fear (*phobos*), self-interest (*kerdos*), and honor (*doxa*). "To improve the world," writes Morgenthau, "one must work with these forces, not against them." Thus, realism accepts the human material at hand, however imperfect that material may be. "It appeals to historical precedent rather than to abstract principles and aims at the realization of the lesser evil rather than of the absolute good." For example, a realist would look to Iraq's own history, explained through its cartography and constellations of ethnic groups, rather than to moral precepts of Western democracy, to see what kind of future Iraq would be immediately capable of following the toppling of a totalitarian regime. After all, good intentions have little to do with positive outcomes, according to Morgenthau. Chamberlain, he explains, was less motivated by considerations of personal power than most other British politicians, and genuinely sought to assure peace and happiness to all concerned. But his policies brought untold sufferings to millions. Winston Churchill, on the other hand, was, in fact, motivated by naked considerations of personal and national power, but his policies resulted in an unrivaled moral effect. (Paul Wolfowitz, the former American deputy secretary of defense, was motivated by the best of intentions in arguing for an invasion of Iraq, believing it would immeasurably improve the human rights situation there, but his actions led to the opposite of what he intended.) Enlarging on this point, simply because a nation is a democracy does not mean that its foreign policy will necessarily turn out to be better or more enlightened than that of a dictatorship. For "the need to marshal popular emotions," says Morgenthau, "cannot fail to impair the rationality of foreign policy itself." Democracy and morality are simply not synonymous. "All nations are tempted—and few have been willing to resist the temptation for long—to clothe their own particular aspirations and actions in the moral purposes of the universe. To know that nations are subject to the moral law," he goes on, "is one thing, while to pretend to know with certainty what is good and evil in the relations among nations is quite another."

Furthermore, states must operate in a much more constrained moral universe than do individuals. "The individual," Morgenthau writes, "may say to himself . . . 'Let justice be done, even if the world perish,' but the state has no right to say so in the name of those who are in its care."[2] An individual has responsibility only for his loved ones, who will forgive him his mistakes so long as he means well. But a state must protect the well-being of millions of strangers within its borders, who in the event of a failed policy will not be so understanding. Thus, the state must be far wilier than the individual.

Human nature—the Thucydidean pantheon of fear, self-interest, and honor—makes for a world of incessant conflict and coercion. Because realists like Morgenthau expect conflict and realize it cannot be avoided, they are less likely than idealists to overreact to it. They understand that the tendency to dominate is a natural element of all human interaction, especially the interactions of states. Morgenthau quotes John Randolph of Roanoke as saying that "power alone can limit power." Consequently, realists don't believe that international institutions by themselves are crucial to peace, because such institutions are merely a reflection of the balance of power of individual member states, which, in the final analysis, determines issues of peace and war. And yet the balance of power system is itself by definition unstable, according to Morgenthau: since every nation, because it worries about miscalculating the balance of power, must seek to compensate for its perceived errors by aiming constantly at a superiority of power. This is exactly what initiated World War I, when Habsburg Austria, Wilhelmine Germany, and czarist Russia all sought to adjust the balance of power in their favor, and gravely miscalculated. Morgenthau writes that it is, ultimately, only the existence of a universal moral conscience— which sees war as a "natural catastrophe" and not as a natural extension of one's foreign policy—that limits war's occurrence.[3]

Following the violence in Iraq from 2003 to 2007 we all claimed for a time to have become realists, or so we told ourselves. But given how Morgenthau defines realism, is that really true? For example, do most of those who opposed the Iraq War on realist grounds also feel that there is not necessarily a connection between democracy and morality? And Morgenthau, remember, who opposed the Vietnam War on grounds of both ethics and national interest, is the realist with whom we can all feel most comfortable. An academic and intellectual his whole life, he never had the thirst for power and position that other realists such as Kissinger and Scowcroft have demonstrated. Moreover, his restrained, almost flat writing style lacks the edginess of a Kissinger or a Samuel Huntington. The fact is, and there's no denying it, realism, even the Morgenthau variety, is supposed to make one uneasy. Realists understand that international relations are ruled by a sadder, more limited reality than that governing domestic affairs. For while our domestic polity is defined by laws, because a legitimate government monopolizes the use of force, the world as a whole is still in a state of nature, in which there is no Hobbesian Leviathan to punish the unjust.[4] Indeed, just beneath the veneer of civilization lie the bleakest forces of human passion, and thus the central question in foreign affairs for realists is: *Who can do what to whom?*[5]

"Realism is alien to the American tradition," Ashley J. Tellis, a senior associate at the Carnegie Endowment in Washington, once told me. "It is consciously amoral, focused as it is on interests rather than on values in a debased world. But realism never dies, because it accurately reflects how states actually behave, behind the facade of their values-based rhetoric."

Realists value order above freedom: for them the latter becomes important only after the former has been established. In Iraq, order, even of totalitarian dimensions, turned out to be more humane than the lack of order that followed. And because world government will forever remain elusive, since there will never be fundamental agreement on the ways of social betterment, the world is fated to be ruled by different kinds of regimes and in some places by tribal and ethnic orders. Realists from the ancient Greeks and Chinese right up through the mid-twentieth-century French philosopher Raymond Aron and his Spanish contemporary José Ortega y Gasset believed war is naturally inherent in the division of humanity into states and other groupings.[6] Indeed, sovereignty and alliances rarely occur in a void; they arise out of differences with others. Whereas devotees of globalization stress what unifies humankind, traditional realists stress what divides us.

And so we come to the map, which is the spatial representation of humanity's divisions—the subject of realist writings in the first place. Maps don't always tell the truth. They are often as subjective as any fragment of prose. European names for large swaths of Africa show, in the words of the late British geographer John Brian Harley, how cartography can be a "discourse of power," in this case of latent imperialism. Mercator projections tend to show Europe larger than it really is. The very bold colorings of countries on the map implies uniform control over hinterlands, which isn't always the case.[7] Maps are materialistic, and therefore morally neutral. They are historically much more a part of a Prussian education than of a British one.[8] Maps, in other words, can be dangerous tools. And yet they are crucial to any understanding of world politics. "On the relatively stable foundation of geography the pyramid of national power arises," writes Morgenthau.[9] For at root, realism is about the recognition of the most blunt, uncomfortable, and deterministic of truths: those of geography.

Geography is the backdrop to human history itself. In spite of cartographic distortions, it can be as revealing about a government's long-range intentions as its secret councils.[10] A state's position on the map is the first thing that defines it, more than its governing philosophy even. A map, explains Halford Mackinder, conveys "at one glance a whole series of generalizations." Geography, he goes on, bridges the gap between arts and sciences, connecting the study of history and culture with environmental factors, which specialists in the humanities sometimes neglect.[11] While studying the map, any map, can be endlessly absorbing and fascinating in its own right, geography, like realism itself, is hard to accept. For maps are a rebuke to the very notions of the equality and unity of humankind, since they remind us of all the different environments of the earth that make men profoundly unequal and disunited in so many ways, leading to conflict, on which realism almost exclusively dwells.

In the eighteenth and nineteenth centuries, before the arrival of political science as an academic specialty, geography was an honored, if not always formalized, discipline in which politics, culture, and economics were often conceived of in reference to the relief map. According to this materialistic logic, mountains and tribes matter more than the world of theoretical ideas. Or, rather, mountains and the men who grow out of them are the first order of reality; ideas, however uplifting and fortifying, only the second.

It is my contention that in embracing realism in the midst of the Iraq War, however uneasily we did so—and for however short a time we did so—what we actually embraced without being aware of it was geography, if not in the overt, imperialistic Prussian sense of the word, then in the less harsh Victorian and Edwardian senses. It is the revenge of geography that marked the culmination of the second cycle in the Post Cold War era, to follow the defeat of geography through air power and the triumph of humanitarian interventionism that marked the end of the first cycle. We were thus brought back to the lowering basics of human existence, where, rather than the steady improvement of the world that we had earlier envisioned, what we accepted was the next struggle for survival, and by association, the severe restraints with which geography burdened us in places such as Mesopotamia and Afghanistan.

And yet within this sad acceptance there is hope: for by becoming more expert at reading the map, we can, helped by technology as the Arab Spring has attested, stretch some of the limits the map inflicts. That is the aim of my study—to have an appreciation of the map so that, counterintuitively, we need not always be bounded by it. For it is not only narrow-mindedness that leads to isolationism, but the overstretching of resources that causes an isolationist backlash.

But first we need to recognize the very centrality of the geographical discipline. "Nature imposes; man disposes," writes the English geographer W. Gordon East. Certainly, man's actions are limited by the physical parameters imposed by geography.[12] But these contours are extremely broad, so that human agency has more than enough room to maneuver. For the Arabs, it turns out, are as capable of democratic practices as any group, even as the spatial arrangement of Libyan tribes and of the mountain ranges in Yemen will continue to play crucial roles in those countries' political development. Geography informs, rather than determines. Geography, therefore, is not synonymous with fatalism. But it is, like the distribution of economic and military power themselves, a major constraint on—and instigator of—the actions of states.

Yale professor Nicholas J. Spykman, the great Dutch American strategist of the early–World War II era, wrote in 1942 that "geography does not argue. It simply is." He goes on:

Geography is the most fundamental factor in the foreign policy of states because it is the most permanent. Ministers come and go, even dictators die, but mountain ranges stand unperturbed. George Washington, defending thirteen states with a ragged army, has been succeeded by Franklin D. Roosevelt with the resources of a continent at his command, but the Atlantic continues to separate Europe from the United States and the ports of the St. Lawrence River are still blocked by winter ice. Alexander I, Czar of all the Russias, bequeathed to Joseph Stalin, simple member of the Communist party, not only his power but his endless struggle for access to the sea, and Maginot and Clemenceau have inherited from Caesar and Louis XIV anxiety over the open German frontier.[13]

And one might add, that despite 9/11 even, the Atlantic Ocean still matters, and, in fact, it is the Atlantic that declares a different foreign and military policy for the United States compared to that of Europe. In the same vein, we can say that Russia, unto this day, is an insecure and sprawling land power, the victim of invasions since before those of the Mongol hordes in the thirteenth century, with only time, distance, and weather as its friends, craving more access to the sea. And because there is no serious geographical impediment between Europe and the Urals, Eastern Europe, despite the collapse of the artificial boundary of the Berlin Wall, is still under threat from Russia, as it has been for centuries. It is also true that anxiety over the German frontier plagued France—like in the time of Louis XIV—through the end of World War II, when the United States finally guaranteed the peace of Europe.

Indeed, geography is the preface to the very track of human events. It is no accident that European civilization had important origins in Crete and the Cycladic islands of Greece, for the former, a "detached fragment of Europe," is the closest European point to the civilization of Egypt, and the latter the closest point to that of Asia Minor.[14] Both, because of their island situations, were for centuries protected against the ravages of invaders, allowing them to flourish. Geography constitutes the very facts about international affairs that are so basic we take them for granted.

What could be a more central fact of European history than that Germany is a continental power and Great Britain an island? Germany faces both east and west with no mountain ranges to protect it, providing it with pathologies from militarism to nascent pacifism, so as to cope with its dangerous location. Britain, on the other hand, secure in its borders, with an oceanic orientation, could develop a democratic system ahead of its neighbors, and forge a special trans-atlantic relationship with the United States, with which it shares a common language. Alexander Hamilton wrote that had Britain not been an island, its military establishment would have been just as overbearing as those of continental Europe, and Britain "would in all probability" have become "a victim to the absolute power of a single man."[15] And yet Britain is an island close to continental Europe, and thus in danger of invasion through most of its history, giving it a particular strategic concern over the span of the centuries with the politics of France and the Low Countries on the opposite shore of the English Channel and the North Sea.[16]

Why is China ultimately more important than Brazil? Because of geographical location: even supposing the same level of economic growth as China and a population of equal size, Brazil does not command the main sea lines of communication connecting oceans and continents as China does; nor does it mainly lie in the temperate zone like China, with a more disease-free and invigorating climate. China fronts the Western Pacific and has depth on land reaching to oil- and natural-gas-rich Central Asia. Brazil offers less of a comparative advantage. It lies isolated in South America, geographically removed from other landmasses.[17]

Why is Africa so poor? Though Africa is the second largest continent, with an area five times that of Europe, its coastline south of the Sahara is little more than a quarter as long. Moreover, this coastline lacks many good natural harbors, with the East African ports that traded vigorously with Arabia and India constituting the exception. Few of tropical Africa's rivers are navigable from the sea, dropping as they do from interior tableland to coastal plains by a series of falls and rapids, so that inland Africa is particularly isolated from the coast.[18] Moreover, the Sahara Desert hindered human contact from the north for too many centuries, so that Africa was little exposed to the great Mediterranean civilizations of antiquity and afterward.

Then there are the great, thick forests thrown up on either side of the equator, from the Gulf of Guinea to the Congo basin, under the influence of heavy rains and intense heat.[19] These forests are no friends to civilization, nor are they conducive to natural borders, and so the borders erected by European colonialists were, perforce, artificial ones. The natural world has given Africa much to labor against in its path to modernity.

Check the list of the world's most feeble economies and note the high proportion that are landlocked.[20] Note how tropical countries (those located between 23.45 degrees north and south latitudes) are generally poor, even as most high-income countries are in the middle and high latitudes. Note how temperate zone, east–west oriented Eurasia is better off than north–south oriented sub-Saharan Africa, because technological diffusion works much better across a common latitude, where climatic conditions are similar, thus allowing for innovations in the tending of plants and the domestication of animals to spread rapidly. It is no accident that the world's poorest regions tend to be where geography, by way of soil suitability, supports high population densities, but not economic growth—because of distance from ports and railheads. Central India and inland Africa are prime examples of this.[21]

In a stunning summation of geographical determinism, the late geographer Paul Wheatley made the observation that "the Sanskrit tongue was chilled to silence at 500 meters," so that Indian culture was in essence a lowland phenomenon.[22] Other examples of how geography has richly influenced the fate of peoples in ways both subtle and obvious are legion, and I will get to more of them in the course of this study.

But before we move on, let me mention the example of the United States. For it is geography that has helped sustain American prosperity and which may be ultimately responsible for America's panhumanistic altruism. As John Adams notes, "There is no special providence for Americans, and their nature is the same with that of others."[23] The historian John Keegan explains that America and Britain could champion freedom only because the sea protected them

"from the landbound enemies of liberty." The militarism and pragmatism of continental Europe through the mid-twentieth century, to
which the Americans always felt superior, was the result of geography,
not character. Competing states and empires adjoined one another on
a crowded continent. European nations could never withdraw across
an ocean in the event of a military miscalculation. Thus, their foreign policies could not be grounded by a universalist morality, and
they remained well armed against one another until dominated by an
American hegemon after World War II.[24] It wasn't only two oceans
that gave Americans the luxury of their idealism, it was also that these
two oceans gave America direct access to the two principal arteries of
politics and commerce in the world: Europe across the Atlantic and
East Asia across the Pacific, with the riches of the American continent
lying between them.[25] And yet these same oceans, by separating America by thousands of miles from other continents, have given America
a virulent strain of isolationism that has persisted to this day. Indeed,
except in its own sphere of influence in the Americas, the United States
zealously resisted great power politics for almost two hundred years:
even the breakdown of the European state system in 1940 failed to
bring America into World War II. It took an attack on Pearl Harbor
in 1941 to do that. Following the war, the United States once more
withdrew from the world, until the aggression of the Soviet Union and
North Korea's attack on South Korea forced its troops back to Europe
and Asia.[26] Since the end of the Cold War, American foreign policy
elites have oscillated between quasi-isolationism and idealist-minded
interventionism: all of this at root because of two oceans.

Geography "has been forgotten, not conquered," writes the Johns
Hopkins University scholar Jakub J. Grygiel.[27] "That technology has
canceled geography contains just enough merit to be called a plausi-
ble fallacy," writes Colin S. Gray, a longtime advisor on military
strategy to the British and American governments. It is not only that,
as we've seen in Iraq and Afghanistan, "the exercise of continuous
influence or control requires," in Gray's words, "the physical pres-

ence of armed people in the area at issue," it is that anyone who truly believes that geography has been pivotally downgraded is profoundly ignorant of military logistics—of the science of getting significant quantities of men and matériel from one continent to another. What I had experienced in traveling with the 1st Marine Division overland through Iraq was only a small part of that logistics exercise, which included getting men and equipment thousands of miles by ship from North America to the Persian Gulf. In a strikingly clairvoyant analysis in 1999, the American military historian Williamson Murray wrote that the approaching new century would make the United States confront once again the "harsh geographic reality" imposed by two oceans, which limit and make almost insanely expensive the deployment of our ground troops to far-off locales. While some wars and rescue missions may be quickly concluded by airborne "raiding" (one thinks of the Israeli attack on Entebbe airport in Uganda in 1976 to rescue hijacked plane passengers), even in those operations, terrain matters. Terrain determines the pace and method of fighting. The Falklands War of 1982 unfolded slowly because of the maritime environment, while the flat deserts of Kuwait and Iraq in the Gulf War of 1991 magnified the effect of air power, even as holding vast and heavily populated stretches of Iraq in the Second Gulf War showed the limits of air power and thus made American forces victims of geography: aircraft can bombard, but they cannot transport goods in bulk, nor exercise control on the ground.[28] Moreover, in many cases still, aircraft require bases reasonably close by. Even in an age of intercontinental ballistic missiles and nuclear bombs, geography matters. As Morgenthau points out, small- and medium-sized states like Israel, Great Britain, France, and Iran cannot absorb the same level of punishment as continental-sized states such as the United States, Russia, and China, so that they lack the requisite credibility in their nuclear threats. This means that a small state in the midst of adversaries, such as Israel, has to be particularly passive, or particularly aggressive, in order to survive. It is primarily a matter of geography.[29]

But to embrace the relief map along with mountains and men is not to see the world irrevocably driven by ethnic and sectarian divides that resist globalization. The story is far more complicated than that. Globalization has itself spurred the rebirth of localisms, built in many cases on ethnic and religious consciousness, which are anchored to specific landscapes, and thus explained best by reference to the relief map. This is because the forces of mass communications and economic integration have weakened the power of many states, including artificially conceived ones averse to the dictates of geography, leaving exposed in some critical areas a fractious, tottering world. Because of communications technology, pan-Islamic movements gain strength across the entire Afro-Asian arc of Islam, even as individual Muslim states themselves are under siege from within.

Take Iraq and Pakistan, which are in terms of geography arguably the two most illogically conceived states between the Mediterranean Sea and the Indian Subcontinent, even as the relief map decrees Afghanistan to be a weak state at best. Yes, Iraq fell apart because the United States invaded it. But Saddam Hussein's tyranny (which I intimately experienced in the 1980s, and was by far the worst in the Arab world), one could argue, was itself geographically determined. For every Iraqi dictator going back to the first military coup in 1958 had to be more repressive than the previous one in order to hold together a state with no natural borders composed of Kurds and Sunni and Shiite Arabs, seething with a well-articulated degree of ethnic and sectarian consciousness.

I realize that it is important not to go too far in this line of argument. True, the mountains that separate Kurdistan from the rest of Iraq, and the division of the Mesopotamian plain between Sunnis in the center and Shiites in the south, may have been more pivotal to the turn of events than the yearning after democracy. But no one can know the future, and a reasonably stable and democratic Iraq is certainly not out of the question: just as the mountains of southeastern Europe that helped separate the Austro-Hungarian Empire from that of the poorer and less developed Ottoman Turkish one, and that helped divide ethnic and confessional groups from one another for centuries in the Balkans, certainly did not doom our interventions there to stop internecine wars. I am not talking here of an implacable force against which humankind is powerless. Rather, I wish to argue for a modest acceptance of fate, secured ultimately in the facts of geography, in order to curb excessive zeal in foreign policy, a zeal of which I myself have been guilty.

The more we can curb this zeal, the more successful will be the interventions in which we do take part, and the more successful these interventions are, the more leeway our policymakers will have in the court of public opinion to act likewise in the future.

I am aware that I am on dangerous ground in raising geography on a pedestal. I will, therefore, in the course of this study, try to keep in mind always Isaiah Berlin's admonition from his celebrated lecture delivered in 1953, and published the following year under the title "Historical Inevitability," in which he condemns as immoral and cowardly the belief that *vast impersonal forces* such as geography, the environment, and ethnic characteristics determine our lives and the direction of world politics. Berlin reproaches Arnold Toynbee and Edward Gibbon for seeing "nations" and "civilizations" as "more concrete" than the individuals who embody them, and for seeing abstractions like "Tradition" and "History" as "wiser than we."[30] For Berlin, the individual and his moral responsibility are paramount, and he or she cannot therefore blame his or her actions—or fate— altogether, or in great part, on such factors as landscape and culture. The motives of human beings matter very much to history; they are not illusions explained away by references to larger forces. The map is a beginning, not an end to interpreting the past and present.

Of course, geography, history, and ethnic characteristics influence but do not *determine* future events. Nevertheless, today's foreign policy challenges simply cannot be solved, and wise choices cannot be made, without substantial reference to these very factors, which Berlin, in his sweeping attack on all forms of determinism, seems at first glance to reject. Reliance on geography and ethnic and sectarian factors could have served us well in anticipating the violence in both the Balkans, following the end of the Cold War, and in Iraq, following the U.S. invasion of 2003. Nevertheless, Berlin's moral challenge holds up well so far as framing the debates that have taken place in the course of the past two decades, about where and where not to deploy American troops abroad.

So what to do? How do we split the difference between recognizing the importance of geography in shaping history and the danger of overemphasizing that very fact? We can take harbor, I think, in Raymond Aron's notion of a "sober ethic rooted in the truth of 'probabilistic determinism,'" because "human choice always operates within certain contours or restraints such as the inheritance of the past."[31] The key word is "probabilistic," that is, in now concentrating on geography we adhere to a partial or hesitant determinism which recognizes obvious differences between groups and terrain, but does not oversimplify, and leaves many possibilities open. As English historian Norman Davies writes: "I have come to hold that Causality is not composed exclusively of determinist, individualist, or random elements, but from a combination of all three."[32] Liberal internationalists, who generally supported intervention in the Balkans but opposed it in Iraq, reflect this spirit of fine distinctions. They intuited, however vaguely, a principal fact of geography: whereas the former Yugoslavia lay at the most advanced, western extremity of the former Ottoman Empire, adjacent to Central Europe, Mesopotamia lay at its most chaotic, eastern reaches. And because that fact has affected political development up through the present, intervention in Iraq would prove to be a stretch.

So what might that modest fate, that hidden hand, have in store for us in the years to come? What can we learn from the map, to forewarn us of possible dangers? Let us review some of the effects of geography on the grand pattern of world history through the eyes of several great scholars of the twentieth century, and then look specifically at geography and human intervention through the eyes of a great man of antiquity. That will prepare us to probe the most time-tested and provocative geopolitical theories from the modern era, and see where they take us in describing the world to come.

Chapter III

HERODOTUS AND HIS SUCCESSORS

During the middle to latter twentieth century, when Hans Morgenthau taught in the political science department at the University of Chicago, two other professors were also forging prodigious academic paths in the history department: William H. McNeill and Marshall G. S. Hodgson. The university was bursting with rigor and talent, and by concentrating on these three professors, I do not mean to slight others. Whereas Morgenthau defined realism for the present age, McNeill quite literally did so for the history of the world and Hodgson for the history of Islam, in massive works of Herodotean scope, in which geography is rarely far out of reach. The very audacity that McNeill and Hodgson showed in the choice of their subjects is to be admired in this current academic era, with its emphasis on narrow specialization—in truth, a necessity as the mass of knowledge steadily accumulates. But to read McNeill and Hodgson is almost to be wistful for a time not that long ago when scholars' horizons were seemingly limitless. Specialization has brought its own unique sort of flowering, but the academy could use more of what these two University of Chicago professors represent. Geography, they demonstrate, is in and of itself a means of thinking broadly.

William Hardy McNeill, born in British Columbia, was in his mid-forties when in 1963 he published *The Rise of the West: A History of the Human Community,* a book which runs well over eight hundred pages. The overarching theme is to challenge the viewpoint of British historian Arnold Toynbee and German historian Oswald Spengler that separate civilizations pursued their destinies independently. Instead, McNeill argues that cultures and civilizations continually interacted, and it has been this interaction that has forged the core drama of world history. If the book is about anything, it is about the vast movements of peoples across the map.

To wit: a northerly movement brought the so-called Danubian cultivators into central and western Europe between 4500 and 4000 B.C. Meanwhile, a southerly movement of pioneer herders and farmers crossed North Africa unto the Strait of Gibraltar, "to meet and mingle with the Danubian flood." But the older hunting populations of Europe were not destroyed, McNeill writes; instead, there was a mixing of populations and cultures.[1] Thus, the heart of the book commences.

Both these population movements, north and south of the Mediterranean, originated from the Fertile Crescent and Anatolia, where political instability was largely a function of geography. "While Egypt lies parallel and peaceful to the routes of human traffic, Iraq is from earliest times a frontier province, right-angled and obnoxious to the predestined paths of man," writes the late British travel writer Freya Stark.[2] Indeed, as McNeill indicates, Mesopotamia cut across one of history's bloodiest migration routes. "As soon as the cities of the plain had been made to flourish," the result of a gently sloping landscape in the lower part of the Tigris-Euphrates valley that carried irrigation water for miles, "they became tempting objects of plunder to the barbarous peoples of the country round about." Moreover, when most of the irrigable land of Mesopotamia came under cultivation, and the fields of one community came into contact with those of another, chronic war emerged, as there was no central authority to settle boundary disputes, or to apportion water in times of shortage. In the midst of this semi-chaos, conquerors like Sargon (2400 B.C.) entered Mesopotamia from the margins of the cultivated zone. Though able to establish a centralized authority, the vanquishing soldiery, after a few generations, McNeill tells us, gave up the military life in favor of the "softer and more luxurious ways" of the towns. And so history began to repeat itself with the arrival of new conquerors.

This is all very reminiscent of the pattern described by the fourteenth-century Tunisian historian and geographer Ibn Khaldun, who notes that while luxurious living strengthens the state initially by furthering its legitimacy, in succeeding generations it leads to decadence, with the process of collapse signaled by the rise of powerful provincial leaders, who then invade and form their own dynasties.[3] Ultimately, the rise of civilization in ancient Iraq led to the most suffocating of tyrannies in order to stave off the disintegration from within: thus we have Tiglath-pileser (twelfth–eleventh centuries B.C.), Ashurnasirpal II (ninth century B.C.), Sennacherib (eighth–seventh centuries B.C.), and others, famous for their cruelty, megalomania, and mass deportations carried out in their name.[4] It is a pattern that culminates in Saddam Hussein: that of a region prone to invasion and fragmentation that required through much of history significant levels of tyranny. But again, one should avoid too constricted a conclusion: for example, between 1921 and 1958, Iraq experienced a modestly well-functioning parliamentary system, which might have continued under slightly altered circumstances. McNeill, Khaldun, and Stark are speaking of historical and geographical tendencies only, and thus avoid the charge of determinism.[5]

Just as geography formed the basis for an extraordinary level of tyranny and bureaucracy in Mesopotamia, McNeill explains how it culminated in somewhat less oppressive rule in Egypt. "Deserts gave the land of Egypt clear-cut and easily defensible boundaries; while the

Nile provided it with a natural backbone and nervous system," so that Mesopotamian levels of oppression weren't necessary along the Nile. "Frontier defense," he goes on, "against outlanders was scarcely a serious problem for the king of Egypt": indeed, because of Egypt's favorable situation vis-à-vis migration routes compared to Mesopotamia's, infiltration by Libyans from the west and Asiatics from the east were relatively minor issues. Egypt was shut off from the south, where there is nothing but bare desert on either side of the river; while in the north there is the Mediterranean Sea. It is probable that for four thousand years Egyptians "never saw an invading host in their midst."[6] The Nile, moreover, was easily navigable, with the flow of the river carrying boats northward, even as the winds generally blowing from north to south carried boats, with the help of sail, southward. Thus was civilization able to dawn in Egypt. "By contrast," McNeill writes, "Mesopotamian rulers could avail themselves of no ready-made natural instrument for securing their centralized authority, but had slowly and painfully to develop [oppressive] law and bureaucratic administration as an artificial substitute for the natural articulation which geography gave to Egypt." Mesopotamia's heavy-handed bureaucracy had further to deal with the capricious rate of flooding of the Tigris and Euphrates, which was not the case with the Nile, and which complexified further the organization of the irrigation system.[7] Even today, both Egypt and Iraq have had dictatorial regimes for long periods, but the fact that Iraq's have been far worse is something that, in part, we can trace to antiquity, and to geography.

Beyond the Middle East were what McNeill calls the "peripheral" civilizations of India, Greece, and China, "on the fringes of the anciently civilized world," which in the cases of the first two derived a good portion of their vitality from the cultures of the Indus River and Minoan Crete. But all three also drew from their interaction with barbarian invaders, even as they were partially protected from them by virtue of geography. For Greece and India on account of their northerly mountains were both "effectively sheltered from the direct impact of steppe cavalry." China was even more isolated, by inhospitable deserts, high peaks, and sheer distance, as thousands of miles separated the Yellow River valley, where Chinese civilization began, from the Middle East and Indian heartlands. The result was three utterly original civilizations, particularly that of the Chinese, that were able to develop separately from the increasingly cultural uniformity of the Greater Desert Middle East, which stretched from North Africa to Turkestan.[8]

McNeill explains that throughout antiquity the ebb and flow of the frontiers between Hellenic, Middle Eastern, and Indian civilizations made for a delicate cultural balance in Eurasia, which, later in the medieval centuries, would be undone by the inundation of steppe peoples from the north, notably the Mongols.[9] It is largely through the Mongols that the Silk Route flourished, especially in the thirteenth and fourteenth centuries, bringing Eurasian civilizations from the Pacific to the Mediterranean into modest contact with one another. Nevertheless, China formed its own separate sphere geographically compared to the civilizations further west, with Tibet, Mongolia, Japan, and Korea all directing their gazes toward the Middle Kingdom, each forging in varying degrees its own civilization. And yet the severe limitations of a high desert environment "made anything more than a protocivilization impossible in Tibet and Mongolia," McNeill writes. Tibetan Lamaists, "always conscious of the Indian Buddhist origins of their faith," in effect opposed Sinification by appealing to the traditions of the rival civilization next door.[10] History, according to McNeill, is a study in fluidity, in which things only seem secure and neatly geographically ordered: more crucially we are always in a state of smaller transitions and cultural interchanges.

While opposing Spengler, Toynbee, and later the "Clash of Civilizations" theory of Harvard professor Samuel Huntington, in emphasizing the interaction of civilizations rather than their separateness, McNeill's The Rise of the West, nevertheless, engages the reader with the whole notion of civilizations formed in large measure by geography, that rise from precisely definable landscapes, achieve their own identity, and then interact with other civilizations, in turn forming new hybrids. In this way, history is woven.[11] McNeill metaphorically describes the process:

> Civilizations may be likened to mountain ranges, rising through aeons of geologic time, only to have the forces of erosion slowly but ineluctably nibble them down to the level of their surroundings. Within the far shorter time span of human history, civilizations, too, are liable to erosion as the special constellation of circumstances which provoked their rise passes away, while neighboring peoples lift themselves to new cultural heights by borrowing from or otherwise reacting to the civilized achievement.[12]

Such erosion and borrowing terrifies the purity of the early-twentieth-century German Oswald Spengler, who writes of the "deep soil ties" that define the best of High Cultures: how the inner evolution of sacral practices and dogmas remain "spellbound in the place of their birth," since, "whatever disconnects itself from the land becomes rigid and hard." High Culture, he goes on, begins in the "pre-urban countryside" and culminates with a "finale of materialism" in the "world-cities." For this dark romantic, who can at once be turgid, hypnotic, profound, and, frankly, at times unintelligible in English translation, cosmopolitanism is the essence of rootlessness, because it is not tied to the land.[13]

That raises the question of the rise and eventual fate of an urban Western civilization, morphing as we speak into a world civilization, and increasingly divorced from the soil. That inquiry will come later in the book. Meanwhile, I want to continue with McNeill, who, through it all, far more so than Spengler even, and far more intelligibly, is attentive to climate and geography.

McNeill writes, for example, that the Aryans developed a different, less warlike cultural personality in India's Gangetic plain than they did in Mediterranean Europe because of the influence of the subcontinent's forests and the monsoonal cycle, which encouraged meditation and religious knowledge. In another example, he writes that Greek Ionia's "precocity" was because of proximity to, and intimate contact with, Asia Minor and the Orient. And yet here, too, McNeill pulls back from outright determinism: for despite Greece's mountainous terrain, which favored the establishment of small political units, i.e., city-states, he is careful to note that in a number of cases, "contiguous expanses of fertile ground were broken up" into different city-states, so that geography can only be part of the story. And above all, of course, there is the history of the Jews, which goes against the entire logic of the geographical continuity of major religions (particularly of Hinduism and Buddhism), and which McNeill therefore takes pains to include: the utter destruction of the Jewish community in Judea, the consequence of the crushing of first- and second-century A.D. revolts by the Romans, did not end Judaism, which went on improbably to evolve and flourish in scattered cities of the western Diaspora, a two-thousand-year-old story averse to the dictates of geography, which shows once again how ideas and human agency matter as much as physical terrain.[14]

And yet, too, there is the story of Europe, reaching back to the dawn of human history, a story very much about the primacy of geography. As McNeill points out, Western Europe had distinct geographical advantages which developments in technology during the so-called Dark Ages brought into play: wide and fertile plains, an indented coastline that allowed for many good natural harbors, navigable rivers flowing northward across these plains and extending the reach of commerce to a greater extent than in the Mediterranean region, and an abundance of timber and metals.[15] Europe's was also a harsh, cold, and wet climate, and as Toynbee, who, like McNeill, was, at a crucial level, not a fatalist, nonetheless writes: "Ease is inimical to civilisation. . . . The greater the ease of the environment, the weaker the stimulus toward civilisation."[16] And thus Europe developed because of a geography that was difficult in which to live but had many natural nodal points of transport and commerce. For civilizations are in many ways brave and fortitudinous reactions to natural environments. Take the proximity of Scandinavia and the military pressure it brought to bear on Western European seaboards, which led to the articulation of England and France as national entities. England, moreover, being smaller than the feudal kingdoms of the continent, and, as Toynbee writes, "possessed of better-defined frontiers [after all, it was an island]," achieved far sooner than its neighbors a national as opposed to a feudal existence.[17]

Of course, some landscapes, the Arctic, for example, prove so difficult that they can lead to civilizational collapse, or to an arrested civilization. What precedes this, according to Toynbee, is a cultural tour de force—say, the Eskimos' ability to actually stay on the ice in winter and hunt seals. But once having accomplished this feat of survival, they are unable to master the environment to the extent of developing a full-fledged civilization. Toynbee, as well as the contemporary UCLA geographer Jared Diamond, write legions about civilizational difficulties and downfalls among the medieval cultures of the Vikings of Greenland, the Polynesians of Easter Island, the Anasazi of the American Southwest, and the Mayans of the Central American jungles, all of which were connected to problems with the environment.[18] Europe, it appears, offered the perfect degree of environmental difficulty, challenging its inhabitants to rise to greater civilizational heights, even as it still lay in the northern temperate zone, fairly proximate to Africa, the Middle East, the Eurasian steppe, and North America; thus its peoples were able to take full advantage of trade patterns as they burgeoned in the course of centuries of technological advancements in navigation and other spheres.[19] Witness Vasco da Gama's mastering of the monsoon winds in the Indian Ocean, which allowed for the outer edges of Eurasia to become a focus of the world's sea lanes under European dominance. But in McNeill's narrative, it is not only the material advancement of Europe, under a challenging physical environment, that leads to the rise of the West, but the closing, as he puts it, of the "barbarian" spaces.[20]

McNeill talks of the "inexorable, if not entirely uninterrupted, encroachment of civilizations upon barbarism":

It was this encroachment which built up the mass and internal variety of the separate civilizations of the world and increased the frequency of contact among them, preparing the way for the spectacular unification of the globe which has occurred during the past three or four centuries.[21]

This civilizational closure of the earth's relatively empty spaces, mainly in the temperate zone, began in a fundamental way with the voyages of discovery: those of da Gama, Columbus, Magellan, and others. And it continued through the well-known stages of revolutions in industry, transport, and communications to the globalization we experience today. In between came the final collapse of the steppe peoples, with Russia, China, and the Habsburg Empire partitioning the relatively empty central Eurasian plains and tablelands. There was, too, the collapse of indigenous populations with the violent securing of the western frontier of the North American continent, and the European colonial encroachment on sub-Saharan Africa.[22] The world, as McNeill describes it, is now finally united under a largely Western, increasingly urbanized culture. Remember that communism, while an extension of the totalitarian tendencies within Eastern Orthodox Christianity, and, therefore, an affront to liberalism, was still an ideology of the industrialized West. Nazism, too, emerged as a pathology of an inflation-wracked, rapidly modernizing West. McNeill is not talking about political unity, but of broad cultural, geographic, and demographic tendencies.

While a central theme of *The Rise of the West* is the closing up of empty spaces on the map, obviously this is true in a relative sense only. The fact that two rail lines coming from opposite directions meet and touch each other does not mean that there still aren't many empty or sparsely inhabited spaces in between. Frontiers may be closed in a formal sense, but the density of human population and electronic interaction keep increasing at a steep rate. And it is this rate of increase that helps to form the political drama of the world we inhabit today. McNeill could consider as united a world where no part of the civilized earth was further than a few weeks from another part.[23] But how does geopolitics change when the remotest places are separated by only a few days, or hours, as in our time? The world was, in a sense, united in the eighteenth and nineteenth centuries, but that world bears little relation in terms of demography and technology to that of the early twenty-first. The core drama of our own age, as we shall see, is the steady filling up of space, making for a truly closed geography where states and militaries have increasingly less room to hide. Whereas mechanized, early-modern armies of a century ago had to cross many miles to reach each other, now there are overlapping ranges of missiles. Geography does not disappear in this scenario, it just becomes, as we shall see, even more critical.

To look at the argument in another way, let me return to Morgenthau. Morgenthau writes that the very imperial expansion into relatively empty geographical spaces in the eighteenth and nineteenth centuries, in Africa, Eurasia, and western North America, deflected great power politics into the periphery of the earth, thereby reducing conflict. For example, the more attention Russia, France, and the United States paid to expanding into far-flung territories in imperial fashion, the less attention they paid to one another, and the more peaceful, in a sense, the world was.[24] But by the late nineteenth century, the consolidation of the great nation-states and empires of the West was consummated, and territorial gains could only be made at the expense of one another.[25] Morgenthau sums up:

> As the balance of power—with its main weight now in three continents—becomes worldwide, the dichotomy between the circle of the great power and its center, on the one hand, and its periphery and the empty spaces beyond, on the other, must of necessity disappear. The periphery of the balance of power now coincides with the confines of the earth.[26]

Whereas Morgenthau's vision, written during the tense, early Cold War years, spells danger, that of his university colleague McNeill, written in a later, more stable phase of the Cold War, spells hope:

> The Han in ancient China . . . put a quietus upon the disorders
> of the warring states by erecting an imperial bureaucratic struc-
> ture which endured, with occasional breakdown and modest
> amendment, almost to our own day. The warring states of the
> twentieth century seem headed for a similar resolution of their
> conflicts.[27]

The fall of the Berlin Wall in 1989 certainly seems to have borne
out McNeill's optimism. Yet the world is arguably as dangerous today
as it was during the Cold War. For the map keeps closing in a multiplicity of ways. Take China: Mao Zedong, at great cost to be sure,
consolidated China as a modern state, and China now rises economically (albeit at a slower pace) and militarily as a great power, filling
up the Eurasian chessboard even more than Morgenthau could have
imagined. Meanwhile, even the remotest parts of the world become
further urbanized, and while Spengler could see the decline of culture
in the desertion of the soil and agricultural life, sprawling and teeming urban conglomerations are, as McNeill intuited, now leading to
the metamorphosis of religion and identity in vigorous and, albeit,
troubling ways:[28] Islam, for example, becomes less of a traditional,
soil-based religion and more of an austere, in some cases ideological, faith, in order to regulate behavior in vast, impersonal slum set-
tings where extended family and kinsmen are less in evidence. This
leads to a Middle East of megacities and other urban concentrations
in the former countryside that, while poor, are generally low in crime,
even as the offshoot is occasionally a destabilizing global terrorism.
Christianity, too, becomes, as a consequence of the stresses of suburban living in the American South and West, more ideological, even as
a loose form of environmental paganism takes root in the cities of
Europe, replacing traditional nationalism, given that the super-state
of the European Union has only abstract meaning to all but the elite.
Meanwhile, war is no longer, as in eighteenth-century Europe, the
"sport of kings," but an instrument of nationalist and religious fa-
naticism, whether on a large scale as in the case of Nazi Germany, or
on a smaller scale as with al Qaeda.[29] Add to that the awful specter of

nuclear weapons in the hands of radicalized elites at both the state and substate level. And in the midst of all these awkward, turbulent shifts, classical geography again rears its head, shaping tensions among the West, Russia, Iran, India, China, Korea, Japan, and so on, all of which we will need to explore in detail. McNeill's thesis of interactions across civilizations has never been truer than today. But it would be a mistake to equate an emerging world culture with political stability: because *space*—precisely because it is more crowded and therefore more precious than ever before—still matters, and matters greatly.

Whereas McNeill's scholarly eye scanned the entire earth, Marshall Hodgson's scope, for our purposes, was narrower, encompassing the Greater Middle East. Still, Hodgson, a passionate Quaker who died at forty-six, demonstrates a prodigious ambition in his three-volume *The Venture of Islam: Conscience and History in a World Civilization,* published in full in 1974, six years after his death. For this largely forgotten University of Chicago historian, so much less well known among contemporary journalists than other distinguished scholars of the Middle East, say, Bernard Lewis of Princeton or John Esposito of Georgetown, has in this monumental work put Islam geographically and culturally, according to McNeill, in the context of the larger currents of world history. Hodgson's style can veer toward the academic and the opaque, but if the reader perseveres, he or she will be rewarded with an explanation as to how Islam was able to emerge, take root, and spread in the fabulous and often speedy way that it did, across not just Arabia and North Africa, but throughout the Indian Ocean littoral, and on land from the Pyrenees to the Tien Shan.[30]

It is important to note that Hodgson wrote much of *The Venture of Islam* in the 1950s and 1960s, when the media spotlight generally gave primacy to the Cold War in Europe. Yet he unfolds his theme in the first volume with the notion that this Eurocentric vision of the world has always been wrong, with the prejudice inherent early in mapping conventions.[31] The "absurdity was disguised by the increasingly widespread use of a drastically visually distortive world map, the Mercator projection, which by exaggerating northward manages to make an artificially bounded 'Europe' look larger than all 'Africa,' and quite dwarf that other Eurasian peninsula, India." Hodgson then proceeds to shift the reader's geographical focus southward and eastward, to what he calls the Oikoumene, the ancient Greek term for the "inhabited quarter" of the world, the temperate zone of the Afro-Asian landmass stretching from North Africa to the confines of western China, a belt of territory he also calls "Nile-to-Oxus."[32] There is a vagueness in these definitions, which at times contradict each other. For example, Nile-to-Oxus connotes a region with Egypt at its western end, whereas the Oikoumene could mean a zone that begins much further west along the Mediterranean's African littoral. The point is that the rigid distinctions of Cold War–area expertise, at their apex when he wrote, with the Middle East sharply differentiated from both Anatolia and the Indian Subcontinent, fall away as Hodgson shows us a more organic geography, delimited by landscape and culture: i.e., that vast and generally parched expanse between the civilizations of Europe and China, Herodotus's world actually, which Hodgson intimates holds the key to world history.

Given how globalization is now erasing borders, regions, and cultural distinctions, Hodgson's deliberately grand and flexible geographic construct is in fact quite useful, for it suggests how inhospitable the relief map can be to fixed and bold lines. In this way, Hodgson helps the reader to visualize the fluid world of late antiquity in which Islam emerged, as well as the world of today, with China and India increasing their economic presence in the Greater Middle East (the Oikoumene of yore), even as the Persian Gulf sheikhdoms do likewise in Africa, thus undoing the artificial divisions we have grown used to.

"The region where Islamicate culture was to be formed can almost be defined negatively," he explains, "as that residual group of lands in which the Greek and the Sanskrit traditions did not have their roots and from which the European and Indic regions were eventually set off. . . . In this sense, our region, in the Axial Age [800 to 200 B.C.], consisted of those lands between the Mediterranean and the Hindu-Kush [Afghanistan] in which Greek and Sanskrit had at best only local or transient growths." Within this wide belt of the Greater Middle East, stretching roughly three thousand miles or more in the lower temperate zone, two geographical features encouraged high culture: the key commercial position, particularly of Arabia and the Fertile Crescent, in terms of the trade routes from one extremity of the Oikoumene to the other, and the very aridity of the region.

This latter point needs explaining. Hodgson tells us that the general lack of water reduced the wealth that could be had by agriculture, and made concentrated holdings of productive land rare, so that rural life was insecure and downgraded in favor of urban life in the oases. Money and power converged in the hands of merchants at the "juncture points" of long-distance Middle East trade routes, particularly when those thoroughfares skirted close to the sea traffic of the Red Sea, Arabian Sea, and Persian Gulf, giving Arab merchants critical accessibility to the prodigious flows of Indian Ocean trade. And because this was a world of trade and contracts, ethical behavior and "just dealing" were paramount for the sake of a stable economic life. Thus, as both the Byzantine and Sassanid empires to the north weakened in Anatolia and Persia, the stage was set in Arabia and the Fertile Crescent for the emergence of a faith that emphasized good ethics over one merely ensuring "the round of the agricultural seasons." Thus, Islam sprung up as much as a merchants' creed as a desert one.[33]

The most important trading center in western and central Arabia was Mecca in the Hejaz, a region close to the Red Sea. It was at the intersection of two major routes. One went south and north, with Mecca the midway point, connecting Yemen and the Indian Ocean ports to Syria and the Mediterranean. The other went west and east, connecting the Horn of Africa on the nearby, opposite coast of the Red Sea to Mesopotamia and Iran on the Persian Gulf. Mecca was located far enough away from the center of Sassanid power in Iran to be independent of it, even as it was exposed to urbane religious and philosophical influences—Zoroastrianism, Manichaeism, Hellenism, Judaism, and so forth—from Persia, Iraq, and Asia Minor. Though

Mecca had no great oasis, it did have sufficient water for camels. It was protected by hills from Red Sea pirates, and possessed a shrine, the Ka'bah, where the sacred tokens of the region's clans were gathered and to which pilgrims came from far and wide. This was the largely geographical context from which the Prophet Muhammad, a respected local merchant and trader who, in his thirties, became preoccupied with how to live a just and pure life, sprang. Rather than a mere backwater camp in the desert, Mecca was a pulsing, cosmopolitan center.[34]

Of course, geography, in Hodgson's intricate tapestry, does not ultimately explain Islam. For a religion by its very definition has its basis more in the metaphysical than in the physical. But he does show how geography contributed to the religion's rise and spread, agglutinated, as Islam was, onto merchant and Bedouin patterns, which were, in turn, creatures of an arid landscape crisscrossed by trade routes.

Bedouin Arabia was bracketed by three agricultural lands: Syria to the north, Iraq to the northeast, and Yemen to the south. Each of these three areas was, in turn, connected to a "political hinterland," a highland region which, in the sixth and seventh centuries, dominated it. For Syria, it was the highlands of Anatolia; for Iraq, it was the highlands of Iran; for Yemen, there was a somewhat weaker interrelationship with the Abyssinian highlands (modern-day Ethiopia). Islam would conquer most of these areas, but geography would partly determine that these clusters of agricultural civilization, particularly Syria and Iraq, the two arcs of the Fertile Crescent, would retain their communal identity and thus become rival centers of Islamic power.[35]

Hodgson's historical sweep of late antiquity and the medieval era in the first two volumes of his epic teaches much about how modern Middle Eastern states, the ostensible results of Western colonialism, actually came about, and why they are less artificial than they have been alleged to be. Egypt, Yemen, Syria, and Iraq, as we have seen, not to mention Morocco, hemmed in by seas and the Atlas Mountains, and Tunisia, heir to ancient Carthage, are all ancient redoubts of civilizations, the legitimate precursors to these modern states, even if the demarcated borders of these states in the midst of flat desert are often arbitrary. Toynbee, lamenting the divisions of the Arab world, alleges that Westernization "gained the upper hand before any Islamic universal state was in sight."[36] But the fact that Islam constitutes a world civilization does not mean it was determined to be one polity, for as Hodgson shows, that civilization had many different population nodes, with a rich pre-Islamic past, that has come into play in the postcolonial era. The Iranian highlands, as Hodgson writes, have always been intrinsically related to the politics and culture of Mesopotamia, something very much in evidence since the American invasion of Iraq in 2003, which opened the door to the reentry of Iran into the region. Indeed, the border between Persia and Mesopotamia, which constantly shifted, was for long periods the Euphrates River itself, now in the heart of Iraq. The Arabs conquered the Sassanid Empire, situated in the heart of the Iranian tableland in A.D. 644, only twenty-two years after Muhammad's flight, or *hegira*, from Mecca to Medina, the event which marks the start of the Islamic era in world history. But the Anatolian highlands were more remote and sprawling, and thus partly on account of geography it would not be until more than four hundred years later, in 1071, that the Seljuk Turks—not the Arabs—captured the Anatolian heartland for Islam, in the Battle of Manzikert against the Byzantine Empire.[37]

The Seljuks were a steppe people from the deep interior of Eurasia, who invaded Anatolia from the east (Manzikert was in eastern Anatolia). But just as the Arabs never succeeded in capturing the mountain fastnesses of Anatolia, the Seljuks, deep inside those very fastnesses, never quite succeeded either in maintaining stable rule over the heart of Islamdom—the Fertile Crescent and the Iranian plateau, to say nothing of the Hejaz and the rest of desert Arabia to the south. This was again geography at work. (Though the Ottoman Turks, heirs to the Seljuks, would conquer Arab deserts, their rule was often weak.) Turkic rule would triumph as far east as Bengal, at the furthest extreme of the Indian Subcontinent, but this was part of a southward population movement across the whole, vast east–west temperate zone of Eurasia. For these Turkic nomads constituted the bulk of the tribes under the infamous Mongol armies (the Mongols themselves, in any case, were a relatively small elite). We will deal with the Mongol hordes and their geopolitical significance later, but it is interesting here to note Hodgson's view that the horse nomadism of the Mongols and Turkic peoples was ultimately more crucial to history than the camel nomadism of the Arabs. Because horses could not endure the aridity of Middle Eastern deserts, and the sheep with which these nomads often traveled required relatively dense forage, the Mongol-led armies avoided distant Arabia, and instead ravaged nearer and more environmentally friendly Eastern Europe, Anatolia, northern Mesopotamia and Iran, Central Asia, India, and China: territories that, taken together, would be of overwhelming strategic importance on the map of Eurasia just prior to the advent of gunpowder warfare. The Mongol-Turkic invasions were arguably the most significant event in world history in the second millennium of the common era, and it was mainly because of the use of certain animals tied to geography.[38]

Hodgson's discussion of the Mongols shows how *The Venture of Islam* is far more than a work of area expertise. To call Hodgson an Arabist or an Islamicist is to inaccurately diminish him. For in his hands, Islam is a vehicle to reveal the most pivotal intellectual, cultural, and geographical trends affecting Afro-Eurasian societies, the entire Old World, in fact, with the Oikoumene of antiquity at its heart. This is not a work of geography per se. Hodgson spends as much time defining Sufi mysticism as he does landscape, to say nothing of the other intellectual and sectarian traditions he unravels. And yet in bringing geography into the discussion in the way that he does, he demonstrates how it interacts with politics and ideology to produce the very texture of history. Take the Ottoman Turks, who eventually replaced their Turkic brethren, the Seljuks, in Anatolia in the late thirteenth century. The "monolithic military caste system" of the Ottomans placed "inherent geographical limits" on the area under their control, in contrast to that of Russia, say, or even of the primitive Mongols. The Ottomans were accustomed to a single grand army, in which the *padishah*, or emperor, must always be present. At the same time, they had to operate out of a single capital city, Constantinople, in the northeastern Mediterranean by the Black Sea, where the sultanate's vast bureaucratic structure was headquartered. "As a result, a major campaign could be carried only so far as a single season's marching would allow": Vienna to the northwest and Mosul to the southeast were consequently the geographical limits of stable Ottoman expansion on land. The army could winter in some years at Sofia or Aleppo, extending its range, though miring it in great logistical difficulties. In general, however, this absolutist system with all the power, both personal and bureaucratic, concentrated in Constantinople had the effect of taking the capital's geographical situation and making it an all-determining factor. This was, after a fashion, the inverse of human agency. And it had the effect of leading to the decay of this military state, since once the Ottoman military's geographical limits were reached, morale as well as rewards declined within the ranks of the soldiery. A less centralized state might have led to a more secure empire, rather than one at the mercy of geography. In the naval realm, too, absolutism exaggerated the tyranny of location, with Ottoman sea power mostly clustered in the Black and Mediterranean seas close to home, with only "transient" success achieved against the Portuguese in the Indian Ocean.[39]

Hodgson, like his colleague in the Chicago history department McNeill, is less an academic in the contemporary sense than an old-world intellectual aided by the rigor of tireless, scientifically minded inquiry, an outgrowth perhaps of his particular Quaker intensity. That is, even in the depths of his exploration of minutiae, he sees the grand sweep. His main stage is the ancient Greek Oikoumene, which also, as it happens, forms much of the material for McNeill's world history, and as we've said, much of the background for Herodotus's fifth-century B.C. *Histories*. It may be no accident that this is precisely the world which occupies current news headlines: that region between the eastern Mediterranean and the Iranian-Afghan plateau. For the Oikoumene is where the Eurasian and African landmasses converge, with many outlets to the Indian Ocean via the Red Sea and Persian Gulf, making it ultra-strategic, as well as a stew of migration patterns and consequently clashing ethnic and sectarian groups. Herodotus's *Histories* captures this unceasing turbulence.

Herodotus is at the heart of my argument for the relevance of McNeill and Hodgson in the twenty-first century. For this Greek, who was born a Persian subject sometime between 490 and 484 B.C. in Halicarnassus, in southwestern Asia Minor, maintains in his narrative about the origins and execution of the war between the Greeks and the Persians the perfect balance between geography and the decisions of men. He advances the *partial* determinism we all need. For he shows us a world where the relief map hovers in the background— Greece and Persia and their respective *barbarian* penumbrae in the Near East and North Africa—even as individual passions are acted out with devastating political results. Herodotus stands for the sensibility we need to recover in order to be less surprised by the world to come.

"Custom is king of all," Herodotus observes, quoting Pindar. Herodotus tells of the Egyptians, who shaved their eyebrows in mourning for a beloved cat, of Libyan tribesmen who wore their hair long on one side and shorn on the other, and smeared their bodies with vermilion. There are the Massagetae, a people who lived east of the Caspian Sea, in what is now Turkmenistan, among whom, when a man grows old, "his relatives come together and kill him, and sheep and goats along with him, and stew all the meat together and have a banquet of it." First there is only the landscape, the historical experience of a people on it, and the manners and ideas that arise out of that experience. Herodotus is a preserver of the memory of civilizations and their geographies, the myths, fables, and even lies that they lived by. He knows that the better a knack a political leader has for *just what's out there*, the less likely he is to make tragic mistakes. The Scythians lived on the far side of the Cimmerian Bosporus, where it is so cold that to make mud in the winter they had to light a fire. As Artabanus warns Darius, the Persian king, to no avail: Do not make war against the Scythians—a swiftly mobile and nomadic people without cities or sown land, who offer no focal point of attack for a large, well-equipped army.[40]

Herodotus's signal strength is his powerful evocation of just what human beings are capable of believing. It is a belief made tangible by the fact that the ancients, living without science and technology, saw and heard differently—more vividly than we do. Landscape and geography were real to them in ways we cannot imagine.

Take the story of Phidippides, a professional runner sent from Athens to Sparta as a herald to plead for help against the Persians. Phidippides tells the Athenians that on Mount Parthenium, en route to Sparta, he saw the god Pan, who bade him ask his countrymen: "Why do you pay no heed to Pan, who is a good friend to the people of Athens, has been many times serviceable to you, and will be so again?" The Athenians are convinced that Phidippides has told the truth, and when their fortunes improved, they set up a shrine to Pan under the Acropolis.

This is more than just a charming story; it may well be the truth as the Athenians related it to Herodotus. The runner probably believed he saw Pan. *He did see Pan.* A vision of the god was likely, given his fatigue, the pantheon inherent in his belief system, and the wonder-filled fear of the physical elements that has since been lost to human beings. The ancient world was "settled so sparsely that nature was not yet eclipsed by man," Boris Pasternak writes in *Doctor Zhivago.* "Nature hit you in the eye so plainly and grabbed you so fiercely and so tangibly by the scruff of the neck that perhaps it really was still full of gods."[41] If rationalism and secularism have taken us so far that we can no longer imagine what Phidippides saw, then we are incapable of understanding—and consequently defending ourselves against—religious movements that reverse the Enlightenment and affect to-day's geopolitics. For while space across the planet has filled up, and the natural world is not what it was, the new geography of slums and shantytowns and neither-nor landscapes likewise manifest an equally intense psychological effect on human beings, in a different way of course. And to understand this new geography, the premium it puts on space, and its consequent psychic impact it helps to first appreciate the antique landscapes as described by Herodotus.

The crux of Herodotus's *Histories* is the lure of that seething-with-culture archipelagic landmass of Greece, lurking just to the west beyond the mountainous tablelands of Persia and Asia Minor. Here is geographical determinism writ large, it would seem, for the peoples of Asia to the east and Greece to the west have fought each other over the millennia, culminating in our own day with the tense relations between Greece and Turkey: a tension that has not led to outright war since the 1920s mainly because of the mass transfers of population that occurred in that decade, creating two neat, uniethnic states. Peace reigned, in other words, only after ethnic cleansing that went according to the dictates of geography. And yet this is ultimately not the line of thinking that Herodotus imparts.

For Herodotus evinces a receptivity to the province of the heart and the attendant salience of human intrigues. He illustrates how self-interest is calculated within a disfiguring whirlwind of passion. Atossa, a wife of Persia's King Darius, appeals to her husband's male vanity in bed while begging him to invade Greece. She does this as a favor to the Greek doctor who has cured a growth on her breast, and who wants to revisit his homeland. It is all about geography, until it becomes all about Shakespeare.

Herodotus's *Histories* at its deepest level is about understanding the complexities of fate: *moira* in Greek, "the dealer-out of portions." And because heroes are the ones who overcome fate, they form the superstructure of Herodotus's narrative. It is none other than Hodgson who notes in his introduction to *The Venture of Islam:*

> Herodotus wrote his history, he said, to preserve the memory of the great deeds done by the Greeks and the Persians: unrepeatable deeds that have an enduring claim to our respect. Those deeds cannot be imitated, though they may be emulated and in some sense perhaps surpassed. But even now we dare call no man great whose deeds cannot somehow measure up to theirs.[42]

Hodgson writes this early in his epic to make it clear that men ultimately have control over their destiny, even as he will often engage for three volumes in the description of grand historical and environmental trends over which, it might seem, individuals have little control. Without the admission of individual struggle, there is no humanism in the study of history, Hodgson says. Thus, he weaves his tapestry of Islam: "a morally, humanly relevant complex of traditions" that assumes the nature of a global force, but started with the actions of individuals in Mecca.

So we are back to the battle against fate, and it is well that we are. For we now need to be especially fortified by the likes of Herodotus, Hodgson, and McNeill, since we are about to enter exceedingly rough terrain: that of geopolitics and the quasi-determinist theories that emanate from it. The fact is, the broad outlines of history have, indeed, been predicted, and might still be again. This is, to say the least, unsettling given how individuals can alter history. But, as we shall see, it is true. The men I am about to introduce should make liberal humanists profoundly uneasy. These men were hardly philosophers: rather, they were geographers, historians, and strategists who assumed that the map determined nearly everything, leaving relatively little room for human agency. Human agency, to the degree that it did matter to them, mattered mainly in regards to military and commercial dominance. Yet it is such men with whom we now have to engage, so as to establish the framework for what we are up against around the world, and what can be achieved in it.

Chapter IV

THE EURASIAN MAP

Times of global upheaval, testing as they do our assumptions about the permanence of the political map, lead to a renaissance in thinking about geography. This is particularly so because geography is the very basis for strategy and geopolitics. Strategy as defined by Napoleon is the art of using time and space in a military and diplomatic manner. Geopolitics constitutes the study of the outside environment faced by every state when determining its own strategy: that environment being the presence of other states also struggling for survival and advantage.[1] In short, geopolitics is the influence of geography upon human divisions.[2] As Napoleon said, to know a nation's geography is to know its foreign policy.[3]

Morgenthau calls geopolitics a "pseudoscience" because it erects "the factor of geography into an absolute." Writing soon after World War II, he had in mind the great British geographer Halford Mackinder, whose turn-of-the-twentieth-century theories were revived in the midst of the Second World War and misused by the Nazis to justify their idea of *Lebensraum*, or German "living space."[4] To be sure, because the aim of geopolitics is to achieve a balance of power, and the Nazis attempted nothing less than to overthrow the balance of power, the Nazis' use of Mackinder was a perversion of Mackinder's own thinking. The balance of power, according to Mackinder, because it grants each nation its security, forms the very basis of freedom.[5] Morgenthau may be too hard on Mackinder. In any case, Morgenthau's aversion to Mackinder, as well as his careful summary of Mackinder's theories, is itself an indication of Mackinder's powerful influence over Western geopolitical thought over many decades. Mackinder keeps getting denounced, and yet remains relevant through it all, especially in eras like our own, with large numbers of American troops still on the ground in the Greater Middle East and Northeast Asia. Clearly, there is some unsettling, underlying truth to his work, though there is also the risk of taking it too far.

Mackinder clearly had a gift. The dictum of his life's work was that geography is the generalist's answer to academic specialization.[6] In 1890, he gave a singular example of how knowledge of geography enriches one's thinking on world affairs:

> Suppose I am told that a certain sample of wheat comes from Lahore, and that I do not know where Lahore is. I look it out in the gazetteer and ascertain that it is the capital of the Punjab. . . . If I know nothing of geography, I shall get up with the idea that Lahore is in India, and that will be about all. If I have been properly trained in geography, the word Punjab will . . . probably connote to me many things. I shall see Lahore in the northern angle of India. I shall picture it in a great plain, at the foot of a snowy range, in the midst of the rivers of the Indus system. I shall think of the monsoons and the desert, of the water brought from the mountains by the irrigation canals. I shall know the climate, the seed time, and the harvest. Kur-

rachee and the Suez Canal will shine out from my mental map.
I shall be able to calculate at what time of the year the cargoes
will be delivered in England. Moreover, the Punjab will be to
me the equal in size and population of a great European country, a Spain or an Italy, and I shall appreciate the market it offers for English exports.[7]

Mackinder's ideas and way of putting things, as we shall now see,
are riveting.

Sir Halford J. Mackinder, the father of modern-day geopolitics, which
Morgenthau so disparages, is famous not for a book, but for a single
article, "The Geographical Pivot of History," published in the April
1904 issue of *The Geographical Journal* in London. Mackinder's thesis is that Central Asia, helping to form as it does the Eurasian Heartland, is the pivot on which the fate of great world empires rests: for
the earth's very layout of natural arteries between mountain ranges
and along river valleys encourages the rise of empires, declared or
undeclared, rather than states. Before exploring how this notion,
slightly redefined, helps illuminate our own geopolitics, it is worth
describing how Mackinder reached his conclusion. For his article,
taking in the whole of history and human settlement patterns, is
the archetype of the geographical discipline, recalling the work of
Herodotus and Ibn Khaldun, and presaging stylistically the work
of McNeill, Hodgson, and the French historian and geographer Fernand Braudel. As Mackinder writes, in the manner of Braudel, "Man
and not nature initiates, but nature in large measure controls."[8]

Mackinder's opening sentence suggests the epic sweep of his
article:

When historians in the remote future come to look back on the
group of centuries through which we are now passing, and see
them fore-shortened, as we to-day see the Egyptian dynasties, it

may well be that they will describe the last 400 years as the Columbian epoch, and will say that it ended soon after the year 1900.[9]

He explains that whereas medieval Christendom was "pent into a narrow region and threatened by external barbarism," the Columbian age—the Age of Discovery—saw Europe expand across the oceans into other continents against "negligible resistances." But from the present time forth, in the post-Columbian age (he writes from the vantage point of 1904), "we shall again have to deal with a closed political system," and this time one of "world-wide scope." Elaborating, he says:

> Every explosion of social forces, instead of being dissipated in a surrounding circuit of unknown space and barbaric chaos, will [henceforth] be sharply re-echoed from the far side of the globe, and weak elements in the political and economic organism of the world will be shattered in consequence.[10]

By perceiving that there was no more room on the planet for European empires to expand, he also understood that European wars would have to be played out on a worldwide scale, something which would come true in World Wars I and II. Yet, as I learned years ago at a seminar at the United States Army's Command and General Staff College at Fort Leavenworth, *attrition of the same adds up to big change.* In other words, while the Age of Discovery had more or less ended by 1900, throughout the twentieth century and up through the present day—and especially looking forward to the coming decades— that closed and crowded map or chessboard of Mackinder's, as I've already indicated, has filled up even more: not just in terms of population, but in terms of the range of weaponry. The Middle East, for example, in the last fifty years alone has gone from a rural society to one of immense megacities. The world, as I've learned as a foreign correspondent for the past thirty years, is even in some of its remotest parts heavily urbanized. We will later revisit in depth all the implications of this newly crowded map, but to do that we must first return to Mackinder and his Eurasia pivot theory.

Mackinder asks us to look at European history as "subordinate" to that of Asia, for he believes that European civilization is merely the outcome of the struggle against Asiatic invasion. Ahead of McNeill by decades, Mackinder points out that Europe became the cultural phenomenon that it is mainly because of its geography: an intricate array of mountains, valleys, and peninsulas—from which individual nations would emerge—set against the immense and threatening flatland of Russia to the east. That Russian flatland was divided between forest to the north and steppe to the south. The earliest incarnations of Poland and Russia were established, as Mackinder explains, wholly in the protective embraces of the northern forest; for out of the naked southern steppe from the fifth to the sixteenth centuries came a succession of nomadic invaders: Huns, Avers, Bulgarians, Magyars, Kalmuks, Cummins, Patzinaks, Mongols, and others. For on the Heartland steppe the land is unceasingly flat, the climate hard, and the vegetable production limited to grass, in turn destroyed by sand, driven by powerful winds. Such conditions bred hard and cruel races of men who had at once to destroy any adversaries they came across or be destroyed themselves, as there was no better means of defense in one spot than in another. It was the union of Franks, Goths, and Roman provincials against these Asiatics that produced the basis for modern France. Likewise, Venice, the Papacy, Germany, Austria, Hungary, and other burgeoning European powers would all originate, or at least mature, through their threatening encounter with Asiatic steppe nomads. As Mackinder writes:

When we reflect that through several centuries of the Dark Ages the Norse pagans in their ships were at piracy on the Northern seas, and the Saracen and Moorish infidels in their ships at piracy on the Mediterranean, and that the horse-riding Turks from Asia raided thus into the very heart of the Christian peninsula when it was clasped by hostile sea-power, we have some idea of the pounding, as between pestle and mortar, which went into the making of modern Europe. The pestle was land-power from the Heartland.[11]

Meanwhile, Russia, protected by forest glades against many a rampaging host, nevertheless fell prey in the thirteenth century to the Golden Horde of the Mongols. Thus would Russia be denied access to the European Renaissance, and branded forever with the bitterest feelings of inferiority and insecurity. The ultimate land-based empire, with no natural barriers against invasion save for the forest itself, Russia would know forevermore what it was like to be brutally conquered, and as a result would become perennially obsessed with expanding and holding territory, or at least dominating its contiguous shadow zones.

Whereas the Mongol invasions out of Central Asia decimated and subsequently changed not only Russia, but Turkey, Iran, India, China, and the northern reaches of the Arab Middle East, Europe in many parts knew no such level of destruction, and thus was able to emerge as the political cockpit of the world.[12] Indeed, given that the Sahara Desert blocked Europe off from almost all of Africa, the macro-destiny of medieval Europe up until the Columbian epoch, according to Mackinder, was to be generally conditioned by what happened on the Asian steppe. And it wasn't only the Mongols that we are talking about; the Seljuk Turks, bursting out of the heartland steppe in the tenth and eleventh centuries, overran much of the Middle East, and it was their ill treatment of Christian pilgrims at Jerusalem that ostensibly led to the Crusades, which Mackinder considers the beginning of Europe's collective modern history.

Mackinder goes on in this vein, laying out for the reader a Eurasia bounded by ice to the north and tropical ocean to the south, which has four marginal regions at its extremities, all of them positioned under the shadow of the vast and pivotal expanse of Central Asia and its Mongol-Turkic hordes. These four marginal regions, as he informs us, correspond not coincidentally to the four great numerical religions: for faith, too, in Mackinder's judgment, is a function of geography. There are the "monsoon lands," one in the east facing the Pacific Ocean, the home of Buddhism; the other in the south facing the Indian Ocean, the home of Hinduism. The third marginal region is Europe itself, watered by the Atlantic to the west, the hub of Christianity. But the most fragile of the four outliers is the Middle East, home of Islam, "deprived of moisture by the proximity of Africa," and "except in the oases . . . thinly peopled" (in 1904, that is). Devoid of forest, dominated by desert, and thus wide open to nomadic invasions and to subsequent upheavals and revolutions, the Middle East is, in addition—because of its propinquity to gulfs, seas, and oceans— particularly vulnerable to sea power (even as it benefits by it). Strictly speaking, the Greater Middle East, in Mackinder's wholly geographic viewpoint, is the ultimate unstable transition zone, the sprawling way station between the Mediterranean world and Indian and Chinese civilizations, registering all the monumental shifts in power politics. This is an altogether consistent precursor to Hodgson's depiction of the Greater Middle East as the Oikoumene of the world of antiquity, which gave birth to three of the great confessional religions (Judaism, Christianity, and Islam), and continued its pivotal role in geopolitics into modern times.

And yet for Mackinder, writing in an age before Big Oil and pipelines and ballistic missiles, the globe's geographical pivot, nevertheless, lies slightly afield. For he brushes aside the Middle East and plows onward with his thesis.

The Columbian epoch, he writes, featured the discovery of the sea route to India around the Cape of Good Hope, thus bypassing the Middle East. Whereas in the Middle Ages, Europe was "caged between an impassable desert to south, an unknown ocean to west . . . icy or forested wastes to north and north-east," and "horsemen and camelmen" to the east and southeast, she now suddenly had access via the Indian Ocean to the entire rimland of southern Asia, to say nothing of her strategic discoveries in the New World.

But while the peoples of Western Europe "covered the ocean with their fleets," Russia was expanding equally impressively on land, "emerging from her northern forests" to police the steppe with her

Cossacks against the Mongol nomads. So just as Portuguese, Dutch, and English mariners triumphantly rounded the Cape, Russia was sweeping into Siberia and sending peasants to sow the southwestern steppe with wheat fields, outflanking the Islamic Iranian world. Toynbee and others would make this point decades later, but Mackinder was among the first.[13] It was an old story this, Europe versus Russia: a liberal sea power—as were Athens and Venice—against a reactionary land power—as was Sparta and Prussia. For the sea, in addition to the cosmopolitan influences it bestows by virtue of access to distant harbors, provides the sort of inviolate border security necessary for liberalism and democracy to take root. (The United States is virtually an island nation bordered by two oceans and the thinly peopled Canadian Arctic to the north. Only to its south is it threatened by the forces of Mexican demography.)

Mackinder notes that in the nineteenth century steam and the Suez Canal increased the mobility of sea power around the southern rimland of Eurasia, even as the development of railways began to act as "feeders for ocean-going commerce." But as he also notes, railways were now beginning to do the same for land power as they already had for sea power, and nowhere so much as in the heartland of Eurasia, which was previously hampered by the lack of stone and timber necessary for road making.

At last, he reaches his main point:

As we consider this rapid review of the broader currents of history, does not a certain persistence of geographical relationship become evident? Is not the pivot region of the world's politics that vast area of Euro-Asia which is inaccessible to ships, but in antiquity lay open to the horse-riding nomads, and is to-day about to be covered with a network of railways?

In Mackinder's view, the centrality of an expanded Russia at the beginning of the twentieth century would replace that of the Mongol hordes, which some might argue had the greatest effect on world history during the second millennium. Just as the Mongols banged at—

and often broke down—the gates of the marginal regions of Eurasia (Finland, Poland, Turkey, Syria, Iraq, Persia, India, and China), so, too, now would Russia, sustained by the cohesiveness of its land-mass, won by the recent development of its railways. For as Mac-kinder writes, "the geographical quantities in the calculation are more measurable and more nearly constant than the human." Forget the czars and in 1904 the commissars-yet-to-be, they are but trivia compared to the deeper, tectonic forces of geography and technology. This is not to say that Mackinder was helped by current events. For within two weeks of his famous lecture, the Japanese navy at-tacked Port Arthur at the southern entrance to Manchuria in the first battle of the Russo-Japanese War. The war ended a year later with the Battle of Tsushima Strait, where the Japanese won a great victory at sea. In other words, while Mackinder was proclaiming the importance of land power, it was sea power that defeated the most sprawling land power on earth in this early conflict of the twentieth century.[14]

Still, Mackinder's seeming determinism prepared us well for the rise of the Soviet Union and its enormous zone of influence in the second half of the twentieth century, as well as for the two world wars in the first half, which were, as the historian Paul Kennedy points out, struggles for Mackinder's "rimlands," running from East-ern Europe to the Himalayas and beyond.[15] From the Russian Revo-lution right up to the dissolution of the Soviet Union, railways in Central Asia and Siberia expanded by 45,000 miles, proving Mac-kinder's point.[16] Cold War containment strategy, moreover, would depend heavily on rimland bases across the Greater Middle East and the Indian Ocean. Indeed, the U.S. projection of power into the rim-lands of Afghanistan and Iraq, and America's tension with Russia over the political fate of Central Asia and the Caucasus—the geo-graphical pivot itself—have given yet more legitimacy to Mackinder's thesis. In his last paragraph, Mackinder raises the specter of Chinese conquests of Russian territory, which would make, he says, China the dominant geopolitical power. If one looks at how Chinese migrants are now demographically claiming parts of Siberia from Russia, even as Russia's political control of its eastern reaches shows strains, one can envision Mackinder being right once more.

Mackinder has been attacked as an arch-determinist and an imperialist. Both charges are to a degree unfair. An educator all his life, he was not by nature extreme or ideological. Mackinder was only an imperialist because Great Britain at the time ran a worldwide empire, and he was an enlightened British patriot, who saw the prospect of human development—and especially democracy—more likely under British influence than under Russian or German. He was subject to the same prejudices of those of his day. He was a determinist only to the extent that geography was his subject, and geography can by its very nature be deterministic. Mackinder especially tried to defend British imperialism in the aftermath of the debilitating Boer War (1899–1902).[17] But a principal theme of his *Democratic Ideals and Reality: A Study in the Politics of Reconstruction* is that human agency can overcome the dictates of geography. "In the long run, however," writes biographer W. H. Parker, paraphrasing Mackinder, "those who are working in harmony with environmental influences will triumph over those who strive against them."[18] This is the very essence of Raymond Aron's "probabilistic determinism," to which most of us can subscribe.[19] In fact, Aron defends Mackinder, believing at heart he is a social scientist rather than a natural scientist, as Mackinder, in Aron's view, believes geography can be conquered through technological innovation.[20] To erase any doubt as to where Mackinder in the end came down on the matter, at the beginning of *Democratic Ideals and Reality*, he writes:

> Last century, under the spell of the Darwinian theory, men came to think that those forms of organization should survive which adapted themselves best to their natural environment. To-day we realize, as we emerge from our fiery trial [of World War I], that human victory consists in our rising superior to such mere fatalism.[21]

Mackinder was opposed to complacency in all its forms. Again, here is a telling example from the beginning of *Democratic Ideals and Reality:*

> The temptation of the moment [in 1919] is to believe that un-
> ceasing peace will ensue merely because tired men are deter-
> mined that there shall be no more war. But international tension
> will accumulate again, though slowly at first; there was a gen-
> eration of peace after Waterloo. Who among the diplomats
> round the Congress table at Vienna in 1814 foresaw that Prus-
> sia would become a menace to the world? Is it possible for us
> so to grade the stream bed of future history as that there shall
> be no more cataracts? This, and no smaller, is the task before us
> if we would have posterity think less meanly of our wisdom
> than we think of that of the diplomats of Vienna.[22]

No, Mackinder was no mere fatalist. He believed that geography and the environment could be overcome, but only if we treat those subjects with the greatest knowledge and respect.

To be sure, Machiavelli's *The Prince* has endured partly because it is an instructional guide for those who do not accept fate and require the utmost cunning to vanquish more powerful forces. So, too, with Mackinder's theories. He sets out a daunting vision that appears overwhelming because of the power of his argument and prose, and so there is the sensation of being bludgeoned into a predetermined reality when in reality he is actually challenging us to rise above it. He was the best kind of hesitant determinist, understanding just how much effort is required of us to avoid tragedy.

Determinism implies static thinking, the tendency to be over-whelmed by sweeping forces and trends, and thus to be unaffected by the ironies of history as they actually unfold. But Mackinder was the opposite. Like a man possessed, he kept revising his 1904 "Pivot" thesis, adding depth and insights to it, taking into account recent events and how they affected it. The real brilliance of "The Geograph-ical Pivot of History" lay in its anticipation of a *global* system at a time when Edwardian-era minds were still employed in exertions over a European *continental* system.[23] That continental system had its roots in the post-Napoleonic Congress of Vienna almost a hundred years earlier, and was in its dying days though few, save for Mackinder and some others, intuited it. The cataclysm of World War I, which erupted a decade after the publication of "The Geographical Pivot of History," pitted Germany-Prussia and czarist Russia against each other on the eastern front, and German land power against British-French maritime power on the western front, thus upholding in a vague manner Mackinder's struggle-for-the-Heartland idea, while at the same time adding complications and adjustments to it. *Democratic Ideals and Reality* was his book-length update to "The Geographical Pivot of History," appearing the same year as the Versailles Peace Conference. He warned the peacemakers "that the issue between sea power and land power had not been finally resolved and that the duel between Teuton and Slav was yet to be fought out," despite a war that had cost millions of lives.[24] "The Geographical Pivot of History" was a theory only; *Democratic Ideals and Reality,* rather, a revised and expanded thesis that was also a far-sighted warning.

The writing in *Democratic Ideals* seethes with description, erudition, and illuminating tangents about both contemporary and antique landscapes, as Mackinder presents the world from both a seaman's and a landsman's perspective. Nile valley civilization, he tells us, thinking like a seaman, was protected on the east and west by deserts, and never suffered from Mediterranean piracy only because of the marshlands of the Delta to the north: this helped provide Egyptian kingdoms with extraordinary levels of stability. To the north of Egypt in the eastern Mediterranean lay the island of Crete, the largest and most fruitful of the Greek islands, and therefore "the first base of sea power" in the Western world, for "the man-power of the sea must be nourished by land fertility somewhere." From Crete, mariners may have settled the Aegean " 'sea-chamber' " that formed the very basis of Greek civilization: Greek sea power flourished until challenged by Persian land power, Mackinder goes on. But the Persian effort failed. It was the half-Greek Macedonians to the north, "in the root of the

Greek Peninsula itself," who finally conquered the whole Aegean. For Macedonia, being more remote from the sea than Greece, bred a race of "landmen and mountaineers," who were more obedient to their rulers even as they were excellent warriors, and yet still close enough to the sea to have a sense of the wider world. It was this Macedonian conquest, making the Aegean a "closed sea"—thus depriving the Greeks and the Phoenicians of their bases—that allowed Alexander the Great, a Macedonian, the luxury to attempt the land conquest of the Greater Near East. Mackinder then illuminates the geographical origins of Roman and later empires, even as he admits that geography is not always an explanation for history: for example, the Saracens from the Sahara in the southern Mediterranean conquered Spain in the northern Mediterranean, while the Romans in the northern Mediterranean conquered Carthage in the southern Mediterranean, in both cases because of the will of men in the form of exceptional sea power.

And yet, as Mackinder suggests, however dramatic the accomplishments of individuals, geographical forces, acting upon human cultures, tend ultimately to win through. For example, there is the case of Petersburg, which Peter the Great made the capital of Russia in "the teeth of a hostile geography," even as culture and highly motivated individuals made its survival technically possible. So in the short run Peter triumphed, and for two centuries "the Russian Empire was ruled from this 'folly.' " But in the end land-bound Moscow—and geography—again won out. Human volition has its limits.[25]

Mackinder's departure point for the post–World War I era is his salient perception from the "Pivot" that we are confronted for the first time in history with a "closed system," in which "political ownership of all the dry land" has been "pegged out." In this new global geography, the dry-land area forms a "vast cape," or "World-Promontory," as he puts it, stretching from the British Isles and Iberia south all the way around the bulge of West Africa and the Cape of Good Hope, and then across the Indian Ocean up to the Indian Subcontinent and East Asia. Thus, Eurasia and Africa together form the

"World-Island," something that as the decades march on will be increasingly a cohesive unit:[26]

> There is one ocean covering nine-twelfths of the globe; there is one continent—the World-Island—covering two-twelfths of the globe; and there are many smaller islands, whereof North America and South America are, for effective purposes, two, which together cover the remaining one-twelfth.[27]

Furthermore, one could say that 75 percent of the human population lives in Eurasia (to speak nothing of Africa), which contains most of the world's wealth, 60 percent of its gross domestic product, and three-quarters of its energy resources.[28]

The implicit assumption in Mackinder's thesis is that Eurasia will dominate geopolitical calculations, even as Europe will be less and less of an entity separate from the rest of Eurasia and Africa. "The Old World has become insular, or in other words a unit, incomparably the largest geographical unit on our globe." From the end of the Napoleonic Wars, with the exception of Portuguese Mozambique, German East Africa, and the Dutch East Indies, British sea power encompassed this "World-Promontory." Mackinder compares the Roman control of the Mediterranean, with its legions along the Rhine frontier, with British domination of the Indian Ocean (the Promontory's chief sea), while the British army stakes out the northwest frontier of India against an encroaching czarist Russia.[29]

The implications of Mackinder's "closed system," in which it is possible to conceive of the entire breadth of Eurasia and Africa as one organic unit, and the further closing of that system throughout the course of the twentieth century and beyond, forms the core point of my own study, from which others will emerge. But it is equally crucial to acknowledge that even a closed system, in which, for example, the Indian Ocean is a vascular center of the world economy, with tankers in the future collecting oil and natural gas from Somalia for deposit in China, is still divided from within by geography. Geography, in fact, becomes all the more important in a closed system, because of that system's propensity to make the effect, say, of a harsh terrain in Afghanistan register politically from one end of the World-Island to the other.

For now, let us return to explore exactly what Mackinder meant by the Heartland, which so much affects the destiny of the World-Island.

Mackinder both begins and sums up his thinking with this oft-quoted grand and simplistic dictum:

Who rules East Europe commands the Heartland:
Who rules the Heartland commands the World-Island:
Who rules the World-Island commands the World.[30]

The first thing to realize here is that Mackinder, rather than being wholly deterministic, is just as much reacting to events that are the upshot of human agency as he is predicting them. Between his publication of "The Geographical Pivot of History" in 1904 and of *Democratic Ideals and Reality* in 1919 came the carnage of World War I, and in the war's aftermath came the Paris Peace Conference, which was taking place as Mackinder's book was going to press. With the collapse of the Austro-Hungarian and Ottoman empires as a result of the war, the diplomats at Versailles had as one of their central purposes the rearrangement of the map of Eastern Europe. And thus Mackinder in his book takes up a cause that he ignored in "The Geographical Pivot of History" fifteen years previously: the "vital necessity that there should be a tier of independent states between Germany and Russia." For as he puts it, "We were opposed to the half-German Russian Czardom because Russia was the dominating, threatening force both in East Europe and the Heartland for half a century. We were opposed to the wholly German Kaiserdom, because Germany took the lead in East Europe from the Czardom, and would then have crushed the revolting Slavs, and dominated East Europe and the

Heartland." Thus, Eastern Europe in Mackinder's view of 1919 becomes the key to the Heartland, from which derives the land power
of Germany and especially that of Russia. For Russia is "knocking at
the landward gates of the Indies," making it opposed to British sea
power, which, in turn, is "knocking at the sea gates of China" around
the Cape of Good Hope and later through the Suez Canal. By proposing a bulwark of independent Eastern European states from Estonia
south to Bulgaria—"Great Bohemia," "Great Serbia," "Great Ruma-
nia," and so on—Mackinder is, in effect, providing nuance to his and
James Fairgrieve's idea of a "crush zone," which Fairgrieve had specifically identified in his writings in 1915, meaning that area liable to
be overrun by either land power originating from the Heartland or by
sea power originating from Western Europe.[31] For if these newly sovereign states can survive, then there is a chance for the emergence of
a Central Europe, in both a spiritual and geopolitical sense, after all.
Mackinder went further, proposing a series of states to the east, as it
were, of Eastern Europe: White Russia (Belarus), Ukraine, Georgia,
Armenia, Azerbaijan, and Daghestan, in order to thwart the designs
of Bolshevik Russia, which he called "Jacobin Czardom." In fact,
with the demise of the Soviet Union in 1991 there would emerge a
line of newly independent states strikingly similar to what Mackinder
had proposed.[32]

But Mackinder, at least initially, was proven wrong in this matter.
He does not seem to have realized, as Toynbee did, that a Europe
whose borders were drawn up on the principle of national self-
determination was liable to be a Europe dominated by Germany—
larger, geographically better positioned, and more powerful than any
of the other ethnically bound states. Indeed, Germany would conquer
Eastern Europe in the 1930s and early 1940s, and Russia, in reaction,
would conquer these newly independent states of Mackinder's buffer
zone, keeping them in a prison of nations from 1945 to 1989. Only
in the last generation has hope arisen that a spiritual Central Europe
can survive between the two land powers of Russia and Germany. So
why did Mackinder, the arch-realist, suddenly go soft, as it were, in
supporting what were, in effect, "Wilsonian" principles of national

self-determination? Because, as one scholar, Arthur Butler Dugan, suggests, Mackinder was, his daring and deterministic theories notwithstanding, a child of his time, "a product of the 'climate of opinion' more than he realized."[33]

Mackinder deep down was a liberal, or at least became one. He imagined the British Commonwealth as becoming an association of cultures and peoples, different but equal; and he believed that a league of democracies would be the best defense against an imperial superpower in the heart of Eurasia (thus foreseeing NATO's struggle against the Soviet Union).[34]

Mackinder's drift toward Wilsonian principles, which began in *Democratic Ideals and Reality,* forms the centerpiece of his revision of his own "Heartland" theory. The theory was first expounded in the "Geographical Pivot" article, without using the term "Heartland." The term was actually coined by Fairgrieve in his own book, *Geography and World Power,* in 1915. To the pivot areas of Central Asia identified in 1904, Mackinder added in 1919 the "Tibetan and Mongolian upland courses of the great rivers of India and China," and the whole broad belt of countries going north to south from Scandinavia to Anatolia, and including Eastern and Central Europe: so that the new Heartland would more or less approximate the Soviet Empire at the height of its power during the Cold War.[35] Or I should say: the Soviet Empire plus Norway, northern Turkey, Iran, and western China. Because the bulk of the Chinese population live not in the west but in the monsoonal coastlands, Mackinder's Heartland is the bulk of interior Eurasia that is relatively sparsely populated, with the demographic immensities of China, India, and the western half of Europe to the sides of it. The Middle East (specifically Arabia and the Fertile Crescent) was neither heavily populated nor part of the Heartland, but as Mackinder writes in 1919, now central to the destiny of the World-Island, because it is the "passage-land" from Europe to the Indies and from the northern part of the Heartland to the southern part, as well as being accessible by several water bodies around the Arabian Peninsula.[36] But the destiny of Arabia, as that of Europe, is heavily influenced by the Heartland; and the most proximate part of the Heartland to Arabia is Iran, a lesson we should bear in mind for our own time. Indeed, the Iranian plateau is critical, and I will deal with it later.

A fascinating exception here is Greece, which is geographically part of the independent tier of buffer states between Germany and Russia, but which Mackinder leaves out of his expanded Heartland of 1919 because Greece, as he says, is so much bounded by water and therefore accessible to sea power. Greece was the first of these states to be liberated from German control in World War I. Here, too, Mackinder showed prescience. "Possession of Greece by a great Heartland power," he writes, "would probably carry with it the control of the World-Island."[37] In fact, that almost happened. After heavy fighting in a civil war between pro-Western and communist guerrillas, Greece became the only one of these buffer lands not to fall within the Soviet orbit after World War II, and later formed with Turkey a strategic southern ridgeline of NATO. The Soviets, as it happened, would go on to lose the Cold War.

According to Mackinder, Europe and the Middle East are much more affected by the Heartland than India and China, whose hundreds of millions of people are self-contained and thus able to peacefully develop. This leads him to predict that the future lies to a large extent in the "Monsoon lands of India and China."[38]

But why is the Heartland so important in the first place? Is control of the broad lowlands and tablelands of the Eurasian interior truly pivotal to world power? Yes, they are rich in oil and strategic minerals and metals, but is that even enough? Mackinder's idea is mechanical in the extreme. And yet, partly as a consequence, it provides a vehicle for explaining so much about the spatial arrangement of states and peoples around the Eastern Hemisphere. It is easier to explain the relationships between one end of Eurasia and the other by having the center of it as a reference point, rather than any coastal margin. The Heartland may best be seen as a register of power around the World-Island rather than the determiner of it. Near the end of *Democratic Ideals and Reality* Mackinder posits that if the Soviet Union emerges from World War I ahead of Germany, "she must rank as the greatest land Power on the globe," because of her ability to garrison the Heartland.[39] The Soviet Union did so eventually emerge, and did so again after World War II. Thus, it came to face off, as Mackinder indicated it would, against the world's preeminent sea power, the United States. It was in quest of sea power—the search for a warm-water port on the Indian Ocean—that the Soviets ultimately invaded Afghanistan, a small part of the Heartland that had eluded its grasp. And by getting entrapped by guerrillas in Afghanistan the Kremlin's whole empire fell apart. Now Russia, greatly reduced in size, tries to reconsolidate that same Heartland—Belarus, Ukraine, the Caucasus, and Central Asia. That, in and of itself, a century after Mackinder put down his theories, constitutes one of the principal geopolitical dramas of our time.

Chapter V

THE NAZI DISTORTION

As heirs to land power, Germans and Russians have over the centuries thought more in terms of geography than Americans and Britons, heirs to sea power. For Russians, mindful of the devastation wrought by the Golden Horde of the Mongols, geography means simply that without expansion there is the danger of being overrun. Enough territory is never enough. Russia's need for an empire of Eastern European satellites during the Cold War, and its use of military power, subversion, and the configuration of its energy pipeline routes all designed to gain back its near-abroad, and thus reconstitute in effect the former Soviet Union, are the wages of a deep insecurity. But Germans, at least through the middle of the twentieth century, were more conscious of geography still. The shape of German-speaking territories on the map of Europe changed constantly from the Dark Ages through modern times, with the unification of a German state occurring only in the 1860s under Otto von Bismarck. Germany stood at the very heart of Europe, a land and sea power both, and thus fully conscious of its ties to maritime Western Europe and to the Heartland of Russia–Eastern Europe. Germany's victories against Denmark, Habsburg Austria, and France were ultimately the result of Bismarck's strategic brilliance, anchored in his acute sense of geography, which was actually the recognition of limits: namely, those Slavic regions to the east and southeast where Germany dare not go. Germany's abjuration of Bismarck's caution led to its loss in World War I, which gave Germans a keener sense of their geographic vulnerability—and possibilities. Historically changeable on the map, lying between sea to the north and Alps to the south, with the plains to the west and east open to invasion and expansion both, Germans have literally lived geography. It was they who developed and elaborated upon geopolitics, or *Geopolitik* in German, which is the concept of politically and militarily dominated space. And it was such geographical theories, which in the first half of the twentieth century owed much to Mackinder, that was to lead to the Germans' undoing—discrediting geography and geopolitics for generations of Germans since World War II.

The rise and fall of *Geopolitik*, in which one theoretician after another both built on and misused the work of his predecessor, began in earnest with Friedrich Ratzel, a late-nineteenth-century German geographer and ethnographer, who coined the idea of *Lebensraum*, or "living space." The concept actually owes its origin to a German immigrant in early-nineteenth-century America, Friedrich List, a journalist, political science professor, business speculator, and friend of Henry Clay, who drew inspiration from the Monroe Doctrine, with its notion of a vast and virtually sovereign geographical area. As for Ratzel, he was also much influenced by the writings of Charles Darwin, and thus developed an organic, somewhat biological sense of geography in which borders were constantly evolving depending upon the size and makeup of the human populations in the vicinity. While we regard borders as static, as the very representation of permanence, legality, and stability, Ratzel saw only gradual expansion, contraction, and impermanence in the affairs of nations. For him the map *breathed* as though a living being, and from this came the idea of the organic-biological state whose expansion was written into natural law.

One of Ratzel's students, a Swede, Rudolf Kjellén, would as a political scientist at the universities in Uppsala and Göteborg coin the word *"Geopolitik."* Kjellén, an intense Swedish nationalist, feared Russian expansionism in quest of the relatively warm waters of the Baltic Sea. He wanted an expansionist Sweden and Finland to counter Russia's designs. While Kjellén found support for his views with members of the aristocracy and upper middle classes, nostalgic for Sweden's past grandeur under kings such as Gustavus Adolfus and Charles XII, there was ultimately too little public support for his views. The appetite for great power preoccupations in Scandinavia, even by the late-nineteenth and early-twentieth centuries, was long past. Kjellén transferred all his hopes to a Greater Germany—to stand forth against Russia and England, both of which he especially detested. Kjellén's German empire-of-the-future, as he cataloged it, included all of Central and Eastern Europe as well as the Channel ports along the French coast, and the Baltic provinces of Russia, Ukraine, Asia Minor, and Mesopotamia (to be connected to Berlin by a great railway). Employing Ratzel's ideas, Kjellén categorized human societies in racial, biological terms, conceiving of the state in terms of the *Volk,* which, if sufficiently virile and dynamic, would require an especially large amount of living space. It is the very glibness and windiness inhabiting the thought of Ratzel and Kjellén that a later generation of murderers would make use of to justify their acts. Ideas matter, for good and for bad, and hazy ideas can be especially dangerous. Whereas legitimate geography shows us what we are up against in the challenges we face around the world, Ratzel's and Kjellén's is an illegitimate geography that annihilates the individual and replaces him with the vast racial multitude.

This is all but prologue to the life of Karl Haushofer, the geopolitician of Nazism and steadfast admirer of Mackinder. The tragic perversion of Mackinder's work by Haushofer, as well as the danger posed by Nazi *Geopolitik,* is elegantly told in a largely forgotten but classic work of political science, *Geopolitics: The Struggle for Space and Power* by Robert Strausz-Hupé, published in 1942. Strausz-Hupé, an Austrian immigrant to the United States, was a faculty member at the University of Pennsylvania and a U.S. ambassador to four countries (including Turkey) during the Cold War years. In 1955 in Philadelphia, he founded the Foreign Policy Research Institute, with which I have been loosely affiliated for two decades. Strausz-Hupé's book, written before the tide turned in the Allies' favor in World War II, was a clear-cut attempt not only to explain the danger of Nazi *Geopolitik* to the fellow citizens of his adopted country, but to explain what geopolitics is and why it is important, so that the forces of good can make use of it in a much different way than the Nazis were doing. Strausz-Hupé thus rescues the reputation of Mackinder and the discipline itself, while performing an act of individual agency in doing his intellectual part to win the war.

Major General Professor Doktor Karl Haushofer was born in 1869 in Munich. His grandfather, uncle, and father all wrote about cartography and travel. Thus was his life marked. Haushofer joined the Bavarian army and in 1909 was appointed artillery instructor to the Japanese army. He became infatuated with the military rise of Japan, with which he advocated a German alliance. Haushofer fought in World War I as a brigade commander, and had as his aide the Nazi Rudolf Hess, to whom he would later dedicate several books. After the war Haushofer was appointed to the chair of geography and military science at the University of Munich, where Hess followed him as a disciple. It was through Hess that Haushofer met the "rising agitator" Adolf Hitler, whom Haushofer would visit and provide academic briefings on geopolitics while Hitler was imprisoned at Landsberg fortress, following the failure of the Beer Hall Putsch of 1923. Hitler was writing *Mein Kampf* at the time, and as a partially educated man, he needed, despite his intuition, to know more about the real world. And here was this university professor who could fill

some of the gaps in his knowledge. Chapter 14 of *Mein Kampf,* which
defines Nazi foreign policy and the Nazi ideal of *Lebensraum,* was
possibly influenced by Haushofer, who was in turn influenced by,
among others, Ratzel, Kjellén, and especially Mackinder. For Mackinder had written that world history has always been made by the
great outward thrusts of landlocked peoples located near Eastern Europe and the Heartland of Eurasia.[1]

Strausz-Hupé takes us on a journey along the line of thought by
which Haushofer came to be mesmerized by his contemporary Mackinder. Mackinder, though obsessed with land power, never actually
denigrated the importance of sea power. But he was pessimistic about
the ability of British sea power to prevent a raid on the Heartland by
German land power. And once in possession of the Heartland, Germany could build a great navy to aid in its conquest of the World-
Island. In the twentieth century, Mackinder explained that, more
than ever, sea power required a broader and deeper landward reach
to take advantage of industrialization. The Industrial Age meant a
world of big states, and the strong ate the weak. Haushofer adopted
this theory of Mackinder "to the opposite German point of view,"
Strausz-Hupé writes, "and concluded that the path to German world
power lay along the lines that had frightened the English, i.e., consolidation of the German and Russian 'greater areas.' " Haushofer, in
the words of Strausz-Hupé, goes positively cloudy and mystical and
nebulous when describing Mackinder's Heartland. It is the "cradle of
world conquerors," "a gigantic citadel reaching from 'the Elbe to the
Amur,' " that is, from central Germany to Manchuria and the Russian
Far East, deep into which Germany can withdraw her vital war industries while its army and navy can strike outward in all directions.[2]

Whereas Mackinder, influenced by Wilsonianism and the need to
preserve the balance of power in Eurasia, recommended in 1919 a
belt of independent states in Eastern Europe, Haushofer, inverting
Mackinder's thesis, calls a few years later for the "extinction of such
states." Haushofer, Strausz-Hupé reports, calls them "bits of states . . .
fragments," whose inhabitants think only in terms of "narrow space,"
which to Haushofer, as Strausz-Hupé explains, "is the unmistakable

symptom of decay." Strausz-Hupé goes on, uncovering Haushofer's "neat logic" about the dissolution of the British Empire and the need to break up the Soviet Union into its component ethnic parts, which will all lean on a Greater Germany, which in Haushofer's view is the only state entitled to national self-determination. For in Haushofer's own words, "one-third of the German people [are] living under alien rule outside the borders of the Reich." German *Geopolitik*, Strausz-Hupé warns, is a world of "acrobatics on the ideological trapeze," with conclusions of "stark simplicity." The German new world order presupposes a Greater East Asia under Japanese hegemony, a U.S.-dominated "Pan-America," and a German-dominated Eurasian Heartland with a "Mediterranean–North African subregion under the shadow rule of Italy." But for Haushofer, this is only an intermediate step: for, according to Mackinder, the Heartland dominates the World-Island and hence the world.[3]

Strausz-Hupé tells us that Mackinder's concept of the Heartland "is colored by the very personal point of view of an Edwardian Englishman." For Mackinder's generation, Russia had been Great Britain's antagonist for almost a century, and consequently British statesmen lived with the fear of a Russia that would control the Dardanelles, consume the Ottoman Empire, and fall upon India. Thus, Mackinder fixated upon a tier of independent buffer states between Russia and maritime Europe, even as he identified the Heartland inside Russia itself as a visual tool of strategy. "Mackinder's vision," Strausz-Hupé writes, "accorded only too well with the morbid philosophy of world power or downfall which explains so much about German national pathology. There is in Mackinder's dogma just the kind of finality for which the Wagnerian mentality yearns." And yet Strausz-Hupé ultimately rescues Mackinder's reputation:

> Mackinder's book—written when the armies had not yet returned from the battlefields—is dignified by a cool detachment and never loses sight of the broad perspectives of history. It is his faith in the individual which his German admirer so woefully lacks. For, though Haushofer likes to stress the part of

heroism in the shaping of history, it is the collective sacrifice of
the battlefield rather than the anonymous struggles of ordinary
men and women . . . which he has in mind.[4]

Strausz-Hupé and Mackinder both believe in human agency, in the
sanctity, as they say, of the individual, whereas the German *Geopolitikers* do not.

Whereas in Mackinder's hands the Heartland is an arresting way
to explain geopolitics, in Haushofer's hands it becomes both a crazed
and dreamy ideology. Yet Strausz-Hupé takes it very seriously, and
informs his fellow Americans to do likewise: "To the Nazis," Strausz-
Hupé writes, Haushofer "transmitted something that the vaporous
cerebrations of Adolf Hitler had failed to provide—a coherent doctrine of empire." While Mackinder saw the future in terms of a balance of power that would protect freedom, Haushofer was determined
to overthrow the balance of power altogether: thus he perverted geopolitics. To wit, just as Haushofer distorted Mackinder, he also distorted Lord George Nathaniel Curzon. Curzon delivered a lecture in
1907 about "Frontiers." Haushofer, inspired by Curzon, wrote a
book entitled *Frontiers,* which was, in fact, about how to break them.
According to Haushofer, only nations in decline seek stable borders,
and only decadent ones seek to protect their borders with permanent
fortifications: for frontiers are living organisms. Virile nations build
roads instead. Frontiers were but temporary halts for master nations.
To be sure, German *Geopolitik* is perpetual warfare for "space," and
thus akin to nihilism. Strausz-Hupé adds:

> It should not be assumed, however, that this perverted use, de-
> structive to world peace as it is, necessarily invalidates all geo-
> political theories; anthropology is no less a science for having
> served as a vehicle to racism.[5]

Haushofer, even within the confines of his own violent worldview,
had few fixed principles. On Hitler's fiftieth birthday, in 1939, he
described the Führer as a "statesman" who combined in his person

"Clausewitz's blood and Ratzel's space and soil."[6] Haushofer greeted the Russo-German pact of 1939 with enthusiasm in an editorial, stressing Germany's need to join its land power forces with those of Russia. Yet after Hitler invaded Russia in 1941, he wrote another editorial, celebrating the invasion as a way to capture the Heartland. Of course, nobody dared criticize Hitler's decision. There is a strong case to be made that Haushofer's specific links to Hitler were greatly exaggerated, even as Haushofer, nevertheless, came to represent a typical Nazi strategic view.[7] In any case, as the war turned badly, Haushofer fell out of favor with the Führer, and was imprisoned in the Dachau concentration camp in 1944. The same year, Haushofer's son, Albrecht, also a geopolitician, was executed for his participation in the army plot against Hitler. This was after Haushofer and his family had been incarcerated. Then there was the fact that Haushofer's wife was part Jewish: the couple was protected from Nazi race laws by Hess, who was imprisoned in Britain in 1941 after a solo flight there to negotiate a separate peace. The contradictions in Haushofer's life must have become too much to bear, as he gradually became aware of the monumental carnage and destruction in a world war that he did his part to bring about. Haushofer's life is a signal lesson in the dangers inherent for men of ideas who seek desperately to ingratiate themselves with those in power. Soon after Germany's defeat and an Allied investigation of him for war crimes, both Haushofer and his wife committed suicide.

Strausz-Hupé's work is not merely designed to discredit Haushofer and rescue the reputation of Mackinder, but to implore Americans to take geopolitics seriously, because if they don't, others of ill intent will, and in the process vanquish the United States. As he writes at the end of his book:

The Nazi war machine is the *instrument* of conquest; *Geopolitik* is the *master plan* designed to tell those who wield the in-

strument what to conquer and how. It is late, but not too late
to profit by the lessons of *Geopolitik.*[8]

For Strausz-Hupé is every inch a realist. Exposing some of the intellectual underpinnings of a totalitarian state's program of conquest
is not enough for him, and in addition is much too easy. He knows
the uncomfortable truth that just as Mackinder's reasoning is flawed
in crucial ways, Haushofer's reasoning, though perverted, does
have a basis in reality. Therefore, Strausz-Hupé's aim is to imbue
Americans—who live in splendid isolation by virtue of being bounded
by two oceans—with a greater appreciation of the geographical discipline, so that the United States can assume its postwar role as a
stabilizer and preserver of the Eurasian balance of power, which the
Nazis, helped by Haushofer, attempted to overturn.

As for the Heartland thesis itself, Strausz-Hupé, who is extremely
skeptical of it to begin with, says that air power—both commercial
and military—may render it meaningless. Nevertheless, he does believe that Industrial Age technology provided the advantage to big
states: large factories, railway lines, and tanks and aircraft carriers
are best taken advantage of by states with depth of distance and territory. "The history of our times appears to reflect, with malignant
fatality, the trend toward empires and super-states predicted by the
Ratzels, Spenglers, and Mackinders."[9] Of course, the postindustrial
age, with its emphasis on smallness—microchips, mobile phones,
plastic explosives—has empowered not only large states but individuals and stateless groups, too, adding only a deeper complexity and
tension to geopolitics. But Strausz-Hupé intuits some of this in his
discussion of frontiers, which he takes up on account of Haushofer's
misuse of Curzon in this matter.

Despite Haushofer's nihilism, Strausz-Hupé will not be intimidated into debunking him outright. For the very fact of frontiers
shows a world beset by political and military divisions. "The sovereign state is, at least by its origins, organized force. Its history begins
in war. Hence its frontiers—be they 'good' or 'bad'—are strategic

frontiers," Strausz-Hupé writes. He tellingly selects a quotation from Curzon in which the latter notes that frontier wars will increase in number and intensity as "the habitable globe shrinks," at which time "the ambitions of one state come into sharp and irreconcilable collision with those of another."[10] In other words, Haushofer is not altogether wrong in his assumption of perpetual conflict. Even after the war, there will be little respite from the tragedy of the human condition. The very crowding of the planet in recent decades, coupled with the advance of military technology, in which time and distance have been collapsed, means that there will be a crisis of "room" on the map of the world.[11] This crisis of room follows from Mackinder's idea of a "closed system." For now let us note that it adds urgency to Strausz-Hupé's plea that America, which for him represents the ultimate source of good in a world of great powers, can never afford to withdraw from geopolitics. For geopolitics and the competition for "space" is eternal. Liberal states will have to gird themselves for the task, lest they leave the field to the likes of Haushofer.

Chapter VI

THE RIMLAND THESIS

Robert Strausz-Hupé was not the only naturalized American to be warning his fellow citizens during the war about the need to take geopolitics out of Nazi hands, restore its reputation, and employ it for the benefit of the United States. Nicholas J. Spykman was born in 1893 in Amsterdam. During the First World War, when the Netherlands was neutral, he traveled extensively as a foreign correspondent in the Near East (1913 to 1919) and in the Far East (1919 to 1920). Following the war, he earned undergraduate and graduate degrees at the University of California, Berkeley, where he also taught, and then went to Yale, where he founded the Institute of International Studies in 1935.[1] He imbued his students with an awareness of geography as the principal means to assess the dangers and opportunities that his adopted country faced in the world. He died of cancer in 1943 at the age of forty-nine, but not before publishing the prior year *America's Strategy in World Politics: The United States and the Balance of*

Power, a book that even more than the work of Mackinder gives us a framework for understanding the Post Cold War world. Spykman, who lived later, in some senses updates Mackinder.

In the vein of Strausz-Hupé, Morgenthau, Henry Kissinger, and other European immigrants in the middle decades of the twentieth century, who brought realism to a country that had given them refuge but which they felt was dangerously naive, Spykman would have none of the idealism and sentimentalism that was a characteristic of much American thinking. Geography is everything, he argues. The United States was a great power less because of its ideas than because, with direct access to the Atlantic and Pacific oceans, it was "the most favored state in the world from the point of view of location."[2] With Spykman there is no respite from the heartlessness of the map and the consequent struggle for space. He writes, "International society is . . . a society without a central authority to preserve law and order." It is in a state of anarchy, in other words. Thus, all states must struggle for self-preservation. Statesmen can strive for the universal values of justice, fairness, and tolerance, but only so far as they do not interfere with the quest for power, which to him is synonymous with survival. "The search for power is not made for the achievement of moral values; moral values are used to facilitate the attainment of power." Such a statement could almost have been made by Karl Haushofer, and there is much tragedy in that realization. But that should not blind us to the fundamental difference between the two men. Spykman, like Mackinder and Strausz-Hupé, believes in the "safety" of "balanced power," not in domination. From that difference flows all the others. For the "balance of power," Spykman is careful to say, corresponds with the "law of nature and Christian ethics" because it preserves the peace.[3]

While Strausz-Hupé focuses down-and-in on Nazi geopolitical theory and in the process defends Mackinder, Spykman focuses up-and-out on the world map to assess the prospects of Nazi domination, as well as to outline the power configurations of a postwar world that he would not live to see. He begins with a geographical explanation about how the United States became a great power.

"History," Spykman says, "is made in the temperate latitudes," where moderate climates prevail, "and, because very little of the land mass of the Southern Hemisphere lies in this zone, history is made in the temperate latitudes of the Northern Hemisphere." It is not that sub-Saharan Africa and the Southern Cone of South America do not matter, for they matter much more in our day than in the past because of transport and communications technology that has allowed every place to affect every other; rather, it is that they still have less worldwide impact than do places in the Northern Hemisphere, and particularly those places in the northern temperate zone. James Fairgrieve, a near-contemporary of Mackinder, explains that because of the lack of solar energy compared to the tropics, human beings in the temperate zones must work harder to deal with greater varieties of weather, and with the differences in seasons that lead to definite times for sowing and harvest: thus, it is in the temperate zones where human beings "advance from strength to strength." And whereas at the South Pole there is a great continent surrounded by an unbroken ring of ocean, around the North Pole there is an ocean surrounded by a near-unbroken ring of land—the land where human beings have been the most productive. Strausz-Hupé is even more specific in this regard, telling us that history is made between "twenty and sixty degrees north latitude." This area includes North America, Europe, the Greater Middle East and North Africa, most of Russia, China, and the bulk of India. Mackinder's "wilderness girdle" is roughly consistent with it, for it takes in the Heartland and adjacent marginal zones of Eurasia. The critical fact about the United States, according to this line of thinking, is that, located below the Canadian Arctic, it occupies the last great, relatively empty tract of the temperate zone that wasn't settled by urban civilization until the time of the European Enlightenment. Furthermore, America initially prospered, Spykman writes, because the east coast, with its estuaries and indentations, provided "innumerable favorable locations for harbors."[4] Ultimately, in this view, geography was the early sustainer of American freedom.

America's great power position exists because the United States is the regional hegemon in the Western Hemisphere, with, as Spykman says, "power to spare for activities outside the New World," so that it can affect the balance of power in the Eastern Hemisphere.[5] This is no mean feat, and something the United States should not take for granted, for it is rooted in the specifics of Latin American geography. No other nation in the world, not China or Russia, is a hegemon of hemispheric proportions. In explaining how this came about, Spykman brings South America—which Mackinder largely ignores—into the discussion of geopolitics. Because of Mackinder's concentration on Eurasia, and particular its Heartland, Mackinder is vital to an understanding of Cold War geography; whereas Spykman has a more organic conception of the entire globe, and thus is more relevant than Mackinder in an age in which every place can affect every other place.

The strategic and geographic heart of the New World is what Spykman calls the "American Mediterranean," that is, the Greater Caribbean Sea, including the Gulf of Mexico. Just as Athens gained effective control of the Greek archipelago by dominating the Aegean, and Rome took command of the Western world by dominating the European Mediterranean, America, Spykman explains, became a world power when it was able, finally, in the Spanish-American War of 1898, to take unquestioned control of the "middle sea," or Caribbean, from European colonial states, which would allow for the construction of the Panama Canal soon after. "No serious threat against the position of the United States can arise in the region itself," he says about the Caribbean basin. "The islands are of limited size, and the topography of Central America, like that of the Balkan peninsula . . . favors small political units. Even the countries of large size like Mexico, Colombia, and Venezuela are precluded by topography, climate, and absence of strategic raw materials from becoming great naval powers." The U.S. Navy can blockade the eastern boundary of the Caribbean and cut these states off from world markets, thus they are in the final analysis dependent on the United States. Spykman's strength, as well as that of other thinkers I cover here, is the ability to see through the hurly-burly of current events and reveal basic truths. And the basic geographical truth of the Western Hemisphere, he says, is that the division inside it is not between North America and South America, but between the area north of the equatorial jungle dominated by the Amazon and the area south of it. It follows that Colombia and Venezuela, as well as the Guianas, although they are on the northern coast of South America, are functionally part of North America and the American Mediterranean. Their geopolitical world is the Caribbean, and they have relatively little to do with the countries south of the Amazonian jungle, despite sharing the same continent: for like the European Mediterranean, the American Mediterranean does not divide but unites. Just as North Africa is part of the Mediterranean world, but is blocked by the Sahara Desert from being part of Africa proper, the northern coast of South America is part of the Caribbean world, and is severed by geography from South America proper. As Spykman explains:

The mountain ranges which bend eastward from the Andes, separate the Amazon basin from the valleys of the Magdalena and the Orinoco and form the southern boundaries of the Guianas. Beyond this lies the enormous impenetrable jungle and tropical forest of the Amazon valley. The river and its tributaries offer an excellent system of communications from west to east but they do not provide transportation for movements north and south.[6]

As for the southern half of South America, geography works to marginalize its geopolitical importance, Spykman explains. The west coast of South America is crushed between the Pacific Ocean and the Andes, the highest mountain range in the world save for the knot of the Himalayas, Karakoram, and Pamirs, which separate China from the Indian Subcontinent. The valleys through the Andes, compared with those through the Appalachians that give the east coast of America access westward, are narrow and few. The rivers are not navigable, so that countries such as Chile and Peru, eight thousand miles across the Pacific from East Asia, and many thousands of miles from either coast of the United States, are far from the main global channels of communication and historical migration, and thus cannot raise great navies. Only central and southern Chile lie in the temperate zone, and as Henry Kissinger once reportedly quipped, Chile is a dagger thrust at Antarctica. As for the east coast of South America, it is, too, remote and isolated. Because South America does not lie directly below North America, but to its east, the populated parts of South America's Atlantic coast, from Rio de Janeiro to Buenos Aires—far to the south, below the thickly wooded Amazon—are no closer to New York than they are to Lisbon. Dominating the American Mediterranean, and separated from the heart of South America by yawning distance and a wide belt of tropical forest, the United States has few challengers in its own hemisphere. The Southern Cone of South America, Spykman writes, is less a "continental neighbor" than an "overseas territory."[7]

But there is a negative flip side to much of this. Yes, the Caribbean basin unites rather than divides, and the trail of cocaine and marijuana from Colombia through Central America and Mexico to the United States shows this in action. The so-called drug war is a salient lesson in geography, which now threatens the U.S. in its hemispheric backyard. The same with the populist, anti-American radicalism of Venezuelan strongman Hugo Chávez, who has been an affront to American global interests not simply because he has been allied with Russia and Iran, but because he has been allied with Russia and Iran from his perch on the Caribbean basin: were he situated below the Amazon rainforest in the Southern Cone, he would have been less of a threat. Globalization—the Information Age, the collapsing of distance, the explosion of labor migration from demographically young countries to demographically graying countries—has brought the U.S. into an uncomfortably closer relationship with an unstable Latin America around the Caribbean. Whereas the Caribbean was previously a place that the U.S. Navy dominated, but which was otherwise separated from the main currents of American society, it is now part of the very fabric of American life. Spykman's ideas presage these developments, even as, obviously, he could not have predicted their specifics.

Writing in the midst of World War II like Strausz-Hupé, before the fortunes of war turned in the Allies' favor, the worldwide threat posed by the Nazis was uppermost in Spykman's mind. Consequently, he saw the separation of the United States from southern South America as of considerable geographical importance: it was a strategic advantage in that the U.S. did not have to master the region, the way it had to master the Caribbean basin; but it was a vulnerability in that the U.S. had no special geographical advantage in the event of the region being threatened by an adversary from Europe. And the Southern Cone, from Rio de Janeiro southward—what Spykman calls the "equidistant zone"—contained the continent's most productive agricultural regions, three-quarters of South America's population, and the major cities of the two most important South American republics at the time, Brazil and Argentina. Even allowing for its geographic insignificance compared to Eurasia, Spykman worried about the Southern Cone becoming part of the encirclement strategy of a hostile power. Just as the geography of the Americas allowed for the emergence of the United States as a hemispheric hegemon, the breakup of the Americas into a free north and an Axis-dominated south would have spelled the end of that preponderance. "Many of the isolationists," he writes, "accepted the policy of hemisphere defense because it seemed a way of avoiding conflict with Germany, but they overlooked the fact that, even if the U.S. could have avoided war with Germany over Europe, it could not have avoided a struggle with Germany for hegemony over South America."[8]

Even though the Axis powers were to be defeated, Spykman's warning still stands, after a fashion. Europe, Japan, and China have made very deep inroads in trade with Spykman's equidistant zone, and there is no guarantee that the United States will remain the dominant outside power in a region in which under 20 percent of its trade is with the U.S., and the flying time from New York to Buenos Aires is eleven hours, the same time it takes to fly from the U.S. to the Middle East. Although his obsession was with winning the war, by his single-minded focus on geography, Spykman is able to show us the world we currently inhabit.

———

Spykman was a generation younger than Mackinder, deriving his frame of reference and inspiration from the English geographer. Latin America constitutes a long tangent from Spykman's central concern about Eurasia, which he shared with Mackinder. Mackinder's work suggests the struggle of Heartland-dominated land power versus sea power, with Heartland-based land power in the better position. Here is Spykman essentially acknowledging the spiritual influence of Mackinder—even if they assessed differently the relative importance of sea and land power:

> For two hundred years, since the time of Peter the Great, Russia has attempted to break through the encircling ring of border states and reach the ocean. Geography and sea power have persistently thwarted her.[9]

Spykman describes the Heartland as vaguely synonymous with the Soviet Empire, bordered by ice-blocked Arctic seas to the north, between Norway and the Russian Far East; and to the south ringed by mountains, from the Carpathians in Romania to the plateaus of Anatolia, Iran, and Afghanistan, and turning northeastward to the Pamir Knot, the Altai Mountains, the plateau of Mongolia, and finally over to Manchuria and Korea. This to him was the world's key geography, which would be perennially fought over. To the north and inside this belt of mountain and tableland lies the Heartland; to the south and outside this belt lie the demographic giants of Europe, South Asia, Southeast Asia, China, and Japan, as well as the oil-rich Middle East. These marginal areas of Eurasia, especially their littorals, was what Spykman called the Rimland. Spykman held that the Rimland was the key to world power; not Mackinder's Heartland, because in addition to dominating Eurasia, the maritime-oriented Rimland was central to contact with the outside world.[10]

Of course, both men are really talking about the same thing; for Mackinder says that he who controls the Heartland is in the best position to capture the Rimland, which then provides through sea power the key to world domination. As Mackinder writes, "If we would take the long view, must we still not reckon with the possibility that a large part of the Great Continent might someday be united under a single sway, and that an invincible sea-power might be based upon it?" This, of course, was the dream of the Soviet Union, to advance to the warm waters of the Indian Ocean through the invasion of Afghanistan and the attempted destabilization of Pakistan in the 1980s, and thus combine sea power and land power.[11]

Still, Spykman with his emphasis on the Rimland has the slight advantage here. Given the present state of the world, with Rimland upheavals in the Greater Middle East and tensions throughout South Asia, as well as the Korean Peninsula, Spykman with his concentration on the Rimland and his more complexified view of geopolitics seems almost contemporary. For the body of Mackinder's theories emerge from the world at the turn of the twentieth century and the First World War; whereas Spykman is arguing from the facts of life of a later war, in which the Heartland was in the hands of an ally, Soviet Russia, and thus not an issue; whereas the Rimland was endangered by the Axis powers.

While the Axis powers lost the war, the competition for the Rimland continued into the Cold War. The Soviet Union constituted the great Heartland power that threatened the Rimland in Europe, the Middle East, the Korean Peninsula, and elsewhere, and was opposed by Western sea power. Consequently, "containment," the Cold War policy against the Soviet Union enunciated in 1946 by the diplomat and Russia expert George Kennan in his Long Telegram, had both a Spykmanesque and Mackinderesque feel. Containment is the peripheral sea power's name for what the Heartland power calls encirclement.[12] The defense of Western Europe, Israel, moderate Arab states, the Shah's Iran, and the wars in Afghanistan and Vietnam all carried the notion of preventing a communist empire from extending control from the Heartland to the Rimland. In his landmark work, *Nuclear Weapons and Foreign Policy,* published in 1957, the young Henry Kissinger writes that "limited war represents the only means for preventing the Soviet bloc, at an acceptable cost, from overrunning the peripheral areas of Eurasia," especially since, as Kissinger continues, the Soviet Union as the Heartland power possesses "interior lines of communications" that allow it to assemble a considerable force "at any given point along its periphery."[13] Poland, Iran, Afghanistan, Vietnam—battlegrounds all in the history of the Cold War, and all were on the periphery of Soviet and Chinese communism. This was Mackinder's world, but with the sensibility of Spykman.

As Spykman looks out from the vantage point of 1942 beyond World War II, we see the anxious foresight of which the geographical discipline is capable. Even as the Allies are losing and the utter destruction of Hitler's war machine is a priority, Spykman worries aloud about the implications of leaving Germany demilitarized. "A Russian state from the Urals to the North Sea," he explains, "can be no great improvement over a German state from the North Sea to the Urals." Russian airfields on the English Channel would be as dangerous as German airfields to the security of Great Britain. Therefore, a powerful Germany will be necessary following Hitler. Likewise, even as the United States has another three years of vicious island fighting with the Japanese military ahead of it, Spykman is recommending a postwar alliance with Japan against the continental powers of Russia and particularly a rising China. Japan is a net importer of food, and inadequate in oil and coal production, but with a great naval tradition, making it both vulnerable and useful. A large, offshore island nation of East Asia, it could serve the same function for the United States in the Far East as Britain serves in Europe. Spykman underscores the necessity of a Japanese ally against a powerful China, even as in the early 1940s China is weak and reeling under Japanese military devastation:

A modern, vitalized, and militarized China . . . is going to be a threat not only to Japan, but also to the position of the Western Powers in the Asiatic Mediterranean. China will be a continental power of huge dimensions in control of a large section of the littoral of that middle sea. Her geographic position will be similar to that of the United States in regard to the American Mediterranean. When China becomes strong, her present economic penetration in that region will undoubtedly take on political overtones. It is quite possible to envisage the day when this body of water will be controlled not by British, American, or Japanese sea power but by Chinese air power.[14]

Perhaps Spykman's most telling observation concerns Europe. Just as he is opposed to both German and Russian domination of Europe, he is also opposed to a united Europe under any circumstances. He prefers a balance of power among states within Europe as more advantageous to American interests than a European federation, even were it to come about peacefully and democratically. "A federal Europe," he writes, "would constitute an agglomeration of force that would completely alter our significance as an Atlantic power and greatly weaken our position in the Western Hemisphere." Because the European Union is still in an intermediate phase of development, with strong national leaders pursuing coordinated, yet ultimately independent, foreign policies, despite the creation of a single currency zone, it is too soon to pass judgment on Spykman's prediction. Yet already one can see that the more united Europe becomes, the greater its tensions with the United States. A true European super-state with armed forces and a single foreign policy at its command would be both a staunch competitor of the U.S., and possibly the dominant outside power in the equidistant zone of southern South America.[15] (Of course, Europe's current financial crisis make this prospect doubtful.)

Here is where Spykman differs markedly from Mackinder and Cold War containment policy.[16] Containment policy, which encouraged a united Europe as a bulwark against Soviet communism, was rooted in the liberal ideals of a free society as well as in geopolitics. George Kennan, when he wrote the Long Telegram, put his faith in the Western way of life, which he believed would outlast the totalitarian strictures of Soviet communism. It followed, therefore, that like-minded democratic European states were to be encouraged in their efforts toward a common political and economic union. Spykman, though, is even more cold-blooded than Kennan—himself a hard-core realist. Spykman will simply not let any elements outside of geographical ones enter into his analysis. Unlike Haushofer, it is not that he doesn't believe in democracy and a free society: rather, it is that he does not feel the existence of it has much of a role in geopolitical analysis. Spykman sees his job not as improving the world, but in saying what he thinks is going on in it. It is this very ice-in-his-veins sensibility that permits him to see beyond Kennan and the Cold War. Thus, in 1942 he can still write about today:

> Only statesmen who can do their political and strategic thinking in terms of a round earth and a three-dimensional warfare can save their countries from being outmaneuvered on distant flanks. With air power supplementing sea power and mobility again the essence of warfare, no region of the globe is too distant to be without strategic significance, too remote to be neglected in the calculations of power politics.[17]

In other words, because of air power and the expeditionary ability of, in particular, the American military to deploy quickly anywhere, the entire earth is in play. But it isn't only in play for us, but for everyone in Mackinder's "closed system," thanks to communications technology, of which air power is related. Nevertheless, the planet is too big a system to be dominated by one hegemon, so, as Spykman writes, there will a "regional decentralization of power," with each big area affecting the other. He intuits a world of multiple hegemons: similar to the multipolarity that we now all talk about, and which exists already in an economic and political sense, but not quite yet in a military one, because of the great distance still separating the United States from other national militaries. But an emerging world of regional behemoths: the United States, the European Union, China, India, and Russia—with middle powers such as Turkey, Iran, Indonesia, Vietnam, Brazil—would bear out his observations.[18]

What will be the dynamics of such a world? Spykman practices futurology in the best way possible, by staring at maps from different angles. His most arresting insights come from a northern polar map. "Two significant features clearly stand out: the concentration of the land masses in the Northern Hemisphere, and their starfishlike dispersion from the North Pole as a center toward Africa and the Cape of Good Hope, South America and Cape Horn, and Australia." Looking at this projection, land is nearly everywhere; whereas if you stare at a southern polar projection, it is water that is nearly everywhere. The northern polar map shows how the northern continents are relatively close to one another, and the southern continents are far apart. Of course, in this projection the distance between the southern continents is exaggerated, yet the map is still symbolic of how far away Australia is from South America, and South America from Africa. Thus, the geographically close relationship between North America and Eurasia is dynamic and constitutes "the base lines of world politics," while those between the southern continents are much less important. Again, he is not saying that South America and Africa are insignificant in and of themselves, only that their relationships with each other are. South America and Africa achieve significance in geopolitics only in their relationships with the northern continents. But the real message about this polar map is the organic relationship between North America and Eurasia. We think of the vast Pacific as separating the west coast of North America from East Asia. But the polar route indicates that it is just a matter of flying north to Alaska and then south, down across the Russian Far East, to the temperate zone of Japan, Korea, and China. The Arctic, especially if it warms, will give new meaning to sea power and especially air power in future decades. Supersonic transport may cut the distance between the west coast of the United States and cities in Asia by two-thirds. The increased use of polar routes will lock the United States, Russia, and China in an ever tighter embrace. Geography, because it will be more accessible, will, counterintuitively, become more crucial.[19] Globalization, understood as the breaking down of walls, results in an increase in the number and intensity of contacts, which

holds out the greater likelihood of both political conflict and cooperation.

Mackinder argues that once the world becomes "a closed political
system, the ultimate geographical reality would make itself felt."[20] By
that he means the recognition of the World-Island as a single unit in
geopolitics, with North America as the most significant of the continental satellites in the surrounding seas. It is the Northern Hemisphere that Mackinder is talking about here, as all of mainland
Eurasia and much of Africa—the components of the World-Island—
fall inside it. Spykman's Rimland thesis fits neatly with this scenario,
with the marginal zones of Europe, the Middle East, the Indian Subcontinent, and the Far East together dominating the seaboard continuum around Eurasia in the Indian and Pacific oceans, buttressed
by their substantial populations, economic development, and hydrocarbon resources: together, they check the Heartland power of Russia, even as Russia gains the warming waters of its northern Arctic
seaboard.[21] Just as the Arctic will be a hub of planes and ships connecting North America with the northern reaches of the World-Island,
the Greater Indian Ocean will form the maritime interstate of the
World-Island's commercial and military traffic, connecting Africa and
the Middle East with East Asia.

Still, the Eurasian Rimland will not be united in any strictly political sense. In a world of multiple regional hegemons, the danger
with which both Mackinder and Spykman were concerned, that of a
single land power dominating Eurasia, or a single sea power dominating the Eurasian Rimland, appears nowhere on the horizon. Not
even the Chinese, with their rising sea power, appear capable of this
achievement, checked as they will be by the American, Indian, Japanese, Australian, and other navies. Nevertheless, as we shall see, a
world of subtle power arrangements, where trade and economics will
erode sheer military might, will still be one of geopolitics governed by
geography, especially in the world's oceans, which will be more
crowded than ever. To see this maritime world better, we will next
turn to another thinker from the late nineteenth and early twentieth
centuries.

Chapter VII

THE ALLURE OF SEA POWER

Whereas Mackinder's emphasis was on land power because of emerging technological developments in rail and road transport, the same Industrial Revolution made American Navy captain Alfred Thayer Mahan, a slightly older contemporary of Mackinder, a proponent of sea power. Mahan thought sea power not only more important than land power in the fight for dominance, but also less threatening to international stability. Mahan noted that it is "the limited capacity of navies to extend coercive force inland" that makes them no menace to liberty. Mahan thought that instead of the Heartland of Eurasia being the geographical pivot of empires, it was conversely the Indian and Pacific oceans that constituted the hinges of geopolitical destiny. For these oceans would allow for a maritime nation to project power around the Eurasian Rimland, affecting political developments inland—thanks to the same rail and road feeder networks—deep into Central Asia. Nicholas Spykman, with his own emphasis on the Rimland around the Indian and Pacific oceans, was as profoundly influenced by Mahan as he was by Mackinder.

Though Mackinder was awed by the strength of Russia, given its control of the Heartland, Mahan, whose book *The Problem of Asia* preceded Mackinder's "The Geographical Pivot of History" article by four years, espied Russia's vulnerability, given its distance from the warm waters of the Indian Ocean. Russia's "irremediable remoteness from an open sea has helped put it in a disadvantageous position for the accumulation of wealth," and, as Mahan goes on, "This being so, it is natural and proper that she should be dissatisfied, and dissatisfaction readily takes the form of aggression." Thus does Mahan reveal the deepest psychological currents—based, in fact, on geography—of the Russian national character. Mahan calls the nations lying to the south of Russia and north of the Indian Ocean the "debatable ground" of Asia, "the zone of conflict between Russian landpower and British seapower." (Spykman, four decades later, will call this area the Rimland.) Of this debatable ground, Mahan emphasizes the importance of China, Afghanistan, Iran, and Turkey. It is no coincidence that in 1900 he is able to identify the pivotal states of geopolitical significance in our own time: for geography is unchangeable.

Geography helped dictate a containment strategy against the Soviet Union from the southern tier of Eurasian states during the Cold War that involved all of these Rimland nations; and geography helps determine the importance of China, as a state and civilization extending from the Eurasian Heartland to the warm waters of the Pacific Rim, even as geography helps determine Afghanistan and Iran as two Heartland nations critical to the destiny of the Middle East. It was Mahan who, in 1902, first used the term "Middle East" to denote the area between Arabia and India that held particular importance for naval strategy. India, he points out, located in the center of the Indian Ocean littoral, with its rear flanks protected by the Himalayan mountain system, is critical for the seaward penetration of both the Middle East and China. Sea power, it emerges, provides the Mahanian means by which a distant United States can influence Eurasia in a Mackinderesque "closed system."[1]

Mahan's ocean-centric view has its flaws. As Robert Strausz-Hupé explains in *Geopolitics*, "In the fact that Britain and the United States clung to the doctrine of Mahan they [Haushofer and the other German *Geopolitikers*] saw Germany's shining opportunity. As long as the Anglo-Saxon powers made that [Mahanian] doctrine—so appealing because it promised security *and* business as usual—the basis of their defense—Germany was assured of just that breathing space she needed for organizing total war."[2] Mahan's sea power doctrine, in other words, concentrating as it did on grand Eurasian security, did not, as aggressive as it was, sufficiently take into account the ability of a land power to quickly lay siege of Europe from Iberia to the Urals.

Yet Mahan did cover his tracks. For he wrote that "the due use and control of the sea is but one link in the chain of exchange by which wealth accumulates."[3] Nevertheless, his thinking was more suited to the sea power expansion of the United States around the world than it was to the preservation of the balance of power within Europe. There was, in Strausz-Hupé's words, a "lusty imperialism" to Mahan, who saw the ultimate goal of American power to be more than just the "sea-to-shining-sea" of Manifest Destiny, but also to encompass the domination of the Caribbean and the Pacific, which would make the United States the world's preponderant power. Mahan held that a nation must expand or decline—for it was impossible for a nation to hold its own while standing still. As a tactician he was often similarly unnuanced, believing in the concentration of naval power through battle fleet supremacy: "the massed fleet of line-of-battle ships."[4]

But Mahan, who published nineteen books in a twenty-year period, beginning in 1883, is hard to pin down: a lusty imperialism was just one side of him. He was also a democrat who, despite his observation that democracies are not friendly to military expenditures, openly preferred democratic to monarchical rule. He did not necessarily feel that a massive fleet was absolutely necessary for the United States, which he believed should cooperate with Great Britain, since naval supremacy was only possible through a coalition. He considered war an unnatural condition of nations, which they, nevertheless, had to tragically prepare for. And he foresaw a multinational system of maritime alliances to guard the global commons. So it is important not to caricature him.[5]

Mahan laid out his overall vision in *The Influence of Sea Power Upon History, 1660–1783,* published in 1890, which affected the thinking of Presidents William McKinley and Theodore Roosevelt—as well as that of Germany's Kaiser Wilhelm II—and helped prompt the naval buildup prior to World War I. Mahan showed that because the sea is the "great highway" or "wide common" of civilization, naval power—the power to protect merchant fleets—had always been the determining factor in global political struggles, especially as "both travel and traffic by water have always been easier and cheaper than by land." The strength of his argument lay as much in its originality as in its comprehensiveness.[6]

Mahan begins his epic with the assertion that "a peaceful, gain-loving nation is not far-sighted, and far-sightedness is needed for adequate military preparation, especially in these days." Mahan is neither a warmonger nor is he championing despotism. In fact, as he points out, it was because of despotism and "fierce avarice" that neither Spain nor Portugal, despite being great sea powers, were in the final analysis great nations. Nonetheless, "Whether a democratic government will have the foresight, the keen sensitiveness to national position," necessary to deter adversaries is "an open question." For the friendly foreign ports that are found the world over do not always endure, he tells us. Not only are nations at peace in general ignorant of the tragedy that comes from not cultivating a tragic sensibility, but their historians are specifically ignorant of the sea, ignorant of the vast expanses of the earth that exert so much influence on the dry-land regions, and contribute to their security and prosperity. Thus, it is urgent, he warns, to write about the history of naval war: particularly because the principles of such war have remained constant, despite the technological advances from oared galley to steamship (and to nuclear-powered aircraft carriers and submarines in our day). Mahan illustrates this by a land-bound army analogy:

When the march on foot was replaced by carrying troops in coaches, when the latter in turn gave place to railroads, the scale of distances was increased, or, if you will, the scale of time diminished; but the principles which dictated the point at which the army should be concentrated, the direction in which it should move, the part of the enemy's position which it should assail, the protection of communications, were not altered.[7]

Mahan embraces the period from 1660, when the sailing ship era "had fairly begun," to 1783, the end of the American Revolution. He notes that George Washington partly attributed America's victory in its war for independence to France's control of the seas—even as decades earlier France had lost the Seven Years' War partly because of its neglect of sea power. Yet Mahan's panoramic commentary on naval tactics, as well as his illustrations about the criticality of the sea in human history, range much further back. It was the Roman control of the water that forced Hannibal "to that long, perilous march through Gaul in which more than half his veteran troops wasted away. Throughout the war, the [Roman] legions passed by water, unmolested and unwearied, between Spain, which was Hannibal's base, and Italy." Mahan points out that there were no great sea battles in the Second Punic War, because Rome's mastery of the Mediterranean was a deciding factor in Carthage's defeat. If the Mediterranean Sea were a flat desert, Mahan writes, and the land were the mountains rising off the desert floor, a dominant navy is the force capable of traveling back and forth across the desert from one mountain range to another at will. This was the case with Rome. But because water is a strange element, and sailors "from time immemorial a strange race apart," we don't hold navies in the high regard that we should. "The navy is essentially a light corps," Mahan goes on, "it keeps open the communications between its own ports; it obstructs those of the enemy; but it sweeps the sea for the service of the land, it controls the desert that man may live and thrive on the habitable globe."[8]

And so, Mahan intones, "It is not the taking of individual ships or convoys" that is crucial; rather, "it is the possession of that overbearing power on the sea which drives the enemy's flag from it, or allows it to appear only as a fugitive" that is so important. And "if a nation be so situated that it is neither forced to defend itself by land nor induced to seek extension of its territory by way of the land, it has, by the very unity of its aim directed upon the sea, an advantage as compared with a people one of whose boundaries are continental."[9]

England and America are so situated, and both have experienced long periods of global power in the course of history. But America's geographical position, Mahan implies, has real disadvantages, too. Yes, America is a massive, well-endowed, virtual island in the temperate zone, independent of the debilitating power struggles in Eurasia, but at the same time it is a yawning distance from Eurasian ports, especially in the Pacific, which inhibits its ability to exert influence over them. The building of a Central American canal in Panama, which he foresees in his book, will bring American merchant and war fleets into greater contact with both ends of Eurasia. But the distance will still be great, and that will be the "cause of enormous expense." Though the real effect of the Panama Canal will be the transformation of the Caribbean from a "terminus" and "place of local traffic" into "one of the great highways of the world," as the ships of not only the United States, but of European nations, transit the canal en route to the Pacific. With this, he says, "it will not be so easy as heretofore" for the United States "to stand aloof from international complications."[10]

Geography, which makes the isthmian canal possible in the first place, also necessitates closer ties between the United States and its Central American and Caribbean neighbors in order to protect the canal and control the seas nearby. By making America physically closer to Asia, and more involved with Europe through shipping, the canal would help effect the eventual enfeeblement of isolationism and the consequent rise of a muscular liberal internationalism in the corridors of power in Washington. But it certainly wasn't destiny, despite the commanding role of geography. For the Panama Canal was the upshot of several phenomena all involving human agency: the Spanish-American War, the great power politics that ultimately denied any European nation a role in the project, the backroom deal-making that resulted in the choice of Panama over Nicaragua, the conquest of disease in the Central American tropics, and above all immense labor and ingenuity. Once again, geography provides the backdrop for what human choice arranges.

And Mahan clearly seeks to influence human choice. In his thumping book, propitiously published the same year that the U.S. Army consolidated the American continent with a virtual final (if hideous) victory in the Indian Wars, and only a few years before the United States would gain, as a result of war, Spain's empire in the Western Pacific as well as dominance in the Caribbean, Mahan issues a call to arms through global sea power. Mahan is not so much a geographer as a historian and tactician. He represents an imperialistic sensibility which carries with it obvious geographical implications. This is the decisive explanation for Spykman's high regard for him. Not that Spykman was an enthusiast of conquest; only that he intuitively grasped, as Mahan did, that America would have no choice but to engage in worldwide power struggles because of its own geographically privileged position in the Western Hemisphere, which gave it influence in the Eastern Hemisphere.

Mahan, as one would expect, had enemies. Sir Norman Angell, in an engaging and spirited defense of pacifism, *The Great Illusion,* published in 1909, condemns Mahan's writings as "very mischievous moonshine." This British journalist and politician, who to his credit was hated by Haushofer, denounces Mahan's assertion that the "extension of national authority over alien communities" can be a dignified enterprise: for "like individuals, nations and empires have souls as well as bodies." Mahan is, in Angell's view, absurdly denying the very tangible reality of the individual and replacing him with the comparatively intangible reality of the state. As Angell argues, "Does anyone think of paying deference to the Russian *moujik* because he happens to belong to one of the biggest empires territorially? Does anyone think of despising an Ibsen . . . or any educated Scandinavian or Belgian or Hollander, because they happen to belong to the smallest nations in Europe?"[11] In other words, Mahan, and by inference Spykman, Mackinder, and the other geographer-geopoliticians, are determinists and essentialists all. Their warlike tendencies emerge from their seeing, as Isaiah Berlin complained, nations and empires as more real than the individuals who encompass them. Again, we can offer only the Haushofer defense: if Mahan and the others did not engage in the sort of determinism which Angell condemns, they would leave the field of grand strategy to those who are truly evil. Alas, we require the moral imperfections of the likes of a Mahan.

In fact, Angell's treatise on why war and great power competition are illogical suffered the misfortune of being published only a few years before World War I, which initiated a century of unprecedented war and conflict in Europe. Angell, unfairly, became a laughingstock in many quarters. I say unfairly because his book, in and of itself, is compulsively readable, as well as brilliantly argued. And his book might have proved clairvoyant were human nature a bit less base than it is. It is because of the flaws in human nature, amplified by divisions imposed by geography, that a writer like Mahan wears so much better over the decades than one like Angell.

In a sign of how the power dynamics of the world are changing, Indian and Chinese strategists avidly read Mahan; they, much more than the Americans, are the Mahanians now: they are building fleets designed for armed encounters at sea, whereas European navies view sea power only in terms of constabulary action. For example, in a 2004 symposium in Beijing, "scholar after scholar quoted Mahan . . . attesting to his influence," write Naval War College professors James R. Holmes and Toshi Yoshihara. "And almost without exception, they quoted the most bellicose-sounding of Mahan's precepts, equating command of the sea to overbearing power that closes the maritime common to an enemy's flag."[12] Since then, as the Chinese navy becomes larger and more wide-ranging, the bent toward Mahan has only intensified in Beijing, especially with the rise of Indian sea power, which the Chinese fear; the Indians, for their part, view the Chinese in similar Mahanian terms. The American Navy, meanwhile, appears to have embraced another theorist. Let me explain.

Julian Corbett, a British historian of the same era, did not so much disagree with Mahan as offer a subtler approach to naval strategy, placing greater emphasis on doing more at sea with fewer ships. Corbett asserts that just because one nation has lost control of the sea, another nation has not necessarily gained it (as Mahan believed). A naval coalition that may appear weak and dispersed can, if properly constituted, have "a reality of strength." Corbett called this a "fleet in being"—a collection of ships that can quickly coalesce into a unified fleet when necessary. This fleet in being would not need to dominate or sink other fleets; it could be effective by seizing bases and policing choke points. Such a deceptively able fleet, Corbett argued, should pursue an "active and vigorous life" in the conduct of limited defense.[13] As it happened, Corbett's book came out after the British Royal Navy had reduced its worldwide presence by leveraging the growing sea power of its allies Japan and the United States.

Now the United States is in a position similar to that of Britain a hundred years ago. America's Navy has been getting smaller in number: from around 600 ships during the Cold War, to 350 during the 1990s, to 280 now, and with the possibility—because of budget cuts and cost overruns—of going down to 250 in the coming years and decades. As such, it is embracing naval allies such as India, Japan, Australia, and Singapore. The U.S. Navy published a document in October 2007, "A Cooperative Strategy for 21st Century Seapower," that is more in the spirit of Corbett, with its emphasis on cooperation, than of Mahan, with its emphasis on dominance. "Our Nation's interests," goes the document, "are best served by fostering a peaceful global system comprised of interdependent networks of trade, finance, information, law, people, and governance." As the U.S. Navy sees it, our world is increasingly interconnected, with the global population clustered in pulsing demographic ganglia near the seas that will be prone to great disruptions, such as asymmetric attacks and natural disasters. Even great power conflicts, the document says, are apt to be subtle and asymmetric. There is little talk here of conventional sea and land battles. The growing naval power of China is not even mentioned. The spirit of "collective security" is everywhere. "No one nation has the resources required to provide safety . . . throughout the entire maritime domain." And in this maritime domain, the document indicates that the Western Pacific and Indian oceans will be the first among equals in strategic importance.[14]

And so the Rimland of Eurasia and the larger World-Promontory (the seaboard of the World-Island), to use the phraseology of Spykman and Mackinder, will have two military realities, it seems. On the one hand, there will be the U.S. Navy, with its declining but still dominant fleet, patrolling, in the spirit of Corbett, in concert with its local allies from Africa to Northeast Asia, in order to keep the seas safe for commerce. On the other hand, there will be the assertion of rising power by China primarily, and India secondarily, each armed with their Mahanian proclivities. Precisely because the Chinese have welcomed this American icon of imperialist ambition, the U.S. Navy will not be able to escape entirely from his spirit. For the eternal struggle of power politics goes on, as much as we might want to escape from it. "To argue that expansion is inherently misguided," writes the University of Chicago political scientist John Mearsheimer, "implies that all great powers over the past 350 years have failed to comprehend how the international system works. This is an implausible argument on its face." And as Mearsheimer goes on, "Since the security benefits of hegemony are enormous" in an anarchic system in which there is no world hegemon, "powerful states will invariably be tempted to emulate the United States and try to dominate their region of the world."[15] So far as his reputation goes, Mahan's best days may lie ahead.

With a Eurasian littoral increasingly crowded with warships in order to accommodate the ambitions of the Chinese, Indians, and others alongside the U.S., even as an ever more practical polar route cuts distances between Eurasia and North America, worldwide hegemonic struggles may only quicken in speed and intensity. Thus, we now need to explore the features of a closed geographic system.

Chapter VIII

THE "CRISIS OF ROOM"

As a visiting professor at the U.S. Naval Academy in Annapolis some years back, I taught a course about future challenges in national security. I started the semester by having the midshipmen read *Fire in the East: The Rise of Asian Military Power and the Second Nuclear Age* by Yale political science professor Paul Bracken. A brief and clairvoyant tour de force that sold poorly when it was published in 1999, Bracken's book is very much in the spirit of Mackinder and Spykman, even as there are no references to them in his text. Bracken, who has served as a consultant to nearly all Post Cold War American government reassessments, draws a conceptual map of Eurasia defined by the ongoing collapse of time and distance, and the filling up of empty spaces—something that William McNeill first alerted us to in the latter chapters of his grand history of humanity. But because Bracken writes during a more dramatic stage of this development, this leads him to declare a "crisis of room." Bracken refers to the idea of the great Hungarian American mathematician John von Neumann, who contended that in the past a sparsely populated geography had acted as a safety mechanism against military and technological advances. Yet von Neumann worried that geography was now losing the battle. Undeniably, the very "finite size of the earth" would increasingly be a force for instability, as military hardware and software condensed distances on the geopolitical map. "This is an easy change to miss," Bracken warns, "because it is gradual."[1]

Let me condense Bracken's thesis into a few pages. For it matters greatly to the development of my own.

While the Americans and Europeans focus on globalization, the appeal of nationalism and military power is growing in Eurasia. Missile and bomb tests, biological warfare programs, and the development of chemical weapons are "the products of a prosperous, liberalizing Asia," Bracken notes. What the West has "failed to recognize" is that the technologies of war and wealth creation have always been closely connected: from Asia's economic rise has come its military rise. In the early Cold War years, Asian military forces were primarily lumbering, World War II–type armies whose primary purpose, though never stated, was national consolidation. "The army was an instrument of mass indoctrination, a giant school with a core curriculum of nationhood." Soldiers helped bring in the crops more often than they honed their battlefield skills. Thus, armies were focused inward, even as many a state army was separated by enormous tracts of mileage from other state armies. But as national wealth accumulated and the computer revolution took hold, Asian militaries from the oil-rich Middle East to the tiger economies of the Pacific developed full-fledged, military-civilian postindustrial complexes, with missiles and fiber optics and cellular phones. At the same time, Eurasian states were becoming bureaucratically more cohesive, allowing their militaries and their leaders to focus outward and away from domestic politics, toward other states—becoming more lethal and professional in the process. Rather than retreat into the countryside in the face of danger, an option in epochs past, now electronic sensors monitor international borders with weapons of mass destruction at the ready. Geography, rather than a cushion, has become a prison from which there is no escape.[2]

"An unbroken belt of countries from Israel to North Korea" (including Syria, Iran, Pakistan, India, and China) "has assembled either nuclear or chemical arsenals and is developing ballistic missiles. A multipolar balance of terror stretches over a 6,000-mile arc," cutting across military and political theaters and "regional studies" departments into which the West divides up Asia. The "death of distance" is upon us, Bracken warns. Take Japan, which ever since North Korea in 1998 fired a missile across it, landing in the Pacific Ocean, is no longer a zone of sanctuary, but an integral part of mainland Asia military space, despite its archipelagic geography. Over the centuries, the concept of Asia was created by Western maritime power, beginning with the Portuguese at the turn of the sixteenth century. It was then deconstructed into separate regions by the Cold War. But in the 1970s, as an economic boom swept East Asia, a large and new region, the "Pacific Basin," was formed, the basis for a return to a holistic map of Asia. This economic success story was possible only because the threat of force was unthinkable: that, in turn, was because there was a military hegemon, the United States, which guaranteed the peace. Now, as Asia returns to being a single organic unit, U.S. power is slowly receding and the military power of China, India, and other indigenous states is rising. Asia is enlarging as regional subunits collapse. It is getting more claustrophobic because of the expansion of both populations and missile ranges; and it is becoming more volatile, because of the accumulation of weaponry without concomitant alliance structures.[3]

As Bracken explains, because of its immense size, for most of history alliances never mattered much in Asia, as armies were too far removed from one another to come to one another's aid. This was unlike the situation in Europe where many powerful states were bunched up against one another in a narrow peninsula. But that is now changing. Across Eurasia missiles and weapons of mass destruction are being built, not infantry forces. The naval and marine patrols of various states, pulsing with technology, are ranging far from home ports in the Indian Ocean and Western Pacific. China, Japan, India, Israel, and other nations are developing communications grids using satellites and underwater listening devices. India, which for most of history found China largely irrelevant to its security concerns, because the two countries were separated by the highest mountains in the world, now has its own satellites and reconnaissance aircraft providing details of Chinese troop movements in Tibet. Meanwhile, the Indian navy has set up a Far Eastern Command in the Andaman Islands, 750 miles east of India proper, to counter a Chinese naval presence that is also far from its home shores. As "Asian industrial power becomes aligned with Asian military power," Bracken writes, the continent is literally running out of room for mistakes and miscalculations, becoming, in effect, "the shrinking Eurasian chessboard."[4]

To this shrinking chessboard, Bracken adds the destabilizing factor of "disruptive technologies": technologies that, rather than help sustain leadership and the current global power structure, "undermine it by disrupting the status quo." Such technologies include computer viruses and weapons of mass destruction, especially nuclear and biological bombs. Bracken writes:

Disruptive technology changes the game. By upsetting existing advantages, it nurtures new skills and fosters different strategies. The resulting uncertainty shakes up the established order and changes the standards by which leadership is measured.[5]

Indeed, disruptive technology, abetted by religious zealotry, brought the Iranian plateau to the doorstep of geographical Palestine, even though Iran and Israel are separated by over eight hundred miles. And Iran is merely part of a trend. As I've indicated, rather than shop only for the latest in Western armaments, China, North Korea, India, Pakistan, and other countries are developing disruptive technologies. In an age of former Third World countries acquiring tactical nuclear weapons, large forward bases like the kind the U.S. military maintained in Saudi Arabia and Kuwait prior to the two Gulf wars may henceforth be vulnerable to enemy attack. Such a development promises to hinder America's projection of power around the Eurasian rimland, and thus pave the way toward a more unstable, multipolar power arrangement. It is the freedom to concentrate military equipment in key locations around the world that has preserved American military might. But nuclear and chemical-biological weapons can destroy these forward sites, or at least render them unusable for a time. "Preservation of the asymmetric situation," Bracken writes, "whereby the greatest military power in Asia is not Asian [but American] depends on arms control"—something which is becoming increasingly problematic as former Third World nations develop disruptive military capabilities. For decades the United States and the Soviet Union used nuclear weapons without actually detonating them for "political maneuvers, implicit threats, deterrence, signaling, drawing lines in the sand, and other forms of psychological advantage." Now more countries will want to do likewise, even as some will be motivated by a rage that is the upshot of poverty, even as they will lack the bureaucratic control mechanisms to responsibly control the use of these weapons. During the Cold War, both superpowers approached nuclear warfare with "detachment and rationality." That may not be the case in what Bracken calls "the second nuclear age," in which Eurasia constitutes a small room crowded with poor countries, some of which are nuclear powers.[6]

"The spread of missiles and weapons of mass destruction in Asia is like the spread of the six-shooter in the American Old West," says Bracken. Cheap and deadly, the six-shooter was an equalizer because it rendered the size and physical strength of a man much less important. Just as the six-shooter changed the balance of power among men in the Old West, so do *poor man's nukes* and other disruptive technologies change the global balance of power.[7]

The spread of nuclear weapons in Asia "makes the world less Eurocentric," and thus greatly accelerates the process of globalization.[8] The geography of Eurasia will become as intimate as the geography of Europe, where a myriad of powerful states, uncomfortably confined within a small space, constantly fought wars, with peace breaking out just as constantly through the practice of balance of power

politics. There will not be the accumulation of masses of thermonu-
clear warheads that we saw during the Cold War, so that the peace
and stability obtained by mutually assured destruction will not necessarily result, even as the damage one state will be able to do to another will be immense and—in a world of crowded megacities—nearly
beyond comprehension. Thus, a closed geography will demand the
ablest practitioners of Metternichian balance of power statecraft in
order to prevent mass violence.

To be sure, we may be entering a world of multidimensional brink-
manship. The shrinking of the map not only obliterates artificial regions invented by Cold War area studies, but also renders less distinct
Mackinder's and Spykman's conception of a specific pivot and adjacent rimlands, since Eurasia has been reconfigured by technology into
an organic whole. For example, military assistance from China and
North Korea to Iran can cause Israel at the other end of the Eurasian
landmass to take specific military actions. Because of vivid television
images, bombs falling on Gaza can now incite crowds in Indonesia.
The U.S. Air Force can attack landlocked Afghanistan from the island
of Diego Garcia in the middle of the Indian Ocean. While local militaries used to be confined to their regions, increasingly the Chinese
and Indian navies will be projecting power from the Gulf of Aden all
the way to the South China Sea and the Sea of Japan—along the
whole navigable rimland, that is. There are many more such examples of political situations in one part of Eurasia echoing and reecho-
ing back from other parts. This does not negate geography, it just
means that we have to add other factors to it. It no longer reigns supreme to the extent that it used to.

The worries of Mackinder and Spykman will not only be intensified
by the disruptive technologies that Bracken concentrates on, but by
the sheer rise of urban populations themselves, which will make the
map of Eurasia only more claustrophobic. In the 1990s, during the
first intellectual cycle of the Post Cold War, when the terms "realist"
and "determinist" were vilified in the heady days following the over-

throw of communism, the ideas of the late-eighteenth century English philosopher Thomas Robert Malthus were mocked by many intellectuals as too grim and fatalistic: for Malthus treats humankind as a species reacting to its physical environment, rather than as a body of self-willed individuals motivated by ideas. Malthus's specific theory—that population increases geometrically while food supplies increase only arithmetically—was wrong. Yet as the years pass, with great fluctuations in world food and energy prices, and teeming multitudes of angry, *lumpen* faithful—young males predominantly—walled off in places like Karachi and Gaza (the Soweto of the Middle East), Malthus, the first philosopher to focus on demography and the political effects of the quality of life among the poor, has been getting more respect. Half the population of the West Bank and Gaza is under fifteen. Indeed, while the population of the Greater Middle East grows from 854 million to over 1.2 billion over the next twenty years, with the Arab world in the midst of nearly doubling its population even as supplies of groundwater greatly diminish, especially in places like Yemen, leading to explosive side effects on politics, the word "Malthusian" will be heard more often.

Though proving Malthus right may be a useless exercise, his general worldview fits well with Bracken's conception of a loss of room in Eurasia. Crowded megacities, beset by poor living conditions, periodic rises in the price of commodities, water shortages, and unresponsive municipal services, will be fertile petri dishes for the spread of both democracy and radicalism, even as regimes will be increasingly empowered by missiles and modern, outwardly focused militaries.

The megacity will be at the heart of twenty-first-century geography. There are already twenty-five cities in the world with a population of over 10 million people, and that number will rise to forty by 2015, with all but two in the former Third World. Greater Tokyo leads with 35 million; Lagos is at the bottom with nearly 12 million. Thirteen of the twenty-five are in South or East Asia. Karachi, Tehran, Istanbul, and Cairo are the megacities in the Greater Middle East. The key fact is that there are many cities in the former Third World which just miss making the list, and that over half of humanity now lives in urban conditions, a statistic that will rise to two-thirds by 2025. There are 468 cities in the world with populations exceeding one million. Almost all urban growth in the future will be in developing countries, specifically in Asia and Africa. We are in an era with a significant percentage of people living in slumlike conditions. During Mackinder's time at the turn of the twentieth century, only 14 percent of humanity were urbanites.

As I've noted, Ibn Khaldun writes in his *Muqaddimah,* or "Introduction" to a world history, that desert nomads, in aspiring to the physical comforts of sedentary life, create the original dynamic for urbanization that is then captured by powerful rulers and dynasties, which in turn, by providing security, allow cities to flourish. But because authority requires luxury, decay eventually sets in, as group solidarity erodes and individuals, through their accumulation of wealth and influence, weaken executive power. Thus, systems grow brittle and fragment, and are superseded by other formations.[9] For the first time in history this process is operating on a global scale. Vast cities and megacities have formed as rural dwellers throughout Eurasia, Africa, and South America migrate toward urban centers from the underdeveloped countryside. As a consequence, the mayors and governors of these conurbations can less and less govern them effectively from a central dispatch point: so that these sprawling concentrations informally break up into suburbs and neighborhood self-help units, whose own local leaders are often motivated by ideals and ideologies originating from afar, by way of electronic communications technology. Radical Islam is, in part, the story of urbanization over the past half-century across North Africa and the Greater Middle East. Urbanization also accounts for the far more progressive demonstrators for democracy who overthrew various Arab regimes in 2011. Forget the image of the Arab as the nomad or inhabitant of an oasis on the steppe-desert. In most instances he is a city dweller, of a crowded and shabby city at that, and is at home in vast crowds. It is the very impersonal quality of urban life, which is lived among strangers, that accounts for intensified religious feeling. For in the village of old, religion was a natural extension of the daily traditions and routine of life among the extended family; but migrations to the city brought Muslims into the anonymity of slum existence, and to keep the family together and the young from drifting into crime, religion has had to be reinvented in starker, more ideological form. In this way states weaken, or at least have to yield somewhat, to new and sometimes extreme kinds of nationalism and religiosity advanced by urbanization. Thus, new communities take hold that transcend traditional geography, even as they make for spatial patterns of their own. Great changes in history often happen obscurely.[10]

A Eurasia and North Africa of vast, urban concentrations, overlapping missile ranges, and sensational global media will be one of constantly enraged crowds, fed by rumors and half-truths transported at the speed of light by satellite channels across the rimlands and heartland expanse, from one Third World city to another. Conversely, the crowd, empowered by social media like Twitter and Facebook, will also be fed by the very truth that autocratic rulers have denied it. The crowd will be key in a new era where the relief map will be darkened by densely packed megacities—the *crowd* being a large group of people who abandon their individuality in favor of an intoxicating collective symbol. Elias Canetti, the Bulgarian-born Spanish Jew and Nobel laureate in literature, became so transfixed and terrified at the mob violence over inflation that seized Frankfurt and Vienna between the two world wars that he devoted much of his life to studying the human herd in all its manifestations. The signal insight of his book *Crowds and Power,* published in 1960, was that we all yearn to be inside some sort of crowd, for in a crowd—or a mob, for that matter—there is shelter from danger and, by inference, from loneliness. Nationalism, extremism, the yearning for democracy are all the products of crowd formations and thus manifestations of seeking to escape from loneliness. It is loneliness, alleviated by Twitter and Facebook, that ultimately leads to the breakdown of traditional authority and the erection of new kinds.

Loneliness is a particular characteristic of urban existence, in which strangers are many and true friends and family relatively few. And so the new urban geography of the former Third World in the twenty-first century will constitute a map of intense, personal long-ing. Indeed, George Orwell's depiction of tyranny rests to a great degree on the human proclivity, however much it may be denied, to trade individual freedom for the enfolding protection and intimate contact of the group. "Always yell with the crowd, that's what I say. It's the only way to be safe," one character declares in Orwell's novel *1984*.[11] Indeed, the Internet, explains the novelist Thomas Pynchon, offers the protection of a virtual crowd, and thus "promises social control on a scale those quaint old twentieth-century tyrants with their goofy mustaches could only dream about."[12] Meanwhile, the media amplify *presentness*, the rage and ecstasy and virtue—whatever the case may be—of the present moment, for good and for bad. In other words, politics in the mass media age will be more intense than anything we have experienced, because the past and future will have been obliterated.

Crowd psychology supplanted by technology was at work in the election of Barack Obama and in the panic selling on Wall Street in 2008. It was at work in the anti-Muslim pogroms in Hindu Gujarat, in India in 2002, in the mass public demonstrations in Europe against the U.S. invasion of Iraq in 2003, in both the pro- and anti-regime demonstrations in Iran in 2009 and 2010, in the mass populist rallies against the Thai government in Bangkok in the same time period, and endemically in the anti-Israel demonstrations in the West Bank and Gaza; and, of course, in the Middle East's year of revolution in 2011, even as the Arab Spring promoted the sanctity of the individual while attacking the power of autocrats who robbed individuals of their dignity.

It is in the megacities of Eurasia principally where crowd psychology will have its greatest geopolitical impact. Ideas do matter as the liberal humanists and anti-determinists proclaim. And it is the very compression of geography that will provide optimal circumstances for new and dangerous ideologies—as well as for healthy democratizing ideas. Mass education, because it produces hosts of badly educated people liberated from fatalism, will contribute to instability. Lack of space will be the key factor. The psychological hearth place of nationalist identity is increasingly the city and not the idealized rural landscapes of the past, even as urban crowds will at times demand maximalist foreign policies from their governments based on this very idealized terrain.

The media will play a crucial role in this process. "No tamer has his animals more under his power" than the media, writes Oswald Spengler in *The Decline of the West*:

> Unleash the people as reader-mass and it will storm through the streets and hurl itself upon the target indicated. . . . A more appalling caricature of freedom of thought cannot be imagined. Formerly a man did not dare to think freely. Now he dares, but cannot; his will to think is only a willingness to think to order, and this is what he feels as *his* liberty.[13]

Spengler is overly pessimistic and cynical. Nevertheless, recall that the hatred Soviets and Americans had for each other was cool and abstract, without a racial basis, separated as they were by oceans and Arctic tundra, during an earlier age of communications technology. But digital big flat television screens of the present and of the future (that, like CNN at airports, you can't turn off!) increasingly make everything up close and personal. Here, again, is Bracken:

> What westerners find difficult to understand is the intensity of the feelings that Asians [and Middle Easterners] bring to these religious and ethnic disputes. Internal disorders could quickly spill over into whole regions, inflamed by mass media that reach across borders and by the political logic that seeks a foreign scapegoat for domestic problems. National leaders could then be backed into a rhetorical corner—a dangerous place for people who have atom bombs at their disposal.[14]

Bracken warns that nationalism is "dangerously underrated" by Western observers, who see it as part of a retrograde past that economic and social progress moves us beyond. "The most important issue of the twenty-first century is understanding how nationalism combines with the newly destructive technologies appearing in Asia." As I've said, the new nuclear powers, like Pakistan, India, and China, will have poor and lower-middle-class populations, and this will abet a resentful, hot-blooded nationalism in an age when the new military symbols are not armies but missiles and nuclear weapons—the latest totemic objects of the crowd.[15]

Though the possession of missiles as objects of pride will strengthen nationalism and therefore the power of some states, making patriotism more potent, the mass psychologies that with the help of the media unite various ethnic, religious, and sectarian groups, as well as groups dedicated to democratic universalism, will dilute the power of other states. Meanwhile, some states will slowly, inexorably lose the battle against globalization, as their bureaucratic capacities are eroded by long-running wars, attendant refugee movements, and the job of administering vast, badly urbanized cities. In sum, as the map of Eurasia gets smaller thanks to technology and population growth, artificial frontiers will begin to weaken inside it.

Understanding the map of the twenty-first century means accepting grave contradictions. For while some states become militarily stronger, armed with weapons of mass destruction, others, especially in the Greater Middle East, weaken: they spawn substate armies, tied to specific geographies with all of the cultural and religious tradition which that entails, thus they fight better than state armies on the same territory ever could. Southern Lebanon's Hezbollah, the former Tamil Tigers of northern Sri Lanka, the Maoist Naxalites in eastern and central India, the various pro-Taliban and other Pushtun tribal groupings in northwestern Pakistan, the Taliban itself in Afghanistan, and the plethora of militias in Iraq, especially during the civil war of 2006–2007, are examples of this trend of terrain-specific substate land forces. For at a time when precision-guided missiles can destroy a specific house hundreds of miles away, while leaving the adjacent one deliberately undamaged, small groups of turbaned irregulars can use the tortuous features of an intricate mountain landscape to bedevil a superpower. In the latter case the revenge of geography is clear. But in the former case, too, those missiles have to be fired from somewhere, which requires a land or a sea base, thus bringing us back to geography, albeit to a less intimate and traditional kind. For Spykman's Indian Ocean Rimland is crucial for the placement of American warships, whose missiles are aimed deep into Iran and Afghanistan, two Heartland states, the latter of which is as riven by tribal conflicts as it was in the time of Alexander the Great. Spykman's and Mackinder's early-twentieth-century constructs coexist with those of antiquity, and both are relevant for our own era.

The very burden of governing vast, poor urban concentrations has made statehood more onerous than at any previous time in history; a reason for the collapse of sclerotic dictatorships, as well as for the weakness of young democracies. A state like Pakistan can have weapons of mass destruction, even as it can barely provide municipal services and protect its population from suicide bombers. States like Nigeria, Yemen, Somalia, to name but a few, barely function, and are besieged by substate militias. The Palestinians, particularly in Gaza, have engaged in violence to protest their condition, even as they have eschewed the compromises required for statehood. The same with Hezbollah in Lebanon, which could have toppled the government in Beirut anytime it wanted, but chose not to. A state has to abide by certain rules and thus makes for an easier target. And so we have a new phenomenon in this age of megacities and mass media: the power of statelessness. "The state is a burden," writes Jakub Grygiel, an associate professor at Johns Hopkins University, so these substate groups "seek power without the responsibility of governing." Modern communications and military technologies allow these groups to organize, to seek help abroad, and to arm themselves with lethal weapons so that the state no longer owns the monopoly on violence. As I've said earlier, whereas the Industrial Revolution was about bigness (airplanes, tanks, aircraft carriers, railways, factories, and so on) the post–Industrial Revolution is about smallness—miniature bombs and plastic explosives that do not require the large territory of a state to deploy. Small stateless groups are beneficiaries of this new age of technology. In fact, there are more and more reasons not to have a state. Grygiel writes:

> The greater the capability of nations to destroy one another, and of the great powers in particular, the more dangerous it is to have a state, especially for groups whose goal is to challenge the existing powers.[16]

A state is a bad fit, he goes on, for those with absolutist goals inspired by religious zeal or ideological extremism that can never be realized by statehood. The mass exodus to slums in our era, by cutting off the link with the traditional countryside, has helped in this process of radicalization along the broad swath of the southern Eurasian rimland. The mass media, to which these groups have access, publicize their demands and in the process further fortify their identities, creating crowd packs of fellow thinkers not necessarily defined by state loyalties. In sum, if we step back a moment and consider the situation, we have a map of Eurasia that is one huge area rather than the smaller divisions of Cold War regions that we have grown used to. This map is overloaded with nodes of contact and communications that never or barely existed before: for in addition to extended cities and overlapping missile ranges and ideologies that reverberate on account of mass media, we will have new roads and ports and energy pipelines connecting the Middle East and Central Asia with the rest of Eurasia from Russia to the Indian Ocean to China. With civilizations densely jammed one against the other, and the media a vehicle for constant verbal outrages, as well as for popular pressure from oppressed groups, the need for quiet behind-the-scenes diplomacy will never be greater. One crisis will flow into the next, and there will be perennial need for everyone to *calm down*. Because of the map's very cohesion and shrinkage, concepts like "Heartland" and "Rimland" and "marginal" zones, which imply a horizontal separating out into large component parts, will in one sense be less relevant, but in another sense will be fraught with consequence because of the perpetual interactions between these areas: a watch, or a computer chip for that matter, is no less complex because of its size, and to understand how that watch or chip works one must still disaggregate it to see how one part affects the other. The airplane, the Internet, the concentration of politics in vast cities that more and more look like one another will, to be sure, erode the importance of the relief map. Indeed, the very orality of the Internet has a way of turning territorial battles into battles of ideas (a reason why the humanism of Isaiah Berlin is something we will desperately need to hold on to). But as states themselves, no matter how well armed, become fragile, precisely because of how democracy and cyberspace will be friendly to subnational and supranational forces, smaller regions will emerge in bolder lines, as they did during the Middle Ages following the breakup of the Roman Empire.

Yet now that we inhabit Mackinder's "closed political system," which, as Bracken notes, has closed much further in the course of the twentieth century, the map is also subject to the law of entropy, meaning a state of equilibrium will eventually set in, with each human habitation on the relief map—not just the megacities—looking increasingly like one another, and be subject to similar passions. The result, according to Ohio State University political science professor Randall L. Schweller, is that "a sort of global ennui" will result, the consequence of overstimulation, "mixed with a disturbingly large dose of individual extremism and dogmatic posturing by states."[17] In other words, the world will be both duller and more dangerous than ever before.

But before the dullness completely sets in, there will upheavals and power shifts and natural geopolitical evolutions that can usefully be described by reference to the relief map.

It is now time to explore in depth various regions of the globe, with a particular emphasis on the super-continent of Eurasia, bearing in mind all that we have learned from these historians, geopoliticians, and other thinkers. For in the chapters that follow, I will try to adhere to their sensibilities as well as to their theories. I will write about Europe, which lies adjacent to Mackinder's Heartland and is so influenced by it; about Russia, Mackinder's Heartland itself; China, which may in future decades come to dominate part of the Heartland and part of Spykman's Rimland; the Indian Subcontinent, which forms the core region of the Rimland; Iran, where the Heartland and Rimland actually meet; the Turkish and Arab Middle East, which approximates Hodgson's Oikoumene; and finally North America, the largest of Mackinder's continental satellites to challenge Eurasia and the World-Island. I will try not to make predictions, but rather to describe geography as it affects history, so as to get some idea of what the future might hold.

Part II

THE EARLY-TWENTY-FIRST-
CENTURY MAP

Chapter IX

THE GEOGRAPHY OF EUROPEAN DIVISIONS

When it comes to contemporary geopolitics, with its frequent upheavals and evolutions, the focus is naturally on Afro-Asia, from the Middle East to China. Europe tends to be left out of the equation, reduced as it often is to a financial story. But this is a mistake. The European Union's population of 500 million is the third largest in the world after China's and India's. The EU's economy of $16 trillion is larger than that of the United States. From its western extremity Europe faces the heart of North America. It is as close to the Southern Cone of South America as is the United States. From its eastern extremity, Europe overlooks Afro-Eurasia. Europe lies at the heart of the Eastern or "Land" Hemisphere, equidistant between the Russian Far East and South Africa.[1] In fact, our geographical explanation of world politics should begin with Europe. The perspective of Mackinder, Spykman, Morgenthau, and some of the other thinkers we have considered is in large part a European one. Thus, to see how the

world has evolved since their day it helps to start where they did. Though Marshall Hodgson is obviously right about the primacy of the Near Eastern Oikoumene, that region will constitute one of the climaxes of our journey, and so we need not commence with it. Not to worry, Europe will lead us organically to geographical consideration of Russia, China, the Indian Subcontinent, and the Greater Middle East. To understand geopolitics in the twenty-first century, we must start with the twentieth, and that means with Europe.

Europe, as we know from Mackinder, has had its destiny shaped by the influx of Asian hordes. And indeed, in the twenty-first century, Europe will continue to be pivotally influenced by its relations with the East, particularly with Russia. The degree to which Central and Eastern Europe can develop a belt of prosperous and stable states from the ashes of communism will go a long way to protect Europe from Russia, and, in the process, convert the dream of a revived *Mitteleuropa* into reality: a dream that liberal intellectuals actually share with Mackinder.

Yet Europe, precisely because of its quest for a wider and deeper unity, will also continue to be bedeviled by its own internal divisions, which, despite the economic form that these rifts now exhibit on the surface—as with German anger over the Greek debt crisis—are in truth the timeless expressions of geography: that is to say, the different development patterns of Germany in northern Europe and Greece in Mediterranean and Balkan Europe. Europe, largely because of how technology facilitates the movement of peoples, will certainly see its history increasingly intertwined with Africa to the south and Asia to the east. But concomitantly, Europe will not be denied its variety within. In other words, the very fact that Europe at the moment faces no conventional military threat could leave it prey to the narcissism of small differences. And that, in turn, could make Spykman's worries about a unified Europe challenging the United States premature.

It is the delicious complexity of Europe's geography, with its multiplicity of seas, peninsulas, river valleys, and mountain masses that have assisted in the formation of separate language groups and nation-states, which will continue to contribute to political and economic disunity in the years to come, despite pan-European institutions. Europe, the map suggests, has a significant future in the headlines.

Europe, in the words of the Oxford archaeologist Barry Cunliffe, is the "westerly excrescence" of the continent of Asia, a massive peninsula which came to dominate world politics in the course of the second millennium A.D. Geography ordained this, as we know from McNeill, and Cunliffe elaborates on McNeill's thesis. Europe lay in a "congenial" ecozone between the deserts of Africa and the ice sheets of the Arctic, with a climate moderated by the Gulf Stream. Europe was rich in resources, with wood, stone, metals, and furs. Most crucially, Europe has a deviating and shattered coastline, indented with many good natural harbors, and cluttered with islands and half-islands. This coastline is 23,000 miles long—an epic length equal to the circumference of the earth. In fact, Europe has a higher ratio of coastline to landmass than any other continent or subcontinent.[2] Europe borders on no fewer than four enclosed and semi-enclosed seas that squeeze the subcontinent, so to speak, into a relatively narrow peninsula: the Mediterranean, the Black, the Baltic, and the North seas; even as Europe has an advantageous riverine topography blessed with cross-peninsula routes—the Rhine, the Elbe, and above all the Danube. The Danube, as the Italian devotee of Central Europe, Claudio Magris, rhapsodizes, "draws German culture, with its dream of an Odyssey of the spirit, towards the east, mingling it with other cultures in countless hybrid metamorphoses."[3] There are, too, the Moravian Gap, the Brenner Pass, and the broad plain through France to the Rhône valley that act as corridors from one part of Europe to another.

This very elaborate interface between land and water, and the fact that Europe is protected from—and yet accessible to—a vast ocean, has led to maritime dynamism and mobility among Europe's peoples, as well as contributing to an intense range of landscapes inside Europe itself. That, in turn, has led to strikingly different human communities, and ultimately to the outbreak of power politics: from warring Athenians, Spartans, Romans, Iberians, Phoenicians, and Scythians and other barbarian tribes in antiquity, to the conflicts between French, Germans, and Russians—and between Prussians, Habsburgs, and Ottomans—in the modern era. Yet despite these divisions, a lowland corridor from the Atlantic to the Black Sea, for example, has allowed travelers for centuries to cross the length of Europe in relative comfort, contributing to Europe's cohesion and superior sense of itself, as ably demonstrated by Magris's prose.[4] Moreover, the fact that distances are short within Europe has been another unifying factor: from Lisbon to Warsaw, that is, from one end of Europe to the other, it is only 1,500 miles.

Geography, in other words, has helped determine that there is an *idea* called Europe, the geographical expression of liberal humanism by way of the post–World War II merging of sovereignty. This pacifying trend, as well as a reaction to devastating military conflict in all historical ages, is also the product of many hundreds of years of material and intellectual advancement. And yet there exists, too, several Europes, at times in conflict with one another. For the economic divisions we see today in the form of a currency crisis actually have a basis in history and geography.

In the years immediately before and after the collapse of the Berlin Wall, as we have seen in an earlier chapter, intellectuals celebrated the concept of Central Europe—of *Mitteleuropa*—as a beacon of multiethnic tolerance and historic liberalism, to which the contiguous Balkans and Third World regions further afield could and should aspire. But in truth, the political heart of twenty-first-century Europe lies slightly to the northwest of *Mitteleuropa*: it starts with the Benelux states, then meanders south along the Franco-German frontier to the approaches of the Alps. To wit, there is the European Commission and its civil service in Brussels, the European Court in The Hague, the treaty town of Maastricht, the European Parliament in Strasbourg, and so on. In fact, all these places lie athwart a line running southward from the North Sea "that formed the centerpiece and primary communications route of the ninth-century Carolingian monarchy," observes the late eminent scholar of modern Europe Tony Judt.[5] The fact that the budding European super-state of our own era is concentrated in Europe's medieval core, with Charlemagne's capital city of Aachen (Aix-la-Chapelle) still at its very center, is no accident. For nowhere on the continent, more so than along this spinal column of Old World civilization, is Europe's sea and land interface quite as rich and profound. In the Low Countries there is the openness to the great ocean, even as the entrance to the English Channel and a string of islands in Holland form a useful protective barrier, giving these small states advantages out of proportion to their size. Immediately in the rear of this North Sea coast is a wealth of protected rivers and waterways, all promising trade, movement, and consequent political development. The loess soil of northwestern Europe is dark and productive, even as the forests provide a natural defense. Finally, the cold climate between the North Sea and the Alps, much more so than the warmer climate south of the Alps, has been sufficiently challenging to stimulate human resolve from the Late Bronze Age forward, with Franks, Alamanni, Saxons, and Frisians settling in late antiquity in Gaul, the Alpine Foreland, and the coastal lowlands. Here, in turn, would be the proving grounds of Francia and the Holy Roman Empire in the ninth century, of Burgundy, Lorraine, Brabant, and Friesland, too, and of city-states like Trier and Liege, all of which collectively displaced Rome, and evolved into polities that today drive the machinery of the European Union.

Of course, before all of the above came Rome, and before Rome ancient Greece: both of which, in William McNeill's choice words, constituting the antechambers of the "anciently civilized" world that began in Egypt and Mesopotamia, and spread from there, through Minoan Crete and Anatolia, to the northern shore of the Mediterranean. Civilization, as we know, took root in warm and protected river valleys such as the Nile and Tigris-Euphrates, and continued its migration into the relatively mild climates of the Levant, North Africa, and the Greek and Italian peninsulas, where living was hospitable with only rudimentary technology.

But though European civilization had its initial flowering along the Mediterranean, it continued to develop, in ages of more advanced

HABSBURG EMPIRE

Habsburg acquisitions 1648–1913 (some lost during that period)

1914 boundary

AUSTRIAN NETHERLANDS

Elbe River

GERMANY

Rhine River

BOHEMIA

Seine River

WÜRTTEM-BERG

Danube River

AUS

STYRIA

Loire River

COUNTY OF BURGUNDY

F R A N C E

VORARLBERG

TYROL

SALZBURG

CARINTHIA

Rhône River

TRENT

VENETIA

GORIZIA

CARNIOL

LOMBARDY

MANTUA

CTY. OF ISTRIA

Adriatic Sea

PARMA

MODENA

TUSCANY

PAPAL STATES

Tiber R.

I T A L Y

Mediterranean Sea

KINGDOM OF NAPLES

Tyrrhenian Sea

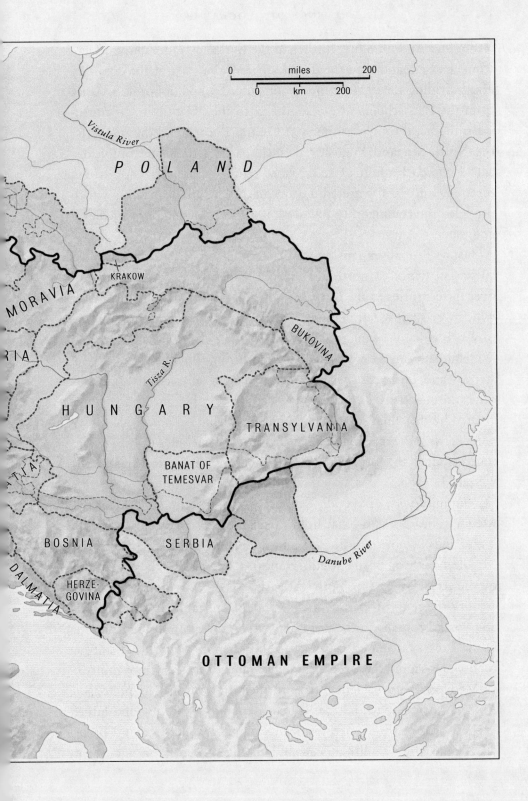

technology and mobility, further to the north in colder climes. Here Rome had expanded in the decades before the start of the common era, providing for the first time political order and domestic security from the Carpathians in the southeast to the Atlantic in the north-west: that is, throughout much of Central Europe and the region by the North Sea and English Channel. Large settlement complexes, called *oppida* by Julius Caesar, emerged throughout this sprawling, forested, and well-watered European black-soil heartland, which provided the rudimentary foundation for the emergence of medieval and modern cities.[6]

Just as Roman expansion gave a certain stability to the so-called barbarian tribes of northern Europe, Rome's breakup would lead over the centuries to the formation of peoples and nation-states with which we are now familiar, and which was formalized by the Treaty of Westphalia following the Thirty Years' War in 1648. As the scholar William Anthony Hay writes, "Pressure from nomadic tribes on the steppes and European periphery started a chain effect that pushed other groups living in more or less settled cultures into the vacuum created by the collapse of Roman power."[7] That is, Rome's collapse, coupled with the onslaught westward from the peoples of the steppe, together aided the formation of national groups in Central and north-western Europe.

Antiquity was, above all, defined by the geographic hold of the Mediterranean, and as that hold "slackened," with Rome losing its hinterlands in northern Europe and the Near East, the world of the Middle Ages was born.[8] Mediterranean unity was further shattered by the Arab sweep through North Africa.[9] Already by the eleventh century the map of Europe has a modern appearance, with France and Poland roughly in their present shapes, the Holy Roman Empire in the guise of a united Germany, and Bohemia—with Prague at its center—presaging the Czech Republic. Thus did history move north.

Mediterranean societies, despite their innovations in politics—Athenian democracy and the Roman Republic—were, by and large, in the words of the French historian and geographer Fernand Braudel, defined by "traditionalism and rigidity." The poor quality of

Mediterranean soils favored large holdings that were, perforce, under the control of the wealthy. And that, in turn, contributed to an inflexible social order. Meanwhile, in the forest clearings of northern Europe, with their richer soils, grew up a freer civilization, anchored by the informal power relationships of feudalism, that would be better able to take advantage of the invention of movable type and other technologies yet to come.[10]

As deterministic as Braudel's explanation may appear, it does work to explain the broad undercurrents of the European past. Obviously, human agency in the persons of such men as Jan Hus, Martin Luther, and John Calvin was pivotal to the Protestant Reformation, and hence to the Enlightenment, that would allow for northern Europe's dynamic emergence as one of the cockpits of history in the modern era. Nevertheless, all that could not have happened without the immense river and ocean access, and the loess earth, rich with coal and iron ore deposits, which formed the background for such individual dynamism and industrialization. Great, eclectic, and glittering empires there certainly were along the Mediterranean in the Middle Ages, notably the Norman Roger II's in twelfth-century Sicily, and lest we forget, the Renaissance flowered first in late medieval Florence, with the art of Michelangelo and the secular realism of Machiavelli. But it was the pull of the colder Atlantic which opened up global shipping routes that ultimately won out against the enclosed Mediterranean. While Portugal and Spain were the early beneficiaries of this Atlantic trade—owing to their protruding peninsular position—their pre-Enlightenment societies, traumatized by the proximity of (and occupation by) North African Muslims, lost ground eventually to the Dutch, French, and English in the oceanic competition. So just as Charlemagne's Holy Roman Empire succeeded Rome, in modern times northern Europe has now succeeded southern Europe, with the mineral-rich Carolingian core winning out in the form of the European Union: in no small measure because of geography.

The medieval Mediterranean was itself divided between the Frankish west and the Byzantine east. For it wasn't only divisions between north and south that both define and plague Europe today, but also those between west and east and, as we shall see, between the northwest and the center. Consider the migration route of the Danube valley that continues eastward beyond the Great Hungarian Plain, the Balkans, and the Black Sea, all the way through the Pontic and Kazakh steppes to Mongolia and China.[11] This geographical fact, along with the flat, unimpeded access to Russia further north, forms the basis for the waves of invasions of mainly Slavic and Turkic peoples from the east that Mackinder details in his "Geographical Pivot of History" article, and which have, as we know, greatly shaped Europe's political destiny. So just as there is a Carolingian Europe and a Mediterranean Europe, there is, too, often as a result of these invasions from the east, a Byzantine-Ottoman Europe, a Prussian Europe, and a Habsburg Europe, all of which are geographically distinct, and that live today through somewhat differing economic development patterns: differing patterns that cannot simply be erased by the creation of a single currency.

For example, in the fourth century A.D., the Roman Empire itself divided into western and eastern halves. Rome remained the capital of the western empire, while Constantinople became the capital of the eastern one. Rome's western empire gave way to Charlemagne's kingdom further north and to the Vatican: Western Europe, in other words. The eastern empire—Byzantium—was populated mainly by Greek-speaking Orthodox Christians, and later by Muslims, when the Ottoman Turks, migrating from the east, captured Constantinople in 1453. The border between these eastern and western empires ran through the middle of what after World War I became the multiethnic state of Yugoslavia. When that state broke apart violently in 1991, at least initially the breakup echoed the divisions of Rome sixteen centuries earlier. The Slovenes and Croats were Roman Catholics, heirs to a tradition that went back from Austria-Hungary to Rome in the West; the Serbs were Eastern Orthodox and heirs to the Ottoman-Byzantine legacy of Rome in the East. The Carpathians, which run northeast of the former Yugoslavia and divide Romania into two parts, partially reinforced this boundary between Rome and Byzantium, and later between the Habsburg emperors in Vienna and the Turkish sultans in Constantinople.[12] Passes and, thus, trade routes existed through these formidable mountains, bringing the cultural repository of *Mitteleuropa* deep into the Byzantine and Ottoman Balkans. But even if the Carpathians were not a hard and fast border, like the Alps, they marked a gradation, a shift in the balance from one Europe to another. Southeastern Europe would be poor not only compared to northwestern Europe, but also in comparison to northeastern Europe, with its Prussian tradition. That is to say: the Balkans were not only poor compared to the Benelux countries, but compared to Poland and Hungary as well.

The collapse of the Berlin Wall brought these divisions into sharp relief. The Warsaw Pact had constituted a full-fledged eastern empire, ruled from Moscow, featuring military occupation and enforced, freeze-frame poverty through the introduction of command economies. During the forty-four years of Kremlin rule, much of Prussian, Habsburg, and Byzantine-Ottoman Europe was locked away in a Soviet prison of nations, collectively known as Eastern Europe. Meanwhile, in Western Europe the European Union was taking shape, first as the Franco-German Coal and Steel Community, then as the Common Market, and finally as the European Union, building out from its Carolingian base of France, Germany, and the Benelux countries to encompass Italy and Great Britain, and later Greece and the Iberian nations. Because of its economic head start during the Cold War years, Carolingian Europe inside NATO has emerged as stronger, for the time being, than Prussian northeastern Europe and Danubian *Mitteleuropa,* which historically were equally prosperous, but for so long were inside the Warsaw Pact.

The Soviet thrust into Central Europe in the latter phases of World War II created this entire turn of events, even as it bore out Mackinder's thesis of Asiatic invasions shaping European destiny. Of course, we shouldn't carry this determinism too far, since without the actions of one man, Adolf Hitler, World War II would not have occurred and there would have been no Soviet invasion in the first place.

But Hitler did exist, and so we are left with the situation as we have it today: the Europe of Charlemagne rules, but because of the resurgence of a united Germany, the balance of power within Europe may shift slightly eastward to the confluence of Prussia and *Mitteleuropa,* with German economic power invigorating Poland, the Baltic states, and the upper Danube. The Mediterranean seaboard and the Byzantine-Ottoman Balkans lag behind. The worlds of the Mediterranean and the Balkans meet in mountainous and peninsular Greece, which despite being rescued from communism in the late 1940s remains among the most economically and socially troubled of European Union members. Greece, at the northwestern edge of Hodgson's Near Eastern Oikoumene, was the beneficiary of geography in antiquity—the place where the heartless systems of Egypt and Persia-Mesopotamia could be softened and humanized, leading to the invention of the West, so to speak. But in today's Europe dominated from the north Greece finds itself at the wrong, orientalized end of things, far more stable and prosperous than places like Bulgaria and Kosovo, but only because it was spared the ravages of communism. Roughly three-quarters of Greek businesses are family-owned and rely on family labor, so that minimum wage laws do not apply, even as those without family connections cannot be promoted.[13] This is a phenomenon that has deep cultural, and therefore historical and geographical roots.

Indeed, geography explains much. As noted in an earlier chapter, when the Warsaw Pact broke up, the formerly captive countries advanced economically and politically almost exactly according to their positions on the map: with Poland and the Baltic states, along with Hungary and the Bohemian end of Czechoslovakia performing the best, and the Balkan countries to the south suffering destitution and unrest. All the vicissitudes of the twentieth century notwithstanding—including the pulverizing effect of Nazism and communism—the legacies of Prussian, Habsburg, and Byzantine and Ottoman rules are still relevant. These empires were first and foremost creatures of geography, influenced as they all were by Mackinderesque migration patterns from the Asiatic east.

Thus, behold again that eleventh-century map of Europe, with the Holy Roman Empire resembling a united Germany at its center. All around are region states: Burgundy, Bohemia, Pomerania, Estonia; with Aragon, Castille, Navarre, and Portugal to the southwest. Think now of the regional success stories in the twenty-first century, mainly in Carolingian Europe: Baden-Württemberg, the Rhône-Alps, Lombardy, and Catalonia. These, as Tony Judt reminds us, are for the most part northerners, who peer down on the so-called backward, lazy, subsidized Mediterranean south, even as they look in horror at the prospect of Balkan nations like Romania and Bulgaria joining the European Union.[14] It is the center versus the periphery, with the losers in the periphery, generally—though not exclusively—in those regions closer geographically to the Middle East and North Africa. But precisely because the Brussels-headquartered European super-state has worked well enough for the northerly subregions like Baden-Württemberg and Catalonia, they have been liberated from their own one-size-fits-all, chain store national governments, and have consequently flourished by occupying historically anchored, economic, political, and cultural niches.

Beyond their dissatisfaction with Europe's losers on the periphery, among prosperous northern Europeans there is an unease over the dissolution of society itself. National populations and labor forces are demographically stagnant in Europe, and consequently graying. Europe will lose 24 percent of its prime, working-age population by 2050, and its population of those over sixty years old will rise by 47 percent in that timeframe. This will likely lead to increased immigration of young people from the Third World to support Europe's aging welfare states. While reports of Muslim domination of Europe have been exaggerated, the percentage of Muslims in major European countries will, in fact, more than double by mid-century, from the current 3 percent to perhaps 10 percent of the population. Whereas in 1913 Europe had more people than China, by 2050 the combined populations of Europe, the United States, and Canada will comprise just 12 percent of the world total, down from 33 percent after World War I.[15] Europe is certainly in the process of being demographically diminished by the rest of Asia and Africa, even as European populations themselves are becoming more African and Middle Eastern.

Indeed, the map of Europe is about to move southward, and once again to encompass the entire Mediterranean world, as it did not only under Rome, but under the Byzantines and Ottoman Turks, too. For decades, because of autocratic regimes that stifled economic and social development—while also being the facilitators of extremist politics—North Africa was effectively cut off from the northern rim of the Mediterranean. North Africa gave Europe economic migrants, and little more. But as North Africa states evolve into messy democracies the degree of political and economic interactions with nearby Europe will, at least over time, multiply (and some of those Arab migrants may return home as new opportunities in their homeland are created by reformist policies). The Mediterranean will become a connector, rather than the divider it has been during most of the postcolonial era.

Just as Europe moved eastward to encompass the former satellite states of the Soviet Union upon the democratic revolutions of 1989, Europe will now expand to the south to encompass the Arab revolutions. Tunisia and Egypt are not about to join the EU, but they are about to become shadow zones of deepening EU involvement. Thus, the EU itself will become an even more ambitious and unwieldy project than ever before. This is in keeping with Mackinder, who argued that the Sahara Desert denoted Europe's real southern boundary because it cut off Equatorial Africa from the north.[16]

Nevertheless, the European Union, albeit beset by divisions, anxieties, and massive growing pains, will remain one of the world's great postindustrial hubs. Thus, the ongoing power shift within it, eastward from Brussels-Strasbourg to Berlin—from the European Union to Germany—will be pivotal to global politics. For, as I will argue, it is Germany, Russia, and, yes, Greece, with only eleven million people, that most perceptively reveal Europe's destiny.

The very fact of a united Germany has to mean comparatively less influence for the European Union than in the days of a divided Germany, given united Germany's geographical, demographic, and economic preponderance in the heart of Europe. Germany's population is now 82 million, compared to 62 million in France, and almost 60 million in Italy. Germany's gross domestic product is $3.65 trillion, compared with France's $2.85 trillion and Italy's $2.29 trillion. More key is the fact that whereas France's economic influence is mainly limited to the countries of Cold War Western Europe, German economic influence encompasses both Western Europe and the former Warsaw Pact states, a tribute to its more central geographical position and trade links with both east and west.[17]

Besides its geographical position astride both maritime Europe and *Mitteleuropa,* Germans have a built-in cultural attitude toward trade. As Norbert Walter, then the senior economist for Deutsche Bank, told me long ago, "Germans would rather dominate real economic activities than strict financial activities. We keep clients, we find out what they need, developing niches and relationships over the decades." This ability is aided by a particularly German dynamism; as the political philosopher Peter Koslowski once explained to me, "because so many Germans started from zero after World War II, they are aggressively modernist. Modernism and middle-class culture have been raised to the status of ideologies here." United Germany is also spatially organized to take advantage of an era of flourishing northern European regions. Because of the tradition of small, independent states arising out of the Thirty Years' War in the seventeenth century—which still guides Germany's federal system—there is no one great pressure cooker of a capital, but rather a series of smaller ones that manage to survive even in an era of a reborn Berlin. Hamburg is a media center, Munich a fashion center, Frankfurt the banking center, and so on, with a railway system that radiates impartially in all directions. Because Germany came late to unification in the second half of the nineteenth century, it has preserved its regional flavor that is so advantageous in today's Europe. Finally, the fall of the Berlin Wall, which, in historical terms, is still recent, with trends taking decades to fully emerge, has reconnected Germany to Central

Europe, re-creating, in exceedingly subtle and informal ways, the First and Second reichs of the twelfth and nineteenth centuries: roughly equivalent to the Holy Roman Empire.

Besides the Berlin Wall's collapse, another factor that has buttressed German geopolitical strength has been the historic German-Polish reconciliation that occurred during the mid-1990s. As former national security advisor Zbigniew Brzezinski writes, "Through Poland, German influence could radiate northward—into the Baltic states—and eastward—into Ukraine and Belarus." In other words, German power is enhanced by both a larger Europe, and also by a Europe in which *Mitteleuropa* reemerges as a separate entity.[18]

A critical factor in this evolution will be the degree to which European, and particularly German, quasi-pacifism holds up in the future. As the Britain-based strategist Colin Gray writes, "Snake-bitten . . . on the Somme, at Verdun, and by the Götterdämmerung of 1945, the powers of West-Central Europe have been convincingly debellicized."[19] Though it hasn't only been the legacy of war and destruction that makes Europeans averse to military solutions (aside from peacekeeping and humanitarian interventions), it has also been the fact that Europe during the Cold War decades had its security provided for by the American superpower, and today faces no palpable conventional threat. "The threat to Europe comes not in the form of uniforms, but in the tattered garb of refugees," says the German American academic and journalist Josef Joffe.[20] But what if, according to Mackinder, Europe's destiny is still subordinate to Asiatic history, in the form of a resurgent Russia?[21] Then there might be a threat. For what drove the Soviet Union to carve out an empire in Eastern Europe at the end of World War II still holds today: a legacy of depredations against Russia by Lithuanians, Poles, Swedes, Frenchmen, and Germans, leading to the need for a cordon sanitaire of compliant regimes in the space between historic Russia and Central Europe. To be sure, the Russians will not deploy land forces to reoccupy Eastern Europe for the sake of a new cordon sanitaire, but through a combination of political and economic pressure, partly owing to Europe's need for natural gas from Russia, Russians could exert undue influence on their former satellites in years to come: Russia supplies some 25 percent of Europe's gas, 40 percent of Germany's, and nearly 100 percent of Finland's and the Baltic states'.[22] Moreover, we may all wake up from Europe's epic economic and currency crisis to a world with greater Russian influence within the continent. Russia's investment activities as well as its critical role as an energy supplier will loom larger in a weakened and newly divided Europe.

So, will a debellicized Germany partly succumb to Russian influence, leading to a somewhat Finlandized Eastern Europe and an even more hollow North Atlantic Treaty Alliance? Or will Germany subtly stand up to Russia through various political and economic means, even as its society remains immersed in a post-heroic quasi-pacifism? The former scenario threatens to prove the fears of Mackinder and other geographers right: that, in a geographical sense, there is no Central Europe or *Mitteleuropa,* only a maritime Europe and a continental one, with a crush zone in between. The latter scenario, on the other hand, would present a richly complex European destiny: one in which Central Europe would fully reappear and flower for the first time since before World War I; and a tier of states between Germany and Russia would equally flourish, as Mackinder hoped for, leaving Europe in peace, even as its aversion to military deployments is geopolitically inconvenient to the United States. In this scenario, Russia would accommodate itself to countries as far east as Ukraine and Georgia joining Europe. Thus, the *idea* of Europe, as a geographical expression of historic liberalism, would finally be realized. Europe went through centuries of political rearrangements in the Middle Ages following the collapse of Rome. And in search of that *idea,* Europe will continue to rearrange itself following the Long European War of 1914–1989.

Indeed, Europe has been in geographical terms many things throughout its history. Following the Age of Exploration, Europe moved laterally westward as commerce shifted across the Atlantic, making cities such as Quebec, Philadelphia, and Havana closer economically to Western Europe than were cities like Kraków and Lvov in Eastern Europe; even as Ottoman military advances as far northwest as Vienna in the late seventeenth century cut off the Balkans from much of the rest of the European subcontinent. Of course, nowadays, Europe is shifting to the east as it admits former communist nations into the European Union, and to the south as it grapples with the political and economic stabilization of the southern shore of the Mediterranean in North Africa.

And in all these rearrangements, Greece, of all places, will provide an insightful register of the health of the European project. Greece is the only part of the Balkans accessible on several seaboards to the Mediterranean, and thus is the unifier of two European worlds. Greece is geographically equidistant between Brussels and Moscow, and is as close to Russia culturally as it is to Europe, by virtue of its Eastern Orthodox Christianity, in turn a legacy of Byzantium. Greece throughout modern history has been burdened by political underdevelopment. Whereas the mid-nineteenth-century revolutions in Europe were often of middle-class origins with political liberties as their goal, the Greek independence movement was a mainly ethnic movement with a religious basis. The Greek people overwhelmingly sided with Russia in favor of the Serbs and against Europe during the 1999 Kosovo War, even if the Greek government's position was more equivocal. Greece is the most economically troubled European nation that was not part of the communist zone during the Cold War. Greece, going back to antiquity, is where Europe—and by inference the West—both ends and begins. The war that Herodotus chronicled between Greece and Persia established a "dichotomy" of West against East that persisted for millennia.[23] Greece barely remained in the Western camp at the beginning of the Cold War, owing to its own civil war between rightists and communists, and the fateful negotiations between Winston Churchill and Joseph Stalin that ultimately made Greece part of NATO. Greece, as Mackinder writes, lies just outside the Eurasian Heartland and is thus accessible to sea power. But possession of Greece in some form by a Heartland power (namely Russia) "would probably carry with it the control of the World-

Island."[24] Of course, Russia is not going to be taking control of Greece anytime soon. Yet it is interesting to contemplate what would have happened during the Cold War had the negotiations between Churchill and Stalin gone differently: imagine how much stronger the Kremlin's strategic position would have been with Greece inside the communist bloc, endangering Italy across the Adriatic Sea, to say nothing of the whole eastern Mediterranean and the Middle East. The Greek financial crisis, so emblematic of Greece's political and economic underdevelopment, rocked the European Union's currency system beginning in 2010, and because of the tensions it wrought between northern and southern European countries was nothing less than the most significant challenge to the European project since the wars of the Yugoslav secession. As Greece ably demonstrates, Europe remains a truly ambitious work in progress: one that will be influenced by trends and convulsions from the south and east in a world reeling from a crisis of room.

Chapter X

RUSSIA AND THE INDEPENDENT HEARTLAND

Alexander Solzhenitsyn opens his epic novel on World War I, *August 1914,* with a rhapsody about the Caucasus range, whose "each single indentation . . . brilliantly white with deep blue hollows . . . towered so vast above petty human creation, so elemental in a man-made world, that even if all the men who had lived in all the past millennia had opened their arms as wide as they could and carried everything they had ever created . . . and piled it all up in massive heaps, they could never have raised a mountain ridge as fantastic as the Caucasus." Solzhenitsyn continues on in this vein, writing about the "snowy expanses," "bare crags," "gashes and ribs," and "vaporous fragments indistinguishable from real clouds."[1]

The Caucasus have throughout history held Russians, especially fierce nationalists like Solzhenitsyn, in fear and awe. Here, between the Black and Caspian seas, is a land bridge where Europe gradually vanishes amid a six-hundred-mile chain of mountains as high as eighteen thousand feet—mesmerizing in their spangled beauty, especially after the yawning and flat mileage of the steppe lands to the north. This is Russia's Wild West, though the mountains lie to the south of Moscow and St. Petersburg. Here, since the seventeenth century, Russian colonizers have tried to subdue congeries of proud peoples: Chechens, Ingush, Ossetes, Daghestanis, Abkhaz, Kartvelians, Kakhetians, Armenians, Azeris, and others. Here, the Russians encountered Islam in both its moderation and implacability. The complex emotional reaction of the Russians to the very fact of the Caucasus, which both tantalize and threaten them, opens a window onto the entire Russian story.

Russia is the world's preeminent land power, extending 170 degrees of longitude, almost halfway around the globe. Russia's principal outlet to the sea is in the north, but that is blocked by Arctic ice many months of the year. Land powers are perennially insecure, as Mahan intimated. Without seas to protect them, they are forever dissatisfied and have to keep expanding or be conquered in turn themselves. This is especially true of the Russians, whose flat expanse is almost bereft of natural borders and affords little protection. Russia's fear of land-bound enemies is a principal theme of Mackinder. The Russians have pushed into Central and Eastern Europe to block nineteenth-century France and twentieth-century Germany. They have pushed toward Afghanistan to block the British in India and to seek a warm water outlet on the Indian Ocean, and have pushed into the Far East to block China. As for the Caucasus, those mountains constitute the barrier that the Russians must dominate in order to be safe from the political and religious eruptions of the Greater Middle East.

Another geographical fact about Russia is its severe cold. The northernmost part of the United States lies at the 49th parallel of north latitude, where Canada begins. But the great mass of Russia lies north of the 50th parallel, so that the Russian population inhabits an even colder climate than do the Canadians, who live mainly along the U.S. border. "Because of latitude, remoteness from open seas, the bar-

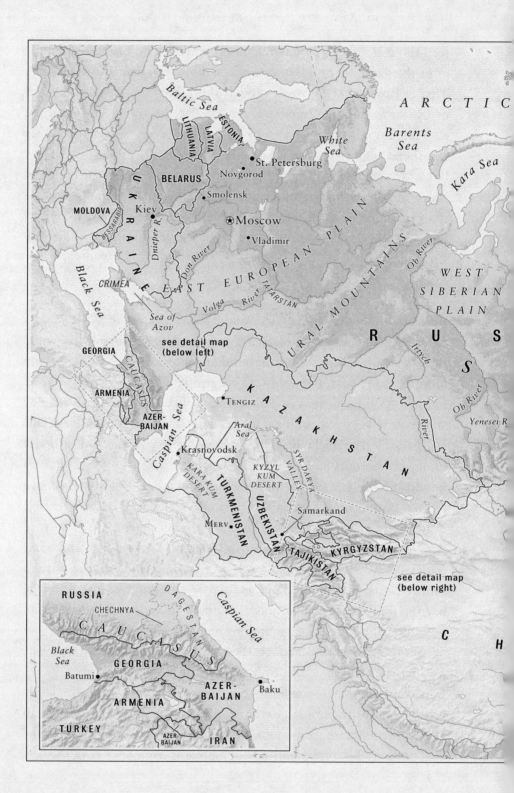

ARCTIC

Barents
Sea

Kara Sea

Baltic Sea

White
Sea

ESTONIA
LITHUANIA
LATVIA

St. Petersburg
Novgorod

BELARUS

Smolensk

MOLDOVA

Kiev

U K R A I N E

Dnieper R.

BESSARABIA

Don River

★ Moscow

Vladimir

E A S T   E U R O P E A N   P L A I N

TATARSTAN

Volga River

U R A L   M O U N T A I N S

Ob River

WEST
SIBERIAN
PLAIN

Black
Sea

CRIMEA

Sea of
Azov

see detail map
(below left)

Irtych

GEORGIA

CAUCASUS

ARMENIA

AZER-
BAIJAN

Caspian Sea

Tengiz

K A Z A K H S T A N

R U S S

Ob River

Yenesei R.

Aral
Sea

River

Krasnovodsk

KARA
KUM
DESERT

KYZYL
KUM
DESERT

SYR DARYA VALLEY

TURKMENISTAN

UZBEKISTAN

Samarkand

MERV

TAJIKISTAN

KYRGYZSTAN

see detail map
(below right)

C

H

RUSSIA

DAGESTAN

CHECHNYA

C A U C A S U S

Caspian Sea

Black
Sea

GEORGIA

Batumi

AZER-
BAIJAN

Baku

ARMENIA

TURKEY

AZER-
BAIJAN

IRAN

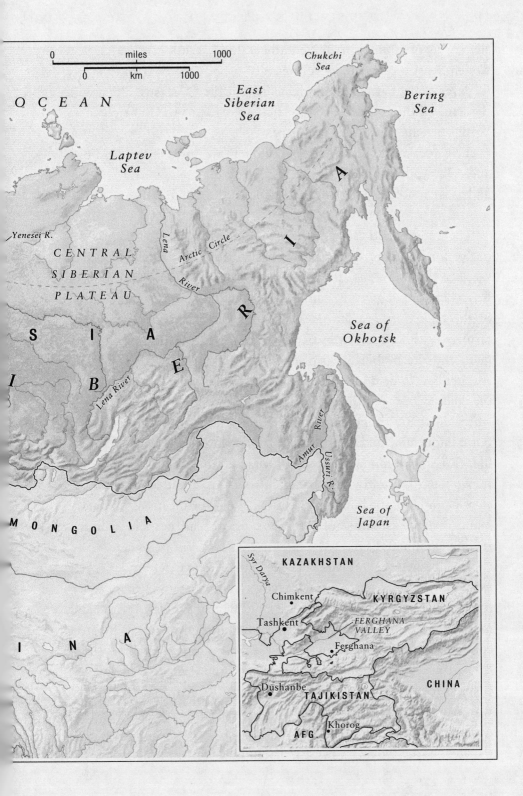

O C E A N

Laptev
Sea

Chukchi
Sea

East
Siberian
Sea

Bering
Sea

Yenesei R.

C E N T R A L

S I B E R I A N

P L A T E A U

Lena River

Arctic Circle

I

A

R

E

B

I

S

I

A

Lena River

Amur River

Ussuri R.

Sea of
Okhotsk

Sea of
Japan

M O N G O L I A

I N A

A

KAZAKHSTAN

Syr Darya

Chimkent

Tashkent

KYRGYZSTAN

FERGHANA
VALLEY

Ferghana

Dushanbe

TAJIKISTAN

CHINA

Khorog

AFG.

miles   1000

km   1000

rier effects of mountains, and continentality," writes geographer Saul Cohen, Russia's climate leaves much of it both too cold and too dry for large-scale, permanent settlement.[2] But the Caucasus, along with the parts of the Russian Far East that are close to the North Korean border, are the exceptions to this principle: so that another attraction of the Caucasus is their relatively mild temperatures at the 43rd parallel.[3] Truly, the Russian climate and landscape are miserably rugged, and as such hold the keys to the Russians' character and to their history.

The intense cold seems to have developed in the Russians "a capacity for suffering, a certain communalism, even a willingness to sacrifice the individual for the common good," writes historian of Russia Philip Longworth, who explains that the short growing season of the high northern latitudes required "interdependence between farmers," as well as "frenetic, strenuous effort, long hours in the field, and the mobilization of children," because both sowing and reaping had to be done in haste. Moreover, low surpluses because of the cold encouraged the elites of the emerging Russian state to control wide areas, killing the incentive of farmers to work harder without compulsion, and contributing to a "violent tendency" in daily life.[4] Russian communism, as well as a certain disdain for personal freedom until recently, have had their roots in a frigid landscape. The clearing of land, the building of churches and fortifications on the icy plain, and the chanting of Orthodox prayers all bespoke a heart-rending communalism.

The northern belt of Russia between the Arctic Circle and the Arctic Ocean is frozen treeless tundra, covered in moss and lichen. When it melts in summer slush covers the land, which is infested with giant mosquitoes. South of the tundra lies the taiga, the world's greatest coniferous forest, stretching from the Baltic to the Pacific. About 40 percent of these regions in Siberia and the Russian Far East are covered in permafrost. Finally, in southern Russia, reaching all the way from the Hungarian plain in the west, through Ukraine, the northern Caucasus, and Central Asia to far-off Manchuria, lies the steppe, the world's vastest grassland, "the great grass road," in the words of Russia scholar W. Bruce Lincoln.[5] As Mackinder writes, the Russians were originally a people huddled in the shielding enclosure of the forest who, for the sake of their own security, had to seek out and conquer—from the High Middle Ages into the early modern era—the incoming Asiatic nomads of the steppe to the south and east. In particular, the protracted and humiliating presence of the Mongols—the Golden Horde near medieval Muscovy and the Blue Horde in Central Asia—which played a role in denying Russia the experience of the Renaissance, gave to the victimized Eastern Orthodox Slavs a commonality, energy, and sense of purpose that was crucial to them being able to eventually break out of the Tatar yoke and roll up large expanses of territory in more recent centuries.[6] The Tatar yoke, according to historian G. Patrick March, instilled in the Russians a "greater tolerance for tyranny," while inuring them to privation and afflicting them with a "paranoid fear of invasion."[7]

Insecurity is the quintessential Russian national emotion. "The desire to find both roots and vindication in history grew partly out of the insecurity of the Eastern Plain," writes Librarian of Congress James H. Billington in his great tome about Russian culture, *The Icon and the Axe*. "Geography, not history," he says, has dominated Russian thinking:

> Harsh seasonal cycles, a few, distant rivers, and sparse patterns of rainfall and soil fertility controlled the lives of the ordinary peasant; and the ebb and flow of nomadic conquerors often seemed little more than the senseless movement of surface objects on an unchanging and unfriendly sea.[8]

In other words, the very flatness of Russia, extending from Europe to the Far East, with few natural borders anywhere and the tendency for scattered settlements as opposed to urban concentrations, has for long periods made for a landscape of anarchy, in which every group was permanently insecure.

Clustered in the forest with their enemies lurking on the steppe, the Russians took refuge in both animism and religion. The springtime festival of Orthodox Easter "acquired a special intensity in the Russian north," writes Billington. The traditional Easter greeting "was not the bland 'Happy Easter' of the modern West, but a direct affirmation of the central fact of sacred history, 'Christ is risen!'" And the reply was, "In truth, risen!" This spoke not only to the ascended Christ but to nature as well. For the long and dark winter was nearly over, with the trees shedding snow and putting out their leaves. Eastern Orthodox Christianity contains more than a hint of paganism. And Russian communism with its Bolshevik emphasis on totality was another form of Russian religion—the secular equivalent of Orthodoxy, according to the early-twentieth-century Russian intellectual Nicolas Berdyaev. As the title of Billington's book shows, the icon was a vivid reminder to the harassed frontiersmen of the power of their Orthodox faith, and the security and higher purpose it brought, while the axe "was the basic implement of Great Russia: the indispensable means of subordinating the forest" to their own purposes.[9]

Russia's religious and communist totality, in other words, harked back to this feeling of defenselessness in the forest close to the steppe, which inculcated in Russians, in turn, the need for conquest. But because the land was flat, and integrally connected in its immensity to Asia and the Greater Middle East, Russia was itself conquered. While other empires rise, expand, and collapse—and are never heard from again, the Russian Empire has expanded, collapsed, and revived several times.[10] Geography and history demonstrate that we can never discount Russia. Russia's partial resurgence in our own age following the dissolution of the Soviet Empire is part of an old story.

Russia's first great empire, and really the first great polity of Eastern Europe, was Kievan Rus, which emerged in the middle of the ninth century in Kiev, the most southerly of the historic cities along the Dnieper River. This allowed Kievan Rus to be in regular contact with the Byzantine Empire to the south, facilitating the conversion of Russians to Orthodox Christianity, which, as we know, would be enriched with the particular intensity that Russians gave to it, on account of their own encounter with a wintry landscape. Geography also decreed that Kievan Rus would demographically constitute a joining of Scandinavian Vikings (traveling down rivers from the north) and the indigenous eastern Slavs. The poor soils in the area meant that large tracts of land had to be conquered for the sake of a food supply, and thus an empire began to form, which brought together two dynamic regional forces, those of the Vikings and of the Byzantines. Russia, as a geographic and cultural concept, was the result.

Kievan Rus perennially struggled against steppe nomads. In the mid-thirteenth century it was finally destroyed by the Mongols under Batu Khan, Genghis's grandson. Successive years of drought in their traditional grazing lands had driven the Mongols westward in search of new pastures for their horses, which were the source of both their food and mobility. And so, the first great attempt at Russian imperial expansion over the Eurasian heartland was overrun.

The result was that, through innumerable movements and countermovements, as well as political dramas that were the stuff of human agency, Russian history shifted gradually north to cities like Smolensk, Novgorod, Vladimir, and Moscow, with Moscow emerging strongest in the later medieval centuries: these medieval centuries were in turn characterized by, as we have seen, autocracy and paranoia, which were partly the consequence of Mongol pressure. Moscow's rise to prominence was helped by its advantageous position for commerce, on the portage routes between the rivers in the basin of the mid- and upper Volga. Bruce Lincoln writes: "Moscow stood at the center of the upland in which the great rivers of European Russia had their beginnings . . . it was a hub from which Russia's river highways zigged and zagged outward like the irregularly shaped spokes of a lopsided wheel."[11] Yet because in this phase of their history the Russians avoided the steppe where the Tatars roamed, they concentrated on further developing the impenetrable forest tracts, where a state could better cohere.[12] Medieval Muscovy was surrounded and virtually landlocked. To the east was only taiga, steppe, and Mongol. To the south, the Turks and Mongols on the steppe denied Muscovy access to the Black Sea. To the west and northwest the Swedes, Poles, and Lithuanians denied it access to the Baltic Sea. Ivan IV, "the Terrible" (1553–1584), had access to only one seaboard, barely usable, in the far north: the White Sea, an inlet of the Arctic Ocean. Threatened on all sides of the infinite plain, the Russians had no choice but to try to break out, which they did under Ivan IV.

Ivan the Terrible is a historical figure of controversy, both a monster and folk hero, whose sobriquet is a misleading translation of *Groznyi,* the Dread, given to him by supporters for his punishment of the guilty. Ivan showed that in his time and place the only antidote to chaos was absolutism. Ivan was Russia's first great imperialist, a role that was partially thrust on him by history and geography. For in 1453, Greek Byzantium was overrun by the Ottoman Turks, and Greek refugees filtered north from Constantinople into Moscow, bringing with them political, military, and administrative expertise vital to empire building. Ivan, upon becoming czar, defeated the Kazan Tatars, which gave him access to the Urals; while later in his reign he took a major step toward the conquest of Siberia by defeating the Mongol khanate of Sibir near the Irtysh River, northwest of present-day Mongolia. Ivan's cruelty and cunning summarized what his people had learned from generations of "patient and supple dealings" with the Asiatics.[13] The speed of the Russian irruption over this vast landscape was such that less than six decades later, in the early seventeenth century, Russians were at the Sea of Okhotsk, on the margins of the Pacific Ocean.

Ivan also eyed the south and southeast, specifically the Muslim khanate of Astrakhan, an offshoot of the Golden Horde which oversaw the estuary of the Volga and the roads to the Caucasus, Persia, and Central Asia. Here was the land of the Nogai Horde, Turkic nomads who spoke a form of Kypchak. Even as the Nogais were political enemies of Muscovy, they traded with the principality, and welcomed Ivan's soldiery to keep the main roads safe. The sea of grasslands was a complex enormity in which Mongols and Tatars, with their armies sometimes overlapping, made war—and also had

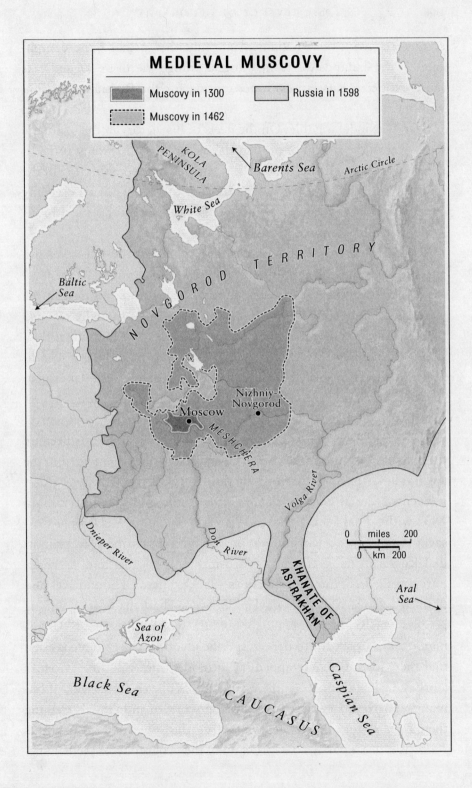

MEDIEVAL MUSCOVY

Muscovy in 1300

Russia in 1598

Muscovy in 1462

KOLA PENINSULA

Barents Sea

Arctic Circle

White Sea

N O V G O R O D   T E R R I T O R Y

Baltic Sea

Nizhniy-Novgorod

Moscow

MESHCHERA

Volga River

Dnieper River

Don River

0 miles 200

0 km 200

Aral Sea

KHANATE OF ASTRAKHAN

Sea of Azov

Caspian Sea

Black Sea

C A U C A S U S

commerce—with the Russians. And remember, as hard and complicated as the flatlands were, the Caucasus range was more so, and thus more exotic to Russian eyes, accounting for the Russian obsession with them.

Ivan was indefatigable. On the heels of his victory in the south, he made war in the region of present-day Estonia and Latvia in order to secure a perch on the Baltic, but was defeated by a combination of the Hanseatic League and the German Order of Livonia. This crucially cut Russia off from the West, even as it was being influenced by its newly taken lands in the Middle East and Asia.

Russia's first thrust at a continental empire in the late sixteenth and early seventeenth centuries established the reputation of the Cossacks, employed by the Russian state to firm up its position in the Caucasus. Though the word "Cossack," or *kazak,* originally referred to a freelance Tatar warrior, the Cossacks came to be individual Russians, Lithuanians, and Poles, who, despairing of the harsh conditions on the estates of their homelands, migrated to the Ukrainian steppes. Here amid the chaotic conditions of a former Mongol frontier, they made their livings as thieves, traders, colonists, and mercenaries, gradually coalescing into irregular units of Ivan's army because they were tough and came cheap. Cossack settlements emerged in the river valleys, principally those of the Don and the Dnieper.[14] As it happens, Nikolai Gogol's classic *Taras Bulba,* published initially in 1835 with a final version a decade later, is a story of the Dnieper Cossacks. Gogol was a Russian nationalist but he saw the real, primordial Russia in the Ukraine (a word meaning "borderland"), whose unremitting and unimpeded steppes—lacking natural boundaries and drained by relatively few navigable rivers—had made its colliding peoples warlike. Although Gogol used the words "Russian," "Ukrainian," and "Cossack" to denote specific identities, he also recognized that these identities overlapped (as local identities still do).[15] Gogol's story is dark with unredemptive violence. While the utter lack of humanity portrayed in these pages is the work of individuals making their own awful choices, it is also true that the violence of *Taras Bulba* is at least partly an expression of the geography of the Russian and Ukrainian steppes, where flatness, continentality, and migration routes lead to conflict and swift changes of fortune.

Ivan IV's empire continued to expand under Boris Godunov (1598–1605), particularly in the southeasterly direction of Stalingrad, the Urals, and the Kazakh steppe. But then medieval Muscovy collapsed, as Kievan Rus had before it, this time with Swedes, Poles, Lithuanians, and Cossacks carving pieces out of the carcass. Medieval Muscovy had fashioned itself as the "Third Rome," the rightful successor of both Rome itself and Constantinople. Hence Muscovy's undoing, known as the Time of Troubles—the result of factionalism in the capital—made it appear that an entire world and civilization were ending. And yet Russia was not finished, in spite of how it seemed at the time. Within a few short years, in 1613, Michael Romanov was installed as the czar, and a new dynasty as well as a new chapter in Russian history commenced.

It was the Romanov dynasty that came to define modern Russia, to give mechanization and further administrative organization to Russian imperialism, an improvement over the somewhat romantic, ad hoc forays of medieval Muscovy. Under the three-hundred-year rule of the Romanovs, Russia subdued Poland and Lithuania, destroyed Sweden, humbled Napoleonic France, took back the Ukraine, expanded into the Crimea and the Balkans at the expense of the Ottoman Turks, and both extended and formalized its hold on the Caucasus, Central Asia, and Siberia unto China and the Pacific. Russia recovered from reverses in the Crimean War (1853–1856) and the Russo-Japanese War (1904–1905). And in keeping with the grand theme of Russian history, that of momentous expansions and equally momentous retreats against the backdrop of a vast, unimpeded geography, the Romanovs lost both Poland and western Russia to Napoleon's Grande Armée in 1812, only to recover within a few weeks and hasten a French withdrawal back to Central Europe that reduced Napoleon's forces to ashes.

Peter the Great, who ruled Russia in the late seventeenth and early eighteenth centuries, was to the Romanov dynasty what Ivan IV had been to medieval Muscovy: an extraordinary individual whose actions demonstrate that geography is only part of the story. Of course, Peter is most well known to history for his building of St. Petersburg on the shores of the Baltic, which he began in 1703, and which entailed a grueling war against the Swedish Empire: with Sweden invading across the Masurian Marshes in the area of Belarus, and the Russians burning crops as part of a scorched earth policy in the dry areas, a tactic that they would later use against both Napoleon and Hitler. And yet Peter's grand achievement of consolidating Russia's Baltic coast, establishing a new capital there that faced toward Europe, in an effort to change Russia's political and cultural identity, would ultimately fail. For with conquests in every other direction, too, Russia remained more properly a Eurasian country, arguably the archetypal one, the only one in fact, straining to be European even as geography and the history of invasions exemplified by the Mongols denied it that status. Alexander Herzen, the great nineteenth-century literary intellectual of Russia, remarked:

> To this day we look upon Europeans and upon Europe in the same way as provincials look upon those who live in the capital, with deference and a feeling of our own inferiority, knuckling under and imitating them, taking everything in which we are different for a defect.[16]

Though Russians should have had nothing to be ashamed of, for they could only be what they were: a people that had wrested an empire from an impossible continental landscape, and were consequently knocking at the gates of the Levant and India, thus threatening the empires of France and Britain. For at about the same time that Herzen wrote those words above, Russian forces took Tashkent and Samarkand on the ancient silk route to China, close to the borders of the Indian Subcontinent.

Whereas the maritime empires of France and Britain faced implacable enemies overseas, the Russians faced them on their own territory, so that the Russians learned from early on in their history to be anxious and vigilant. They were a nation that in one form or another was always at war. Again, the Caucasus provide a telling example in the form of the Muslim Chechens of the north Caucasus, against whom the armies of Catherine the Great fought in the late eighteenth century, and continued fighting under succeeding czars throughout the nineteenth, to say nothing of the struggles in our own time. This was long after more pliable regions of the Caucasus further south, such as Georgia, had already come under czarist control. Chechen belligerency stemmed from the difficulty of earning a living from the stony mountain soil, and from the need to bear arms to protect sheep and goats from wild animals. Because trade routes traversed the Caucasus, the Chechens were at once guides and robbers.[17] And though converts to Sufi Islam—often less fanatical than other branches of the faith—they were zealous in defense of their homeland from the Orthodox Christian Russians. In the Caucasus, writes the geographer Denis J. B. Shaw, "the Russian, Ukrainian and cossack settlement of the 'settler empire' came into conflict with the stout resistance of the mountain peoples. Most of these peoples, apart from the majority of the Osetians, are Islamic in culture, and this reinforced their determination to fight the Russian intruder." Because of their fear of the independent spirit of the people of the north Caucasus, the Bolsheviks refused to incorporate them into a single republic and split them up, only to rejoin them into artificial units that did not conform to their linguistic and ethnic patterns. Thus, Shaw goes on, "the Karbardians were grouped with the Balkars, despite the fact that the former have more in common with the Cherkessians and the latter with the Karachay." Stalin, moreover, exiled the Chechens, Ingush, Kalmyks, and others to Central Asia in 1944, for their alleged collaboration with the Germans.[18]

The Caucasus have contributed mightily to making the face of Russian imperialism hard. Such, as we've said, is often the destiny of land powers, who have often the need to conquer.

So the Russians pressed on, inspiring Mackinder to formulate his pivot theory by a surge of Russian railway building in the second half of the nineteenth century: fifteen thousand miles of lines between 1857 and 1882, so that Moscow was connected with the Prussian

frontier to the west and with Nizhniy-Novgorod to the east, as well
as with the Crimea on the shore of the Black Sea to the south. Moreover, between 1879 and 1886, Russian engineers built a rail line from
Krasnovodsk, on the eastern shore of the Caspian, to Merv, more
than five hundred miles to the east, close to the borders of Persia and
Afghanistan; by 1888 that line reached another three hundred miles
northeastward to Samarkand. (And a spur was built from Merv south
to near the Afghan border.) These new arteries of empire followed
Russian military advances in the Kara Kum (Black Sand) and Kyzyl
Kum (Red Sand) deserts south of the Central Asian steppe, in the area
of present-day Turkmenistan and Uzbekistan. Because of the proximity of the Indian Subcontinent, where British power was then at its
zenith, this bout of Russian imperial activity joined the "Great Game"
between Russia and Britain for the control of Asia. Meanwhile, a line
was built to connect Baku, on the western shore of the Caspian, with
Batumi, on the Black Sea, so as to span the Caucasus. And in 1891,
the Russians began a railway from the Urals to the Pacific, four thousand miles away, through Siberia and the Far East, and all the forests,
mountains, swamplands, and permafrost in between. By 1904 there
were 38,000 miles of railways in Russia, a fact that gave St. Petersburg access to eleven time zones, all the way to the Bering Strait between Russia and Alaska. Motivating this latest Russian version of
Manifest Destiny was, once again, insecurity: the insecurity of a land
power that had to keep attacking and exploring in all directions or
itself be vanquished.

On a relief map of Eurasia a great fact stands out—one that explains
the story of Russia. From the Carpathian Mountains in the west to
the Central Siberian plateau in the east there is nothing but lowland
plains, with the Urals in between as but a small eruption on this flat,
continent-sized landscape. This plain, which includes Mackinder's
Heartland, extends from the Arctic Ocean inlets of the White and
Kara seas to the Caucasus, and to the Hindu Kush and Zagros mountains in Afghanistan and Iran, so that Russian imperialism has always

been tempted by the vague hope of a warm water outlet on the close-by Indian Ocean. But it wasn't only in the cases of the Caucasus and Afghanistan where Russians ventured beyond the core region of this great plain and deep into the mountains. From the early seventeenth century into the twentieth, Russians—Cossacks, fur trappers, and traders—bravely reached beyond the Yenesei River, from western into eastern Siberia and the Far East, a frigid immensity of seven major mountain ranges 2,500 miles across where the frost can last nine months of the year. While the conquest of Belarus and the Ukraine was natural because of the close affinity and common, inter-twined history of these lands with Russia, in Siberia the Russians carved out an entirely new "boreal riverine empire."[19] As W. Bruce Lincoln writes in his magesterial history, *The Conquest of a Continent: Siberia and the Russians,* "the conquest that has defined her [Russian] greatness has been in Asia," not Europe.[20] The drama that played out in eastern Siberia and beyond summed up the Russian historical experience in its most intense form. Philip Longworth writes:

> The harshness of the climate has made them hardy and endur-ing; the immensity of their landscape and the low density of settlement, as well as the brevity of the growing season, have encouraged both cooperation and coercion in social relation-ships, for Russians have needed a greater degree of organiza-tion than most peoples in order to survive. . . . In the past this need has favored centralized, authoritarian forms of govern-ment and discouraged more participatory forms.[21]

The Yenesei swells to a flood as much as three miles wide and is the sixth longest river in the world. It flows north for 3,400 miles from Mongolia to the Arctic. Much more so than the Urals, it is the true dividing line between two Russias—between western and eastern Siberia, with thousands of miles of lowland plain beckoning on its western bank and thousands of miles of plateau and snowy moun-tains on its eastern bank. The British traveler Colin Thubron writes that "it is the flow of the river out of emptiness, like something incarnate, time-bearing, at once peaceful and rather terrible, which tightens my stomach." At another, more northerly point along the river, beyond the Arctic Circle, he goes on: "the earth is flattening out over its axis. The shoreline is sinking away. Nothing, it seems, has ever happened here. So . . . history becomes geology."[22]

The lure of animal furs first brought explorers to this glacial back-of-beyond. Later it would be the natural resources: oil, natural gas, coal, iron, gold, copper, graphite, aluminum, nickel, and a plethora of other metals and minerals, as well as the electric power generated by Siberia's mighty rivers: for just as the Yenesei divides western and eastern Siberia, the equally majestic Lena divides eastern Siberia from the Russian Far East. Indeed, whereas the great rivers of Siberia flow south to north, their tributaries stretch east and west, "like the intersecting branches of . . . mammoth trees," creating a great portage system.[23]

The mines punctuating this landscape were to constitute the heart of the czarist and Soviet penal systems. Indeed, the geography of Siberia has been a synonym for cruelty and strategic wealth, making Russia over the decades both a morally dark and an energy-rich power. The sudden appearance of Russia among the great powers of Europe in the early 1700s was related to the rich supplies of iron ore found in the Ural forests, fit for making cannons and muskets, so necessary for waging modern war. Likewise, in the mid-1960s, the discovery of vast fields of oil and natural gas in northwestern Siberia would make Russia an energy hyperpower in the early twenty-first century.[24] Siberia's conquest also achieved something else: it brought Russia into the geopolitics of the Pacific, and into conflict with both Japan and China. It has been the Russian conflict with China that was at the heart of Cold War dynamics, even as that conflict could be central to America's own strategy for dealing with both powers in the twenty-first century.[25]

Unlike the Irtych, Ob, Yenesei, and Lena, the Amur River flows not south to north, but west to east, linking up with the Ussuri River to form today's border between the Russian Far East and Chinese

Manchuria. This frontier region, known as Amuria to the north of the Chinese border and Ussuria to the east of it, has been fought over between czarist Russia and Qing (Manchu) China since the mid-seventeenth century, when Russian freebooters entered the region, to be followed by Muscovite soldiers, and later by diplomats at a time when the Manchus were distracted by their conquests of Taiwan and parts of the mainland. This process culminated in 1860 when a weak China with a decaying dynasty was forced to accept the transfer of 350,000 square miles of territory from Chinese to Russian sovereignty, creating the current frontiers.[26] Now that China is strong and Russia comparatively weak this border is again coming under pressure from Chinese settlers and corporations seeking to move north, in order to take advantage of this region's oil, natural gas, timber, and other resources. Geography commands a perennially tense relationship between Russia and China, obscured by their tactical, somewhat anti-U.S. alliance of the moment. In July 2009, Chief of the Russian General Staff Nikolai Makarov made a slide presentation in which it was reportedly said that "NATO and China . . . are the most dangerous of our geopolitical rivals."[27]

What this geography illuminates is something that is often forgotten: that Russia has historically been very much a part of East Asian power dynamics. The Russo-Japanese War of 1904–1905 was partially instigated by Japan's demand that Russia acknowledge Chinese sovereignty in Manchuria (as well as Japan's freedom to intervene in Korea), to which the Russians objected. That war's ending, in addition to humiliating the czarist regime, even more so constituted a humiliation of Qing China, as it was fought over land that the Manchus considered part of their patrimony. To wit, Russia's defeat still left it in control of Amuria and Ussuria, which the Manchus coveted.

More so than the Russo-Japanese War, in which Russia lost the southern half of Sakhalin Island and parts of southern Manchuria (which according to geographic logic should have belonged to China anyway), it was the Russian Revolution of 1917 and its chaotic aftermath that really shook loose Russia's control of its own Far East. China, Japan, and the United States (an emerging Far Eastern power in its own right) took control of pieces of the Trans-Siberian Railway between Lake Baikal in the west and the port of Vladivostok in the east, while Vladivostok itself came under Japanese occupation between 1918 and 1922. Eighty thousand Japanese troops occupied the Amur region during this period.

Gradually, though, Lenin's Red Army turned the tide of the civil war against the White Russian antirevolutionaries. Consequently, the new Soviet state was able to take back the territories on its margins: especially in the ethnic Turkic areas of the Central Asian deserts, where the Bolsheviks feared they were vulnerable to attack from the British in India, acting through Afghanistan. The Bolsheviks, notwithstanding their professed ideology about the unity of all the workers of the world, were realists when confronted with the "age-old problem" of a sprawling land power: the threat of attack on its peripheries. Whoever ruled Russia had to face the fact of a cursedly flat landmass spilling into contiguous states in several directions. To compensate, the Bolsheviks became Russian imperialists like the czars before them: Moldovans, Chechens, Georgians, Azeris, Turkmens, Uzbeks, Kazakhs, Tajiks, Kyrgyz, Buriat-Mongols, Tatars, and others all came under their sway. The Bolsheviks easily rationalized their conquests: after all, they had given the blessing of communism to these peoples, even as they awarded them Soviet republics of their own.[28] Following the dictates of geography, however subconsciously, the Bolsheviks moved the capital back eastward to Moscow from St. Petersburg on the Baltic, restoring the largely Asiatic reality that was always central to Russia's being. In place of the semi-modernized regime bestowed by Peter the Great, which ruled Russia from its Baltic "window on the West," there now arose a state ruled from the Kremlin, the historic semi-Asiatic seat of medieval Muscovy.[29] The new Soviet Union consisted of three Union Republics—Russia, Ukraine, and Belarus—and eleven Autonomous Republics and subregions. But because many of these republics did not neatly overlap with ethnic borders—for example, there was a large Tajik minority in Uzbekistan and a larger Uzbek one in Tajikistan—secession was impossible without civil war, and so the Soviet Union became a prison of nations.

This prison of nations was as aggressive as ever in the twentieth century, even as it had more cause for insecurity than ever before. In 1929 Soviet infantry, cavalry, and aircraft attacked the western edge of Manchuria to seize control of a railroad passing through Chinese territory. In 1935 the Soviet Union made a virtual satellite out of western China's Xinjiang Province, while Outer Mongolia became the Mongolian People's Republic, strongly aligned with the Soviet Union. Meanwhile, in European Russia, the signing of the 1939 Russo-German pact allowed Stalin to annex eastern Poland, eastern Finland, Bessarabia, and the Baltic states of Lithuania, Latvia, and Estonia. Russia, under the guise of the Soviet Union, now stretched from Central Europe to the Korean Peninsula. And yet, as events would demonstrate, Russia was still not secure. Geography continued to have a say in the matter. Hitler's 1941 invasion eastward across the plain of European Russia brought German troops to the outskirts of Moscow and within reach of the Caspian Sea, until they were stopped at Stalingrad in early 1943. At the end of the war, the Soviets exacted their revenge, giving vent to centuries of geographical insecurity going back to the Mongol depredations against Kievan Rus.

Following the collapse of Nazi Germany and fascist Japan, the Soviet Union effectively acquired the entire eastern half of Europe by erecting a system of communist satellite states, the loyalty of which was guaranteed in most cases by the presence of Soviet troops, who had surged back across the flat plain westward—back across the Dnieper, the Vistula, and the Danube—as the logistics of Hitler's war machine failed amid the vastness of European Russia, much as Napoleon's had the century before. This Soviet Eastern European empire now stretched deeper into the heart of Central Europe than had the Romanov Empire of 1613–1917, and included all of the territory promised Russia in the Nazi-Soviet pact.[30] At the opposite end of the Soviet Union, Moscow took possession of Sakhalin and the Kuril Islands north of Japan, adjoining the Russian Far East. The chaotic and weakened state of China following the Japanese occupation and the struggle for power between Mao Zedong's communists and Chiang Kai-shek's nationalists allowed for a large Russian troop presence in Manchuria, the consolidation of a pro-Soviet Outer Mongolia, and a friendly communist regime in the northern half of the Korean Peninsula. In the Korean Peninsula the great land power of the Soviet Union—and that of soon-to-be-communist China—would encounter the sea power of the United States, helping to facilitate the Korean War five years after World War II. For the upshot of World War II was the creation of Mackinder's Heartland power in the form of Soviet Russia, juxtaposed with Mahan's and Spykman's great sea power in the form of the United States. The destinies of Europe and China would both be affected by the very spread of Soviet power over the Heartland, even as the Greater Middle East and Southeast Asia in the Eurasian rimland would feel the pressure of American sea and air power. This was the ultimate geographical truth of the Cold War, which the ideology of communism coming from Moscow and the ideal of democracy coming from Washington obscured.

But the Cold War, which seemed interminable to those like myself who had grown up during the period, proved to be merely another phase of Russian history that ended according to the familiar dictates of Russian geography. Mikhail Gorbachev's attempt to reform Soviet communism in the 1980s revealed the system for what it actually was: an inflexible empire of subject peoples, inhabiting in many cases the steppe-land and mountainous peripheries of the Russian forests and plains. Once Gorbachev himself, in effect, announced that the ideological precepts on which the empire rested were deeply flawed, the whole system began to fall apart with the marginal pieces breaking off from the Russian center much as they had following the failure of Kievan Rus in the middle of the thirteenth century, medieval Muscovy in the early seventeenth, and the Romanov Empire in the early twentieth. This is why historian Philip Longworth notes that repeated expansion and collapse over a generally flat topography has been a principal feature of Russian history. In fact, as geographer and Russian specialist Denis Shaw explains, while the open frontier and the military burden which that engendered "fostered the centralization of the Russian state"—indeed, the power of the czars was legendary—Russia was, nevertheless, a weak state, because the czars did not develop sturdy administrative institutions in the far-flung provinces. This made Russia even more open to invasion.[31]

In 1991, when the Soviet Union officially disbanded, Russia was reduced to its smallest size since before the reign of Catherine the Great. It had lost even Ukraine, the original heartland of Kievan Rus. But despite the loss of Ukraine and the Baltic states, the Caucasus, and Central Asia, despite the military uncertainties of Chechnya, Dagestan, and Tatarstan, and despite the emergence of Outer Mongolia as an independent state free of Moscow's tutelage, Russia's territory still surpassed that of any other nation on earth, covering over a third of mainland Asia, with land borders still stretching over almost half of the world's time zones from the Gulf of Finland to the Bering Sea. And yet this vast and naked expanse—no longer guarded by mountains and steppes at its fringes—now had to be protected by a population that was only a little over half that of the former Soviet Union.[32] (Russia's population was smaller than that of Bangladesh, in fact.)

Perhaps never before in peacetime was Russia so geographically vulnerable. In all of Siberia and the Far East there were only 27 million people.[33] Russia's leaders lost no time in assessing the dire situation. Less than a month after the dissolution of the Soviet Union, Russian foreign minister Andrei Kozyrev told *Rossiyskaya Gazeta* that "we rapidly came to understand that geopolitics is replacing ideology."[34] "Geopolitics, persistently demonized during the days of the Soviet Union," writes University of Edinburgh professor emeritus John Erickson, "has returned with a vengeance to haunt post-Soviet Russia." Gone were the denunciations of geopolitics as the tool of capitalist militarism: not only was geopolitics as a discipline rehabilitated in Russia, but so were the reputations of Mackinder, Mahan, and Karl Haushofer even. In "unabashed neo-Mackinderian style," the old-guard communist leader Gennady Zyuganov declared that Russia had to restore control of the "Heartland."[35] Given the ups and downs of Russian history, in addition to its new geographical vulnerabilities, Russia had no choice but to become a revisionist power, intent on regaining—in some subtle or not so subtle form—its near-abroad in Belarus, Ukraine, Moldova, the Caucasus, and Central Asia, where 26 million ethnic Russians still lived. During the lost decade of the 1990s, when Russia teetered on the brink of economic collapse and was consequently weak and humiliated, a new cycle of expansion was nevertheless being nurtured. The Russian ultranationalist Vladimir Zhirinovsky suggested that the southern Caucasus as well as Turkey, Iran, and Afghanistan now all had to come under Russian domination. While Zhirinovsky's extremism was not shared by the majority of Russians, he still tapped into a vital undercurrent of Russian thinking. Truly, Russia's present weakness in Eurasia has made geography itself a turn-of-the-twenty-first-century Russian obsession.

Of course, the Soviet Union would never be reconstituted. However, a looser form of union reaching to the borders of the Middle East and the Indian Subcontinent might still be attainable. But what would be the uplifting rallying cry behind it? What would be the idea with which the Russians could morally justify the next wave of expansion? Zbigniew Brzezinski in *The Grand Chessboard: American Primacy and Its Geostrategic Imperatives* writes that in the 1990s Russians began to resurrect the nineteenth-century doctrine of Eurasianism as an alternative to communism, in order to lure back the non-Russian peoples of the former Soviet Union.[36] Eurasianism fits nicely with Russia's historical and geographical personality. Sprawling from Europe to the Far East, and yet anchored in neither, Russia, in the way of no other country, epitomizes Eurasia. Moreover, a closed geography featuring a crisis of room in the twenty-first century—one that erodes the divisions of Cold War area specialists—makes more palpable the very idea of Eurasia as a continental, organic whole. But while Eurasia may become an ever more useful concept for geographers and geopoliticians in the coming years, that doesn't mean that Georgians, Armenians, or Uzbeks, with all the historical and emotional baggage that goes with such ethnic identities, will begin to think of themselves as "Eurasians." The Caucasus are the Caucasus precisely because they are a cauldron of ethnic identities and conflicts: identities that with the collapse of Cold War power blocs have the potential to become even more richly developed. The same holds true to a large extent for Central Asia. Even if Russians and, say, Kazakhs can suppress their ethnic rivalry through a "Eurasian Union" of sorts, Eurasianism does not appear to be something that people will die for; or something that will send a chill up their spine; especially as Ukrainians, Moldovans, Georgians, and others pine to be Europeans. But if Eurasianism can suppress differences however slightly in some quarters of the former Soviet Union, and therefore help stability, is it not worthwhile in its own right?

Just as geography is not an explanation for everything, neither is it a solution. Geography is merely the unchanging backdrop against which the battle of ideas plays out. Even when geography is a unifier— as in the case of America or Great Britain, or India or Israel—the ideals of democracy and liberty and Zionism (with its spiritual element) have, nevertheless, been basic to national identity. And when a people have nothing else to unite them except geography, as in the case of Egypt under former dictator Hosni Mubarak or Japan under the former ruling Liberal Democratic Party, then the state is afflicted by an overpowering malaise: stable it may be, thanks to geography, but that is all. Thus Russia, shorn of czardom and communism, requires an uplifting, unifying ideal beyond geography if it is to succeed in attracting back former subject peoples, particularly at a time when its own meager population is rapidly diminishing. Indeed, because of low birth rates, high death rates, a high rate of abortion, and low immigration, Russia's population of 141 million may drop to 111 million by 2050. (Accelerating this are the toxic levels of water and soil pollution, as part of a general environmental degradation.) Meanwhile, Russia's nominal Muslim community is increasing and may make up as much as 20 percent of the country's population within a decade, even as it is based in the north Caucasus and the Volga-Ural area, as well as in Moscow and St. Petersburg, so that it has a tendency toward regional separatism, while also possessing the ability to engage in urban terrorism. Chechen women have more than a third as many children as their Russian counterparts. To be sure, a mere appeal to geography—which is really what Eurasianism and the attendant Commonwealth of Independent States are about—will probably not allow for the rebirth of a Russian empire to compete with Kievan Rus, medieval Muscovy, the Romanov dynasty, and the Soviet Union.

Dmitri Trenin, director of the Carnegie Moscow Center, argues that in the twenty-first century, "the power of attraction trumps that of coercion," and, therefore, "Soft power should be central to Russia's foreign policy." In other words, a truly reformed Russia would be in a better position to project influence throughout its Eurasian peripheries. For the Russian language is the lingua franca from the Baltics to Central Asia, and Russian culture, "from Pushkin to pop music," is still in demand. A Russian-language television station could, in the event of an intellectually revitalized Russia, "become a sort of al Jazeera for Russophones." In this way of thinking, liberal democracy is the only ideal that could allow Russia to once again achieve what in its eyes is its geographic destiny.[37] Such an idea dovetails with Solzhenitsyn's remark in 1991 that "the time has come for an uncompromising *choice* between an empire of which we ourselves are the primary victims, and the spiritual and physical salvation of our own people."[38]

In fact, there is a geographic side to Trenin's analysis. He argues that Russia should put more emphasis on its extremities—Europe and the Pacific—than on its Eurasian heartland. A stress on cooperation with Europe would move Russia attitudinally westward. The population map of Russia shows that despite a territory that occupies eleven time zones, the overwhelming majority of Russians live in the extreme west adjacent to Europe. Thus, true political and economic reform merged with demographics could make Russia an authentic European country. As far as the Pacific is concerned, "Russia would do well to think of Vladivostok as its twenty-first-century capital," Trenin writes. Vladivostok is a cosmopolitan seaport, in close proximity to Beijing, Hong Kong, Seoul, Shanghai, and Tokyo, the world's most economically dynamic region.[39] Indeed, because the old Soviet

Union regarded its Far East as an area to exploit for raw materials rather than as a gateway to the Pacific Rim, the economic rise of East Asia that began in the 1970s and has continued through the present completely bypassed Russia.[40] Trenin says that it is past time to rectify that—for Russia is suffering as a result. China, which, rather than Russia, followed the lead of its fellow Pacific Rim countries Japan and South Korea in adopting market capitalism, is now emerging as the great power in Eurasia. Beijing has given $10 billion in loans to Central Asia, helped Belarus with a currency swap, gave a billion dollars in aid to Moldova at the other end of the continent, and is developing an area of influence in the Russian Far East. For Russia, a corresponding strategy would be to politically attach itself to Europe and economically attach itself to East Asia. Thus would Russia solve its problems in the Caucasus and Central Asia—by becoming truly attractive to those former Soviet republics, whose peoples are themselves desirous of the freedoms and living standards that obtain at the western and eastern edges of Eurasia.

Russia actually had a chance for a similar destiny a century ago. Had power in Russia at a particularly fragile moment in 1917 not been wrested by the Bolsheviks, it is entirely possible, likely even, that Russia would have evolved in the course of the twentieth century into a poorer and slightly more corrupt and unstable version of France and Germany, anchored nevertheless to Europe, rather than becoming the Stalinist monster that it did. After all, the ancien régime, with its heavily German czardom, its French-speaking nobles, and bourgeois parliament in the European capital of St. Petersburg, was oriented westward, even if the peasantry was not so.[41] Again, while the relief map of Russia spreads across Asia, Russia's population map favors Europe.

The Bolshevik Revolution was a total rejection of this quasi-Western orientation. Likewise, the low-dose authoritarianism of Vladimir Putin since 2000, both as president and later as prime minister, is a rejection of the cold turkey experiment with Western democracy and market capitalism that brought a chaotic Russia to its knees in the 1990s, following the collapse of communism. Putin and

Russian president Dimitri Medvedev in recent years have not been quite orienting Russia toward Europe and the Pacific, and consequently have not been reforming Russia in order to make it more of an attractive power to its former subject peoples. (Indeed, in trade, foreign investment, technology, infrastructure, and educational attainment, the "clouds have darkened" for Russia under Putin.[42]) Though Putin is not strictly speaking an imperialist, Russia's latest empire-in-the-making is being built on the wealth of Russia's immense natural resources which are desperately needed at the European periphery and in China, with the profits and coercion that go along with that. Putin and Medvedev have had no uplifting ideas to offer, no ideology of any kind, in fact: what they do have in their favor is only geography. And that is not enough.

Russia boasts the world's largest natural gas reserves, the second largest coal reserves, and the eighth largest oil reserves, much of which lie in western Siberia between the Urals and the Central Siberian plateau. This is in addition to vast reserves of hydropower in the mountains, rivers, and lakes of eastern Siberia at a time in history when water shortages are critical for many nations, especially China. Putin has used energy revenues for a quadrupling of the military budget, the air force in particular, during his first seven years in office. And the military budget has gone up ever since. Because of geography—Russia, as I've said, has no clear-cut topographical borders save for the Arctic and Pacific oceans—Russians appear to accept "the deep-seated militarization" of their society and the "endless search for security through the creation of a land-based empire," which Putin through his energy caliphate has given them.[43] Rather than liberalize Russia and unleash its soft power potential throughout the former Soviet Union and the adjacent Eurasian rimland, Putin has opted for neo-czarist expansionism, which his country's abundant natural resources make possible for the short term.

Yet even Putin has not altogether given up on the European dimension of Russian geography. To the contrary, his concentration on Ukraine as part of a larger effort to re-create a sphere of influence in the near-abroad is proof of his desire to anchor Russia in Europe, albeit on nondemocratic terms. Ukraine is the pivot state that in and of itself transforms Russia. Abutting the Black Sea in the south and former Eastern European satellites to the west, Ukraine's very independence keeps Russia to a large extent out of Europe. With Greek and Roman Catholics in the western part of Ukraine and Eastern Orthodox in the east, western Ukraine is a breeding ground for Ukrainian nationalism while the east favors closer relations with Russia. In other words, Ukraine's own religious geography illustrates the country's role as a borderland between Central and Eastern Europe. Zbigniew Brzezinski writes that without Ukraine, Russia can still be an empire, but a "predominantly Asian" one, drawn further into conflicts with Caucasian and Central Asian states. But with Ukraine back under Russian domination, Russia adds 46 million people to its own Western-oriented demography, and suddenly challenges Europe, even as it is integrated into it. In this case, according to Brzezinski, Poland, also coveted by Russia, would become the "geopolitical pivot" determining the fate of Central and Eastern Europe and, therefore, of the European Union itself.[44] The struggle between Russia and Europe, and in particular between Russia and Germany-France, goes on, as it has since the Napoleonic Wars, with the fate of countries like Poland and Romania hanging in the balance. Communism may have collapsed, but Europeans still need natural gas from Russia, 80 percent of which comes via Ukraine.[45] The victory in the Cold War changed much, to be sure, but it did not altogether mitigate the facts of geography. And a resurgent Russia, writes Australian intelligence analyst Paul Dibb, might be willing to "contemplate disruption in order to create strategic space."[46] As the 2008 invasion of Georgia showed, Putin's Russia is not a status quo power.

Ukraine, under severe pressure from Russia, has agreed to extend the lease of Russia's Black Sea Fleet base in return for lower natural gas prices, even as the Kremlin tries to put Ukraine's network of gas pipelines under its control. (Ukraine is also dependent on Russia for much of its trade.) Not all pipeline geography in Eurasia works in Russia's favor, though. There are the pipelines that bring Central Asian hydrocarbons to China. Pipelines bring Azerbaijan's Caspian

Sea oil across Georgia to the Black Sea and via Turkey to the Mediterranean, thus avoiding Russia. There is also a plan for a natural gas pipeline from the Caspian across the southern Caucasus and Turkey, through the Balkans, to Central Europe, which also avoids Russia. Meanwhile, though, Russia is planning its own gas pipeline southward under the Black Sea to Turkey, and another westward under the Black Sea to Bulgaria. Turkmenistan, on the far side of the Caspian, exports its natural gas through Russia. Thus, even with diverse energy supplies, Europe—especially Eastern Europe and the Balkans—will still be dependent on Russia to a significant degree. The future of Europe, as in the past, hinges in Mackinderesque fashion to a significant extent on developments to the east.

Russia has other levers, too: a powerful naval base lodged between Lithuania and Poland on the Baltic Sea; the presence of large Russian-speaking minorities in the Baltic States, Caucasus, and Central Asia; a pro-Russian Armenia; a Georgia that is threatened by the pro-Russian breakaway provinces of Abkhazia and South Ossetia; missile test sites and an air base in Kazakhstan; an air base in Kyrgyzstan in range of Afghanistan, China, and the Indian Subcontinent; and a Tajikistan that permits Russian troops to patrol its border with Afghanistan. Moreover, it was a Russian-orchestrated media campaign and economic pressure that helped oust Kyrgyz president Kurmanbek Bakiyev from power in 2010, for the crime of hosting an American air base.

In many of these places, from Chechnya in the north Caucasus to Tajikistan next door to China, Russia must deal with a resurgent Islam over a vast southern frontier that is historically part of a Greater Persian cultural and linguistic realm. Therefore, Russia's recovery of its lost republics, by the establishment of a sphere of influence over them, definitely requires a friendly Iran that does not compete with Russia in these areas, and does not export Islamic radicalism. Russia, for reasons rooted in geography, can only offer meager help in America's campaign against the Iranian regime.

———

Yet despite all these advantages, history will likely not repeat itself in the sense of another Russian empire emerging in the early twenty-first century. This is because of particular historical and geographical circumstances that adhere in Central Asia.

Russia began to solidify control in Central Asia in the early nineteenth century, when Russian trade in the area increased, even as on the Kazakh steppe, for example, anarchy reigned with no point of political domination above that of local clan authorities.[47] The Soviets in the early twentieth century created individual states out of the vast Central Asian steppe and tableland that did not cohere with ethnic borders, so that if any tried to secede from the Soviet Union it would have been impossible—leading to interethnic war. The Soviets were afraid of pan-Turkism, pan-Persianism, and pan-Islamism, for which the splitting up of ethnic groups was a partial panacea. This created a plethora of anomalies. The Syr Darya valley begins in an Uzbek-populated part of Kyrgyzstan and passes through Uzbekistan, then through Tajikistan before returning to Uzbekistan and ending up in Kazakhstan. The road linking the Uzbek capital of Tashkent to the Uzbek province of Ferghana must pass through Tajikistan. To get from Dushanbe, the capital of Tajikistan, to the ethnic-Tajik areas of Khojent and Khorog one must pass through Uzbekistan and Kyrgyzstan. The town of Chimkent, close to Uzbekistan, is predominantly Uzbek, but is "attached" to Kazakhstan. The predominantly Tajik-populated city of Samarkand is in Uzbekistan, and so forth. What emerged in Central Asia, therefore, was less ethnic nationalism than "Sovietism" as a technique of control and power. But while Sovietism survives, even after the breakup of the Soviet Union, the ethnic Russians in the region have been marginalized, and in some places there exists strong hostility against them. Nevertheless, pan-Turkism and pan-Persianism remain relatively weak. Iran has been Shiite since the sixteenth century, whereas Tajiks and the other Persianized Muslims of Central Asia are mainly Sunni. As for the Turks, only recently has modern Turkey sought to become a focal point of the Muslim world.[48]

Sovietism and the lack of complete identification of each state with a single ethnic group has ironically led to a modest stability in Central

Asia, occasional unrest in the Ferghana valley and elsewhere notwithstanding. (Though, I must say, the region remains a potential tinderbox.) This dynamic, buttressed by extreme wealth in natural resources, has given some of these states significant bargaining power with the principal Eurasian states—Moscow and Beijing—who can be played off one against the other. (Russia needs Central Asian gas to transport to European markets, which gives Russia leverage over Europe; but Russia's position is being threatened by China's own purchase of Central Asian gas.)[49] Central Asia's bounty is immense. Kazakhstan's Tengiz oil fields alone are thought to contain twice as much oil as the Alaskan North Slope.[50] Turkmenistan's annual natural gas output is the third highest in the world. Kyrgyzstan was the largest producer of mercury and antimony in the Soviet Union, and has large deposits of gold, platinum, palladium, and silver.[51] This wealth in natural resources, as well as lingering resentment over Soviet occupation, has led, for instance, to Uzbekistan opening its railway bridge to Afghanistan to NATO traffic without at least initially consulting Russia; to Turkmenistan diversifying its energy routes rather than relying completely on Russia; and to Kazakhstan turning to European rather than Russian engineers to exploit its geologically "tricky" petroleum reserves in the Caspian Sea shelf.[52]

Thus, a Russian sphere of influence will be challenging to preserve, and will be held hostage in some degree to the fickleness of global energy prices, given how Russia's own economy essentially runs on natural resources, just like the Central Asian ones. Russia's new empire, if it does emerge, will likely be a weak reincarnation of previous ones, limited not just by flinty states in Central Asia but by the rising influence in Central Asia of China, and to a lesser extent of India and Iran. China has invested over $25 billion in Central Asia. It is paying for a two-thousand-mile highway across Kazakhstan. There are daily flights between the Kazakh city of Almaty and the western Chinese city of Urumqui, and Chinese goods fill Central Asian markets.[53]

Kazakhstan may be the ultimate register of Russian fortunes in Eurasia. Kazakhstan is a prosperous middle-income state by Central

Asian standards that is geographically the size of Western Europe, with a GDP larger than all the other Central Asian states combined. Kazakhstan's new capital, Astana, is located in the ethnic Russian north of the country, which hothead Russian nationalists wanted to annex after the fall of the Soviet Union: at that time, of nine oblasts along Kazakhstan's three-thousand-mile northern border with Russia, in eight of them, in their northern parts, the population was almost 90 percent non-Kazakh.[54] The ceremonial buildings of Astana, designed by Sir Norman Foster, constitute a Kazakh rebuke to Russian ambitions regarding their country. The reinvention of Astana cost $10 billion. It is linked to the south of the country by high-speed trains.[55] Kazakhstan is truly becoming an independent power in its own right. It is developing three super-giant "elephant" oil, gas, and condensate fields, two on the Caspian Sea, with major investment from Western multinationals. A new oil pipeline from the Caspian to western China will soon be completed. Kazakhstan is about to become the world's largest producer of uranium. It has the world's second largest chromium, lead, and zinc reserves, the third largest manganese reserves, the fifth largest copper reserves, and ranks in the top ten for coal, iron, and gold.

Kazakhstan *is* Mackinder's Heartland! It is rich in all the world's strategic natural resources and smack in the middle of Eurasia—overlapping, as it does, western Siberia and Central Asia—and stretches 1,800 miles from the Caspian Sea in the west to Outer Mongolia in the east. The Urals peter out in Kazakhstan's northwest; the foothills of the Tien Shan begin in Kazakhstan's southeast. Kazakhstan's climate is so continental in its extremes that before dawn in winter Astana's temperature can be minus 40 degrees Fahrenheit. Mackinder believed that some great power or superpower would control the Heartland. But in our age the Heartland lies in the hands of its indigenous inhabitants, even as great powers like Russia and China fight over its energy resources. Russia may influence Kazakhstan, and in ways severely pressure it. In the final analysis, the Russian and Kazakh economies are interwoven and Kazakhstan cannot defend itself against the Russian military. But Kazakhstan will always have the option of turning toward China if the likes of Putin or his successor become too heavy-handed; in any event, the chances that Russia would be willing to suffer the international disapproval and diplomatic isolation that an invasion of Kazakhstan would precipitate are slim. In 2008, Georgia, a country forty times smaller than Kazakhstan, with a third the population and with few natural resources, may have exposed the limits of Russian military adventurism on the super-continent. Indeed, when Kyrgyzstan made a subtle plea for Russian troops to intervene against ethnic riots in 2010, Russia did not opt for a major intervention, afraid of getting bogged down in a mountainous Central Asian country on the far side of Kazakhstan.

Another restraining factor against Russian military action in Central Asia is China, whose influence in the region has grown at the expense of Russia, and with whom Russia shares a long border in the Far East. Reasonably good Russian-Chinese relations will provide momentum to the Shanghai Cooperation Organization: a group of which Kazakhstan is a member, which seeks to unite Eurasian powers, mainly autocratic, in an effort to counter the influence of the United States. The wages of Russian-Chinese enmity are greater influence for the United States and Europe in Eurasia. Thus, Russia will discipline its behavior in Central Asia and likely forswear any attempt to reclaim parts of Mackinder's Heartland by force.

One word of caution regarding this analysis: Russia's hand may be weakened in Central Asia because of the rise of China and the desire of Central Asians to do more business with nonthreatening, high-technology countries like South Korea and Japan. But while Russia's military options are somewhat constrained, Russia can still move troops around Central Asia in a way that no other power can, and Central Asians do harbor a certain nostalgia in these politically volatile times for the peace and security that was the old Soviet Union.

Nevertheless, Dmitri Trenin of the Carnegie Moscow Center could well be right: Russia's best real hope in the long run is to liberalize its economy and politics, in order to make Russia attractive to the Kazakhs and other former subject peoples. For the Heartland, with the collapse of communism and the onset of globalization, has become a power in its own right. Kazakhstan, which is more than double the land area of the other Central Asian states combined, demonstrates it. Mackinder, who feared the horizontal separation of the world into classes and ideologies, believed that along with the balance of power, it was provincialism—the vertical separation of the world into small groups and states—that helps guarantee freedom.[56]

Chapter XI

THE GEOGRAPHY OF CHINESE POWER

At the end of his famous article "The Geographical Pivot of History," Mackinder has a disturbing reference to China. After elucidating why the interior of Eurasia forms the fulcrum of geostrategic world power, he posits that the Chinese "might constitute the yellow peril to the world's freedom, just because they would add an oceanic frontage to the resources of the great continent, an advantage as yet denied to the Russian tenant of the pivot region."[1] Leave aside the inherent racist sentiment of the era, as well as the hysterics with which the rise of any non-Western power is greeted, and concentrate instead on Mackinder's analysis: that whereas Russia is a land power whose only oceanic frontage is mainly blocked by Arctic ice, China is, too, a continental-sized power, but one whose virtual reach extends not only into the strategic Central Asian core of the former Soviet Union, with all of its mineral and hydrocarbon wealth, but also to the main shipping lanes of the Pacific three thousand miles away, where China enjoys a nine-thousand-mile coastline with many good natural harbors, most of which are ice-free. (Mackinder actually feared that China would one day conquer Russia.) Furthermore, as Mackinder wrote in 1919 in *Democratic Ideals and Reality*, if Eurasia conjoined with Africa forms the "World-Island"—the heart of the dry-land earth, four times the size of North America, with eight times the population—then China, as Eurasia's largest continental nation with a coastline in both the tropics and the temperate zone, occupies the globe's most advantageous position. Mackinder predicts at the conclusion of *Democratic Ideals and Reality* that, along with the United States and the United Kingdom, China would eventually guide the world by "building for a quarter of humanity a new civilization, neither quite Eastern nor quite Western."[2] A patriotic imperialist to the last, Mackinder naturally included Great Britain in this exalted category. Nevertheless, using only the criteria of geography and demography, his prediction about China has at least so far proved accurate.

The fact that China is blessed by geography is something so basic and obvious that it tends to be overlooked in all the discussions about its economic dynamism and national assertiveness over recent decades. Thus, a look at the map through the prism of Chinese history is in order.

While Russia lies to the north of 50 degrees north latitude, China lies to the south of it, in roughly the same range of temperate latitude as the United States, with all the variations in climate and the benefits which that entails.[3] Harbin, the main city of Manchuria, lies at 45 degrees north latitude, the same as Maine. Beijing is near 40 degrees north latitude, the same as New York. Shanghai, at the mouth of the Yangzi River, lies at 30 degrees north latitude, the same as New Orleans. The Tropic of Cancer runs through the southern extremity of China and also cuts just below the Florida Keys.

China is only somewhat less of a continent than the United States. The United States, bounded by two oceans and the Canadian Arctic, is threatened only by the specter of Mexican demography to its

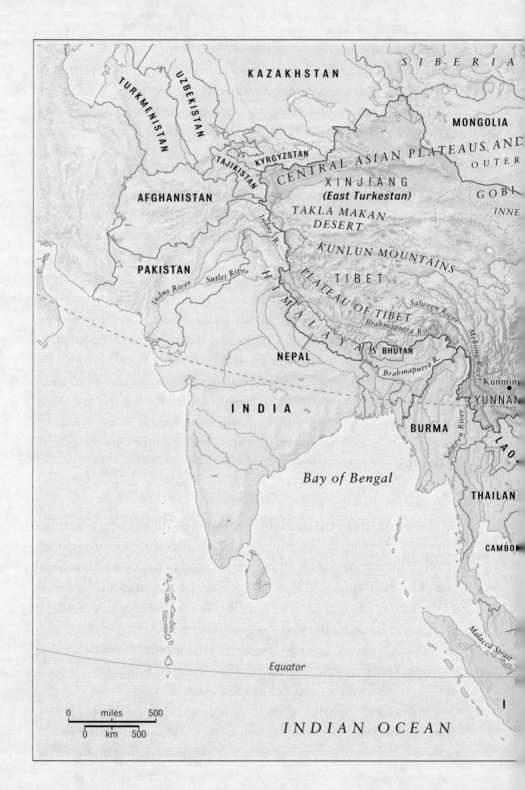

TURKMENISTAN

UZBEKISTAN

KAZAKHSTAN

SIBERIA

MONGOLIA

TAJIKISTAN

KYRGYZSTAN

CENTRAL ASIAN PLATEAUS AND

OUTER

AFGHANISTAN

XINJIANG
(East Turkestan)

GOBI

INNE

TAKLA MAKAN
DESERT

Indus R.

KUNLUN MOUNTAINS

PAKISTAN

TIBET

Sutlej River

Indus River

PLATEAU OF TIBET

H
I
M
A
L
A
Y
A
S

Salween River

Brahmaputra River

NEPAL

BHUTAN

Brahmaputra R.

Kunmin

YUNNAN

INDIA

BURMA

Salween River

Mekong River

LAO

Bay of Bengal

THAILAN

CAMBO

I

Malacca Strait

Equator

INDIAN OCEAN

0   miles   500

0   km   500

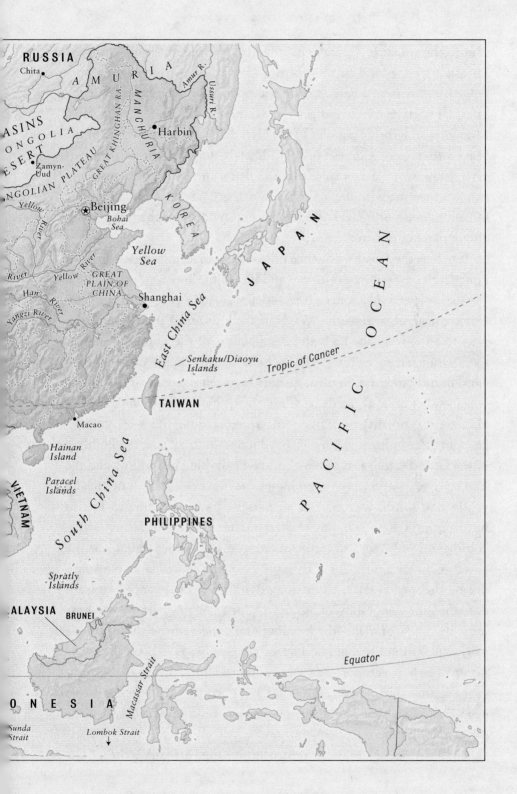

south. The threat to China came mainly over the millennia from the Eurasian steppe-land to the north and northwest, the same steppe-land that threatened Russia from the opposite direction: so that the interplay between the indigenous Chinese and the Manchurians, Mongols, and Turkic peoples of the high desert has formed one of the central themes of Chinese history. That is why the capital cities of early Chinese dynasties were often built on the Wei River, upstream from its meeting with the Yellow, where there was enough rainfall for sedentary agriculture, yet safe from the nomadism of the Inner Mongolian plateau just to the north.

Whereas the "neat" sequence of forest, prairie, high desert, mountain, and coast—crossed in the middle by the north–south flowing Mississippi and Missouri rivers—defines American geography, in China the great rivers—the Wei, Han, Yellow, and Yangzi—run from west to east, from the high and dry uplands of the Eurasian interior to the moister agricultural lands closer to the Pacific coast.[4] These agricultural lands are, in turn, divided between the comparatively dry wheat-millet area of northern China, with its short growing season, akin to the northern Midwest of America, and the wet, double-cropping rice culture of China's productive south. Thus, the building of the Grand Canal between 605 and 611, linking the Yellow and the Yangzi rivers—and China's famine-prone north with its economically productive south, with its rice surpluses—had, according to British historian John Keay, "a similar effect to the building of the first transcontinental railroads in North America."[5] The Grand Canal was the key to Chinese unity. For it eased the north's conquest of the south during the medieval Tang and Song dynasties, which helped consolidate the core geography of agrarian China. Again, here we see how individual acts of men—the building of a canal—prove more historically crucial than the simple fact of geography. For given the grave differences between northern and southern China, in the early medieval era the split between the two Chinas which had lasted for two centuries might well have become permanent, like that between the eastern and western Roman empires.[6]

But as the late Harvard professor John King Fairbank writes, "The contrasts between North and South China are superficial compared with those between the pastoral nomadism of the plateaus of Inner Asia and the settled villages based on the intensive agriculture of China." By Inner Asia, Fairbank means something quite comprehensive: "the wide arc running from Manchuria through Mongolia and Turkestan to Tibet." China's sense of itself, he goes on, is based on the cultural difference that obtains between this surrounding belt of desert and the sown of China proper, that is, between the pastoral and the arable.[7] China's ethnic geography reflects this "core-periphery structure," with the core being the arable "central plain" (*zhongyuan*) or "inner China" (*neidi*), and the periphery being the pastoral "frontiers" (*bianjiang*) or "outer China" (*waidi*).[8]

This is what the building of the Great Wall was ultimately about. The Great Wall, writes political scientist Jakub Grygiel, "served to reinforce the ecological distinction that translated into political differences."[9] Indeed, to the early Chinese, agriculture meant civilization itself: the Central or Middle Kingdom, *Zhongguo,* which owed nothing to the surrounding pastoral peoples. From this followed the kind of cultural certainty that China would share with Western Christendom.[10] From the late Zhou Dynasty in the third century B.C., arable China would begin to absorb barbarian and quasi-barbarian elements.[11] And later, beginning with the Han Dynasty in the second century B.C., the Chinese would encounter other cultures—Roman, Byzantine, Persian, and Arab—and thus develop a comparative, *regional* sense of space.[12] The fact that the Chinese state today includes both desert and sown, on a continental scale no less, reflects the culmination of a long and thus far triumphant historical process which, in turn, provides the geographic basis for Chinese power—at least for the time being.

This process of enlargement began with the "cradle" area around the Wei and lower Yellow rivers in the northern part of the cultivable zone just south of Manchuria and Inner Mongolia, which flourished during the western Zhou Dynasty three thousand years ago.[13] Because pastoral Inner Asia had no crop agriculture, its sparse population, about one-sixteenth that of the cradle area, could not properly

survive without access to it.[14] Thus China grew outward from the Wei
and lower Yellow rivers, though recent archaeological excavations do
indicate civilizational development in southeastern China and northern Vietnam during this time.[15] During the Warring States period
(403–221 B.C.), which saw the number of polities shrink from 170 to 7,
Chinese civilization moved further southward into rice- and tea-
growing areas, to include the region of present-day Shanghai. Even
so, political power remained in the north, which embraced the region
of present-day Beijing.[16] It was the Qin that emerged victorious from
the Warring States period—the dynasty from which, according to
some etymologies, China got its name. By the first century B.C., under
the Han Dynasty (which had supplanted the Qin), China included all
of the cultivable heartland from the headwaters of the Yellow and
Yangzi rivers to the Pacific coast, and from the Bohai Sea by the Korean Peninsula to the South China Sea. A combination of diplomatic
overtures and military forays allowed Han emperors to establish feu-
datories among the Xiongnu, that is, the nomadic Huns, in Outer
Mongolia and East Turkestan (Xinjiang), as well as in southern Manchuria and the northern part of Korea.

A pattern had developed. China's settled agricultural civilization
had to constantly strive to create a buffer against the nomadic peoples
of the drier uplands bordering it on three sides, from Manchuria
counterclockwise around to Tibet.[17] This historical dilemma was
structurally similar to that of the Russians, who also required buffers.
But while the Russians were spread across eleven time zones with a
meager population, China was much more cohesive and relatively
densely populated from antiquity. With less to fear, comparatively
speaking, China became a less militarized society. Nevertheless, China
produced dynasties of particular energy and aggressiveness. Under the
Tang emperors of the eighth century, military prowess burgeoned
along with literature and the arts. Tang armies threaded their way
through the space between Mongolia and Tibet to establish protector-
ates all over Central Asia as far as Khorasan in northeastern Iran,
further enabling the Silk Route. Concomitantly, the Tang emperors
fought wars with the Tibetans to the southwest with help from the

Turkic Uighurs to the northwest. It was always a matter of maneuvering amid the peoples of the steppe-lands, rather than fighting them all at once. In fact, the soldiery constituted only one of the Tang state's tools. "Confucian doctrine," writes British historian John Keay, "formulated during the 'Warring States' era and partly in reaction to it, was adamant about civilian control over military affairs."[18] Among the "glories of old China," writes Fairbank, was a "reasoned pacifism," for one of the Confucian myths of the state was "government by virtue."[19] This pacifism, according to historians, is sometimes blamed for the fact that just as China invaded the grasslands and plateau areas, the pastoral nomads in turn invaded China. In A.D. 763 Tibetan forces actually sacked the Tang capital of Chang'an. More significantly, the Jin, Liao, and Yuan dynasties—all products of the northern grasslands—would manifest Inner Asian military aggression against China throughout the Middle Ages. This went along with the failure of the indigenous Song and Ming dynasties, despite their revolutionary military technology, to gain back the steppe-lands. Inner Asia, from Tibet and East Turkestan across Mongolia to the Far Eastern borderland with Russia, was only taken back by the Manchu Qing Dynasty in the seventeenth and eighteenth centuries. (It was during this period that the multiethnic territory controlled by the Chinese state today was "staked out," as well as envisioned: Taiwan was acquired in 1683.)[20] In sum, China became a vast continent in and of itself by virtue of its continual backwards and forwards interactions with an Inner Asian steppe-land that stretched unto Mackinder's Heartland, and this is what drives the political reality of China today.

Indeed, the question now becomes whether the dominant Hans, who comprise more than 90 percent of China's population and live mainly in the arable cradle of China, are able to permanently keep the Tibetans, Uighur Turks, and Inner Mongolians who live on the periphery under control, with the minimum degree of unrest. The ultimate fate of the Chinese state will hinge on this fact, especially as China undergoes economic and social disruptions.

For the time being, China is at the peak of its continental power, even as the wounds of its territorial rape by the nations of Europe,

Russia, and Japan are still, by China's own historical standards, extremely fresh. For in the nineteenth century, as the Qing Dynasty became the sick man of East Asia, China lost much of its territory—the southern tributaries of Nepal and Burma to Great Britain; Indochina to France; Taiwan and the tributaries of Korea and Sakhalin to Japan; and Mongolia, Amuria, and Ussuria to Russia.[21] In the twentieth century came the Japanese takeovers of the Shandong Peninsula and Manchuria in the heart of China. And this was all in addition to the humiliations forced on the Chinese by the extraterritoriality agreements of the nineteenth and early twentieth centuries, whereby Western nations got control of parts of Chinese cities. Now fast-forward to the 1950s, when maps started appearing in Chinese secondary schools of a Greater China that included all of these lost areas, as well as eastern Kazakhstan and Kyrgyzstan. Mao Zedong, who had consolidated continental China for the first time since the High Qing, was clearly an irredentist who had internalized the wounds of a once vast and imperial state surviving the centuries only to be humiliated in the recent past.[22] Given these vicissitudes of China's history, this may be one flaw in Mao's thinking that we might actually forgive. While the rulers of China in the second decade of the twenty-first century may not be so heartless in their outlook as Mao, China's history can, however, never be far from their minds. Though China's current borders encompass Manchuria, Inner Mongolia, East Turkestan, and Tibet—all the surrounding plateaus and grasslands, that is—the very economic and diplomatic strategies of China's rulers today demonstrate an *idea* of China that reaches beyond the territorial extent of even the China of the eighth-century Tang and the eighteenth-century High Qing. China, a demographic behemoth with the world's most energetic economy for the past three decades, is, unlike Russia, extending its territorial influence much more through commerce than coercion.

Geography indicates that while China's path toward ever greater global power may not be linear—its annual GDP growth rates of over

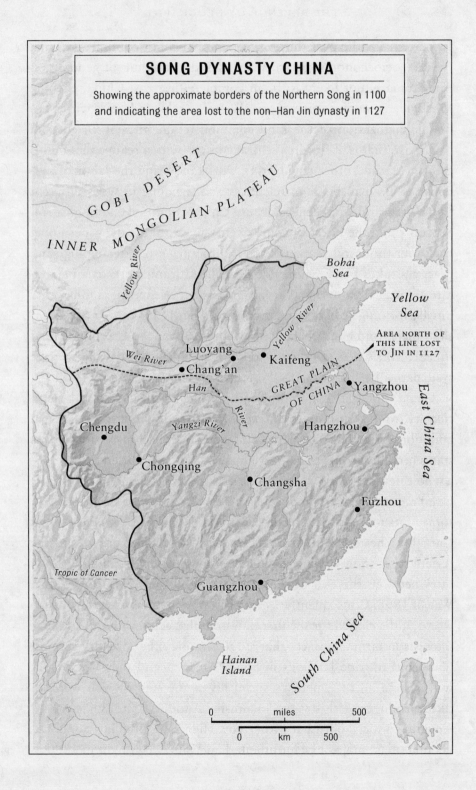

SONG DYNASTY CHINA

Showing the approximate borders of the Northern Song in 1100
and indicating the area lost to the non–Han Jin dynasty in 1127

GOBI DESERT

INNER MONGOLIAN PLATEAU

Yellow River

Bohai
Sea

Yellow
Sea

Wei River

Luoyang

Kaifeng

Yellow River

AREA NORTH OF
THIS LINE LOST
TO JIN IN 1127

Chang'an

Han

GREAT PLAIN

River

OF CHINA

Yangzhou

East China Sea

Chengdu

Yangzi River

Hangzhou

Chongqing

Changsha

Fuzhou

Tropic of Cancer

Guangzhou

Hainan
Island

South China Sea

0   miles   500

0   km   500

10 percent for the past thirty years simply cannot continue—China, even in socioeconomic disarray, will stand at the hub of geopolitics. And China is not likely to be in complete disarray. China, echoing Mackinder, combines an extreme, Western-style modernity with a hydraulic civilization of the kind common to the ancient Orient and Near East: that is, it features central control, with a regime that builds great water and other engineering works requiring the labor of millions.[23] This makes China relentless and dynamic in ways different from Western democracies. Because China's nominal communist rulers constitute the latest of some twenty-five Chinese dynasties going back four thousand years, the absorption of Western technology and practices takes place within the disciplined framework of an elaborate cultural system: one that has unique experience in, among other things, forming tributary relationships. "The Chinese," a Singaporean official told me, "charm you when they want to charm you, and squeeze you when they want to squeeze you, and they do it quite systematically."

China's internal dynamism, with all of its civil unrest and inefficiencies, to say nothing of an economic slowdown, creates external ambitions. Empires are often not sought consciously. Rather, as states become stronger, they develop needs and—counterintuitively— a whole new set of insecurities that lead them to expand in an organic fashion. Consider the American experience. Under the stewardship of some of its more forgettable presidents—Rutherford B. Hayes, James Garfield, Chester Alan Arthur, Benjamin Harrison, and so on—the American economy chugged quietly along with high annual growth rates between the end of the Civil War and the Spanish-American War of 1898. Consequently, as America traded more with the outside world, it developed for the first time complex economic and strategic interests in far-flung places that led to, among other military actions, Navy and Marine landings in South America and the Pacific. This was despite all of America's social ills at the time, which were, in turn, products of this very dynamism. Another factor that caused America to focus outward was its consolidation of the interior continent. The last major battle of the Indian Wars was fought in 1890.

China is also consolidating its land borders and beginning to focus outward. Unlike America, China does not come armed with a missionary approach to world affairs. It has no ideology or system of government it seeks to spread. Moral progress in international politics is an American goal, not a Chinese one. And yet China is not a status quo power: for it is propelled abroad by the need to secure energy, metals, and strategic minerals in order to support the rising living standard of roughly a fifth of humanity. Indeed, China is able to feed 23 percent of the world's population from 7 percent of the arable land—"by crowding some 2,000 human beings onto each square mile of cultivated earth in the valleys and flood plains," as Fairbank points out.[24] It now is under popular pressure to achieve something similar—that is, provide a middle-class lifestyle for much of its urban population.

To accomplish this task, China has built advantageous power relationships both in contiguous territories and in distant locales rich in the very resources it requires to fuel its growth. Because what drives China beyond its official borders has to do with a core national interest—economic survival and growth—China can be defined as an über-realist power. It seeks to develop an eerie, colonial-like presence throughout the parts of sub-Saharan Africa that are well endowed with oil and minerals, and wants to secure port access throughout the South China Sea and adjacent Indian Ocean, which connect the hydrocarbon-rich Arab-Persian world to the Chinese seaboard. Having little choice in the matter, Beijing cares little about the type of regime with which it is engaged; it requires stability, not virtue as the West conceives of it. And because some of these regimes—such as those in Iran, Sudan, and Zimbabwe—are either benighted or authoritarian, or both, China's worldwide scouring for resources brings it into conflict with the missionary-oriented United States, as well as with countries like India and Russia, against whose own spheres of influence China is bumping up. What frequently goes unnoticed is that these countries, and others in Southeast Asia, Central Asia, and the Middle East, are places which came under the influence of one Chinese dynasty or another in the past. Even Sudan is not far from the area of the Red Sea visited by the Ming Dynasty admiral Zheng He in the early fifteenth century. China is merely reestablishing, after a fashion, its imperial domain.

China does not pose an existential threat. The possibility of a war between the United States and China is extremely remote. There is a military threat from China, but as we will see, it is indirect. The challenge China poses at its most elemental level is geographic—notwithstanding critical issues such as debt, trade, and climate change. China's emerging area of influence in Eurasia and Africa—in Mackinder's "World-Island"—is growing, not in a nineteenth-century imperialistic sense, but in a more subtle manner better suited to the era of globalization. Simply by securing its economic needs, China is shifting the balance of power in the Eastern Hemisphere, and that will substantially concern the United States. On land and at sea, abetted by China's favorable location on the map, Beijing's influence is emanating from Central Asia to the Russian Far East, and from the South China Sea to the Indian Ocean. China is a rising continental power, and as Napoleon famously said, the policies of such states are inherent in their geography.

China's position on the map of Central-East Asia is, as I have indicated, advantageous. But in other ways twenty-first-century China is dangerously incomplete. There is the example of Mongolia (geographic "Outer Mongolia") to the north: a giant blob of territory that looks as though it has been bitten away from China, which borders Mongolia to the south, west, and east. Mongolia, with one of the world's lowest population densities, is being threatened by the latest of Eurasia's great historical migrations—that of an urban Chinese civilization with a tendency to move north. China has already flooded its own Inner Mongolia with Han Chinese immigrants, and Outer Mongolians worry that they are next to be demographically conquered. Having once conquered Outer Mongolia by moving the line of cultivation northward, China may be poised to conquer Mongolia through globalization. China covets the oil, coal, uranium, and other strategic minerals and rich, empty grasslands of its former Qing-Manchu possession.[25] Its building of access roads into Mongolia has to be seen in this light. With its unchecked industrialization and urbanization, China is the world's leading consumer of aluminum, copper, coal, lead, nickel, zinc, tin, and iron ore, all of which Mongolia has in abundance. China's share of world metal consumption has jumped from 10 percent to 25 percent since the late 1990s. Consequently, Chinese mining companies have been seeking large stakes in Mongolia's underground assets. Given that China has absorbed Tibet, Macau, and Hong Kong on the mainland, Mongolia will be a trip wire for judging future Chinese intentions. Indeed, the Mongolian-Chinese border in 2003 when I visited it near the town of Zamyn-Uud was nothing but an artificial boundary on the flat and gradually descending Gobi Desert. The Chinese border post was a brightly lit, well-engineered arc signifying the teeming and industrialized monolith to the south, encroaching on the sparsely inhabited Mongolian steppe-land of felt tents and scrap iron huts. Keep in mind, though, that such demographic and economic advantages can be a double-edged sword in the event of ethnic unrest in Chinese Inner Mongolia. The very extent of Chinese influence, by encompassing so much of the pastoral periphery, can expose weaknesses peculiar to multiethnic states. Moreover, another factor that could upend China's plans is Mongolia's own fast-track economic development of late, which is drawing a plethora of business investors from the world over, thus limiting Beijing's influence.

North of Mongolia, as well as north of China's three provinces of Manchuria, lies the Russian Far East, an interminable stretch of birch forest lying between Lake Baikal and Vladivostok. This numbing vastness, roughly twice the size of Europe, has a meager population of 6.7 million that is in the process of falling further to 4.5 million people. Russia, as we have seen, expanded into this area in the nineteenth and early twentieth centuries during a fit of nationalist imperialism and at a time of Chinese weakness that is long past. In few other areas is the Russian state so feeble as in its eastern third, and particularly that part of it close to China. Yet on the other side of the frontier, inside Manchuria, are 100 million Chinese, a population density sixty-two times greater than that in eastern Siberia. Chinese migrants have been filtering across this border. For example, the Siberian city of Chita, north of Mongolia, has a large and growing population of ethnic Chinese. Resource acquisition is the principal goal of Chinese foreign policy, and Russia's demographically barren Far East is filled with large reserves of natural gas, oil, timber, diamonds, and gold. "Russia and China might operate a tactical alliance, but there is already tension between them over the Far East," writes David Blair, a correspondent of London's *Daily Telegraph*. "Moscow is wary of large numbers of Chinese settlers moving into this region, bringing timber and mining companies in their wake."[26] Here, as in Mongolia, it is not a question of an invading army or of formal annexation, but of creeping Chinese demographic and corporate control over a region, large parts of which used to be held by China during both the Ming and Qing dynasties.

During the Cold War, border disputes between the Soviet Union and China ignited into military clashes in which hundreds of thousands of troops were massed in this Siberian back-of-beyond—fifty-three Soviet army divisions by 1969 on the Russian side of the Amur and Ussuri rivers. Mao's China responded by deploying one million troops on its side of the border, and building bomb shelters in major cities. To help relieve pressure on his western flank, so as to concentrate on the Far East, Soviet leader Leonid Brezhnev launched the policy of détente with the United States. For its part, China saw itself as virtually surrounded by the Soviet Union, the Soviet satellite state of Mongolia, a pro-Soviet North Vietnam and its own Laotian client, and pro-Soviet India. All these tensions led to the Sino-Soviet split, which the Nixon administration was able to take advantage of in its opening to China in 1971–1972.

Could geography once again drive apart Russia and China, whose current alliance is mainly tactical? And could the beneficiary be, as in the past, the United States? Though this time, with China the greater power, the United States might conceivably partner with Russia in a strategic alliance to balance against the Middle Kingdom, so as to force China's attention away from the First Island Chain in the Pacific and toward its land borders. Indeed, the ability to hamper the growth of a Chinese naval presence close to Japan, South Korea, and Taiwan will require American pressure from bases in Central Asia close to China, as well as a particularly friendly relationship with Russia. Pressure on land can help the United States thwart China at sea.

However, another scenario might play out, far more optimistic and beneficial to the inhabitants of northern Manchuria and the Russian Far East themselves. In this version, which harks back to the period before 1917, Chinese trade and demographic infiltration of Amuria and Ussuria lead to an economic renaissance in the Russian Far East that is embraced by a more liberal government in Moscow, which uses the development to better position the port of Vladivostok as a global hub of northeast Asia. Pushing the scenario further, I would posit the emergence of a better regime in North Korea, leading to a dynamic Northeast Asian region of open borders centered around the Sea of Japan.

China's frontier with the former Soviet republics of Central Asia is not so much incomplete as arbitrary, and, therefore, to a degree ahistorical. China stretches too far into the heart of Eurasia, and yet doesn't stretch far enough. Xinjiang, China's westernmost province, means "New Dominion," and what is dominated by the Chinese is East Turkestan, an area made even more remote from China's demographic heartland by the intervention of the Gobi Desert. Though China has been a state in some form or other for three thousand years, Xinjiang only became part of China in the middle of the eighteenth century, when the Qing (Manchu) emperor Qianlong conquered huge areas of western territory, consequently doubling the size of China and fixing a "firm western border" with Russia.[27] Since then, writes the late British diplomat and travel writer Sir Fitzroy Maclean, the history of the province "has been one of sustained turbulence."[28] There have been revolts and periods of independent Turkic rule right up to the 1940s. In 1949, Mao Zedong's communists marched into Xinjiang and forcibly integrated it with the rest of China. But as recently as 1990, and again in 2009, there have been riots and bloodshed against Chinese rule by the ethnic Turkic Uighurs, a subdivision of Turks who ruled Mongolia from 745 to 840, when the Kyrgyz drove them into East Turkestan. The Uighurs, numbering some eight million, are less than one percent of China's population, but they comprise 45 percent of Xinjiang's, which is China's largest province—twice the size of Texas.

Indeed, China's population is heavily concentrated in the coastal areas near the Pacific and in the riverine lowlands and alluvial valleys in the center of the country, with the drier plateaus, often at altitudes of twelve thousand feet, in the vast west and southwest relatively empty, even as they are the homes of the anti-Chinese Uighur and Tibetan minorities. The original China, as noted, emerged out of the Yellow and particularly the Wei river valleys, where humankind probably existed in prehistory, and from where China as a civilizational concept began to organically spread along great rivers, which to the Chinese served the purpose that roads did for the Romans. Here in this hearth of Chinese civilization, the land was crisscrossed by "myriad rivers, canals, and irrigation streams that fed lush market gardens and paddies"; here "the seasonal flooding . . . returned needed nutrients to the soil."[29] Nowadays, Chinese territory simply overlaps not only this riverine heartland, but Turkic Central Asia and historic Tibet besides, and that is Beijing's salient cartographic challenge, even as it comports well with China's imperial history. In Beijing's eyes there is no alternative to Chinese control over its contiguous tablelands. For as the mid-twentieth-century American China hand Owen Lattimore reminds us: "The Yellow River derives its water from the snows of Tibet," and for "part of its course it flows near the Mongolian steppe."[30] Tibet, with the headwaters of the Yellow, Yangzi, Mekong, Salween, Brahmaputra, Indus, and Sutlej rivers, may constitute the world's most enormous storehouse of freshwater, even as China by 2030 is expected to fall short of its water demands by 25 percent.[31] Securing these areas, under whose soil also lie billions of tons of oil, natural gas, and copper, has meant populating them over the decades with Han Chinese immigrants from the nation's demographic heartland. It has also meant, in the case of Xinjiang, an aggressive courting of the independent ethnic Turkic republics of Central Asia, so that the Uighurs will never have a political and geographical rear base with which to contest Beijing's rule.

In Central Asia, as in eastern Siberia, China competes fiercely with Russia for a sphere of influence. Trade between China and former Soviet Central Asia has risen from $527 million in 1992 to $25.9 billion in 2009.[32] But the means of Beijing's sway will for the moment be two major pipelines, one carrying oil from the Caspian Sea across Kazakhstan to Xinjiang, and the other transporting natural gas from the Turkmenistan-Uzbekistan border, across Uzbekistan and Kazakhstan, to Xinjiang. Again, no troops will be necessary as Greater China extends into Mackinder's Eurasian Heartland, the upshot of an insatiable demand for energy and the internal danger posed by its own ethnic minorities.

In all of this, China is not risk-averse. Eyeing some of the world's last untapped deposits of copper, iron, gold, uranium, and precious gems, China is already mining for copper in war-torn Afghanistan, just south of Kabul. China has a vision of Afghanistan (and of Pakistan) as a secure conduit for roads and energy pipelines that will bring natural resources from Indian Ocean ports, linking up with Beijing's budding Central Asian dominion-of-sorts. China has been "exceptionally active" building roads that will connect Xinjiang with Kyrgyzstan, Tajikistan, and Afghanistan. Within Afghanistan itself, a Chinese firm, the China Railway Shistiju Group, is "defying insecurity" by building a roadway in Wardak Province. China is improving rail infrastructures that approach Afghanistan from several directions.[33] Thus, as the United States moves to defeat al Qaeda and irreconcilable elements of the Taliban, it is China's geopolitical position that will be enhanced. Military deployments are ephemeral: roads, rail links, and pipelines can be virtually forever.

Like the Taklamakan Desert of Xinjiang, the sprawling, mountainous Tibetan plateau, rich in copper and iron ore, accounts for much of the territory of China, thus clarifying the horror with which Beijing views Tibetan autonomy, let alone independence. Without Tibet there is a much reduced China and a virtually expanded Indian

Subcontinent: this explains the pace of Chinese road and rail projects across the Tibetan massif.

If you accept Pakistan, with its own Chinese-built road and Indian Ocean port project, as a future zone of Greater China, and put the relatively weak states of Southeast Asia into the same category, then India, with its billion-plus population, is a blunt geographic wedge puncturing this grand sphere of Chinese influence. A map of Greater China in Zbigniew Brzezinski's *The Grand Chessboard* makes this point vividly.[34] Indeed, India and China—with their immense populations; rich, venerable, and very different cultural experiences; geographic proximity; and fractious border disputes—are, despite their complementary trading relationship, destined by geography to be rivals to a certain degree. And the issue of Tibet only inflames this rivalry, even as it is a core function of it. India hosts the Dalai Lama's government-in-exile in Dharamsala, which enables him to keep the cause of Tibet alive in the court of global opinion. Dan Twining, a senior fellow for Asia at the German Marshall Fund in Washington, has written that recent Indian-Chinese border tensions "may be related to worries in Beijing over the Dalai Lama's succession," given the possibility that the next Dalai Lama might be named outside China—in the Tibetan cultural belt that stretches across northern India, Nepal, and Bhutan.[35] This belt includes the Indian state of Arunachal Pradesh, which China also claims, as it is part of the Tibetan plateau and thus outside the lowlands which geographically define the Indian Subcontinent. China has also been expanding its military influence into the unstable, Maoist-dominated Himalayan buffer state of Nepal, which India has countered with an Indian-Nepalese defense cooperation agreement of its own. China and India will play a Great Game not only here, but in Bangladesh and Sri Lanka, too. China's pressure on India from the north, which helped ignite a border war between India and China in 1962, must continue as a means to help consolidate its hold on Tibet. This assumes that in an increasingly feverish world media environment the romantic cause of Tibetan nationalism will not dissipate, and may even intensify.

Of course, one might well argue that borders with so many troubled regions will constrain Chinese power, and thus geography is a hindrance to Chinese ambitions. China is virtually surrounded, in other words. But given China's economic and demographic expansion in recent decades, and its reasonable prospects for continued, albeit reduced, economic growth—with serious bumps, mind you—into the foreseeable future, China's many land borders can also work as a force multiplier: for it is China encroaching on these less dynamic and less populated areas, not the other way around. Some explain that the presence of failed and semi-failed states on China's borders—namely Afghanistan and Pakistan—is a danger to Beijing. I have been to those borders. They are in the remotest terrain at exceedingly high elevations. Few live there. Pakistan could completely unravel and it would barely be noticed on the Chinese side of the border. China's borders aren't the problem: the problem is Chinese society, which, as it becomes more prosperous, and, as China's economic growth rate slows, raises the specter of political upheaval of some sort. And serious upheaval could make China suddenly vulnerable on its ethnic peripheries.

China's most advantageous outlet for its ambitions is in the direction of the relatively weak states of Southeast Asia. Here, too, China's geography is incomplete. China dominated Vietnam during the first millennium of the modern era. China's Yuan Dynasty (of Mongol descent) invaded Burma, Siam, and Vietnam in the late thirteenth century. Chinese migration to Thailand dates back many centuries. The lack of a Great Wall in China's southeast was not only because of the rugged forests and steep mountain folds between China and Burma, but because Chinese expansion along this entire frontier from Burma in the west to Vietnam in the east was more fluid than in the north of China, according to Lattimore.[36] There are few natural impediments separating China from parts of Burma, and from Thailand, Laos, and Vietnam. The likely capital of a Mekong River prosperity sphere, linking all the countries of Indochina by road and river traffic, is Kunming in China's Yunnan Province, whose dams will provide the electricity consumed by Thais and others in this demographic cockpit of the world. For it is here in Southeast Asia, with its 568 million people, where China's 1.3 billion people converge with the Indian Subcontinent's 1.5 billion people.

First and foremost among the states of Southeast Asia, with the largest, most sprawling landmass in the region, is Burma. Burma, too, like Mongolia, the Russian Far East, and other territories on China's artificial land borders, is a feeble state abundant in the very metals, hydrocarbons, and other natural resources that China desperately requires. The distance is less than five hundred miles from Burma's Indian Ocean seaboard—where China and India are competing for development rights—to China's Yunnan Province. Again, we are talking about a future of pipelines, in this case gas from offshore fields in the Bay of Bengal, that will extend China's reach beyond its legal borders to its natural geographical and historical limits. This will occur in a Southeast Asia in which the formerly strong state of Thailand can less and less play the role of a regional anchor and inherent balancer against China, owing to deep structural problems in Thai politics: the royal family, with an ailing king, is increasingly less of a stabilizing force; the Thai military is roiled by factionalism; and the citizenry is ideologically split between an urban middle class and an up-and-coming rural class. China, flush with cash, is developing bilateral military relationships with Thailand and other Southeast Asian countries, even as America's own military presence, as exemplified by annual regional exercises like Cobra Gold, lessen in importance for the United States, ever since America's energies have been diverted to its Middle Eastern wars. (Of course, this is now changing: as the Obama administration vows a pivot toward Asia and away from the Middle East, in order to confront a militarily more powerful China.)[37]

Further afield in Southeast Asia, both Malaysia and Singapore are heading into challenging democratic transitions of their own, as both of their adept, nation-building strongmen, Mahathir bin Mohammed and Lee Kuan Yew, pass from the scene. Because all ethnic Malays are Muslim, Islam is racialized in Malaysia, and the result is intercommunal divides between the Malay, Chinese, and Indian communities. Creeping Islamization has led to seventy thousand Chinese leaving

Malaysia over the past two decades, even as the country falls further under the shadow of China economically, with most of Malaysia's imports coming from there. Chinese themselves may be unpopular in Malaysia, but China "the state" is too big to resist. The quiet fear of China is most clearly revealed by the actions of Singapore, a city-state strategically located near the narrowest point of the Strait of Malacca. In Singapore, ethnic Chinese dominate ethnic Malays by a margin of 77 percent to 14 percent. Nevertheless, Singapore fears becoming a vassal state of China, and has consequently developed a long-standing military training relationship with Taiwan. Recently retired Minister Mentor Lee Kuan Yew has publicly urged the United States to stay militarily and diplomatically engaged in the region. The degree to which Singapore can maintain its feisty independence will, like developments in Mongolia, be a gauge of Beijing's regional clout. Indonesia, for its part, is caught between the need of a U.S. naval presence to hedge against China and the fear that if it looks too much like a U.S. ally, it will anger the rest of the Islamic world. The Free Trade Area inaugurated recently between China and ASEAN (Association of South East Asian Nations) demonstrates the tributary relationship that is developing between China and its southern neighbors. China's divide-and-conquer strategy has each ASEAN country negotiating separately with China, rather than as a unit. China uses ASEAN as a market for its high-value manufactured goods, while it imports low-value agricultural produce from Southeast Asia: a classic colonial-style relationship.[38] This has led to Chinese trade surpluses, even as ASEAN countries are becoming a dumping ground for industrial goods produced by China's relatively cheap urban labor. In fact, the trade gap between China and ASEAN has widened five-fold in the first decade of the twenty-first century. Look at recent history: from 1998 to 2001, Malaysian and Indonesian exports to China "nearly doubled," as did Philippine exports to China from 2003 to 2004. From 2002 to 2003, combined exports from all of the ASEAN states to China grew by 51.7 percent, and by 2004 "China had become the region's leading trade partner, surpassing the United States."[39] Yet China's economic dominance is also benevolent, in that China is serving as an engine of modernization for all of Southeast Asia. The complicating factor in this scenario is Vietnam, a historic foe of China with a large army and strategically located naval bases that might serve as a potential hedge against China, along with India and Japan. But even Vietnam, with all of its fears regarding its much larger northern neighbor, has no choice but to get along with it. China may still be in the early phases of its continental expansion, so its grasp of the periphery is nascent. The key story line of the next few decades may be the manner in which China accomplishes this. And if it can accomplish this, what kind of regional hegemon will China be?

Mongolia, the Russian Far East, Central Asia, and Southeast Asia are all natural zones of Chinese influence and expansion, even though no political borders will change. But China is most incomplete on the Korean Peninsula, where political borders could well shift—if one accepts the argument that in a world increasingly penetrated by information technology, the hermetic North Korean regime has few good prospects. This makes North Korea the true pivot of East Asia, whose unraveling could affect the destiny of the whole region for decades to come. Jutting out from Manchuria, of which it is a natural geographical appendage, the Korean Peninsula commands all maritime traffic in northeastern China and, more particularly, traps in its armpit the Bohai Sea, home to China's largest offshore oil reserve. In antiquity, the kingdom of Goguryeo covered southern Manchuria and the northern two-thirds of the Korean Peninsula. Goguryeo paid tribute to China's Wei Dynasty, even as it later fought a war with it. Parts of Korea, especially in the north, came under the sway of the Han Dynasty in antiquity and under the Qing Dynasty in early modern times. China will never annex any part of Korea, yet it remains frustrated by Korean sovereignty. China has supported the late Kim Jong-il's and Kim Jong-un's Stalinist regime, but it covets North Korea's geography—with its additional outlets to the Pacific close to Russia—far more, and thus has plans for the peninsula beyond the reign of the deceased "Dear Leader" and his son, who have caused Beijing no end of headaches. China would like eventually to dispatch its thousands of North Korean defectors to build a favorable political base for Beijing's gradual economic takeover of the Tumen River region—where China, North Korea, and the Russian Far East intersect, with good port facilities on the Pacific fronting Japan. China's goal for North Korea must be a more modern, authoritarian, Gorbachevian buffer state between it and the vibrant middle-class democracy of South Korea.

But not even China is in control of events in North Korea. In other divided country scenarios of the past decades—Vietnam, Germany, Yemen—the forces of unity have ultimately triumphed. But in none of these cases was unification achieved through a deliberate process. Rather, it happened in sudden, tumultuous fashion that did not respect the interests of all the major parties concerned. Nevertheless, it is more likely than not that China, even though it fears reunification, will eventually benefit from it. A unified Greater Korean state could be more or less under Seoul's control, and China is South Korea's biggest trading partner. A reunified Korea would be a nationalist Korea, with undercurrents of hostility toward its larger neighbors, China and Japan, that have historically sought to control and occupy it. But Korea's enmity toward Japan is significantly greater, as Japan occupied the peninsula from 1910 to 1945. (There are still disputes between Seoul and Tokyo over the Tokdo/Takeshima islets in what Koreans call the East Sea and Japanese the Sea of Japan.) Meanwhile, the economic pull from China will be stronger than from Japan. A reunified Korea tilting slightly toward China and away from Japan would be one with little or no basis for a continued U.S. troop presence, and that, in turn, would fuel Japanese rearmament. In other words, it is easy to conceive of a Korean future within a Greater China, even as there are fewer U.S. troops on the ground in Northeast Asia.

Thus, with China making inroads into Mackinder's Central Asian Heartland, it is also likely to have significant influence in Spykman's Rimland, of which Southeast Asia and the Korean Peninsula are parts.

China's land borders at this point in history seem to beckon with more opportunities than hazards. This brings to mind the University of Chicago's John J. Mearsheimer's comment in *The Tragedy of Great*

Power Politics that "the most dangerous states in the international system are continental powers with large armies."[40] Yet China only partially fits that description. True, China is in its own way an expanding land power and the People's Liberation Army ground force numbers some 1.6 million troops, the largest in the world. But as I've indicated, with the exception of the Indian Subcontinent and the Korean Peninsula, China is merely filling vacuums more than it is ramming up against competing states. Moreover, as the events of 2008 and 2009 showed, the PLA ground force will not have an expeditionary capability for years to come. In those years, the PLA had to respond to an earthquake emergency in Sichuan, to ethnic unrest in Tibet and Xinjiang, and to the security challenge of the Olympics in Beijing. What these "trans-regional mobility exercises" as the Chinese call them, indicated, according to Abraham Denmark of the Center for Naval Analysis, was an ability by the PLA to move troops from one end of continental China to another, but not an ability to move supplies and heavy equipment at the rate required. The only conceivable circumstances for the PLA to cross beyond China's borders would be through a process of miscalculation, in the event of another land war with India, or to fill a void in the event of the collapse of the North Korean regime, which might also draw in American and South Korean troops in the mother of all humanitarian emergencies. (North Korea's population is poorer than Iraq, with much less of a modern history of responsible self-government.) The very fact that China has the luxury to fill power vacuums on its vast frontiers without the backup of a truly expeditionary ground force indicates how China is probably more secure on land than it has been in decades, or centuries.

Chinese diplomats have been busy in recent years settling remaining border disputes with the Central Asian republics and with its other neighbors (India being a striking exception).[41] While the accords may not be on China's terms, the very fact of such a comprehensive approach from Beijing is an indication of a strong strategic direction. China has signed military agreements with Russia, Kazakhstan, Kyrgyzstan, and Tajikistan. "The stabilization of China's land borders may be one of the most important geopolitical changes in Asia of the past few decades," writes Jakub Grygiel.[42] There is no longer a Soviet army bearing down on Manchuria like during the Cold War, a time when under Mao Zedong China concentrated its defense budget on its army, and pointedly neglected the seas. The significance of this cannot be overstated. Since antiquity China has been preoccupied with land invasions of one sort or another. The Great Wall of China was built in the third century B.C. ostensibly to keep out Turkic invaders. It was a Mongol invasion from the north that led to the end of Ming forays in the Indian Ocean in the fifteenth century. Relatedly, it is the current favorable situation on land, more than any other variable, that has allowed China to start building a great navy and reestablish the Pacific and maybe even Indian oceans as part of its geography. Whereas coastal city-states and island nations, big and small, pursue sea power as a matter of course, a continental and historically insular nation like China does so partly as a luxury: the mark of a budding empire-of-sorts. In the past, the Chinese, secure in their fertile river valleys, were not forced by poverty to take to the sea like the Norsemen who lived in a cold and sterile land. The Pacific Ocean offered the Chinese little, and was in many respects a road to nowhere, unlike the Mediterranean and Aegean seas, populated as they were with islands in an enclosed maritime space. It was the early-nineteenth-century German philosopher Georg Wilhelm Friedrich Hegel who explained that the Chinese, unlike the Europeans, lacked the boldness for sea exploration, tied as the Chinese were to the agricultural cycles of their plains.[43] The Chinese probably never heard of Formosa (Taiwan) until the thirteenth century, and didn't settle it until the seventeenth century, after Portuguese and Dutch traders had established stations on the island.[44] Thus, merely by going to sea in the manner that it is, China demonstrates its favorable position on land in the heart of Asia.

East Asia now pits Chinese land power against American sea power, with Taiwan and the Korean Peninsula as the main focal points. For decades, China was preoccupied on land where America, particularly since its misadventure in Vietnam, had no appetite to go. America still has no such appetite in Asia, especially after its ordeals in Iraq and Afghanistan. But China is in the early stages of becoming a sea power as well as a land power: that is the big change in the region.

In terms of geography, China is as blessed by its seaboard and its proximity to water as it is by its continental interior. China dominates the East Asian coastline on the Pacific in the temperate and tropical zones, and on its southern border is close enough to the Indian Ocean to contemplate being linked to it in years ahead by roads and energy pipelines. But whereas China is in a generally favorable position along its land borders, it faces a more hostile environment at sea. The Chinese navy sees little but trouble and frustration in what it calls the First Island Chain, which, going from north to south, comprises Japan, the Ryuku Islands, the so-called half-island of the Korean Peninsula, Taiwan, the Philippines, Indonesia, and Australia. All of these places, save for Australia, are potential flashpoints. Scenarios include the collapse of North Korea or an inter-Korean war, a possible struggle with the United States over Taiwan, and acts of piracy or terrorism that conceivably impede China's merchant fleet access to the Malacca and other Indonesian straits. There are, too, China's territorial disputes over the likely energy-rich ocean beds in the East and South China seas. In the former, China and Japan have conflicting claims of sovereignty to the Senkaku/Diaoyu Islands; in the latter, China has conflicting sovereignty claims with Taiwan, the Philippines, and Vietnam to some or all of the Spratly Islands, and with Vietnam over the Paracel Islands. (China also has other serious territorial conflicts in the South China Sea with Malaysia and Brunei.) Particularly in the case of the Senkaku/Diaoyu Islands, the dispute does carry the benefit of providing Beijing with a lever to stoke nationalism, whenever it might need to. But otherwise it is a grim seascape for Chinese naval strategists. For looking out from its Pacific coast onto this First Island Chain, they behold a sort of "Great Wall in reverse," in the words of Naval War College professors James Holmes and Toshi Yoshihara: a well-organized line of American allies, with the equivalent of guard towers stretching from Japan to Australia, all potentially blocking China's access to the larger ocean. Chinese strategists see this map and bristle at its navy being so boxed in.[45]

China's solution has been notably aggressive. This may be somewhat surprising: for in many circumstances, it can be argued that naval power is more benign than land power. The limiting factor of navies is that despite all of their precision-guided weapons, they cannot by themselves occupy significant territory, and thus it is said are no menace to liberty. Navies have multiple purposes beyond fighting, such as the protection of commerce. Sea power suits those nations intolerant of heavy casualties in fighting on land. China, which in the twenty-first century will project hard power primarily through its navy, should, therefore, be benevolent in the way of other maritime nations and empires in history, such as Venice, Great Britain, and the United States: that is, it should be concerned mainly with the free movement of trade and the preservation of a peaceful maritime system. But China has not reached that stage of self-confidence yet. When it comes to the sea, it still thinks territorially, like an insecure land power, trying to expand in concentric circles in a manner suggested by Spykman. The very terms it uses, "First Island Chain" and "Second Island Chain," are territorial terms, which, in these cases, are seen as archipelagic extensions of the Chinese landmass. The Chinese have absorbed the aggressive philosophy of Alfred Thayer Mahan, without having graduated yet to the blue-water oceanic force that would make it possible for China to apply Mahanian theory. In November 2006, a Chinese submarine stalked the USS *Kitty Hawk* and provocatively surfaced within torpedo firing range. In November 2007, the Chinese refused entry to the *Kitty Hawk* Carrier Strike Group into Hong Kong harbor, despite building seas and deteriorating weather (the *Kitty Hawk* did make a visit to Hong Kong in early 2010). In March 2009, a handful of Chinese ships harassed the American surveillance ship the USNS *Impeccable* while it was openly conducting operations outside China's twelve-mile territorial limit in the South China Sea. The Chinese ships blocked passage and pretended to ram the *Impeccable,* forcing the *Impeccable* to respond with fire hoses. These are not the actions of a great power, serene in its position of dominance and recognizing a brotherhood of the sea with other world navies, but of a rising and still immature power, obsessed with the territorial humiliations it suffered in the nineteenth and twentieth centuries.

China is developing asymmetric and anti-access niche capabilities, designed to deny the U.S. Navy easy entry to the East China Sea and other coastal waters. Analysts are divided over the significance of this. Robert S. Ross of Boston College believes that "until China develops situational awareness capability and can degrade U.S. counter-surveillance technologies, it possesses only a limited credible access-denial operations." Andrew F. Krepinevich of the Center for Strategic and Budgetary Assessments believes that whatever technical difficulties China may momentarily be encountering, it is on the way to "Finlandizing" East Asia.[46] Thus, while it has modernized its destroyer fleet, and has plans for an aircraft carrier or two, China is not buying naval platforms across the board. Rather, China has been building four new classes of nuclear- and conventional-powered attack and ballistic missile submarines. According to Seth Cropsey, former deputy undersecretary of the Navy, China could field a submarine force larger than the U.S. Navy's within the foreseeable future. The Chinese navy, he goes on, plans to use over-the-horizon radars, satellites, seabed sonar networks, and cyberwarfare in the service of antiship ballistic missiles with maneuverable reentry vehicles, which, along with its burgeoning submarine fleet, will be part of its effort to rebuff U.S. naval access to large portions of the Western Pacific. This is not to mention China's improving mine warfare capability, the aquisition of Russian Su-27 and Su-30 fourth-generation jet fighters, and 1,500 Russian surface-to-air missiles deployed along China's coast. Moreover, the Chinese are putting their fiber-optic systems underground and moving defense capabilities deep into western China, out of naval missile range—all the while developing an offensive strategy designed to be capable of striking that supreme icon of American wealth and power: the aircraft carrier. China will field a fifth-generation fighter between 2018 and 2020, even as the United States slows or stops production of the F-22.[47] The strategic geography of the Western Pacific is changing thanks to Chinese arms purchases.

China likely has no intention of ever attacking a U.S. aircraft carrier. China is not remotely capable of directly challenging the U.S. militarily. The aim here is dissuasion: to amass so much offensive and defensive capability along its seaboard that the U.S. Navy will in the future think twice and three times about getting between the First Island Chain and the Chinese coast. That, of course, is the essence of power: to affect your adversary's behavior. Thus is Greater China realized in a maritime sense. The Chinese, by their naval, air, and missile acquisitions, are evincing a clear territoriality. The U.S.-China relationship, I believe, will not only be determined by such bilateral and global issues as trade, debt, climate change, and human rights, but more importantly by the specific geography of China's potential sphere of influence in maritime Asia.

Pivotal to that sphere of influence is the future of Taiwan. Taiwan illustrates something basic in world politics: that moral questions are, just beneath the surface, often questions of power. Taiwan is often discussed in moral terms, even as its sovereignty or lack thereof carries pivotal geopolitical consequences. China talks about Taiwan in terms of consolidating the national patrimony, unifying China for the good of all ethnic Chinese. America talks about Taiwan in terms of preserving a model democracy. But Taiwan is something else: in Army general Douglas MacArthur's words, it is "an unsinkable aircraft carrier" that dominates the center point of China's convex seaboard, from which an outside power like the United States can "radiate" power along China's coastal periphery, according to Holmes and Yoshihara.[48] As such, nothing irritates Chinese naval planners as much as de facto Taiwanese independence. Of all the guard towers along the reverse maritime Great Wall, Taiwan is, metaphorically, the tallest and most centrally located. With Taiwan returned to the bosom of mainland China, suddenly the Great Wall and the maritime straitjacket it represents would be severed. If China succeeds in consolidating Taiwan, not only will its navy suddenly be in an advantageous strategic position vis-à-vis the First Island Chain, but its national energies, especially its military ones, will be just as dramatically freed up to look outward in terms of power projection, to a degree that has so far been impossible. Though the adjective "multipolar" is thrown around liberally to describe the global situation, it will be the virtual fusing of Taiwan with the mainland that will mark in a military sense the real emergence of a multipolar world.

According to a 2009 RAND study, the United States will not be able to defend Taiwan from Chinese attack by 2020. China is ready with cyber-weapons, an air force replete with new fourth-generation fighter jets, submarine-launched ballistic missiles, and thousands of missiles on the mainland targeting both Taiwan and Taiwan's own fighter jets on the ground. The Chinese, according to the report, defeat the U.S. with or without F-22s, with or without the use of Kadena Air Base in Japan, and with or without the use of two carrier strike groups. The RAND report emphasizes the air battle. The Chinese would still have to land tens of thousands of troops by sea and would be susceptible to U.S. submarines. Yet the report, with all its caveats, does highlight a disturbing trend. China is just a hundred miles away, but the United States must project military power from half a world away in a Post Cold War environment in which it can less and less depend on the use of foreign bases. China's anti-access naval strategy is not only designed to keep out U.S. forces in a general way, but to ease the conquest of Taiwan in a specific way. The Chinese military can focus more intensely on Taiwan than can America's, given all of America's global responsibilities. That is why the American quagmires in Iraq and Afghanistan have been particularly devastating news for Taiwan.

Even as China envelops Taiwan militarily, it does so economically and socially. Taiwan does 30 percent of its trade with China, with 40 percent of its exports going to the mainland. There are 270 commercial flights per week between Taiwan and the mainland. Two-thirds of Taiwanese companies, some ten thousand, have made investments in China in the last five years. There are direct postal links and common crime fighting, with half a million mainland tourists coming to the island annually, and 750,000 Taiwanese residing in

China for half the year. In all there are five million cross-straits visits each year. There will be less and less of a need for an invasion when subtle economic warfare will achieve the same result. Thus, we have seen the demise of the Taiwan secessionist movement.[49] But while a future of greater integration appears likely, the way it develops will be pivotal for great power politics. Were the United States simply to abandon Taiwan, that could undermine America's bilateral relationships with Japan, South Korea, the Philippines, Australia, and other Pacific allies, let alone with India and even some states in Africa, which will begin to doubt America's other bilateral commitments, thus encouraging them to move closer to China, allowing for a Greater China of truly hemispheric proportions to emerge. The United States and Taiwan must look at qualitative, asymmetric ways of their own to counter China militarily. The aim is not to be able to defeat China in a straits war, but to make a war too costly for China to seriously contemplate, and thus pry loose functional Taiwanese independence long enough for China to become a more liberal society, so that the United States can continue to maintain credibility with its allies. In this way, Taiwan's layered missile defense and its three hundred antiaircraft shelters, coupled with a sale of $6.4 billion worth of weapons to Taiwan, announced by the Obama administration in early 2010, is vital to America's position in Eurasia overall. The goal of transforming China domestically is not a pipe dream. Remember that the millions of Chinese tourists who come to Taiwan watch its spirited political talk shows and shop in its bookstores with their subversive titles. A more open China is certainly more of a possibility than a repressive one. But a more democratic China could be an even more dynamic great power than a repressive China, in an economic, cultural, and hence in a military sense.

Beneath Taiwan on the map looms the South China Sea, framed by the demographic cockpit of mainland Southeast Asia, the Philippines, and Indonesia, with Australia further afield. A third of all seaborne commercial goods worldwide and half of all the energy requirements for Northeast Asia pass through here. As the gateway to the Indian Ocean—the world's hydrocarbon interstate, where China is involved in several port development projects—the South China Sea must in some future morrow be virtually dominated by the Chinese navy if Greater China is truly to be realized. Here we have the challenges of piracy, radical Islam, and the naval rise of India, coupled with the heavily congested geographic bottlenecks of the various Indonesian straits (Malacca, Sunda, Lombok, and Macassar), through which a large proportion of China's oil tankers and merchant fleet must pass. There are also significant deposits of oil and gas that China hopes to exploit, making the South China Sea a "second Persian Gulf" in some estimations, write Naval War College professors Andrew Erickson and Lyle Goldstein.[50] Spykman noted that throughout history states have engaged in "circumferential and transmarine expansion" to gain control of adjacent seas: Greece sought to control the Aegean, Rome the Mediterranean, the United States the Caribbean, and now, according to this logic, China the South China Sea.[51] Indeed, the South China Sea with the Strait of Malacca unlocks the Indian Ocean for China the same way control over the Caribbean unlocked the Pacific for America at the time of the building of the Panama Canal.[52] And just as Spykman called the Greater Caribbean—in order to underscore its importance—the "American Mediterranean," we can call the South China Sea the *Asian Mediterranean,* since it will be at the heart of political geography in coming decades.[53] China may seek to dominate the South China Sea in a similar way that the Americans dominated the Caribbean, while America, playing by different rules now, will seek along with allies like Vietnam and the Philippines to keep it a full-fledged international waterway. It is fear of China—not love of America—that is driving Hanoi into Washington's arms. Given the history of the Vietnam War, it may seem disorienting to witness this emerging relationship between two erstwhile enemies; but consider the fact that precisely by defeating America in a war means Vietnam is a confident country with no chip on its shoulder, and thus psychologically free to enter into an undeclared alliance with the United States.

———

China is using all forms of its national power—political, diplomatic, economic, commercial, military, and demographic—to expand virtually beyond its legal land and sea borders in order to encompass the borders of imperial China at its historical high points. Yet there is a contradiction here. Let me explain.

As I've indicated, China is intent on access denial in its coastal seas. In fact, scholars Andrew Erickson and David Yang suggest "the possibility that China may be closer than ever to mastering" the ability to hit a moving target at sea, such as a U.S. carrier, with a land-based missile, and may plan a "strategically publicized test sometime in the future."[54] But access denial without the ability to protect its own sea lines of communication makes an attack on an American surface combatant (let alone a naval war with the United States) futile, since the U.S. Navy would maintain the ability to cut off Chinese energy supplies by interdicting Chinese ships in the Pacific and Indian oceans. Of course, the Chinese seek to influence American behavior, rather than ever fight the United States outright. Still, why even bother with access denial if you never intend to carry it out? Jacqueline Newmyer, who heads a Cambridge, Massachusetts, defense consultancy, explains that Beijing has "the aim of creating a disposition of power so favorable to the PRC [People's Republic of China] that it will not actually have to use force to secure its interests."[55] Therefore, just as Taiwan builds up its defenses without the intention of clashing with China, China does likewise with respect to the United States. All parties are seeking to alter the behavior of other parties while avoiding war. The very demonstrations of new weapons systems (if Erickson and Yang are right), let alone the building of port facilities and listening posts in the Pacific and Indian oceans, as well as the large amounts of military aid that Beijing is providing to littoral states that come between Chinese territory and the Indian Ocean, are all displays of power that by their very nature are not secret. Still, there is a hard, nasty edge to some of this: for example, the Chinese are constructing a major naval base on the southern tip of Hainan Island, smack in the heart of the South China Sea, featuring underground facilities for up to twenty nuclear and diesel-electric submarines. Such activity goes beyond influencing the other party's behavior to being an assertion in its own right of Monroe Doctrine–style sovereignty over the surrounding waters. It would seem that the Chinese are constructing Greater China first, at the heart of which will be the South China Sea and Southeast Asia, even while they have a longer-term plan for a blue-water force, with which will come the ability to protect their own sea lines of communication to the Middle East across the Indian Ocean, and thus make a military conflict with the United States less unreasonable to contemplate from a Chinese perspective. (China has no motive to go to war with the United States. But motives can change over the years and decades, thus it is prudent to track air and naval capabilities instead.) In the meantime, as Taiwan slips closer into China's embrace, the more likely it is that the Chinese military can divert its attention to the Indian Ocean and the protection of hemispheric sea lanes. The Chinese have more and more raw material equities to protect in sub-Saharan Africa at the Indian Ocean's opposite end: oil markets in Sudan, Angola, and Nigeria; iron ore mines in Zambia and Gabon; and copper and cobalt mines in the Democratic Republic of the Congo, all to be connected by Chinese-built roads and railways, in turn linked to Atlantic and Indian ocean ports.[56] To be sure, control and access to sea lines of communication are more important now than during Mahan's years, and American preponderance over such routes may not be destined to continue forever.

This all means that America's commitment to prolong the de facto independence of Taiwan has implications that go far beyond the defense of the island itself. For the future of Taiwan and North Korea constitute the hinges on which the balance of power in much of Eurasia rests.

The current security situation in Asia is fundamentally more complicated and, therefore, more unstable than the one that existed in the decades after World War II. As American unipolarity ebbs, with the relative decline in size of the U.S. Navy, and with the concomitant rise of the Chinese economy and military (even at slower rates than before), multipolarity becomes increasingly a feature of Asian power relationships. The Chinese are building underground submarine pens on Hainan Island and developing antiship missiles. The Americans are providing Taiwan with 114 Patriot air defense missiles and dozens of advanced military communications systems. The Japanese and South Koreans are engaged in across-the-board modernization of their fleets—with a particular emphasis on submarines. And India is building a great navy. These are all crude forms of seeking to adjust the balance of power in one's favor. There is an arms race going on, and it is occurring in Asia. This is the world that awaits the United States when it completes its withdrawal from both Iraq and Afghanistan. While no one state in Asia has any incentive to go to war, the risks of incidents at sea and fatal miscalculations about the balance of power—which everyone is seeking to constantly adjust—will have a tendency to increase with time and with the deepening complexity of the military standoff.

Tensions at sea will be abetted by those on land, because as we have seen, China is filling vacuums that will in due course bring it into uneasy contact with Russia and India. Empty spaces on the map are becoming crowded with more people, strategic roads and pipelines, and ships in the water, to say nothing of overlapping concentric circles of missiles. Asia is becoming a closed geography, with a coming crisis of "room," as Paul Bracken wrote back in 1999. That process has only continued, and it means increasing friction.

So how might the United States stay militarily engaged while working to preserve the stability of Asia? How does the United States protect its allies, limit the borders of Greater China, and at the same time avoid a conflict with China? For China, if its economy can keep growing, could constitute more embryonic power than any adversary the United States faced during the twentieth century. Being an offshore balancer as some suggest may not be completely sufficient. Major allies like Japan, India, South Korea, and Singapore require the U.S. Navy and Air Force to be in "concert" with their own forces, as one high-ranking Indian told me: an integral part of the landscape and seascape, rather than merely lurking over some distant horizon.

But what exactly does a concert of powers look like on the high seas and Spykmanesque Rimland of Eurasia? A plan that made the rounds in the Pentagon in 2010 sketches out an American naval cartography of the twenty-first century that seeks to "counter Chinese strategic power . . . without direct military confrontation." It does so while envisioning a U.S. Navy down from the current 280 ships to 250, and a cut in defense spending by 15 percent. Drawn up by a retired Marine colonel, Pat Garrett, the plan is worth describing because it introduces into the Eurasian Rimland equation the strategic significance of Oceania, just at a time when the American military footprint is growing dramatically on the island of Guam.

Guam, Palau, and the Northern Mariana, Solomon, Marshall, and Caroline island groups are all either U.S. territories, commonwealths with defense agreements with the United States, or independent states that because of their poverty may well be open to such agreements. The U.S. position in Oceania exists courtesy of the spoils of the 1898 Spanish-American War and the blood of Marines in World War II, who liberated these islands from the Japanese. Oceania will grow in importance because it is sufficiently proximate to East Asia, while lying just outside the anti-access bubble in the process of being expanded by China's DF-21 and more advanced antiship missiles. Future bases in Oceania are not unduly provocative, unlike bases on the "guard towers" of Japan, South Korea, and (until the 1990s) the Philippines. Guam is only four hours flying time from North Korea and only a two-day sail from Taiwan. Most significantly, as outright U.S. possessions, or functionally dependent on the United States for their local economies, the United States can make enormous defense investments in some of these places without fear of being evicted.

Already, Andersen Air Force Base on Guam is the most commanding platform in the world for the projection of U.S. hard power. With 100,000 bombs and missiles and 66 million gallons of jet fuel at any one time, it is the Air Force's biggest strategic gas-and-go anywhere. Its runways are filled with long lines of C-17 Globemasters, F/A-18 Hornets, and the like. Guam is also home to an American submarine squadron and an expanding naval base. Guam and the nearby Northern Mariana Islands, U.S. possessions both, are almost equidistant between Japan and the Strait of Malacca.

Then there is the strategic potential of the southwestern tip of Oceania, signified by the offshore anchorages of the Australian-owned Ashmore and Cartier Islands, and the adjacent seaboard of western Australia itself, from Darwin to Perth: all looking out from below the Indonesian archipelago to the Indian Ocean, which is emerging as the vascular center of the world economy, with oil and natural gas transported across its width from the Middle East to the burgeoning middle classes of East Asia. The U.S. Navy and Air Force, according to Garrett's plan, would take advantage of Oceania's geography in order to constitute a "regional presence in being" located "just over the horizon" from the virtual borders of Greater China and the main shipping lanes of Eurasia.[57] A "regional presence in being" is a variant of the British naval strategist Julian Corbett's "fleet in being" of a hundred years ago, a dispersed collection of ships that can quickly coalesce into a unified fleet when necessary; whereas "just over the horizon" reflects a confluence of offshore balancing and participation in a concert of powers.[58]

The concept of strengthening the U.S. air and sea presence on Oceania reflects a compromise between resisting Greater China at all costs and acceding somewhat to a future Chinese navy role in policing the First Island Chain, while at the same time making China pay a steep price for military aggression on Taiwan. Without ever saying so, this vision allows one to contemplate a world in which American "legacy" bases would be scaled back somewhat on the First Island Chain, even as American ships and planes continue to patrol it, in and out of China's anti-access bubble. Meanwhile, the plan envisages a dramatic expansion of American naval activity in the Indian Ocean. To achieve this, the United States would not have hardened bases, but rather austere "operating locations" and defense agreements in Singapore, Brunei, and Malaysia; and on island nations scattered about the Indian Ocean, such as the Comoros, Seychelles, Mauritius, Reunion, Maldives, and Andamans, a number of which are managed directly or indirectly by France and India, both U.S. allies. This sustains the freedom of navigation in Eurasia along with unimpeded energy flows. The plan deemphasizes existing American bases in Japan and South Korea, and diversifies the U.S. footprint around Oceania to replace the overwhelming stress on Guam, thus moving away from easily targeted "master" bases. For in an age of prickly sovereignty, defended by volatile mass medias, hardening foreign bases make them politically indigestible to local populations. Guam, as a U.S. territory, is the exception that proves the rule. The United States experienced such difficulty with the use of its bases in Turkey prior to the Iraq War in 2003, and for a short time with the use of bases in Japan in 2010. The American Army presence in South Korea is now less embattled mainly because the number of troops stationed there has dropped from 38,000 to 25,000 in recent years, while downtown Seoul has largely been abandoned by the U.S. military.

In any case, the American hold on the First Island Chain is beginning to be pried loose. Local populations are less agreeable to foreign bases, even as a rising China serves as both an intimidator and attractor that can complicate America's bilateral relations with its Pacific allies. It is about time that this is happening. To wit, the 2009–2010 crisis in American-Japanese relations, with an inexperienced new Japanese government wanting to rewrite the rules of the bilateral relationship in Tokyo's favor, even as it talked of developing deeper ties with China, should have occurred years before. The paramount American position in the Pacific is an outdated legacy of World War II, which left China, Japan, and the Philippines devastated: nor can the division of Korea, a product of fighting that ended six decades ago, and left the U.S. military with a dominant position on the peninsula, last forever.

Meanwhile, a Greater China is emerging politically and economically in Central-East Asia and in the Western Pacific, with a significant naval dimension in the East and South China seas, while at the same time Beijing is involved in port-building projects and arms transfers on the Indian Ocean littoral. Only substantial political and economic turmoil inside China could alter this trend. But just outside the borders of this new power realm will likely be a stream of American warships, perhaps headquartered in many cases in Oceania, and partnered with warships from India, Japan, and other democracies, all of whom cannot resist the Chinese embrace, but at the same time are forced to balance against it. Given time, a Chinese blue-water force could become less territorial as it grows in confidence, and thus be drawn into this very alliance structure. Moreover, as political scientist Robert S. Ross points out in a 1999 article that is as relevant now as it was then, because of the particular geography of East Asia, the struggle between China and the United States will remain more stable than that between the Soviet Union and the United States. That is because American maritime power during the Cold War was not enough to contain the Soviet Union; a significant land force in Europe was also required. But even given a faintly pro-Chinese Greater Korea, no such land force will ever be required around the Rimland of Eurasia, in which the U.S. Navy will be pitted against a weaker Chinese one.[59] (The size of the U.S. land force in Japan is diminishing, and is in any case directed not at China, but at North Korea.)

Still, the very fact of Chinese economic power—increasingly accompanied by military power—will lead to a pivotal degree of tension in the years ahead. To paraphrase Mearsheimer's argument from *The Tragedy of Great Power Politics,* the United States, as the regional hegemon in the Western Hemisphere, will seek to prevent China from becoming the regional hegemon over much of the Eastern Hemisphere.[60] This could be the signal drama of the age. Mackinder and Spykman would not be surprised.

Chapter XII

INDIA'S GEOGRAPHICAL DILEMMA

As the United States and China become great power rivals, the direction in which India tilts could determine the course of geopolitics in Eurasia in the twenty-first century. India, in other words, looms as the ultimate pivot state. It is, according to Spykman, a Rimland power writ large. Mahan noted that India, located in the center of the Indian Ocean littoral, is critical for the seaward penetration of both the Middle East and China. But even as the Indian political class understands at a very intimate level America's own historical and geographical situation, the American political class has no such understanding of India's. Yet if Americans do not come to grasp India's highly unstable geopolitics, especially as it concerns Pakistan, Afghanistan, and China, they will badly mishandle the relationship. India's history and geography since early antiquity constitute the genetic code for how the world looks from New Delhi. I begin by placing the Indian Subcontinent in the context of Eurasia in general.

——

With Russia dominating the landmass of Eurasia, even as it is sparsely populated, the four great centers of population on the super-continent are on its peripheries: Europe, India, Southeast Asia, and China. Chinese and European civilizations, as the geographer James Fairgrieve wrote in 1917, grew outward in organic fashion from the nurseries of the Wei River valley and the Mediterranean.[1] Southeast Asia's civilizational development was more elaborate: with Pyu and Mon peoples, followed by Burmans, Khmers, Siamese, Vietnamese, Malays, and others—in turn, influenced by southward migrations from China—coagulating along river valleys like the Irrawaddy and Mekong, as well as on islands like Java and Sumatra. India is another case entirely. Like China, India is possessed of geographical logic, framed as it is by the Arabian Sea to the west and southwest, by the Bay of Bengal to the east and southeast, by the mountainous Burmese jungles to the east, and by the Himalayas and the knot of the Karakoram and Hindu Kush to the north and northwest. India, also like China, is internally vast. But to a lesser extent than China, India lacks a singular nursery of demographic organization like the Wei valley and lower Yellow River, from which a polity could expand outward in all directions.

Even the Ganges River valley did not provide enough of a platform for the expansion of a unitary Indian state unto the subcontinent's deep, peninsular south: for the subcontinent's various river systems besides the Ganges—Brahmaputra, Narmada, Tungabhadra, Kaveri, Godavari, and so on—further divide it. The Kaveri Delta, for example, is the core of Dravidian life, much as the Ganges is of that of the Hindi-speaking peoples.[2] Moreover, India has (along with Southeast Asia) the hottest climate and most abundant and luxuriant landscape of all the Eurasian population hubs, and therefore its inhabitants, Fairgrieve tells us, lacked the need to build political structures for the organization of resources, at least on the scale that the temperate zone Chinese and Europeans did. This last point, of course, may seem overly deterministic, and perhaps inherently racist in its

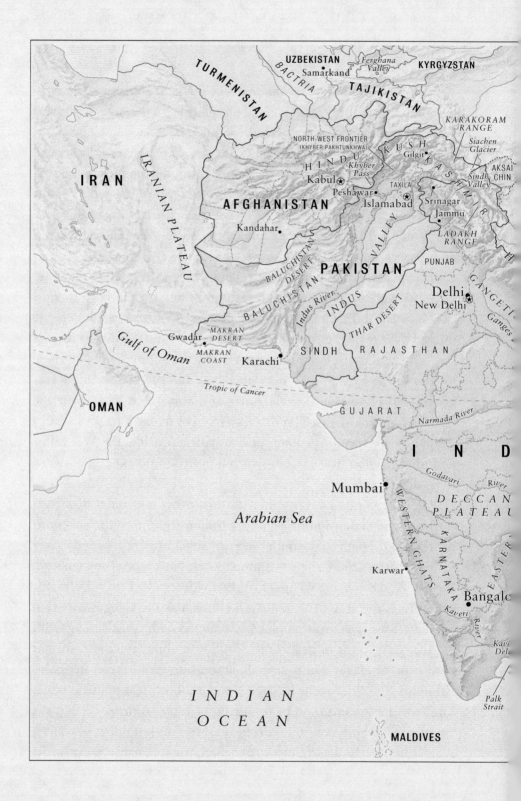

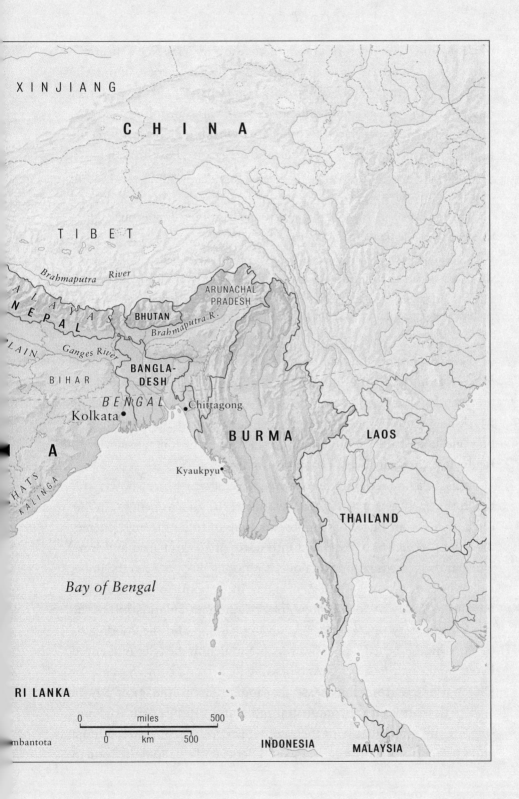

XINJIANG

CHINA

TIBET

Brahmaputra   River

A L A Y A S

ARUNACHAL
PRADESH

NEPAL

BHUTAN

Brahmaputra R.

LAIN

Ganges River

BIHAR

BANGLA-
DESH

BENGAL

Kolkata•

•Chittagong

A

BURMA

LAOS

•Kyaukpyu

HATS

KALINGA

THAILAND

Bay of Bengal

RI LANKA

0   miles   500

0   km   500

mbantota

INDONESIA

MALAYSIA

stark simplicity: a feature common to the era in which Fairgrieve wrote. Yet as in the case of Mackinder, who worried about the "yellow peril" that China supposedly represented, Fairgrieve's larger analysis of India is essentially valid, as well as insightful.

For while obviously constituting its own unique civilization, the Indian Subcontinent, because of the above reasons, has through much of its history lacked the political unity of China, even as it has been open to concentrated invasions from its northwest, the least defined and protected of its frontier regions, where India is dangerously close to both the Central Asian steppe and the Persian-Afghan plateau, with their more "virile," temperate zone civilizations.[3] Motivating these invasions throughout history has been the welcoming fecundity, reinforced by not too excessive rainfall, that characterizes the plain of the Punjab, watered as it is by the Indus River and its tributaries at exactly the point where the Persian-Afghan plateau drops to the floor of the subcontinent. Indeed, it is the thundering invasions and infiltrations from West and Central Asia that have disrupted the quest for unity and stability in the subcontinent well into the modern era. As Mackinder said in one of his lectures: "In the British Empire there is but one land frontier on which warlike preparation must ever be ready. It is the Northwest Frontier of India."[4]

India's advantages and disadvantages as it seeks great power status in the early twenty-first century inhere still in this geography. As the late historian Burton Stein notes, a map of India through the medieval era would have extended into parts of Central Asia and Iran, while at the same time showing only a tenuous link between the Indus valley in the northwest and peninsular India south of the Ganges.[5] For just as today's China represents a triumphant culmination of the relationship between the Inner Asian steppe-land and the floodplains of the Chinese heartland, India was for millennia heavily influenced by its higher-altitude shadow zones, which, unlike in the case of China, it has yet to dominate, so that India remains the lesser power.

The ties between subcontinental India and southeastern Afghanistan are obvious because of their contiguity, yet those between India and the Central Asian steppe-land and between India and the Iranian plateau are equally profound. India and Iran have shared the predicament of being on the receiving end of Mongol onslaughts from Central Asia, even as the dynamism of Iranian culture, abetted by invasions since the time of the Achaemenids (sixth to fourth centuries B.C.), led to Persian being the official language of India until 1835.[6] For India's sixteenth- and seventeenth-century Mughal emperors "became the embodiment of Persian culture," notes the late historian K. M. Panikkar, "and celebrated Nauroz [Persian New Year] with traditional festivities and popularized Persian techniques in art."[7] Meanwhile, Urdu, the official language of Pakistan—the state occupying the Indian Subcontinent's northwestern quadrant—draws heavily on Persian (as well as Arabic) and is written in a modified Arabic script.[8] India, thus, is both a subcontinent and a vital extremity of the Greater Middle East. Here is where we can really understand William McNeill's point about the mixing and melding of civilizations.

And so the key to understanding India is the realization that while as a subcontinent India makes eminent geographical sense, its natural boundaries are, nevertheless, quite weak in places. The result has been various states throughout history that do not conform to our spatial idea of India, and in fact lie astride it. In fact, the present Indian state still does not conform to the borders of the subcontinent, and that is the heart of its dilemma: for Pakistan, Bangladesh, and to a lesser extent Nepal also lie within the subcontinent, and pose significant security threats to India, robbing India of vital political energy that it would otherwise harness for power projection throughout much of Eurasia.

It is not that human settlement from early antiquity forward doesn't adhere to subcontinental geography; rather, it is that India's geography is itself subtle, particularly in the northwest, telling a different story than the map reveals at first glance. At first glance, the relief map shows a brown layer of mountains and tableland neatly marking off the cool wastes of middle Asia from the green tropical floor of the subcontinent along the present border between Afghanistan and Pakistan. But the descent from Afghanistan to the Indus

River, which runs lengthwise through the middle of Pakistan, is exceedingly gradual, so that for millennia similar cultures occupied both the high plateaus and the lowland, riverine plains, whether Harappan, Kushan, Turkic, Mughal, Indo-Persian, Indo-Islamic, or Pushtun, to name but a few. And this is to say nothing of the alkaline deserts of Makran and Baluchistan that unite Iran with the subcontinent; or the medieval sea traffic that united Arabia with India by virtue of the predictable monsoon winds. "The frontier of Al-Hind," as South Asia scholar André Wink—echoing an Arab term—calls the whole region from eastern Iran to western India, dominated by Persianized Muslim populations, has throughout history been very much a fluid cultural organism, so that defining state borders is inherently problematic.[9]

The map of Harappan civilization, a complex network of centrally controlled chieftaincies in the late fourth to mid-second millennia B.C., is telling. According to the archaeological remains, the two major cities were Moenjodaro and Harappa, both alongside the Indus in upper Sindh; so that the Indus, rather than a border differentiating the subcontinent from Inner Asia, constituted the heart of a civilization in its own right. The outlines of the Harappan world stretched from Baluchistan northeast up to Kashmir and then southeast down almost to both Delhi and Mumbai, skirting the Thar Desert: that is, it nearly touched present-day Iran and Afghanistan, covered much of Pakistan, and extended into both northwestern and western India. It was a complex geography of settlement that adhered to landscapes capable of supporting irrigation, even as it suggested how a vast subcontinent had many natural subdivisions within it.

Aryans may have infiltrated from the Iranian plateau, and together with the subcontinent's autochthonous inhabitants were part of a process that consolidated the political organization of the Gangetic plain in northern India around 1000 B.C. This led to sets of monarchies between the eighth and sixth centuries B.C., culminating with the Nanda Empire, which in the fourth century B.C. stretched across northern India and the Gangetic plain from the Punjab to Bengal. In 321 B.C., Chandragupta Maurya dethroned Dhana Nanda and founded the Mauryan Empire, which came to envelop much of the subcontinent, except for the deep south, and thus for the first time in history encouraged the *idea* of India as a political entity conforming with the geography of South Asia. Burton Stein suggests that the merging of so many city-states and chieftaincies into a single coherent system was, in addition to the "vigorous commerce" between them, partially inspired by the threat posed by Alexander the Great, who was on the verge of conquering the Ganges River valley were it not for a mutiny of his soldiers in 326 B.C. Another factor aiding unity was the emergence of the new, pan-subcontinental ideologies of Buddhism and Jainism that "captured the loyalty of commercial peoples," as Stein writes.[10]

The Mauryan kings embraced Buddhism, and ran their empire on Greek and Roman imperial practices that had seeped across the spinal route of migration in the temperate zone from the Aegean basin and West Asia into India. Nevertheless, it required all manners of human ingenuity to hold the Mauryan Empire together. Chandragupta's advisor might have been one Kautilya, who penned a political classic, the *Arthashastra,* or "Book of the State," which shows how a conqueror can create an empire by exploiting the relationships between various city-states: any city-state that touches one's own should be considered an enemy, because it will have to be subdued in the course of empire building; but a distant city-state that borders an enemy should be considered a friend. Because holding such an immense subcontinental empire together was difficult, Kautilya believed in complex alliance networks, and in benevolence toward the conquered, whose way of life should be preserved.[11] The Mauryan was a decentralized empire, to say the least, with a heartland in the eastern Gangetic plain and four regional centers by the time of Chandragupta's grandson Ashoka: Taxila in the northwest, outside the Pakistani capital of Islamabad; Ujjain on the Malwa plateau in western-central India; Suvarnagiri in the southern Indian state of Karnataka; and Kalinga along the Bay of Bengal south of Kolkata.

It was an extraordinary achievement this early in history, with only primitive means of transport and communications available, for one empire to cover so much of the subcontinent. The Mauryans demonstrated the potential for a single state to employ geographic logic over a vast area for quite some time. Alas, the decline of the Mauryans led to the familiar invasions from the northwest, notably through the Khyber Pass: Greeks in the second century B.C. and Scythians in the first century B.C. This encouraged the redivision of the subcontinent into regional dynasties: Sunga, Pandyan, Kuninda, and so on. The Kushan Empire emerged in the first century A.D. in Bactria, where northern Afghanistan meets Tajikistan and Uzbekistan, and its Indo-European rulers conquered territory from the Ferghana valley in the demographic heart of Central Asia to Bihar in northeastern India. The very map of the Kushana domain is mindboggling to our modern sensibilities, overlapping as it does former Soviet Central Asia, Afghanistan and Pakistan, and much of northern India's Gangetic plain. The Kushan Empire follows river valleys on one hand, but crosses mountain ranges on the other, so that it both follows and contradicts geography. It also constitutes a signal lesson in the fact that current borders may not necessarily indicate the last word in political organization of Central and South Asia.

The Gupta Empire (A.D. 320–550) restored a semblance of unity over the subcontinent, governing from the Indus in the west to Bengal in the east, and from the Himalayas in the north to the Deccan plateau in the center, albeit most of the south was outside its control, even as the Gupta rulers suffered incursions from Central Asian horsemen driving down from the northwest into Rajasthan and the western Gangetic plain. Moreover, as in the way of the Mauryan, the Gupta was less a unitary state than a weak system of client states united by trade and tribute to the Ganges core. It was from the non-Gupta south that the devotional form of Hinduism spread north to the Ganges. Southern peninsular India, marked heavily by Dravidian languages, as opposed to the Sanskritic languages spoken in the north, was truly a region unto itself, separated from the north by the Deccan plateau and under the maritime influence of the Middle East and Indochina. For more than six centuries following the Gupta decline, which was hastened by the influx of Huns from Central Asia, came a congeries of small states indicating, yet again, that India was not quite China, with the latter's greater propensity for centralization and political unity. Indeed, the post-Gupta kingdoms, in Stein's words, were "defined less by administration than by language, sectarian affiliations and temples."[12]

From the seventh through sixteenth centuries, writes Fairgrieve, Muslim peoples successively entered India. "The Arabs, as was natural, came first by land along the coast, and by sea coasting along the shores, but they effected nothing permanent; the Turks next," he goes on, "from a little before A.D. 1000 onward, over the plateau of Iran and through Afghanistan. In little over a century, largely because of disputes between Hindu rulers, the whole northern plain had acknowledged Mohammedan rule."[13] In the south, Baluchistan and Sindh were part of the same "desert girdle" that extended unto Mesopotamia.[14] The Indian Subcontinent was indeed grafted to the Greater Middle East. Among the highlights: Iraqi Arabs in the early eighth century occupied parts of Sindh, Punjab, Rajasthan, and Gujarat. The Turkic Mamluk warrior Mahmud of Ghazni, headquartered in eastern Afghanistan, united in his early-eleventh-century empire present-day Iraqi Kurdistan, Iran, Afghanistan, Pakistan, and northwestern India as far as Delhi, and raided Gujarat to the south on the Arabian Sea. From the thirteenth to the early sixteenth century, the so-called Delhi Sultanate featured rule over northern India and parts of the south by the Turkic Tughluq, the Afghan Lodi, and other dynasties from Central Asia.

The choice of Delhi as the capital of India for these invaders was very much a function of geography. As Fairgrieve writes, "Sind and the Indus Valley, including the Punjab . . . form but the antechamber to India, to which there is a comparatively narrow passage, 150 miles wide, between the Indian desert and the Himalayas. At the exit from this passage stands Delhi."[15] At Delhi's back was the Islamic world; in front of it the Hindu world. (By this time Buddhism had virtually disappeared from India, the land of its birth, to move eastward and northeastward.) Geography has determined that the subcontinent in the northwest is less a fixed frontier than an interminable series of gradations, beginning in Iran and Afghanistan, and ending in Delhi: again, proof of McNeill's idea in his grand history of human civilization.

The Mughal Empire was a cultural and political expression of this fact. Few empires have boasted the artistic and religious eclecticism of the Mughals. They ruled India and parts of Central Asia vigorously from the early 1500s to 1720 (after which the empire declined rapidly). Mughal is the Arabic and Persian form of Mongol, which was applied to all foreign Muslims from the north and northwest of India. The Mughal Empire was founded by Zahir-ud-din-Muhammad Babur, a Chaghtai Turk, born in 1483 in the Fergana valley in today's Uzbekistan, who spent his early adulthood trying to capture Tamarlane's (Timur's) old capital of Samarkand. After being decisively defeated by Muhammad Shaybani Khan, a descendant of Genghis Khan, Babur and his followers headed south and captured Kabul. It was from Kabul that Babur swept down with his army from the high plateau of Afghanistan into the Punjab. Thus, he was able to begin his conquest of the Indian Subcontinent. The Mughal or Timurid Empire, which took form under Akbar the Great, Babur's grandson, had a nobility composed of Rajputs, Afghans, Arabs, Persians, Uzbeks, and Chaghtai Turks, as well as of Indian Sunnis, Shiites, and Hindus, not to mention other overlapping groups; it was an ethnic and religious world that began in southern Russia to the northwest and by the Mediterranean to the west.[16] India was very much a depository of ongoing cultural and political trends in the adjoining Middle East.

Kabul and Kandahar were a natural extension of this venerable Delhi-based dynasty, yet the strongly Hindu area in southern India around present-day Bangalore—India's high-technology capital—was much less so. Aurangzeb, the "world-seizer," under whose rule in the late seventeenth century the Mughal Empire reached the zenith of its expansion, was an old man in his eighties still fighting Maratha insurgents in India's south and west. He died in 1707 in his camp on the Deccan plateau, unable to subdue them. The Deccan has, in Panikkar's words, "always formed the great middle rampart of India," unable to be subdued by the peoples of the Gangetic valley. Moreover, the west-to-east flow of rivers in a subcontinent oriented from north to south has, as Aurangzeb's experience demonstrates, made it difficult for the north to govern the south until relatively late in history. Put simply: there are relatively few geographical connecting links between northern and southern India.[17] In fact, it was this long-running and intractable insurgency in southern India that sapped the cohesion and morale of the northern Mughal elite. Aurangzeb's pre-occupation with the great Maratha warriors—to the exclusion of imperial problems elsewhere—made it easier for the Dutch, French, and British East India companies to gain footholds on the coast, which led eventually to British rule in India.[18]

To emphasize the point: Aurangzeb's situation was that of Delhi-based rulers going back hundreds of years, as well as of even older rulers in the subcontinent stretching back to antiquity. That is, the vast region that today encompasses northern India along with Pakistan and much of Afghanistan was commonly under a single polity, even as sovereignty over southern India was in doubt. Thus, for Indian elites, to think of not only Pakistan but Afghanistan, too, as part of India's home turf is not only natural but historically justified. The tomb of Babur is in Kabul, not in Delhi. This does not mean that India has territorial designs on Afghanistan, but it does mean that New Delhi cares profoundly about who rules Afghanistan, and wishes to ensure that those who do rule there are friendly to India.

The British, unlike previous rulers of India, constituted a sea power much more than a land power. It was from the sea, as evinced by the Bombay, Madras, and Calcutta presidencies that were to become the focal points of their rule, that the British were able to conquer India. Consequently, it was the British who, following more than two millennia of invasions and migrations from the west and northwest, restored to India as a political fact the basic truth of its geography: that it is indeed a subcontinent. A 1901 map of India wonderfully demonstrates this: showing a plethora of British-built rail lines ranging in arterial fashion over the whole of the subcontinent—from the Afghan border to the Palk Strait near Ceylon in the deep south, and from Karachi in present-day Pakistan in the west to Chittagong in present-day Bangladesh in the east. Technology had allowed for the subcontinent's vast internal space to be finally united under one polity, rather than divided among several, or administered under some weak imperial alliance system.

True, the Mughals (along with, to a lesser extent, the Maratha Confederacy in the early modern era) were the precursors to this achievement, with their ability to ably administer much of the subcontinent. But Mughal rule, as brilliant as it was, had signified yet another Muslim invasion from the northwest, one that to this day is denigrated by Hindu nationalists. Yet Great Britain, the sea power, was a neutral in the historical drama between Hindus and Muslims: a drama whose basis lay in geography; with the bulk of India's Muslims living both in the northwest, from where invasions had nearly always come, and in East Bengal—the agriculturally rich, eastern terminus of the Gangetic plain, where Islam spread with a thirteenth-century Turkic-Mongol invasion and the clearing of the forest.[19]

The British may have united the Indian Subcontinent with modern bureaucracy and a rail system in the late nineteenth and early twentieth centuries, but by the hastened, tumultuous manner of their leaving in 1947, they helped redivide it in a way that was both more profound and more formalized than any previous imperial sundering. For in the past, the places where, for example, the Indo-Greeks met the Gupta Empire, or where the Mughal Empire met the Maratha Confederacy, did not signify—as such borders do today—barbed wire and minefields and different passports and war-by-media, which all belong to a later phase of technology. The divide now is a hardened legal and partly civilizational one, and became thus less because of geography than because of the decisions of men.

In short, from the historical perspective of India, Pakistan constitutes much more than even a nuclear-armed adversary, a state sponsor of terrorism, and a large, conventional army breathing down its neck on the border. Pakistan, lying to India's northwest, where the mountains meet the plain, is the very geographical and national embodiment of all the Muslim invasions that have swept down into India throughout its history. Pakistan looms to the northwest of India, just as the great Muslim invasion forces of yore once did. "Pakistan," writes George Friedman, the founder of Stratfor, a global intelligence firm, "is the modern-day remnant of Muslim rule over medieval India," even as Pakistan's southwest is the subcontinental region first occupied by Arab Muslims invading from Iran and southern Afghanistan.[20]

To be sure, Indian decision makers are not anti-Muslim. India is home to 154 million Muslims, the third largest Muslim population in the world after Indonesia and Pakistan itself. India has had three Muslim presidents. But India is a secular democracy by virtue of the fact that it has sought to escape from the politics of religion in order to heal the Hindu-Muslim divide in a predominantly Hindu state. Pakistan, as an Islamic republic, to say nothing of its radical elements, is in some ways an affront to the very liberal fundamentals on which India is based.

The fact that India's fear of Pakistan—and vice versa—is existential should not surprise anyone. Of course, India could defeat Pakistan in a conventional war. But in a nuclear exchange, or a war by terrorism, Pakistan could achieve a parity of sorts with India. And it goes beyond that: since it isn't only Pakistan that encompasses, after a fashion, the threat of another Mughal onslaught without the Mughals' redeeming cosmopolitanism; it is Afghanistan, too. For as we know, the border separating Pakistan from Afghanistan is largely a mirage, both today and in history. The crags and canyons of Pakistan's North-West Frontier Province (officially Khyber Pakhtunkhwa), bordering Afghanistan, are utterly porous. Of all the times I crossed the Pakistan-Afghanistan border, I never did so legally. Even at the official Khyber border post, tens of thousands of ethnic Pushtuns pass through weekly without showing identity papers, while hundreds of jingle trucks pass daily uninspected. The lack of procedures attests not only to the same tribes on both sides of the frontier, but to the tenuous nature of the Afghan and Pakistani states themselves, the ultimate cause of which is their lack of geographical coherence as the heart of Indo-Islamic and Indo-Persianate continuums through which it is nearly impossible to draw lines. The Achaemenid, Kushan, Indo-Greek, Ghaznavid, Mughal, and other empires all took in both Afghanistan and Pakistan as part of their dominions, which either threatened India or also included portions of it. Then there is the Central Asian Timur (Tamerlane) and the Turkmen Nader Shah the Great, who in 1398 and in 1739 respectively both vanquished Delhi from imperial bases in present-day Iran, Afghanistan, and Pakistan.

This is a rich history that few in the West know of, while sections of the Indian elite know it in their bones. When Indians look at their maps of the subcontinent they see Afghanistan and Pakistan in the northwest, just as they see Nepal, Bhutan, and Bangladesh in the northeast, as all part of India's immediate sphere of influence, with Iran, the Persian Gulf, the former Soviet Central Asian republics, and Burma as critical shadow zones. Not to view these places as such, is, from the vantage point of New Delhi, to ignore the lessons of history and geography.

As this record of imperial to-ing and fro-ing over the course of millennia shows, Afghanistan and the war there is not just another security issue for India to deal with. Only in the Western view is Afghanistan part of Central Asia; to Indians it is part of their subcontinent.[21] Afghanistan's geography makes it central not only as a principal invasion route into India, for terrorists in our day as for armies in days past, but as a strategically vital rear base for Pakistan, India's primary enemy.

While India's geographic logic is not perfect, Pakistan, right-angled to the course of invasions past, has, in the opinion of many, no geographic logic at all, and Afghanistan far too little. Pakistan can be viewed as an artificial puzzle piece of a territory, straddling the frontier between the Iranian-Afghan plateau and the lowlands of the subcontinent, encompassing the western half of the Punjab, but not the eastern half, crazily uniting the Karakoram in the north (some of the highest mountains in the world) with the Makran Desert almost a thousand miles away to the south by the Arabian Sea.[22] Whereas the Indus should be a border of sorts, the Pakistani state sits on both of its banks. Pakistan is the home of four major ethnic groups, each harboring hostility to the others and each anchored to a specific region: Punjab to the northeast, Sindh to the southeast, Baluchistan to the southwest, and the Pushtun-dominated North-West Frontier. Islam was supposed to have provided the unifying glue for the state but it has signally failed in this regard: even as Islamic groups in Pakistan have become more radical, Baluch and Sindhis continue to see Pakistan as a foreign entity overlorded by the Punjabis, with the Pushtuns in the northwest drawn more into the Taliban-infected politics of the Afghan-Pakistani border area. Without the Punjabi-dominated army, Pakistan might cease to exist—reduced to a rump of an Islamic Greater Punjab, with semi-anarchic Baluchistan and Sindh drawn closer into the orbit of India.

Founded in 1947 by Mohammed Ali Jinnah, a London-Bombay intellectual, the son of a merchant from Gujarat, Pakistan was built on an ideological premise: that of a homeland for the Muslims of the Indian Subcontinent. And it was true, the majority of the subcontinent's Muslims lived in West and East Pakistan (which became Bangladesh in 1971), yet many tens of millions of Muslims remained in India proper, so that Pakistan's geographical contradictions rendered its ideology supremely imperfect. Indeed, millions of Muslims and Hindus became refugees upon Pakistan's creation. The fact is that the subcontinent's history of invasions and migrations makes for a plenteous ethnic, religious, and sectarian mix. For example, India is the birthplace of several religions: Hinduism, Buddhism, Jainism, and Sikhism. Zoroastrians, Jews, and Christians have lived in India for hundreds and thousands of years. The philosophy of the Indian state accepts this reality and celebrates it; the philosophy of the Pakistani state is far less inclusive. That is partly why India is stable and Pakistan is not.

But geography in this case is subject to different interpretations. From another perspective, Pakistan makes impressive geographic sense as a civilizational intermediary and conduit of trade routes connecting the subcontinent with Central Asia, the heart of the Indo-Islamic world; because André Wink's concept of the Indo-Muslim

Al-Hind is hard to define in terms of modern borders, one may ask, why is Pakistan any more artificial than India? After all, Lahore in Pakistan was as much a mother lode of Mughal rule as Delhi in India. The real geographic heart of the northern subcontinental plain is the Punjab, and that is split between the two countries, making neither whole from any historical or geographical view. Just as northern India grows out of the demographic core of the Ganges, Pakistan, it could be argued, grows out of that other vital demographic core, the Indus and its tributaries. In this telling, the Indus, rather than a divider, is a uniter.[23] This point is best expressed in Aitzaz Ahsan's *The Indus Saga and the Making of Pakistan*. A member of the late Benazir Bhutto's Sindh-based Pakistan People's Party, Ahsan asserts that the "critical dividing line" throughout history within the subcontinent is the "Gurdaspur-Kathiawar salient": running southwest from Gurdaspur in eastern Punjab to Kathiawar in Gujarat on the Arabian Sea, a line that approximates the present India-Pakistan border.[24]

But here is the conundrum. During the relatively brief periods in history when the areas of India and Pakistan were united—the Mauryan, Mughal, and British—there was no issue about who dominated the trade routes into Central Asia (Afghanistan and beyond). During the rest of history, there was also no problem, because whereas empires like the Kushana, Ghaznavid, and Delhi Sultanate did not control the eastern Ganges, they did control both the Indus *and* the western Ganges, so that Delhi and Lahore were under the rule of one polity, even as Central Asia was also under their control—so, again, no conflict. Today's political geography is historically unique, however: an Indus valley state and a powerful Gangetic state both fighting for control of an independent Central Asian near-abroad.

Because the Indus and its tributaries, with Punjab at the heart, is the demographic core of the Indus-to-Oxus region, encompassing today's Pakistan and Afghanistan, it is not inappropriate from a historical or geographical sense that, for example, Pakistan's Inter-Services Intelligence Directorate (ISI), dominated by Punjabis, has a strong hand in the terrorist and smuggling operations of the Haqqani Network, which, in turn, operates throughout Indus-to-Oxus. ISI is most interested in controlling the south and east of Afghanistan; that would leave the area north of the Hindu Kush to affect a merger of sorts with the Oxus and trans-Oxus region of southern Uzbekistan and southern Tajikistan—a revival of ancient Bactria. Truly, the early-twenty-first-century map could look like an ancient one.

As for Afghanistan itself—so central, as we have seen, to India's geopolitical fortunes over the course of history—let us consider it for a moment. It is a country with a life expectancy of forty-four years, with a literacy rate of 28 percent (and far lower than that for women), with only 9 percent of females attending secondary schools, and with only a fifth of the population enjoying access to potable water. Out of 182 countries, Afghanistan ranks next to last on the United Nations' Human Development Index. Iraq, on the eve of the U.S. invasion in 2003, was ranked 130, and its literacy rate is a reasonable 74 percent. While in Iraq urbanization stands at 77 percent, so that reducing violence in Greater Baghdad during the troop surge of 2007 had a calming effect on the entire country, in Afghanistan urbanization stands at only 30 percent: meaning that counterinsurgency efforts in one village or region may have no effect on another.

Whereas Mesopotamia, with large urban clusters over a flat landscape, is conducive to military occupation forces, Afghanistan is, in terms of geography, barely a country at all. It is riven by cathedral-like mountain ranges within its territory, which help seal divisions between Pushtuns and Tajiks and other minorities, even as comparatively little in the way of natural impediments separates Afghanistan from Pakistan, or Afghanistan from Iran. Looking at the relief map, and noting that more than half of the world's 42 million Pushtuns live inside Pakistan, one could conceivably construct a country called Pushtunistan, lying between the Hindu Kush mountains and the Indus River, thus overlapping the Afghani and Pakistani states.

Afghanistan only emerged as a country of sorts in the mid-eighteenth century, when Ahmad Khan, leader of the Abdali contingent in the Persian army of Nader Shah the Great, carved out a buffer zone between Persia and a crumbling Mughal empire in the Indian Subcontinent, which was later to evolve into a buffer zone between czarist Russia and British India. Thus the case can be made that with the slow-motion dissolution of the former Soviet Empire in Central Asia, and the gradual weakening of the Pakistani state, a historic re-alignment is now taking place that could see Afghanistan disappear on the political map: in the future, for example, the Hindu Kush (the real northwestern frontier of the subcontinent) could form a border between Pushtunistan and a Greater Tajikistan. The Taliban, the up-shot of Pushtun nationalism, Islamic fervor, drug money, corrupt warlords, and hatred of the American occupation, may, in the words of Asian specialist Selig Harrison, merely be the vehicle for this tran-sition that is too broad and too grand to be in any way deterred by a foreign military run by impatient civilians back in Washington.

But there is another reality to counter this one: one that eschews such determinism. The fact that Afghanistan is larger than Iraq with a more dispersed population is basically meaningless, since 65 per-cent of the country lives within thirty-five miles of the main road system, which approximates the old medieval caravan routes, making only 80 out of 342 districts key to centralized control. Afghanistan has been governed more or less from the center since Ahmad Khan's time: Kabul, if not always a point of authority, was at least a point of arbitration. Especially between the early 1930s and the early 1970s, Afghanistan experienced moderate and constructive government under the constitutional monarchy of Zahir Shah, a descendant of Ahmad Khan. The major cities were united by a highway system on which it was safe to travel, even as malaria was on the point of eradication through estimable health and development programs. Toward the end of this period, I hitchhiked and rode local buses across Afghanistan, never felt threatened, and was able to send books and clothes back home through functioning post offices. There was, too, a strong Afghan national identity distinct from that of Iran or Pakistan or the Soviet Union. A fragile webwork of tribes it might have been, but it was also developing as more than just a buffer state. Pushtunistan might be a reality, but as in the way of dual citizenship, so very definitely is Afghanistan. Blame for the three coup d'états in Kabul in the 1970s that led to the country's seemingly never-ending agony of violence rests as much with a great and contiguous power, the Soviet Union, as with the Afghans. As part of a process to firmly secure the country within its sphere of influence, the Soviets unwittingly destabilized Afghan politics, which led to their December 1979 invasion. For Afghanistan, as a geographical buffer between the Iranian plateau, the Central Asian steppes, and the Indian Subcontinent, is breathtakingly strategic, and thus has been coveted by not just Russians, but also by Iranians and Pakistanis, even as Indian policymakers have been obsessed with it.

An Afghanistan that falls under Taliban sway threatens to create a succession of radicalized Islamic societies from the Indian-Pakistani border to Central Asia. This would be, in effect, a Greater Pakistan, giving Pakistan's Inter-Services Intelligence Directorate the ability to create a clandestine empire composed of the likes of Jallaluddin Haqqani, Gulbuddin Hekmatyar, and Lashkar-e-Taiba: able to confront India in the manner that Hezbollah and Hamas confront Israel. Conversely, an Afghanistan at peace and governed more or less liberally from Kabul would give New Delhi the ability to extricate itself from its historical nemesis on its northwestern frontier, as well as to challenge Pakistan on both its western and eastern borders. That is why during the 1980s India supported the Soviet puppet regime in Kabul of Mohammed Najibullah, which was secular and even liberal compared with some of the pro-Pakistani Islamist mujahidin trying to topple it: for the same reason India now supports Hamid Karzai's Kabul government.

A stable and reasonably moderate Afghanistan becomes truly the hub of not just southern Central Asia, but of Eurasia in general. Mackinder's Heartland exists in terms of the "convergence" of interests of Russia, China, India, and Iran in favor of transport corridors through Central Asia. And the most powerful drivers of Eurasian trade routes are the Chinese and Indian economies. Estimates for overland Indian trade across Central Asia to European and Middle Eastern markets foresee a growth of over $100 billion annually. It is only because Afghanistan remains at war that New Delhi is not connected by trucks, trains, and trans-Caspian ships to Istanbul and Tbilisi; or to Almaty and Tashkent by road and rail. Nevertheless, India has contributed significantly to building Afghanistan's road network, along with Iran and Saudi Arabia. The Indian-funded Zaranj–Delaram highway connects western Afghanistan to the Iranian port of Chah Bahar on the Arabian Sea.[25] Indians can taste the benefits that a quiescent Afghanistan can bring them, even as it has been violent for more than three decades. For a quiescent Afghanistan would spur road, rail, and pipeline construction not only in all directions across Afghanistan, but across Pakistan, too, and therein lies the ultimate solution to Pakistan's own instability. Though a region at peace benefits India most of all, because its economy dwarfs that of any other state save for China.

But that is not the situation that currently obtains. For now, the Greater Indian Subcontinent features among the least stable geopolitics in the world. The register of empires and invasions constitutes a living history because of its relevance to deep-seated insecurities and political problems of today. In many ways, Greater India is like a map of early modern Europe, only worse because of nuclear weapons. In early modern Europe, there were competing ethnic and national groups that were in the process of congealing into bureaucratic states, even as they were engaged in complex balance of power arrangements that because of their frequent interactions and subsequent miscalculations broke down occasionally into open warfare. Modern nationalism was in a young and vigorous phase, as it is in South Asia today. But unlike the multipolarity of early modern Europe, South Asia evinces a bipolar struggle between India and Pakistan, with Afghanistan as one battleground, and the disputed Himalayan state of Kashmir as another one. Unlike the bipolarity of the superpowers, however, there is nothing cool, dispassionate, or ritualistic about this conflict. This is not a clash of ideologies in which the opposing parties have no religious or historical hatred for each other, and are separated by the wide berth of a hemisphere and Arctic ice. This is a clash between a Hindu-majority, albeit secular, state and a Muslim one, both in full-blooded phases of modern nationalism, and separated by a crowded, common border, with capitals and major cities nearby. Less than two hundred miles separate Pakistan's Indus River heartland from northern India's Ganges River heartland.[26] In addition to everything else about this geography, it is a closed and claustrophobic one, the kind that Paul Bracken describes well in his cogitation of a new nuclear age.

India desperately wants to escape from this geography and from this history. Its very competition and fixation with China forms an element of this escape. India's rivalry with China is not like the one with Pakistan at all: it is more abstract, less emotional, and (far more significantly) less volatile. And it is a rivalry with no real history behind it.

It has been nearly half a century since India fought a limited war with China over a disputed Himalayan border, in which combat occurred at altitudes of fourteen thousand feet in the Aksai Chin region near Kashmir in the northwest and in Arunachal Pradesh near Bhutan in the northeast. The background to this 1962 war, in which over 2,000 soldiers were killed and 2,744 wounded, was the 1959 uprising in Tibet that sent the Dalai Lama into exile in India, following the 1950 Chinese invasion of Tibet. An independent or autonomous Tibet that was even vaguely pro-Indian would make Chinese strategists exceedingly nervous. Given the tensions of the Tibet crisis, China saw the establishment of Indian outposts north of disputed border lines as a casus belli, and in one month of fighting in the autumn overran Indian forces. Neither side deployed its navy or air force, and so the fighting was limited to remote regions where few people lived, as opposed to the Indian-Pakistani border, that in addition to passing through swamps and deserts, cuts through the agriculturally rich Punjab inhabited by millions.

The Indo-Chinese border is still in some areas a matter of dispute. The Chinese have built roads and airfields throughout Tibet, and India now falls into the arc of operations of Chinese fighter pilots, even as the Indian air force is the world's fourth largest, with over 1,300 aircraft spread over sixty bases. Indian satellites and reconnaissance aircraft provide intelligence on Chinese troop movements in Tibet. Then there is the rise of both countries' navies. The rise of the Chinese navy was covered in the preceding chapter. Because India has no equivalent of the Mediterranean, no enclosed seas and clusters of islands to lure sailors, even as the earth is warm and productive, India until recently has been more or less a land-bound nation framed against the open ocean. But that has suddenly changed with advances in military technology that have compressed oceanic geography, and with the development of the Indian economy, which can finance major shipbuilding and acquisitions. Another factor driving India seaward is the threat of China itself, as China's own naval aspirations move it beyond the Western Pacific into the Indian Ocean.

China has been helping to build or upgrade ports around India: in Kyaukpyu, Burma; Chittagong, Bangladesh; Hambantota, Sri Lanka; and Gwadar, Pakistan. In all of these countries China is providing substantial military and economic aid, and political support. China, as we know, already has a great merchant fleet and aspirations for a blue-water oceanic navy that will guard its interests and protect its trade routes between the hydrocarbon-rich Middle East and China's Pacific coast. This is occurring at the same time that India has aspirations for a Monroe Doctrine–style presence throughout the Indian Ocean from southern Africa to Australia. The greatly overlapping naval spheres of interest aggravate the border issues in the Himalayan north that are still outstanding. China is merely seeking to protect its own sea lines of communications with friendly, state-of-the-art harbors along the way. But India feels surrounded. The futuristic possibility of a Pakistani-Chinese naval center of operations near the entrance to the Persian Gulf in Gwadar has led to the expansion of the Indian naval port of Karwar on the Arabian Sea. The port and energy pipelines China is building at Kyaukpyu in Burma have caused India to initiate its own port and energy complex at Sittwe, fifty miles to the north, as India and China quicken their competition for routes and resources in western Indochina.

Still, one can only repeat, the Indian-Chinese rivalry represents a new struggle without the force of history behind it. The interactions that India and China have had in the distant past have usually been productive: most famously the spread of Buddhism from India to China in middle and late antiquity, as Buddhism went on to become the established religion of the Tang Dynasty. Despite the issue of Tibet, in which Tibetan autonomy or independence is in India's geopolitical interest but clearly harmful to that of China, the high wall of the Himalayas essentially cuts the two countries' populations off from each other. Only in recent decades, as indigenous militaries in the East have developed sea, air, and missile power, has a new Eurasian-wide geography of conflict come sharply into focus. The death of distance, much more than civilizational divides, is what ails India-China relations today. Only Indian policy elites worry about China, while the problem of Pakistan consumes the entire country, northern India especially. Moreover, India and China constitute among the world's most dynamic and complementary trading relationships. In a way, the tension between India and China illustrates the problems of success: the momentous economic development that both New Delhi and Beijing can now utilize for military purposes, especially for expensive air and naval platforms. Certainly, the new India-China rivalry richly demonstrates Bracken's point that the technologies of war and wealth creation go hand in hand, and the finite size of the earth is increasingly a force for instability, as military hardware and software shrink mileage on the geopolitical map.

To wit, for the first few decades following the Cold War, India and China had relatively low-tech ground forces that were content to watch their own borders and to serve as bulwarks for national consolidation. Thus, they did not threaten each other. But as planes, missiles, and warships entered their military inventories, even as their armies became more expeditionary, suddenly they saw each other at opposite sides of a new battlespace. This is not only true of India and China, but of states across the broad sweep of Eurasia—Israel, Syria, Iran, Pakistan, North Korea, and so on, who are in a new and deathly geographical embrace of overlapping missile ranges.

Behold, then, the Indian Subcontinent. Bounded by seas and mountains, it is still internally vast, and its lack of a natural basis for early political unity and organization shows up still, for China remains better organized and more efficiently governed than India, despite China's lack of democracy. China adds more miles of highways per year than India has in total. Indian ministries are overbearing and weak reeds compared to China's. China may be wracked by strikes and demonstrations, but India is wracked by violent insurrections; notably that of the Maoist-trending Naxalites in the central and eastern portions of the country. In this regard, Fairgrieve's description of a "less advanced" civilization compared to some external ones still holds.[27]

He who sits in Delhi, with his back to Muslim Central Asia, must worry still about unrest up on the plateaus to the northwest. The United States will draw down its troops in Afghanistan, but India will still have to live with the results, and therefore remain intimately engaged. India is faced with a conundrum. Its great power status in the new century will be enhanced by its very political and military competition with China, even as it remains pinned down by frontiers with weak and semi-dysfunctional states inside the subcontinent. We have discussed Afghanistan and Pakistan, but there are Nepal and Bangladesh, too, to momentarily consider.

Following the dismantling of its monarchy and the coming to power of former Maoist insurgents, the Nepalese government barely controls the countryside where 85 percent of its people live. Never having been colonized, Nepal did not inherit a strong bureaucratic tradition from the British. Despite the aura bequeathed by the Himalayas, the bulk of Nepal's population live in the dank and humid lowlands along the barely policed border with India. I have traveled through this region: it is in many ways indistinguishable from the Gangetic plain. If the Nepalese government cannot increase state capacity, the state itself could gradually dissolve. Bangladesh, even more so than Nepal, has no geographical defense to marshal as a state: it is the same ruler-flat, aquatic landscape of paddy fields and scrub on both sides of the border with India; the border posts, as I have discovered, are run-down, disorganized, ramshackle affairs. This artificially shaped blotch of territory—in succession Bengal, East Bengal, East Pakistan, and Bangladesh—could metamorphose yet again amid the gale forces of regional politics, Muslim religious extremism, and climate change. Like Pakistan, the history of Bangladesh is one of military and civilian regimes, few of which have functioned well enough. Millions of Bangladeshi refugees have already crossed the border into India as illegals. And yet the Bangladeshi government struggles on, improving its performance as of this writing. It could yet succeed as a hub of overland trade and pipeline routes connecting India, China, and a future free and democratic Burma.

The subcontinent from early antiquity was politically divided, and that is what ails it still. Now let us look at the extreme north, where the Karakoram meet the Himalayas. Here is the territory of Kashmir, crammed in between Pakistan, Afghanistan, India, and China. The northern areas of the Karakoram Range, with the town of Gilgit, are held by Pakistan and claimed by India, as is the slice of Azad ("Free") Kashmir to the west. The Ladakh Range in the heart of Kashmir, with the towns of Srinagar and Jammu, are administered by India and claimed by Pakistan, as is the Siachen Glacier to the north. To the far north and northeast lie the Shaksam valley and Aksai Chin, administered by China and claimed by India. Furthermore, the Indian state of Jammu and Kashmir (the Ladakh Range) has a Muslim majority of 75 percent, a fact that has helped fuel jihadist rebellions for years. The late Osama bin Laden in his pronouncements railed against Hindu India's domination of Kashmir. And yet much of Kashmir is high-altitude, uninhabitable badlands. But wars have been fought on these territories and over them, and may be fought still. The Chinese fought India in 1962 because they wanted to build a road from Xinjiang to Tibet through eastern Kashmir. India fought China to obstruct the common border between China and Pakistan.

Kashmir, like Palestine, because of the effect of cyberspace and new media, could still fire hatred among millions, putting a solution to its tangle of problems further out of reach. For the very technologies that defeat geography also have the capability of enhancing geography's importance. The subcontinent is a blunt geographical fact, but defining its borders will go on indefinitely.

Whereas Chinese dynasties of old almost completely fall within the current borders of China, the dynasties to which India is heir, as we have seen, do not. Thus, India looks to Afghanistan and its other shadow zones with less serenity than does China to its shadow zones. India is a regional power to the degree that it is entrapped by this geography; it is a potential great power to the degree that it can move beyond it.

Chapter XIII

THE IRANIAN PIVOT

As University of Chicago scholar William McNeill has told us, India, China, and Greece all lay "on the fringes of the anciently civilized world," protected as they were by mountains, deserts, and sheer distance.[1] Of course, this protection was partial, for as we know, Greece was ravaged by Persia, China by the Mongols and the Turkic steppe people, and India by a surfeit of Muslim invaders. Nevertheless, geography provided enough of a barrier for three great and unique civilizations to take root. Lying in the immense space between these civilizations, as noted in an earlier chapter, was what McNeill's Chicago colleague Marshall Hodgson referred to as the Oikoumene, an antique Greek term for the "inhabited quarter" of the world: this is Herodotus's world, the parched temperate zone of the Afro-Asian landmass stretching from North Africa to the margins of western China, a belt of territory Hodgson also calls Nile-to-Oxus.[2]

Hodgson's vision captures brilliantly several key and contradic-

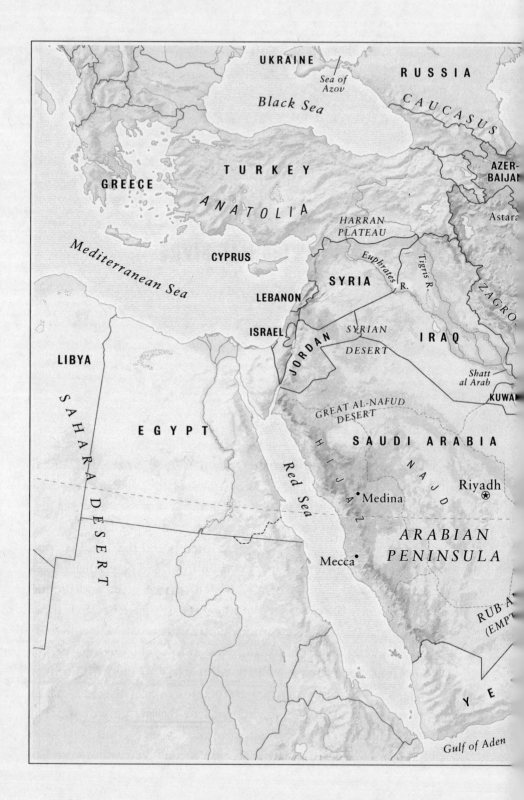

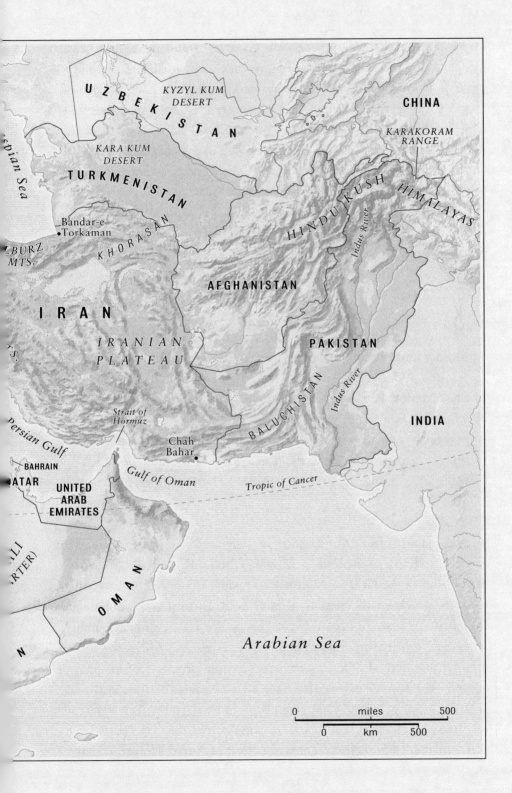

UZBEKISTAN

KYZYL KUM
DESERT

CHINA

KARAKORAM
RANGE

KARA KUM
DESERT

TURKMENISTAN

aspian Sea

HINDU KUSH

HIMALAYAS

Bandar-e
Torkaman

KHORASAN

Indus River

LBURZ
MTS.

IRAN

AFGHANISTAN

IRANIAN
PLATEAU

PAKISTAN

T.S.

BALUCHISTAN

Indus River

Strait of
Hormuz

INDIA

ersian Gulf

BAHRAIN

Chah
Bahar

ATAR

UNITED
ARAB
EMIRATES

Gulf of Oman

Tropic of Cancer

ALI
RTER)

N

OMAN

Arabian Sea

0   miles   500

0   km   500

tory facts: that the Oikoumene—the Greater Middle East—is an easily definable zone existing between Greece, China, and India, distinctly separate from all three, even as it has had pivotal influence on each of them, so that the relationships are extremely organic; and that whereas the Greater Middle East is united by Islam and the legacies of horse and camel nomadism—as opposed to the crop agriculture of China and India—it is also deeply divided within by rivers, oases, and highlands, with great ramifications for political organization to this day. The disparity between the Greater Middle East and China, say, is especially telling. John King Fairbank, the late Harvard China expert, writes:

> The cultural homogeneity of ancient China as revealed by the archaeological record contrasts remarkably with the multiplicity and diversity of peoples, states, and cultures in the ancient Middle East. Beginning about 3000 B.C., Egyptians, Sumerians, Semites, Akkadians, Amorites . . . Assyrians, Phoenicians, Hittites, Medes, Persians, and others jostled one another in a bewildering flux of . . . warfare and politics. The record is one of pluralism with a vengeance. Irrigation helped agriculture in several centers—the Nile, the Tigris-Euphrates, and the Indus valleys. . . . Languages, writing systems, and religions proliferated.[3]

This classical legacy of division remains with us most profoundly across the chasm of the millennia, and is therefore crucial to the volatile politics of the Greater Middle East today. While Arabic has come to unify much of the region, Persian and Turkish predominate in the northern plateau regions, and this is not to mention the many languages of Central Asia and the Caucasus. As Hodgson shows, many individual Middle Eastern states, while products of arbitrary, colonial-era map drawing, also have a sturdy basis in antiquity, that is, in geography. Yet the very multiplicity of these states, as well as the religious, ideological, and democratizing forces that operate within them, further reify their designation as part of Alfred Thayer Mahan's debatable ground. Indeed, the supreme fact of twenty-first-century world politics is that the most geographically central area of the dry-land earth is also the most unstable.

In the Middle East we have, in the words of the scholars Geoffrey Kemp and Robert E. Harkavy, a "vast quadrilateral," where Europe, Russia, Asia, and Africa intersect: with the Mediterranean Sea and the Sahara Desert to the west; the Black Sea, the Caucasus, the Caspian Sea, and the Central Asian steppe-land to the north; the Hindu Kush and the Indian Subcontinent to the east; and the Indian Ocean to the south.[4] Unlike China or Russia, this quadrilateral does not constitute one massive state; nor, like the Indian Subcontinent, is it even overwhelmingly dominated by one state, which might provide it with at least some semblance of coherence. Nor is it, like Europe, a group of states within highly regulated alliance structures (NATO, the European Union). Rather, the Middle East is characterized by a disorderly and bewildering array of kingdoms, sultanates, theocracies, democracies, and military-style autocracies, whose common borders look formed as if by an unsteady knife. To no surprise of the reader, this whole region, which includes North Africa, the Horn of Africa, Central Asia, and, to a degree, the Indian Subcontinent, constitutes, in effect, one densely packed axis of instability, where continents, historic road networks, and sea lanes converge. What is more, this region comprises 70 percent of the world's proven oil reserves and 40 percent of its natural gas reserves.[5] Too, this region is prone to all the pathologies mentioned by Yale professor Paul Bracken: extremist ideologies, crowd psychology, overlapping missile ranges, and profit-driven mass media as dedicated to their point of view as Fox News is to its. In fact, with the exception of the Korean Peninsula, nuclear proliferation is more of a factor in the Middle East than in any other area.

The Middle East is also in the midst of a youth bulge, in which 65 percent of the population is under the age of thirty. Between 1995 and 2025, the populations of Iraq, Jordan, Kuwait, Oman, Syria, the West Bank, Gaza Strip, and Yemen will have doubled. Young populations, as we have seen in the Arab Spring, are the most likely to force upheaval and change. The next generation of Middle Eastern rulers, whether in Iran or in the Arab states, will not have the luxury to rule as autocratically as their predecessors, even as democratic experiments in the region show that while elections are easily accomplished, stable and liberal democratic orders are processes that can take generations to refine. In the Middle East, youth bulges and the communications revolution have ignited a string of messy, Mexico-style scenarios (the replacement of decisive one-party states with more chaotic multifactional and multiparty ones), but without Mexico's level of institutionalization, which, as limited as it is, remains ahead of most countries in the Middle East. Dealing with an authentically democratic Mexico has been harder for the United States than with a Mexico under effective one-party rule. Bristling with advanced armaments, to say nothing of weapons of mass destruction, the Middle East of the next few decades will make the recent era of Arab-Israeli state conflict seem almost like a romantic, sepia-toned chapter of the Cold War and Post Cold War, in which calculations of morality and strategic advantage were relatively clear-cut.

Hodgson's Nile-to-Oxus essentially means Egypt to Central Asia, with Egypt as shorthand for all of North Africa. This terminology comprises both the southern, desert-and-plains component of the Middle East, which is Arab, and the northern mountainous tableland, which is non-Arab, and which begins by the Black Sea and ends by the Indian Subcontinent. The sprawling northern plateau region might also be dubbed Bosporus-to-Indus. Bosporus-to-Indus has been heavily influenced by migrations from Central Asia; Nile-to-Oxus by that, too, as well as by heavy sea traffic in the Mediterranean, the Red Sea, and the Indian Ocean. The fact that the Middle East is the intersection point of continents, with an internal geography more intricate than any save Europe, but vaster and spread across twice as many time zones as Europe, makes it necessary for the sake of this discussion to disaggregate the region into constituent parts. Obviously, electronic communications and air travel have overcome geography in recent times, so that crises are defined by political interactions across the entire region. For example, the Israelis intercept a flotilla carrying relief supplies for Gaza and crowds in Turkey, Iran, and throughout the Arab world are inflamed. A fruit and vegetable vendor in south-central Tunisia immolates himself and not only does Tunisia erupt in demonstrations against dictatorial rule, but also much of the Arab world. Still, much can be discerned by studying the map and its inherent divisions.

When looking at a map of the Middle East, three geographical features stand out above others: the Arabian Peninsula, the Iranian plateau, and the Anatolian land bridge.

The Arabian Peninsula is dominated by the kingdom of Saudi Arabia, yet it also includes other important countries. In fact, Saudi Arabia, with a population of only 28.7 million, contains much less than half of all the peninsula's inhabitants. But Saudi Arabia's annual population growth rate is nearly 2 percent: if that high rate continues, its population will double in a few decades, putting enormous strain on resources, given that the country is located on steppe-land and water-starved desert. Close to 40 percent of Saudis are under fifteen years of age. Forty percent of Saudi Arabia's young men are unemployed. The political pressures arising from such a young population for jobs and education will be immense. Saudi Arabia's power derives not from the size of its population, which in fact is a liability, but from the fact that it leads the world in oil reserves, with 262 billion barrels, and is fourth in the world in natural gas reserves, with 240 trillion cubic feet.

The geographical cradle of the Saudi state, and of the extreme Sunni religious movement known as Wahhabism associated with it, is Najd: an arid region in the center of the Arabian Peninsula, lying between the Great al-Nafud Desert to the north and the Rub al-Khali or Empty Quarter to the south: to the east is the coastal strip of the Persian Gulf; to the west the mountains of Hijaz. The word "Najd" means upland. And its general elevation varies from five thousand feet in the west to under 2,500 feet in the east. The late-nineteenth-century British explorer and Arabist Charles M. Doughty described Najd thus:

> The shrieking suany and noise of tumbling water is, as it were, the lamentable voice of a rainless land in all Nejd villages. Day and night this labour of the water may not be intermitted. The strength of oxen cannot profitably draw wells of above three or four fathoms and, if God had not made the camel, Nejd, they say, had been without inhabitant.[6]

Najd is truly the heart of what Hodgson called camel-based nomadism. It was from the bastion of Najd that Wahhabi fanatics in recent centuries set off on raids in all directions. Though the Hijaz, adjacent to the Red Sea, held the holy cities of Mecca and Medina, the Wahhabist Najdis considered the pilgrimages to the various holy places (with the exception of the *haj* to the Kaaba in Mecca) to be a form of paganism. While the holy cities of Mecca and Medina connote Muslim religiosity in the Western mind, the truth is somewhat the opposite: it is the very pilgrimage of Muslims from all over the Islamic world that lends a certain cosmopolitanism to these holy cities and to the surrounding Hijaz. The Hijaz, "with its young, urbane, religiously varied population, has never fully accommodated to Saudi and Wahabi rule," writes career CIA officer Bruce Riedel.[7] The people of the Hijaz look to the Red Sea, Egypt, and Syria for cultural sustenance, not to the austere desert of Najd with its Wahhabis. The core fact of this history is that the Wahhabis were unable to hold permanently the peripheries of the Arabian Peninsula, even as their adversaries found it equally difficult to hold the heartland of Najd. The Saudi Arabia that exists today, while a tribute to the vision and skills of one man in the first half of the twentieth century, Abdul Aziz ibn Saud—the Najdi who conquered Hijaz in 1925—holds true to this geographical design.[8] The state is focused on Najd and its capital, Riyadh, and does not include the seaboard skeikhdoms of the Persian Gulf, nor Oman and Yemen.

The fundamental danger to Najd-based Saudi Arabia is Yemen. Though Yemen has only a quarter of Saudi Arabia's land area, its population is almost as large, so that the all-important demographic core of the Arabian Peninsula is in its mountainous southwest corner, where sweeping basalt plateaus, rearing up into sand castle formations and volcanic plugs, embrace a network of oases densely inhabited since antiquity. The Ottoman Turks and the British never really controlled Yemen. Like Nepal and Afghanistan, Yemen, because it was never truly colonized, did not develop strong bureaucratic institutions. When I traveled in the Saudi-Yemeni border area some years back it was crowded with pickup trucks filled with armed young men, loyal to this sheikh or that, even as the presence of the Yemeni government was negligible. Estimates of the number of firearms within Yemen's borders go as high as eighty million—almost three for every Yemeni. I will never forget what an American military expert told me in the Yemeni capital of Sana'a: "In Yemen you've got well over twenty million aggressive, commercial-minded, and well-armed people, all extremely hardworking compared with the Saudis next door. It's the future, and it terrifies the hell out of the government in Riyadh."

Saudi Arabia is synonymous with the Arabian Peninsula in the way that India is synonymous with the subcontinent. But while India is heavily populated throughout, Saudi Arabia constitutes a geographically nebulous network of oases separated by vast waterless tracts. Thus, highways and domestic air links are crucial to Saudi Arabia's cohesion. While India is built on an idea of democracy and religious pluralism, Saudi Arabia is built on loyalty to an extended family. And yet whereas India is virtually surrounded by semi-dysfunctional states, Saudi Arabia's borders disappear into harmless desert to the north, and are shielded by (in the most part, Bahrain excepted) sturdy, well-governed, self-contained sheikhdoms to the east and southeast: sheikhdoms that, in turn, are products of history and geography. It was because the territories of present-day Kuwait, Bahrain, Qatar, and the United Arab Emirates all lay along the trade route of the nineteenth century's greatest maritime power, Great Brit-

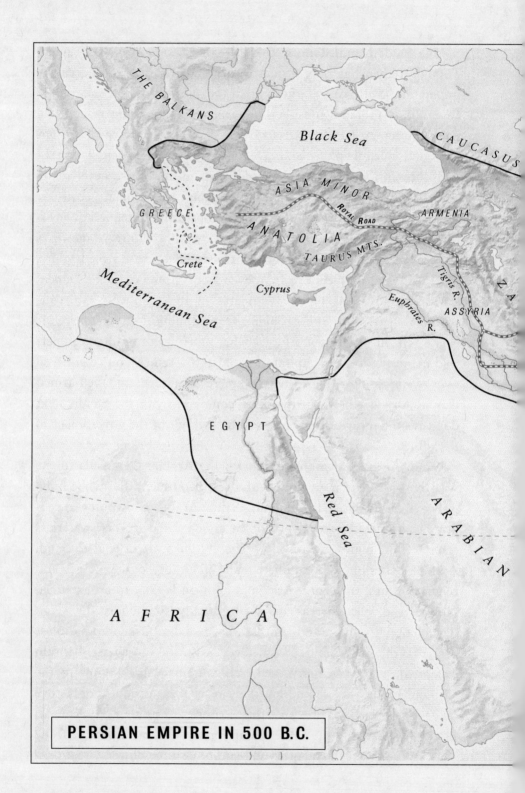

THE BALKANS

Black Sea

CAUCASUS

ASIA MINOR

GREECE

ANATOLIA

ARMENIA

ROYAL ROAD

TAURUS MTS.

ZA

Crete

Tigris R.

Cyprus

Euphrates R.

ASSYRIA

Mediterranean Sea

EGYPT

Red Sea

ARABIAN

AFRICA

PERSIAN EMPIRE IN 500 B.C.

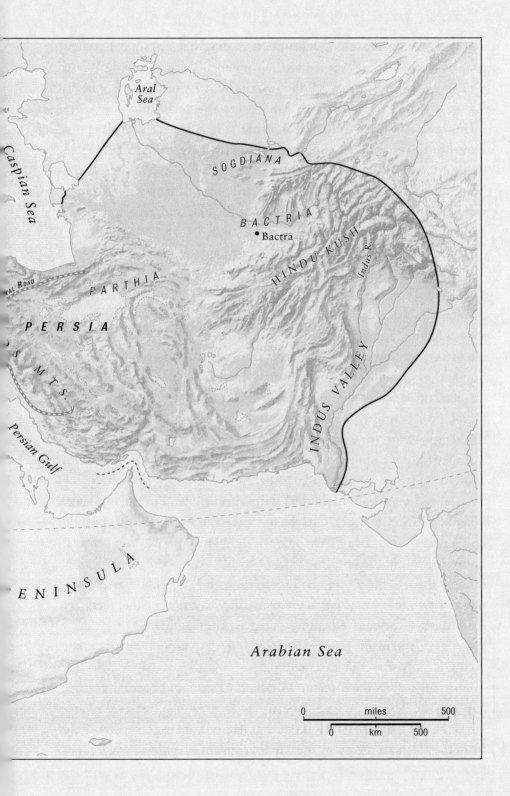

Caspian Sea

Aral
Sea

SOGDIANA

BACTRIA

• Bactra

HINDU-KUSH

Indus R.

AL ROAD

PARTHIA

PERSIA

S MTS.

INDUS VALLEY

Persian Gulf

ENINSULA

Arabian Sea

miles
0   500

km
0   500

ain, and particularly along its route to India, that Britain negotiated deals with its skeikhs that led to their independence following World War II. Large oil deposits tell the rest of the story of these "Eldorado States," in the words of British Arabist Peter Mansfield.[9]

In sum, within the Arabian Peninsula, it remains in the highly populous southwest where Saudi Arabia is really vulnerable: from where weapons, explosives, and the narcotic leaf qat flow in from across the Yemeni border. The future of teeming, tribalized Yemen will go a long way to determining the future of Saudi Arabia, and geography perhaps more than ideas has much to do with it.

The Iranian plateau, on the other hand, is synonymous with only one country: Iran. Iran's population of 74 million is two and a half times that of Saudi Arabia, and is along with Turkey's and Egypt's the largest in the Middle East. Moreover, Iran has impressively gotten its population growth rate down to way below one percent, with only 22 percent of its population below the age of fifteen. Thus, Iran's population is not a burden like Saudi Arabia's, but an asset. One could argue that, for example, Turkey has an even bigger population, a similarly low population growth rate, and a higher literacy rate. Moreover, Turkey has a stable agricultural economy and is more industrialized than Iran. I will deal with Turkey later. For the moment, note that Turkey is situated to the northwest of Iran, closer to Europe and much further away from major Sunni Arab population centers. Turkey also is in the bottom ranks of hydrocarbon producers. Iran is number three in the world in oil reserves, with 133 billion barrels, but number two in natural gas reserves, with 970 trillion cubic feet. Yet it is Iran's locational advantage, just to the south of Mackinder's Heartland, and inside Spykman's Rimland, that, more than any other factor, is truly something to behold.

Virtually all of the Greater Middle East's oil and natural gas lies either in the Persian Gulf or the Caspian Sea regions. Just as shipping lanes radiate from the Persian Gulf, pipelines radiate and will radiate from the Caspian region to the Mediterranean, the Black Sea, China, and the Indian Ocean. The only country that straddles both energy-producing areas is Iran, stretching as it does from the Caspian to the Persian Gulf.[10] The Persian Gulf possesses by some accounts 55 percent of the world's crude oil reserves, and Iran dominates the whole Gulf, from the Shatt al Arab on the Iraqi border to the Strait of Hormuz 615 miles away. Because of its bays, inlets, coves, and islands—excellent places for hiding suicide, tanker-ramming speedboats—Iran's coastline inside the Strait of Hormuz is 1,356 nautical miles; the next longest, that of the United Arab Emirates, is only 733 nautical miles. Iran also has 300 miles of Arabian Sea frontage, including the port of Chah Bahar near the Pakistani border. This makes Iran vital to providing warm water access to the landlocked Central Asian countries of the former Soviet Union. Meanwhile, the Iranian coast of the Caspian in the far north, wreathed by thickly forested mountains, stretches for nearly four hundred miles from Astara in the west, on the border with former Soviet Azerbaijan, around to Bandar-e Torkaman in the east, by the border with Turkmenistan.

A look at the relief map of Eurasia shows something more. The broad back of the Zagros Mountains sweeps down through Iran from Anatolia in the northwest to Baluchistan in the southeast. To the west of the Zagros range, the roads are all open to Mesopotamia. When British area specialist and travel writer Freya Stark explored Iranian Luristan in the Zagros Mountains in 1934, she naturally based herself out of Baghdad, not Tehran.[11] To the east and northeast, the roads are open to Khorasan and the Kara Kum (Black Sand) and Kyzyl Kum (Red Sand) deserts of Turkmenistan and Uzbekistan respectively. For just as Iran straddles the rich energy fields of both the Persian Gulf and the Caspian Sea, it also straddles the Middle East proper and Central Asia. No Arab country can make that claim (just as no Arab country sits astride two energy-producing areas). In fact, the Mongol invasion of Iran, which killed hundreds of thousands of people at a minimum, and destroyed the *qanat* irrigation system, was that much more severe precisely because of Iran's Central Asian prospect. Iranian influence in the former Soviet republics of the Caucasus and Central Asia is potentially vast, even as these same former Soviet

republics, because of ethnic compatriots in northern Iran, could theo-
retically destabilize the Iranian state. Whereas Azerbaijan on Iran's
northwestern border contains roughly eight million Azeri Turks, there
are twice that number in Iran's neighboring provinces of Azerbaijan
and Tehran. The Azeris were cofounders of the Iranian polity. The first
Shiite shah of Iran (Ismail in 1501) was an Azeri Turk. There are important Azeri businessmen and ayatollahs in Iran. The point is that
whereas Iran's influence to the west in nearby Turkey and the Arab
world is well established, its influence to the north and east is equally
profound; and if the future brings less repressive regimes both in Iran
and in the southern, Islamic tier of the former Soviet Union, Iran's influence could deepen still with more cultural and political interactions.

Moreover, Iran, as we know from the headlines, has had, at least
through 2011, an enviable political position by the Mediterranean: in
Hamas-controlled Gaza, Hezbollah-controlled southern Lebanon,
and Alawite Syria. Yet one interpretation of history and geography
suggests an Iranian breakout in all directions. In the palace of the
sixth-century Sassanian Persian emperors at Ctesiphon, south of
modern-day Baghdad, there were empty seats beneath the royal
throne for the emperors of Rome and China, and for the leader of the
Central Asian nomads, in case those rulers came as suppliants to
the court of the king of kings.[12] The pretensions of Iranian rulers have
not lessened with modernity; in this way the clerics are much like the
late shah. That is ultimately why Moscow must tread carefully regarding its relations with Iran. A century ago Russia had a zone of
influence in northern Iran. Though Russia is comparatively weaker
now, proximity and contiguity do matter.

Iran, furthermore, is not some twentieth-century contrivance of
family and religious ideology like Saudi Arabia, bracketed as it is by
arbitrary borders. Iran corresponds almost completely with the Iranian plateau—"the Castile of the Near East," in Princeton historian
Peter Brown's phrase—even as the dynamism of its civilization reaches
far beyond it. Iran was the ancient world's first superpower. The Persian Empire, even as it besieged Greece, "uncoiled, like a dragon's
tail . . . as far as the Oxus, Afghanistan and the Indus valley," writes

Brown.[13] W. Barthold, the great Russian geographer of the turn of the twentieth century, concurs, situating Greater Iran between the Euphrates and the Indus, and identifying the Kurds and Afghans as essentially Iranian peoples.[14]

Of the ancient peoples of the Near East, only the Hebrews and the Iranians "have texts and cultural traditions that have survived to modern times," writes the linguist Nicholas Ostler.[15] Persian (Farsi) was not replaced by Arabic, like so many other tongues, and is in the same form today as it was in the eleventh century, even as it has adopted the Arabic script. Iran has a far more venerable record as a nation-state and urbane civilization than most places in the Arab world and all the places in the Fertile Crescent, including Mesopotamia and Palestine. There is nothing artificial about Iran, in other words: the very competing power centers within its clerical regime indicate a greater level of institutionalization than almost anywhere in the region save for Israel and Turkey. Just as the Middle East is the quadrilateral for Afro-Eurasia, that is, for the World-Island, Iran is the Middle East's very own universal joint. Mackinder's pivot, rather than in the Central Asian steppe-land, should be moved to the Iranian plateau just to the south. It is no surprise that Iran is increasingly being wooed by both India and China, whose navies may at some point in the twenty-first century share dominance with that of the United States in the Eurasian sea lanes. Though Iran is much smaller in size and population than those two powers, or Russia or Europe for that matter, Iran, because it is in possession of the key geography of the Middle East—in terms of location, population, and energy resources—is, therefore, fundamental to global geopolitics.

There is, too, what British historian Michael Axworthy calls the "Idea of Iran," which, as he explains, is as much about culture and language as about race and territory.[16] Iran, he means, is a civilizational attractor, much as ancient Greece and China were, pulling other peoples and languages into its linguistic orbit: the essence of soft power, in other words, and so emblematic of McNeill's concept of one civilization and culture influencing another. Dari, Tajik, Urdu, Hindi, Bengali, and Iraqi Arabic are all either variants of Persian or significantly influenced by it. That is, one can travel from Baghdad to Calcutta and remain inside a Persian cultural realm of sorts. A brief scan of Iranian history, with an emphasis on old maps, further clarifies this dynamism.

Greater Iran began back in 700 B.C. with the Medes, an ancient Iranian people who established, with the help of the Scythians, an independent state in northwestern Iran. By 600 B.C., this empire reached from central Anatolia to the Hindu Kush (Turkey to Afghanistan), as well as south to the Persian Gulf. In 549 B.C., Cyrus (the Great), a prince from the Persian house of Achaemenes, captured the Median capital of Ecbatana (Hamadan) in western Iran, and went on a further bout of conquest. The map of the Achaemenid Empire, governed from Persepolis (near Shiraz) in southern Iran, shows antique Persia at its apex, from the sixth to fourth centuries B.C. It stretched from Thrace and Macedonia in the northwest, and from Libya and Egypt in the southwest, all the way to the Punjab in the east; and from the Transcaucasus and the Caspian and Aral seas in the north to the Persian Gulf and the Arabian Sea in the south. This was Bosporus-to-Indus, including the Nile. No empire up to that point in world history had matched it. While the fifth-century B.C. wars between Persia and Greece dominate Western attitudes toward ancient Iran, with our sympathies lying with the Westernized Greeks as opposed to the Asiatic Persians, it is also the case that, as Hodgson notes, the Oikoumene, under the relative peace, tolerance, and sovereignty of Achaemenid Persia and later empires, provided a sturdy base for the emergence and prospering of the great confessional religions.[17]

"The Parthians," Axworthy writes, "exemplified the best of Iranian genius—the recognition, acceptance, and tolerance of the complexity of the cultures . . . over which they ruled."[18] Headquartered in the northeastern Iranian region of Khorasan and the adjacent Kara Kum, and speaking an Iranian language, the Parthians ruled between the third century B.C. and the third century A.D., generally from Syria and Iraq to central Afghanistan and Pakistan, including Armenia and Turkmenistan. Thus, rather than Bosporus-to-Indus or Nile-to-Oxus like Achaemenid Persia, the Parthian Empire constitutes a more realistic vision of a Greater Iran for the twenty-first century. And this is not necessarily bad. For the Parthian Empire was extremely decentralized, a zone of strong influence rather than of outright control, which leaned heavily on art, architecture, and administrative practices inherited from the Greeks. As for the Iran of today, it is no secret that the clerical regime is formidable, but demographic, economic, and political forces are equally dynamic, and key segments of the population are restive.

The medieval record both cartographically and linguistically follows from the ancient one, though in more subtle ways perhaps. In the eighth century the political locus of the Arab world shifted eastward from Syria to Mesopotamia: that is, from the Umayyad caliphs to the Abbasid ones. The Abbasid Caliphate at its zenith in the middle of the ninth century ruled from Tunisia eastward to Pakistan, and from the Caucasus and Central Asia southward to the Persian Gulf. Its capital was the new city of Baghdad, close upon the old Sassanid Persian capital of Ctesiphon; and Persian bureaucratic practices, which added whole new layers of hierarchy, undergirded this new imperium. The Abbasid Caliphate became more a symbol of an Iranian despotism than of an Arab sheikhdom. Some historians have labeled the Abbasid Caliphate the equivalent of the "cultural reconquest" of the Middle East by the Persians under the guise of Arab rulers.[19] The Abbasids succumbed to Persian practices just as the Umayyads, closer to Asia Minor, had succumbed to Byzantine ones. "Persian titles, Persian wines and wives, Persian mistresses, Persian songs, as well as Persian ideas and thoughts, won the day," writes historian Philip K. Hitti.[20] The Persians also helped determine medieval Baghdad's monumental brick architecture and circular ground plan.

"In the western imagination," writes Peter Brown of Princeton, "the Islamic [Abbasid] empire stands as the quintessence of an oriental power. Islam owed this crucial orientation neither to Muhammad nor to the adaptable conquerors of the seventh century, but to the massive resurgence of eastern, Persian traditions in the eighth and ninth centuries." It wasn't so much Charles Martel at Tours in 732 who "brought the Arab war machine to a halt," but the very foundation of Baghdad, which replaced the dynamism of Bedouin cavalry with that of an imperial and luxurious Persian administration.[21]

Not even the thirteenth-century Mongol conquest of Baghdad, which laid waste to Iraq, and particularly to its irrigation system (as it did in Iran), a devastation from which Iraq never completely recovered, could halt the vitality of Persian arts and letters. The poetry of Rumi, Iraqi, Sa'adi, and Hafez all prospered in the wake of Hulagu Khan's assault, which had reduced Mesopotamia to a malarial swamp. Nostalgic for their Sassanid ancestors, who had ruled an empire greater than their Parthian predecessors and almost equal to that of the Achaemenids, Persian artists and scholars embellished the intellectual and linguistic terrain of a succession of non-Persian empires—Abbasid, Ghaznavid, Seljuk, Mongol, and Mughal. Persian was the Mughal court language, as well as the diplomatic one for the Ottomans. In the medieval centuries, the Persians may not have ruled directly from Bosporus-to-Indus, as they did in antiquity, but they dominated literary life to the same extent. The "Iranian Empire of the Mind," as Axworthy calls it, was the potent idea that served to magnify Iran's geographically envious position, so that a Greater Iran was a historically natural phenomenon.[22] Arnold Toynbee poses this tantalizing hypothetical: if Tamerlane (Timur) had not turned his back on northern and central Eurasia and his arms against Iran in 1381, the relationship between Transoxiana and Russia might have been the "inverse" of what they actually became in modern times, with a state roughly the size of the Soviet Union ruled not by Russians from Moscow, but by Iranians ruling from Samarkand.[23]

As for Shiism, it is very much a component of this idea—despite the culturally bleak and oppressive aura projected by the Shiite clergy from 1979 through at least the first decade of the twenty-first century. While the arrival of the Mahdi in the form of the hidden Twelfth Imam means the end of injustice, and thus is a spur to radical activism, little else in Shiism necessarily inclines the clergy to play an overt political role; Shiism even has a quietest strain that acquiesces to the powers that be, and which is frequently informed by Sufism.[24] Witness the example set by Iraq's leading cleric of recent years, Ayatollah Ali Sistani, who only at pivotal moments makes a plea for political conciliation from behind the scenes. Precisely because of the symbiotic relationship between Iraq and Iran throughout history, with its basis in geography, it is entirely possible that in a post-revolutionary Iran, Iranians will look more toward the Shiite holy cities of Najaf and Karbala in Iraq for spiritual direction than toward their own holy city of Qom; or that Qom will adopt the quietism of Najaf and Karbala.

The French scholar Olivier Roy tells us that Shiism is historically an Arab phenomenon that came late to Iran, but which eventually led to the establishment of a clerical hierarchy for taking power. Shiism was further strengthened by the tradition of a strong and bureaucratic state that Iran has enjoyed since antiquity, relative to those of the Arab world, and which is, as we know, partly a gift of the spatial coherence of the Iranian plateau. The Safavids brought Shiism to Iran in the sixteenth century. Their name comes from their own militant Sufi order, the Safaviyeh, which had originally been Sunni. The Safavids were one of a number of horse-borne brotherhoods of mixed Turkish, Azeri, Georgian, and Persian origin in the late fifteenth century which occupied the mountainous plateau region between the Black and Caspian seas, where eastern Anatolia, the Caucasus, and northwestern Iran come together. In order to build a stable state on the Farsi-speaking Iranian plateau, these new sovereigns of eclectic linguistic and geographical origin adopted Twelver Shiism as the state religion, which awaits the return of the Twelfth Imam, a direct descendant of Muhammad, who is not dead but in occlusion.[25] This development was, of course, not preordained by history or geography, and depended greatly on various personalities and circumstances. Had, for example, the Ilkhanid ruler Oljaitu, the scion of a Mongol khanate, not converted to Twelver Shiism in the thirteenth century, the development of Shiism in northwestern Iran might have been different, and who knows how events might have transpired henceforth. In any case, Shiism had been gathering force among various Turkic orders in northwestern Iran, laying the groundwork for the emergence of Safavid Shah Ismail, who imposed Shiism in the wake of his conquests, and brought in Arab theologians from present-day southern Lebanon and Bahrain to form the nucleus of a state clergy.[26]

The Safavid Empire at its zenith stretched thereabouts from Anatolia and Syria-Mesopotamia to central Afghanistan and Pakistan—yet another variant of Greater Iran through history. Shiism was an agent of Iran's congealment as a modern nation-state, even as the Iranianization of non-Persian Shiite minorities during the sixteenth century also helped in this regard.[27] Iran might have been a great state and nation since antiquity, but the Safavids with their insertion of Shiism onto the Iranian plateau retooled Iran for the modern era.

Indeed, revolutionary Iran of the late twentieth and early twenty-first centuries is a fitting expression of this powerful and singular legacy. Of course, the rise of the ayatollahs has been a lowering event in the sense of the violence done to—and I do not mean to exaggerate—the voluptuous, sophisticated, and intellectually stimulating traditions of the Iranian past. (Persia—"that land of poets and roses!" exclaims the introductory epistle of James J. Morier's *The Adventures of Hajji Baba of Ispahan*.)[28] But comparison, it is famously said, is the beginning of all serious scholarship. Compared to the upheavals and revolutions in the Arab world during the early and middle phases of the Cold War, the regime ushered in by the 1978–1979 Iranian Revolution was striking in its vitality and modernity. The truth is, and this is something that goes directly back to the Achaemenids of antiquity, everything about the Iranian past and present is of a high quality, whether it is the dynamism of its empires from Cyrus to Mahmoud Ahmadinejad (who can deny the sheer Iranian talent for running terrorist networks in Lebanon, Gaza, and Iraq, which is, after all, an aspect of imperial rule!), or the political thought and writings of its Shiite clergy; or the complex efficiency of the bureaucracy and security services in cracking down on dissidents. Tehran's revolutionary order has constituted a richly developed governmental structure with a diffusion of power centers: it was never a crude one-man thugocracy like the kind Saddam Hussein ran in neighboring Arab Iraq. Olivier Roy tells us that the "originality" of the Iranian Revolution lies in the alliance between the clergy and the Islamist intelligentsia:

The Shiite clergy is incontestably more open to the non-Islamic corpus than the Sunni [Arab] ulamas. The ayatollahs are great readers (including of Marx and Feuerbach): there is something of the Jesuit or Dominican in them. Hence they combine clear philosophical syncretism with an exacting casuistic legalism. . . . The twofold culture of the Shiite clergy is striking: highly traditionalist . . . and yet very open to the modern world.[29]

In fact, it is this relatively advanced and modernist strain that makes the "Shiite imagination," in Roy's words, "more easily adaptable to the idea of revolution": an idea which, in turn, requires a sense of history and social justice combined with that of martyrdom. The Sunni Arab world, though it has had its reformers and modernizers, like Muhammad Abduh and Rashid Rida in the late nineteenth and early twentieth centuries, simply lacked for too long the exposure to Western political philosophers such as Hegel and Marx to the degree of Iran: whose mullahs, in the vein of Hegel and Marx, base their moral superiority on an understanding of the purpose of history. Unlike the conservatism of the Afghan mujahidin or the suffocating military regimes of the Arab world, revolutionary Iran in the 1980s saw itself as part of a fraternity that included the Sandinistas in Nicaragua and the African National Congress in South Africa.[30] Though clerical rule descended in recent years to mere brutal repression—the mark of a tired regime in its decadent, Brezhnevite phase—the very doctrinal and abstract nature of the infighting that still occurs behind closed doors is testament to the elevated nature of Iranian culture. The Iranian state has been stronger and more elaborately organized than any in the Greater Middle East, save for Turkey and Israel, and the Islamic Revolution did not dismantle the Iranian state, but, rather, attached itself to it. The regime maintained universal suffrage and instituted a presidential system, even if the clerics and security services abused it through an apparently rigged election in 2009.

Again, what made the clerical regime in Iran so effective in the pursuit of its interests, from Lebanon to Afghanistan, was its merger with the Iranian state, which itself is the product of history and geography. The Green Movement, which emerged in the course of massive anti-regime demonstrations following the disputed election of 2009, is very much like the regime it sought to topple: greatly sophisticated by the standards of the region (at least until the Jasmine Revolution in Tunisia two years later), and thus another demonstration of the Iranian genius. The Greens constituted a world-class democracy movement, having mastered the latest means in communications technology—Twitter, Facebook, text messaging—to advance their organizational throwweight, and having adopted a potent mixture of nationalism and universal moral values to advance their cause. It took all the means of repression of the Iranian state, subtle and not, to drive the Greens underground. Were the Greens ever to take power, or to facilitate a change in the clerical regime's philosophy and foreign policy toward moderation, Iran, because of its strong state and dynamic idea, would have the means to shift the whole groundwork of the Middle East away from radicalization; providing political expression for a new bourgeoisie with middle-class values that has been quietly rising throughout the Greater Middle East, and which the American obsession with al Qaeda and radicalism obscured until the Arab Spring of 2011.[31]

To speak in terms of destiny is dangerous, since it implies an acceptance of fate and determinism, but clearly given Iran's geography, history, and human capital, it seems likely that the Greater Middle East, and by extension Eurasia, will be critically affected by Iran's own political evolution, for better or for worse.

The best indication that Iran has yet to fulfill such a destiny lies in what has not quite happened yet in Central Asia. Let me explain. Iran's geography, as noted, gives it frontage on Central Asia to the same extent that it has on Mesopotamia and the Middle East. But the disintegration of the Soviet Union has brought limited gains to Iran, when one takes into account the whole history of Greater Iran in the region. The very suffix "istan," used for Central Asian countries and which means "place," is Persian. The conduits for Islamization and civilization in Central Asia were the Persian language and culture. The language of the intelligentsia and other elites in Central Asia up through the beginning of the twentieth century was one form of Persian or another. Yet as Roy and others recount, after 1991, Shiite Azerbaijan to the northwest adopted the Latin alphabet and turned to Turkey for tutelage. As for the republics to the northeast of Iran, Sunni Uzbekistan oriented itself more toward a nationalistic than an Islamic base, for fear of its own homegrown fundamentalists: this makes it wary of Iran. Tajikistan, Sunni but Persian speaking, seeks a protector in Iran, but Iran is constrained for fear of making an enemy of the many Turkic-speaking Muslims elsewhere in Central Asia.[32] What's more, being nomads and semi-nomads, Central Asians were rarely devout Muslims to start with, and seven decades of communism only strengthened their secularist tendencies. Having to relearn Islam, they are both put off and intimidated by clerical Iran.

Of course, there have been positive developments from the viewpoint of Tehran. Iran, as its nuclear program attests, is among the most technologically advanced countries in the Middle East (in keeping with its culture and politics), and as such has built hydroelectric projects and roads and railroads in these Central Asian countries that will one day link them all to Iran—either directly or through Afghanistan. Moreover, a natural gas pipeline now connects southeastern Turkmenistan with northeastern Iran, bringing Turkmen gas to Iran's Caspian region, and thus freeing up Tehran's own gas production in southern Iran for export via the Persian Gulf. (This goes along with a rail link built in the 1990s connecting the two countries.) Turkmenistan has the world's fourth largest natural gas reserves, and has committed its entire gas exports to Iran, China, and Russia. Hence, the possibility arises of a Eurasian energy axis united by the crucial geography of three continental powers all up through 2011 opposed to Western democracy.[33] Iran and Kazakhstan have built an oil pipeline connecting the two countries, with Kazakh oil being pumped to Iran's north, even as an equivalent amount of oil is shipped from Iran's south out through the Persian Gulf. Kazakhstan and Iran will also be linked by rail, providing Kazakhstan with direct access to the Gulf. A rail line may also connect mountainous Tajikistan to Iran, via Afghanistan. Iran constitutes the shortest route for all these natural-resource-rich countries to reach international markets.

So imagine an Iran athwart the pipeline routes of Central Asia, along with its substate, terrorist empire-of-sorts in the Greater Middle East. Clearly, we are talking here of a twenty-first-century successor to Mackinder's Heartland Pivot. But there is still a problem.

Given the prestige that Shiite Iran still enjoys in some sectors of the Arab world, to say nothing of Shiite south Lebanon and Shiite Iraq—because of the regime's implacable support for the Palestinian cause and its inherent anti-Semitism—it is telling that this ability to attract masses outside its borders does not similarly carry over into Central Asia. One issue is that the former Soviet republics maintain diplomatic relations with Israel, and simply lack the hatred toward the Jewish state that may still be ubiquitous in the Arab world, despite the initial phases of the Arab Spring. But there is something larger and deeper at work: something that limits Iran's appeal not only in Central Asia but in the Arab world as well. That something is the very persistence of its suffocating clerical rule that while impressive in a negative sense—using Iran's strong state tradition to ingeniously crush a democratic opposition and torture and rape people—has also dulled the linguistic and cosmopolitan appeal that throughout history has accounted for a Greater Iran in a cultural sense. The Technicolor disappeared from the Iranian landscape under this regime, and was replaced by grainy black-and-white.

Some years back I was in Ashgabat, the capital of Turkmenistan, from whose vantage point Tehran and Mashad over the border in Iranian Khorasan have always loomed as cosmopolitan centers of commerce and pilgrimage, in stark contrast to Turkmenistan's own sparsely populated, nomadic landscape. But while trade and pipeline politics proceeded apace, Iran held no real magic, no real appeal for Muslim Turkmens, who are mainly secular and were put off by the mullahs. As extensive as Iranian influence is by virtue of its in-your-face challenge to America and Israel, I don't believe we will see the true appeal of Iran, in all its cultural glory, until the regime liberalizes or is toppled. A democratic or quasi-democratic Iran, precisely because of the geographical power of the Iranian state, has the possibility to energize hundreds of millions of fellow Muslims in both the Arab world and Central Asia.

Sunni Arab liberalism could be helped in its rise not only because of the example of the West, or because of a democratic yet dysfunctional Iraq, but also because of the challenge thrown up by a newly liberal and historically eclectic Shiite Iran. And such an Iran might do what two decades of Post Cold War Western democracy and civil society promotion have failed to, that is, lead to a substantial prying loose of the police state restrictions in former Soviet Central Asia.

Iran's Shiite regime was able for a time to inspire the lumpen Sunni faithful and oppressed throughout the Middle East against their own tired, pharaonic governments, some of which have since fallen. Through its uncompromising message and nimble intelligence services, Iran for a long time ran an unconventional, postmodern empire of substate entities including Hamas in Palestine, Hezbollah in Lebanon, and the Mahdi movement in southern Iraq. And yet the Iranian regime was quietly despised at home in many quarters, where the concept of Islamic Revolution, because Iranians have actually experienced it, has meant power cuts, destruction of the currency, and mismanagement. The battle for Eurasia, as I have explained, has many fronts, all increasingly interlocked with one another. But the first among equals in this regard is the one for the hearts and minds of Iranians, who comprise, along with Turks, the Muslim world's most sophisticated population. Here is where the struggle of ideas meets the dictates of geography: here is where the liberal humanism of Isaiah Berlin meets the quasi-determinism of Halford Mackinder.

For as irresistible and overpowering seem the forces of geography, so much still hangs on a thread. Take the story of the brilliant eighteenth-century post-Safavid conqueror Nader Shah. Of Turkic origin, from Khorasan in northeastern Iran, Nader Shah's Persian Empire stretched from the Transcaucasus to the Indus. His sieges numbered Baghdad, Basra, Kirkuk, Mosul, Kandahar, and Kabul, places that bedevil America in the early twenty-first century, and which were rarely strangers to Iranian rule. Had Nader Shah, as Michael Axworthy writes, not become deranged in the last five years of his life, he could have brought about in Iran "a modernizing state capable of resisting colonial intervention" from the British and Russians in the nineteenth century. But rather than be remembered as the Peter the Great of Persia, who might have dramatically altered Iranian history from then on for the better, his regime ended in misrule and economic disaster.[34]

Or take the fall of the Shah in 1979. Henry Kissinger once told me that had Jimmy Carter's administration handled the rebellion against the Shah more competently in the late 1970s, the Shah might have survived and Iran would now be like South Korea, a dynamic regime, with an imperfectly evolved democracy, that always has its minor disagreements with the United States, but which is basically an ally. The Shah's regime, in his view, was capable of reform, especially given the democratic upheaval in the Soviet Empire that would come a decade later. Though blaming President Carter for the Shah's fall may be too facile, the possibilities raised by even a slightly different outcome to the Iranian Revolution are still intriguing. Who knows? I do know that when I traveled throughout Iran in the 1990s, having come recently from Egypt, it was the former that was much less anti-American and anti-Israeli than the latter. Iran's relatively benign relationship with the Jews stretches from antiquity through the reign of the late Shah. Iran's population contains hope and possibilities.

Or take the opportunity offered to the United States following the attacks of September 11, 2001, when both Ayatollah Ali Khamenei and President Mohammed Khatami condemned the Sunni al Qaeda terrorism in no uncertain terms and Iranians held vigils for the victims in the streets of Tehran, even as crowds in parts of the Arab world cheered on the attacks; or the help Iran gave to the U.S.-led coalition against the Taliban later that year; or the Iranian offer for substantial talks following the fall of Baghdad in the spring of 2003. These are all indications that history, up to this point in time, did not need to turn out as it did. Other outcomes were possible.

Geography dictates that Iran will be pivotal to the trend lines in the Greater Middle East and Eurasia, and it may dictate how it will be pivotal, but it cannot dictate for what purpose it will be pivotal. That is up to the decisions of men.

As I write, true to the innovative imperialist traditions of its medieval and ancient past, Iran has brilliantly erected a postmodern military empire, the first of its kind: one without colonies and without the tanks, armor, and aircraft carriers that have been the usual accompaniments of power. Rather than classic imperialism—invasion and occupation—Iran, notes author and former CIA field officer Robert Baer, is a superpower within the Middle East by virtue of a "three-pronged strategy of proxy warfare, asymmetrical weapons and an appeal to the . . . downtrodden," particularly legions of young and frustrated males. Hezbollah, Tehran's Arab Shiite proxy in Lebanon, Baer points out, "is the de facto state" there, with more military and organizational heft, and more communal commitment, than the official authorities in Beirut possess. In Gaza, Shiite Iran's furtive military and financial aid, and its "raw anticolonial message," seduced poor Palestinians trapped in Soweto-like conditions, who were alienated from contiguous Sunni Arab states run by the likes of the former dictator Mubarak.[35] Iran, a thousand miles away to the east, felt closer to these downtrodden Palestinians than did Gaza's border with Egypt under Mubarak's rule. This, too, was the Iranian genius. Then, at least through 2011, there were the friendly governments in Syria and Iraq, the former of which clung to Iran for dear life as its only real ally, and the latter of which has a political establishment enmeshed with the Iranian intelligence services, which can help stabilize the country or destabilize it, as they wish. Finally, there is the Persian Gulf itself, where Iran is the only major power with its long and shattered coastline opposite small and relatively weak Arab principalities, each of which Tehran can militarily defeat on its own, undermine through local fifth-column Shiite populations, especially in Bahrain as we have seen, or economically damage through terrorism in the Strait of Hormuz.

Though forbidding and formidable, that most important element, again, having to do with enlightenment, is absent. Unlike the Achaemenid, Sassanid, Safavid, and other Iranian empires of yore, which were either benign or truly inspiring in both a moral and cultural sense, this current Iranian empire of the mind rules mostly out of fear and intimidation, through suicide bombers rather than through poets. And this both limits its power and signals its downfall.

Iran, with its rich culture, vast territory, and teeming and sprawling cities, is, in the way of China and India, a universe unto itself, whose future will overwhelmingly be determined by internal politics and social conditions. Yet if one were to isolate a single hinge in calculating Iran's fate, it would be Iraq. Iraq, history and geography tell us, is entwined in Iranian politics to the degree of no other foreign country. The Shiite shrines of Imam Ali (the Prophet's cousin and son-in-law) in Najaf and the one of Imam Hussain (the grandson of the Prophet) in Karbala, both in central-southern Iraq, have engendered Shiite theological communities that challenge that of Qom in Iran. Were Iraqi democracy to ensure even a modicum of stability, the freer intellectual atmosphere of the Iraqi holy cities could have an impact on Iranian politics. In a larger sense, a democratic Iraq will serve as an attractor force of which Iranian reformers might in the future take advantage. For as Iranians become more deeply embroiled in Iraqi politics, the very propinquity of the two nations with a long and common border might work to undermine the more repressive of the two systems. Iranian politics will become gnarled by interaction with a pluralistic, ethnically Arab Shiite society. And as the Iranian economic crisis continues to unfold, ordinary Iranians could well up in anger over hundreds of millions of dollars being spent by their government to buy influence in Iraq, Lebanon, and elsewhere. This is to say nothing of how Iranians will become increasingly hated inside Iraq as the equivalent of "Ugly Americans." Iran would like to simply leverage Iraqi Shiite parties against the Sunni ones. But that is not altogether possible, since that would narrow the radical Islamic universalism it seeks to represent in the pan-Sunni world to a sectarianism with no appeal beyond the community of Shiites. Thus, Iran may be stuck trying to help form shaky Sunni-Shiite coalitions in Iraq and to keep them perennially functioning, even as Iraqis develop greater hatred for the intrusion into their domestic affairs. Without justifying the way that the 2003 invasion of Iraq was planned and executed, or rationalizing the trillions of dollars spent and the hundreds of thousands of lives lost in the war, in the fullness of time it might very well be that the fall of Saddam Hussein began a process that will result in the liberation of two countries; not one. Just as geography has facilitated Iran's subtle colonization of Iraqi politics, geography could also be a factor in abetting Iraq's influence upon Iran.

The prospect of peaceful regime change—or evolution—in Iran, despite the temporary fizzling of the Green Movement, is still greater now than in the Soviet Union during most of the Cold War. A liberated Iran, coupled with less autocratic governments in the Arab world—governments that would be focused more on domestic issues because of their own insecurity—would encourage a more equal, fluid balance of power between Sunnis and Shiites in the Middle East: something which would help keep the region nervously preoccupied with itself and on its own internal and regional power dynamics, much more than on America and Israel.

Additionally, a more liberal regime in Tehran would inspire a broad cultural continuum worthy of the Persian empires of old: one that will not be constrained by the clerical forces of reaction.

A more liberal Iran, given the large Kurdish, Azeri, Turkomen, and other minorities in the north and elsewhere, may also be a far less centrally controlled Iran, with the ethnic peripheries drifting away from Tehran's orbit. Iran has often been less a state than an amorphous, multinational empire. Its true size would always be greater and smaller than any officially designated cartography. While the northwest of today's Iran is Kurdish and Azeri Turk, parts of western Afghanistan and Tajikistan are culturally and linguistically compatible with an Iranian state. It is this amorphousness, so very Parthian, that Iran could return to as the wave of Islamic extremism and the perceived legitimacy of the mullahs' regime erodes.[36]

Chapter XIV

THE FORMER OTTOMAN EMPIRE

If the Iranian plateau is the most pivotal geography in the Greater Middle East, then the land bridge of Anatolia, or Asia Minor, follows in importance naturally from it. Just as the Iranian plateau is completely covered by one country, Iran, so is the Anatolian land bridge, by Turkey. Together, these two countries, defined by mountains and plateaus overlooking desert Arabia from the north, boast a combined population of almost 150 million people, slightly larger than that of all the twelve Arab countries to the south which comprise the Fertile Crescent and the Arabian Peninsula. One would have to add Egypt and the rest of North Africa stretching to the Atlantic in order for the Arabs to demographically overwhelm the weight of Turkey and Iran.

Turkey and Iran—crucial parts of both Mackinder's wilderness girdle and Spykman's Rimland—also contain the Middle East's richest agricultural economies, as well as its highest levels of industrialization and technological know-how. The very existence of Iran's nuclear program, and the indigenous ability of Turkey to follow suit if—for the sake of national prestige—it wished, contrasts sharply with Saudi Arabia and other Arab countries, which lack the intellectual capacity for their own such programs, and would therefore require a technology transfer from an existing nuclear power like Pakistan.

Turkey, like Iran, constitutes its own major region, influencing clockwise the Balkans, the Black Sea, Ukraine and southern Russia, the Caucasus, and the Arab Middle East. Especially in comparison to the Arab world, Turkey, writes Stratfor strategist George Friedman, "is a stable platform in the midst of chaos."[1] However, while Turkey impacts all the places around it, Turkey's position as a land bridge bracketed between the Mediterranean to the south and the Black Sea to the north makes it, in part, an island nation. The lack of dry-land contiguity means that though Turkey influences the surrounding area, it is not geographically pivotal in the way that Iran is to its neighbors. Turkey's influence in the Balkans to the west and Syria and Mesopotamia to the south is primarily economic, though in the former Yugoslavia it has lately become involved in post-conflict mediation. Only in the Caucasus, and particularly in Azerbaijan, where the language is very close to Turkish, does Turkey enjoy the level of diplomatic influence that can dramatically affect daily politics.

Turkey, it is true, controls the headwaters of the Tigris and Euphrates: a terrific geographical advantage, giving it the ability to cut off the supply of water to Syria and Iraq. But were Turkey to actually do this, it would constitute the equivalent of an act of war. Thus, Turkey must be subtle in pressing this advantage. It is the fear that Turkey might reduce the water flow, through upriver diversions for its own agricultural development purposes, that can give Turkey considerable influence over Arab politics. A relatively new geopolitical fact that is often overlooked is the Southeast Anatolia Project, whose centerpiece is the Ataturk Dam, twenty-five miles north of Sanliurfa near the Syrian border. Almost two thousand square miles of arable land in the Harran plateau is being irrigated via gravity-flow water diverted from this dam. The whole Euphrates River dam sys-

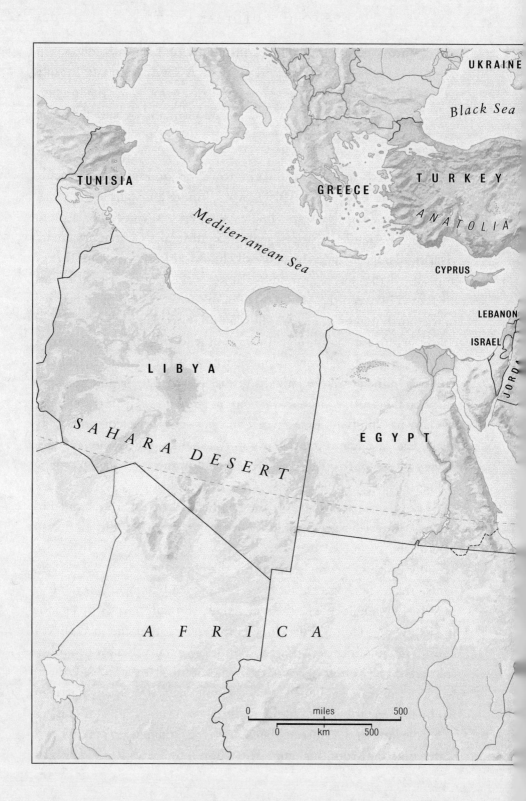

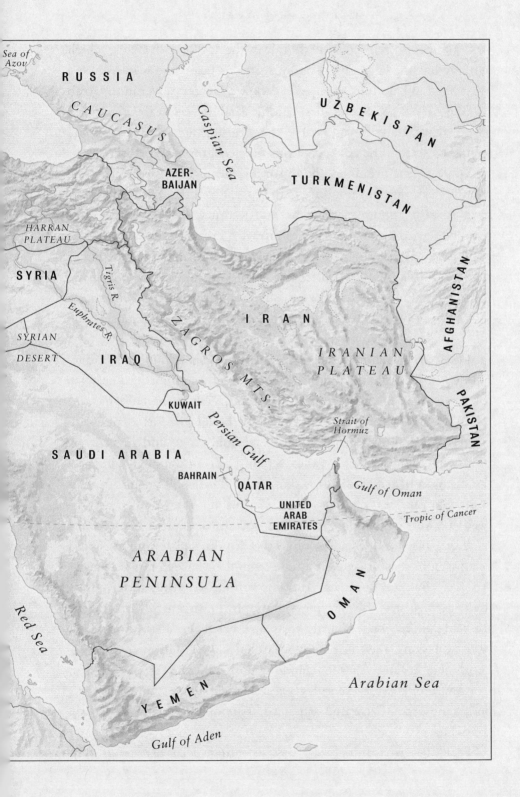

Sea of
Azov

RUSSIA

CAUCASUS

Caspian Sea

UZBEKISTAN

AZER-
BAIJAN

TURKMENISTAN

HARRAN
PLATEAU

SYRIA

Tigris R.

Euphrates R.

SYRIAN

DESERT

IRAQ

ZAGROS MTS.

IRAN

IRANIAN
PLATEAU

AFGHANISTAN

PAKISTAN

KUWAIT

Persian Gulf

Strait of
Hormuz

SAUDI ARABIA

BAHRAIN

QATAR

Gulf of Oman

UNITED
ARAB
EMIRATES

Tropic of Cancer

ARABIAN

PENINSULA

OMAN

Red Sea

YEMEN

Arabian Sea

Gulf of Aden

tem, planned in the 1970s and built in the 1980s and 1990s, which actually has the capacity to pump water as far as the water-starved West Bank in Palestine, will make Turkey a greater power in the Arab Middle East in the twenty-first century than it was in the twentieth. The heightened political profile that Turkey has adopted of late should be seen in the context of this new geographical reality.

While recent headlines show Turkey turning its attention to the Middle East, this was not always the case. From the rise of the Ottoman Turkish Empire in the thirteenth century, the Ottomans were mainly focused on their northwest, toward Europe, where the wealth and lucrative trade routes were. This was a pattern that had begun in the late Middle Ages, when the ascent of Central Europe and of the Carolingian Empire acted like a magnet for Turkish tribes, who themselves had gravitated westward across Anatolia to the Balkans, to the most fertile agricultural lands in Asia Minor's immediate vicinity. Turkey may be synonymous with the entire Anatolian land bridge, but (as with Russia) the nation's demographic and industrial heft has for centuries been clustered in the west, adjacent to the Balkans, and relatively far from the Middle East. But though the Ottomans were clustered near Europe, Anatolia's exceedingly high and rugged terrain, with each mountain valley separated from the next, hindered the creation of tribal alliances that might have challenged Ottoman control in the areas closer to the Caucasus and the Middle East. Indeed, because geography made for social "disruption" in eastern Anatolia, organized dynasties like the Seljuks and Ottomans could rule for hundreds of years at a time from their base in faraway western Anatolia, i.e., European Turkey, without worrying about unrest in the east.[2] Just as the dizzying topography of eastern Siberia and the Russian Far East made it hard to organize a challenge to the European-based Russians, the same with Anatolia and the Ottoman Turks— except that because Anatolia had long borders with seas, the rulers in Constantinople were much less paranoid about incursions on their peripheries than were the Russians. Anatolia is compact; Russia sprawling.

Thus, Turkish demography has accentuated Turkish geography.

Anatolia is further removed from the Middle Eastern heartland than the Iranian plateau, and the northwestern spatial arrangement of the Turkish population in recent centuries has only made it more so. Ottoman military forays into Central Europe, which had the flavor of nomadic wanderings and culminated in 1683 with the siege of Vienna, were eased by Europe's own political fragmentation. France, Great Britain, and Spain were focused on outmaneuvering one another, and on their colonies in the New World across the Atlantic. Venice was involved in a long struggle with Genoa. The Papacy was entangled in other crises. And the Slavs of the southern Balkans were divided against themselves, another case of a mountainous geography encouraging social and political division. Finally, as the early-twentieth-century foreign correspondent Herbert Adams Gibbons writes, "From Europe, Asia Minor and more could be conquered: from Asia, no portion of Europe could be conquered."[3] He meant that in order to truly consolidate the barren stretches of Anatolia and expand into the Middle East, the Ottoman Turks first required the wealth that only the conquest of the Balkans could provide. Facilitating this fluid arrangement between Europe and the Middle East was the location of the Ottoman capital of Constantinople, a safe harbor granting access to the Balkans, the Mediterranean, and North Africa, while also the terminus of caravan routes from Persia, the Caucasus, and beyond.

Arising from this geography came a sprawling, multinational empire that by the late nineteenth century was in its death throes, with the Ottoman Sultanate only giving up the ghost in the aftermath of its defeat in World War I. Mustafa Kemal Ataturk (Father Turk), the only undefeated Ottoman general, who forged a modern state in Anatolia following the imperial losses in the Balkans and the Middle East, was an authentic revolutionary: that is, he changed his people's value system. He divined that the European powers had defeated the Ottoman Empire not on account of their greater armies, but on account of their greater civilization, which had produced the greater armies. Turkey would henceforth be Western, he said, marching culturally and politically toward Europe. Thus, he abolished the Muslim religious courts, forbade men to wear the fez, discouraged women from wearing the veil, and replaced the Arabic script with the Latin one. But as revolutionary as these acts were, they were also the culmination of a Turkish obsession with Europe going back centuries. Though Turkey remained neutral during most of World War II, Kemalism—the pro-Western, secularist doctrine of Kemal Ataturk—guided Turkey's culture and particularly its foreign policy right up through the end of the first decade after the Cold War. Indeed, for years Turkey entertained hopes of joining the European Union, a fixation that Turkish officials made clear to me during many visits to the country in the 1980s and 1990s. But in the first decade of the twenty-first century it became apparent that Turkey might never gain full membership in the EU. The reason was blunt, and reeked of geographical and cultural determinism: though Turkey was a democracy and a member of NATO, it was also Muslim, and thus not wanted. The rejection was a shock to the Turkish body politic. More important, it merged with other trends in society that were in the process of issuing a grand correction to Turkish history and geography.

Actually, the European orientation that Ataturk imposed on Turkey entailed a contradiction. Ataturk was born and brought up in Salonika, in northern Greece, among Greeks, Jews, and other minorities. He was a man of Europe, in other words, as Salonika in the late nineteenth century was a multilingual outpost of cosmopolitanism. Likewise, Ataturk's definition of nationality was strikingly modern. For he oft declared that whoever says he is a Turk, speaks Turkish, and lives in Turkey is a Turk, even if he be a Jew or Christian. He moved the capital to Ankara, in the heart of Anatolia, from Istanbul (Constantinople) in European Turkey, because of Istanbul's association with the ancien régime. And he made no effort to regain lost Ottoman provinces in the Balkans or the Middle East: rather, his strategy was to build a uniethnic Turkish state out of the heartland of Anatolia, which would be firmly anchored toward Europe and the West. The keeper of the Kemalist flame would be the Turkish military, for authentic democracy was a thing to which Kemalism never got around during Ataturk's lifetime. The problem, and this would take decades to play out, was that by focusing on Anatolia, he unwittingly emphasized Islamic civilization, which was more deeply rooted in Asia Minor than in the European Turkey of Constantinople and the sultanate. Furthermore, democracy, as it developed in Turkey in fits and starts between periodic military coups, delivered the electoral franchise to the mass of working-class and devout Turks in the Anatolian hinterlands.

For the first few decades of Republican Turkey's existence, the wealth and power resided with the military and with the ultra-secular Istanbul elite. During this period, American officials had the luxury of proclaiming Turkey's democratic status even as the Turkish generals were responsible for its pro-Western foreign policy. That began to change in the early 1980s, when the newly elected prime minister, Turgut Ozal, a devout Muslim with Sufi tendencies from central Anatolia, enacted a series of reforms that liberalized the statist economy. A slew of large firms were privatized and import controls loosened. This led to the creation of a nouveau riche middle class of devout Muslims with real political power. Nevertheless, Ozal's genius in the later years of the Cold War was to stay politically anchored to the West, even as he softened the arch-secularist tendency of Kemalism to give religious Muslims a larger stake in the system. Turkey became at once more Islamist and more pro-American. Ozal's Islamism allowed him to reach out to the Kurds, who were united with the Turks in religion but divided by ethnicity. The Turkish generals, supremely uncomfortable with Ozal's religiosity, stayed in control of national security policy, which Ozal did not challenge, because he and the generals were in broad agreement about Turkey as a NATO bulwark on Spykman's Rimland of Eurasia facing off against the Soviet Union.

Ozal died suddenly in 1993 at age sixty-five, after ten years as prime minister and president. This had profound repercussions for the future of Turkey, another instance about how the lives and deaths of individual men and women affect the destiny of geopolitics as much as geography, which retains its primacy mainly because it is permanent. Because Ozal in his own person held together apparent contradictions—pro-Islamism and pro-Americanism—his death shattered a tenuous national consensus, though this took some years to unfold. For a decade after Ozal's death, Turkey had uninspiring secularist leaders, even as economic power and Islamic devoutness continued to burgeon in the Anatolian heartland. By late 2002, the whiskey-sipping secular elite was discredited, and an election delivered an absolute parliamentary majority to the Islamist Justice and Development Party led by Recep Tayyip Erdogan, the former mayor of Istanbul. Istanbul, while the home of the secular elite, was also the home of millions of poor devout Turks who had migrated in from the Anatolian countryside in search of jobs to pry their way into the lower middle class; it was these millions to whom Erdogan had given a voice.

When Erdogan assumed control, he gave power to a wave of Islamism, strengthened by Ozal, that had been creeping back into Turkish life under the radar screen of official Kemalism. In 1945, there were 20,000 mosques in Turkey; in 1985, 72,000, and that number has since risen steadily, out of proportion to the population. According to some studies, almost two-thirds of urban working-class Turks prayed daily, as well as most rural Turks, percentages that have only gone up in recent years.[4] A revived Islam has competed extremely well with the secular ideologies of the right (fascism) and the left (Marxism) "as a savior of the disillusioned urban youth," for whom Kemalism was not a "socio-ethical system" to guide daily life, writes the London-based author and journalist Dilip Hiro. Once a normal nationalism tied to Islam took root, Kemalism gradually lost its "raison d'être."[5]

Yet when the Turkish Parliament voted in March 2003 against allowing U.S. troops to stage in Turkey for an invasion of Iraq, it was not really the Islamist Justice Party that undermined the American position, but the secularists, who, by this point, had joined Europeans in their anti-Americanism as a reaction to the unsubtle post-9/11 rhetoric and deportment of the George W. Bush administration. The disastrous outcome of the Iraq invasion, which led to sectarian warfare inside Iraq, even as no weapons of mass destruction were found, roughly coincided with the realization that Turkey would not be admitted to the EU. The upshot of these dramatic events—coming at a time when Turkey had a new, popular, and deeply entrenched Islamist government—was to shift the political and cultural pendulum dramatically in the country toward the Middle East and away from the West for the first time in literally centuries.

In a sense, as I've said, the United States was hoist on its own petard. For decades American leaders had proclaimed democratic Turkey as a NATO, pro-Israel bastion in the Middle East, even as they knew that Turkish foreign and security policy was in the hands of its military. Finally, in the early twenty-first century, Turkey had emerged as truly politically, economically, and culturally democratic, reflecting the Islamic nature of the mass of Turks, and the result was a relatively anti-American, anti-Israeli Turkey.

In the autumn of 1998, in Kayseri in central Anatolia, I interviewed leading Turkish Islamists, including Abdullah Gul, Turkey's current president. The occasion was a meeting and rally of the Virtue Party, which later disbanded and reorganized itself as the Justice Party. The Virtue Party was itself a reincarnation of the Islamic Welfare Party, which had been untainted by corruption and sought to bring about the social justice that had existed under Ottoman Islam. In my report on those meetings, published in 2000, I got a big thing right and a big thing wrong. The big thing I got right was that these people, though a minority party, were about to be become a majority in a few years. And their fundamental theme was democracy: the more democratic Turkey became, the more their Islamist power would increase; for they linked the West with Turkey's autocratic military power structure, which was ironic, but true.

"When will the United States support democracy in Turkey?" the man next to me at the Virtue Party dinner had asked. "Because until now it has been supporting the military." Before waiting for my answer, he added: "I have been to Israel, and there, democracy is more developed than in Turkey."[6]

And that was the big thing I got wrong. Because moderate Turkish Islamists were then relatively open-minded about Israel, I assumed they would always be so. In fact, circumstances would change dra-

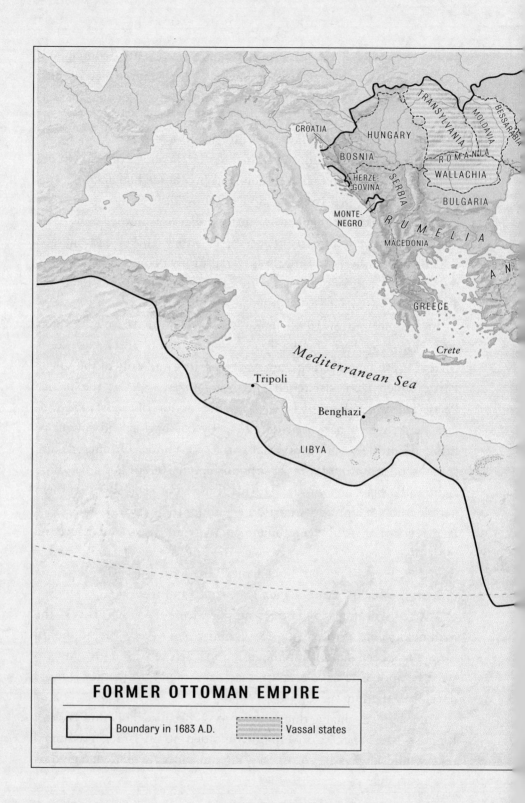

CROATIA

HUNGARY

TRANSYLVANIA

MOLDAVIA

BESSARABIA

BOSNIA

ROMANIA

HERZE-
GOVINA

SERBIA

WALLACHIA

MONTE-
NEGRO

BULGARIA

R U M E L I A

MACEDONIA

A N

GREECE

Crete

Mediterranean Sea

Tripoli

Benghazi

LIBYA

FORMER OTTOMAN EMPIRE

Boundary in 1683 A.D.   Vassal states

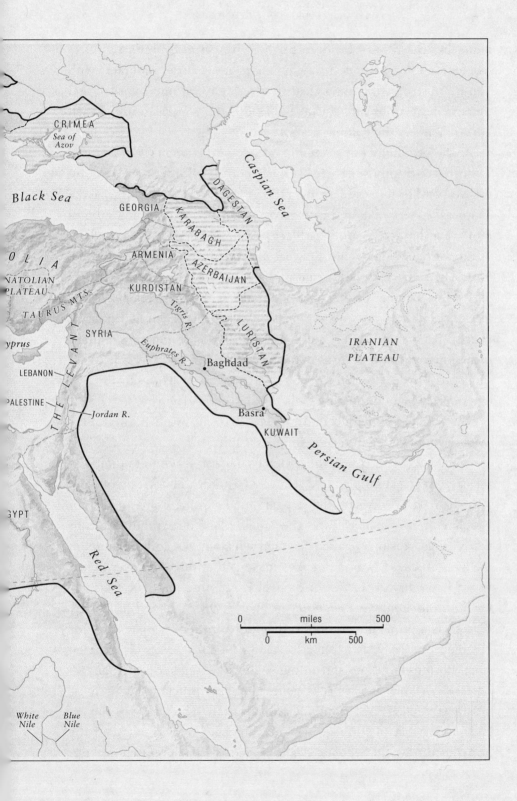

CRIMEA

Sea of
Azov

Black Sea

Caspian Sea

GEORGIA

DAGESTAN

KARABAGH

ARMENIA

AZERBAIJAN

OLIA

ANATOLIAN
PLATEAU

KURDISTAN

Tigris R.

LURISTAN

IRANIAN
PLATEAU

TAURUS MTS.

SYRIA

Euphrates R.

yprus

LEBANON

Baghdad

PALESTINE

Jordan R.

Basra

KUWAIT

Persian Gulf

GYPT

Red Sea

White
Nile

Blue
Nile

| 0 | miles | 500 |
| 0 | km | 500 |

matically: the result of the Turks' own historical evolution as electronic communications brought them into closer contact with
pan-Islamist thought (the defeat of geography in other words), and
the specific actions and mistakes of both the American and Israeli
governments in the coming years.

At the beginning of the second decade of the twenty-first century,
Turkish geography mirrored Turkish politics. Bordering Greece in
the west and Iran in the east, Bulgaria in the northwest and Iraq in the
southeast, Azerbaijan in the northeast and Syria in the south, even as
more than half of Anatolia is Black Sea or Mediterranean coastline,
Turkey is truly equidistant between Europe, Russia, and the Middle
East. The same with its foreign and national security policy. Turkey
was still a member of NATO, cooperated with U.S. intelligence services, maintained an embassy in Israel, and had facilitated indirect
peace talks between Israel and Syria. But it was conducting military
incursions against the Kurds in northern Iraq, was helping Iran avoid
sanctions for developing a nuclear weapon, and was politically and
emotionally behind the most radical Palestinian groups.

The Israeli commando raid in May 2010 against a flotilla of six
ships bringing humanitarian supplies from Turkey to the Hamas-
controlled Gaza Strip, and the ferocious Turkish reaction to that, was
the catalyst for announcing to the world Turkey's historic pivot from
West to East. Turks saw the struggle for Palestine not as an Arab-
Israeli fight, in which as Turks they could play no part, but as a conflict pitting Muslims against Jews, in which Turks could champion
the Muslim cause. Among the key insights that often get overlooked
in the late Harvard professor Samuel P. Huntington's *The Clash of
Civilizations and the Remaking of World Order,* of which Turkey
represents a prime illustration, is that globalization, while a force for
unity on one level, is a force for civilizational tension on another,
since it brings large and spread-out solidarity groups together; and so
while the Islamic world lacks political cohesion, Islamic consciousness nevertheless rises alongside globalization. Thus, the Islamic aspect of Turkish identity grows. This happens at a time when the
non-Western world becomes healthier, more urbane, and more liter-

ate, so that there is a rise in the political and economic power of middle tier nations such as Turkey.[7]

Turks helped lead the House of Islam for almost 850 years, from the Seljuk Turk victory over the Byzantines at the 1071 Battle of Manzikert in eastern Anatolia to the defeat of the Ottoman Empire by the Western Allies in 1918. Only for the past century have the Arabs really been at the head of Muslim civilization. In fact, until the Iranian Revolution of 1978–1979, even the then 50 million Muslims in Iran were largely invisible to the West; just as 75 million Muslims in present-day Turkey were largely invisible until the Gaza flotilla crisis erupted at the same time that the Turks made a deal with Iran to accept its enriched uranium, and voted against sanctioning Iran at the United Nations. Suddenly, Western publics and media woke up to the blunt geographical fact of Turkey.

Then in 2011 came the uprisings against tired autocracies across North Africa and the Middle East, a beneficiary of which in a historical and geographical sense was Turkey. Ottoman Turkey ruled North Africa and the Levant for hundreds of years in the modern era. While this rule was despotic, it was not so oppressive as to leave a lasting scar in the minds of today's Arabs. Turkey is an exemplar of Islamic democracy that can serve as a role model for these newly liberated states, especially as its democracy evolved from a hybrid regime, with generals and politicians sharing power until recently—a process that some Arab states will go through en route to freer systems. With 75 million people and a healthy economic growth rate until recently, Turkey is also a demographic and economic juggernaut that can project soft power throughout the Mediterranean. It simply has advantages that other major Mediterranean states proximate to North Africa—Greece, Italy, and Spain—do not.

Yet there are key things to know about Turkish Islam, which indicate that the West may find a silver lining in Turkey's rise in the Middle East.

Indeed, if we knew a little more about Jalal ed-Din Rumi, the thirteenth-century founder of the Turkic *tariqat* that was associated with the whirling dervishes, we would have been less surprised by

Islam's compatibility with democracy, and Islamic fundamentalism might not seem so monolithic and threatening. Rumi dismissed "immature fanatics" who scorn music and poetry.[8] He cautioned that a beard or mustache on a cleric is no sign of wisdom. Rumi favored the individual over the crowd, and consistently spoke against tyranny. Rumi's legacy is more applicable to democratizing tendencies in the Muslim world than are figures of the Arab and Iranian pantheons with whom the West is more familiar. The eclectic nature of Turkish Islam, as demonstrated by Rumi, goes together with Turkey's very Westernization. Turkey's democratic system, though imperfect and influenced for too long by an overbearing military, incorporated orthodox Islamic elements for decades. Unlike quite a few Arab states and Iran, Turkey's industrial base and middle class were not created out of thin air by oil revenues. Again, we have geography to thank for the advanced level of human development in Turkey compared to most places in the Middle East. Turkey's position as a land bridge not only connects it to Europe, but made for a wave of invasions by Central Asian nomads that invigorated Anatolian civilization, of which Rumi's poetry is an example. It was the Ottoman Empire that played a large role in bringing European politics—at least the Balkan variety of it—into intimate contact with that of the Middle East. The national independence struggles of the nineteenth century in Serbia, Bulgaria, Romania, and Greece encouraged the rise of Arab nationalist societies in Damascus and Beirut. Similarly, modern terrorism was born at the beginning of the twentieth century in Macedonia and Bulgaria, before filtering into Greater Syria.

In the early twenty-first century, Turkey boasted a vibrant and politically dominant Islamic movement, an immense military capability compared to almost any country in the Middle East save Israel, an economy that had grown 8 percent annually for many years, and still managed over 5 percent growth during the worldwide recession, and a dam system that made Turkey a water power to the same extent that Iran and Saudi Arabia were oil powers. These factors, seen and unseen, allow Turkey to compete with Iran for the locus of Islamic leadership and legitimacy. For years Turkey had been almost as lonely as Israel in the Middle East. Its Ottoman era overlordship complicated its relationship with Arabs, even as its relations with neighboring Syria were overtly hostile, and those with Baathist Iraq and fundamentalist Iran tense. In 1998, Turkey was actually on the brink of war with Syria over Damascus's support for the radical antiTurkish Kurdistan Workers' Party. During this time Turkey maintained a virtual military alliance with Israel, confirming its status as a Middle East pariah. But all of this began to change with Erdogan's and the Justice Party's assumption of power, which came at the same time as the West's downward plunge in Turkish public opinion, owing to Turkey's virtual rejection by the European Union and an increasingly truculent right-wing America and right-wing Israel.

Turkey did not withdraw from NATO, nor break diplomatic relations with Israel. Rather, under Erdogan's foreign minister, Ahmet Davutoglu, Turkey adopted a policy of "no problems" with its immediate neighbors, which in particular meant historical rapprochements with Syria, Iraq, and Iran. Because of Turkey's economy, so much more technologically advanced than its neighbors—and growing faster, too—Turkey's robust influence in the Balkans to the west and the Caucasus to the east was already an established fact. Bulgaria, Georgia, and Azerbaijan were all flush with Turkish appliances and other consumer goods. But it was the Turkish championing of the Palestinians, and the intense popularity of the Turkish people which that engendered in Gaza, that made Turkey an integral organizational fact in the Arab world to a degree it had not enjoyed since Ottoman times. Neo-Ottomanism might have been a specific strategy developed by Davutoglu, but it also constituted a natural political evolution: the upshot of Turkey's commanding geographical and economic position made suddenly relevant by its own intensifying Islamization. Neo-Ottomanism's attractiveness rested on the unstated assumption that Turkey lacked both the means and the will in this era of globalization to actually carve out a new-old empire in the Middle East; rather, it rested on Turkey's normalization of relations with its former Arab dependencies, for whom Ottoman rule was distant enough, and benign enough, at least when viewed across the span of the decades and centuries, so as to welcome Turkey back into the fold now that it had turned hostility against Israel up several notches.

Davutoglu's real innovation was reaching out to Iran. The civilizations of the Anatolian and Iranian plateaus, Turkic and Persian respectively, have had a long and complex relationship: Persian, as I've said, was the diplomatic language of the Ottoman Turkish Empire, even as the Ottomans and Safavid Persians were long at odds militarily in the sixteenth and early seventeenth centuries. One can say that the Turkish and Iranian peoples are rivals, while, nevertheless, their cultures and languages deeply intertwine; Rumi wrote in Persian, though he spent most of his life in Turkey. Moreover, neither Turkey nor Iran has suffered a colonial relationship at the hands of the other. Geographically, their spheres of influence, though overlapping, are to a large degree separate, with Iran lying laterally to the east of Turkey. During the Shah's reign, both Turkey and Iran were pro-Western, and even when Iran turned radical under the mullahs, Ankara was careful to maintain correct relations with Tehran. There is little historically shocking about Ankara's embrace of the ayatollahs, even as in a contemporary political context it had considerable shock value.

Consider: the United States, under a universally popular president at the time, Barack Obama, was trying desperately, along with its European allies, to forestall Iran's march to obtaining nuclear weapons, so as to prevent Israel from launching an attack on Iran; a nuclear Iran would change the balance of power in the Middle East dramatically against the West, while an Israeli attack against Iran might even be worse in terms of destabilizing the region. Yet in May 2010, Turkey, along with Brazil, acted through a series of dramatic diplomatic maneuvers to help Iran evade economic sanctions and thus gain critical time in order to make such a bomb. By agreeing to enrich Iran's uranium, Turkey acquired yet more stature in the Islamic world to go along with that which it has acquired by supporting Hamas in Gaza. Iran has the potential "to help Turkey realize its core strategic goal of becoming an energy hub, delivering natural gas and oil [from Iran] to the markets of Western Europe."[9] With Turkey an energy transfer nexus for Iran, as well as for hydrocarbons coming from the Caspian Sea across the Caucasus, even as Turkey holds the power to divert as much as 90 percent of Iraq's water intake from the Euphrates and 40 percent of Syria's, Turkey joins Iran as a Middle East hyperpower, with pipelines running in all directions filled with oil, natural gas, and water—the very basis of industrial life.[10]

Before the Oil Age, as I've suggested, Turkey advanced into the Balkans and Europe in order to develop the economic capacity so that it could also advance into the Middle East. In the Oil Age, it is the other way around. As Turkey becomes a European conduit for Iranian and Caspian Sea oil, it becomes too important an economic factor for Europe to ignore. Rather than be merely a land bridge, albeit the largest land bridge on the globe, Turkey—a G-20 country—has become a core region in and of itself, which, along with Iran, has the capacity to neutralize the Arab Fertile Crescent, whose societies are beset by internal upheaval caused by decades of sterile national security regimes.

Furthermore, the move by Turkey and Brazil to safeguard Iran's enriched uranium was more than a rogue action of little practical consequence to help fundamentalist Iran acquire a nuclear bomb. It reflected the rise of middle-level powers around the world, as more and more millions from developing countries joined the middle class.

The silver lining for the West is the following: without the ascent of Turkey, revolutionary Iran becomes the dominant power in the Middle East; but with Turkey's aggressive rise as a Middle Eastern power for the first time since the collapse of the Ottoman Empire, Iran will have competition from next door—for Turkey can at once be Iran's friend and competitor. And don't forget, Turkey still belongs to NATO, and it still has relations with Israel, however frayed. As difficult as it has become for the West to tolerate, Turkey's Islamist leadership still represents a vast improvement over the mind-set of the Iranian clerical government. Turkey can still act as a mediator between Israel and Muslim countries, just as Iran holds the potential yet to modify its own politics, either through political upheaval or through the wages of the regime's own longevity and contradictions.

What is clear is that as the Cold War fades from memory, both Turkey and Iran will have their geographies further unleashed in order to play intensified roles in the Arab Middle East. Turkey is no longer yoked so strongly to NATO, even as NATO is a weak reed of its former self. And with the end of the Saddam Hussein regime in Iraq—itself a vestige of Cold War, Soviet-style police states—Iran is enmeshed in the politics of the Arab world as never before. It is all quite subtle: Turkey works in concert with Iran even as it balances against it. At the same time, Iraq emerges as a predominantly Shiite alternative to Iran, however weak Iraq may be at the moment. Assisting Turkey and Iran has been the revolution in global communications that, at least in their cases, allows people to rise above ethnicity and truly embrace religion as an identity group. Thus, Turks, Iranians, and Arabs are all Muslims, and all are united against Israel and to some extent against the West. And so with the enhanced geographical factors of Turkey and Iran affecting the Arab world, the vast quadrilateral of the Middle East is more organically interconnected than ever before.

Unlike the cases of Turkey and Iran, the Arab countries that lie between the Mediterranean Sea and the Iranian plateau had little meaning before the twentieth century. Palestine, Lebanon, Syria, and Iraq were but geographical expressions. Jordan wasn't thought of. When we remove the official lines on the map, we find a crude finger painting of Sunni and Shiite population clusters that contradict national borders. Inside these borders, the central governing authorities of Lebanon and Iraq barely operate. The one in Syria is tyrannical but under intense siege from its own masses (and may not last to the time this book is published); the one in Jordan is an absolute monarchy but probably only has a future as a constitutional one. (Jordan's main reason for existing always goes unstated: it acts as a buffer state for other Arab regimes who fear having a land border with Israel.) When U.S. president George W. Bush toppled the Iraqi dictatorship, it was thought at the time that he had set history in motion in the Arab world, roiling it to a greater degree than any Western figure since Napoleon. But then came the democratic rebellions of the Arab Spring, which had their own internal causes unrelated to what Bush had done. In any case, the post-Ottoman state system that came about in the aftermath of World War I is under greater stress than ever before. Western-style democracy may not exactly follow, but some form of liberalization eventually must, helped by the revolution in Egypt, and by the transition away from Cold War–era Arab police states, which will make the transition in Central Europe and the Balkans away from communism seem effortless by comparison. Indeed, the Levant is currently characterized by collapsing authoritarian regimes and democracies here and there that are unable to get anything done. The aggressive energy that characterizes the leaderships of Turkey and Iran, partly a product of their geographies, has for decades been almost nowhere apparent in the Arab world—another reason why the Arab world has now entered a period of epochal political transition.

Truly, the 2011 Arab uprisings that swept away several regimes were about the power of communications technology and the defeat of geography. But as time passes, the geographies of Tunisia, Libya, Egypt, Yemen, Syria, and other countries will reassert themselves. Tunisia and Egypt are age-old clusters of civilizations, whose statehoods originate in antiquity, whereas Libya and Yemen, for example, are but vague geographies, whose statehoods were not established until the twentieth century. Western Libya around Tripoli (Tripolitania) was always oriented toward the rich and urbane civilizations of Carthage in Tunisia, whereas eastern Libya around Benghazi (Cyrenaica) was always oriented toward those of Alexandria in Egypt. Yemen was rich and populous from antiquity forward, but its many mountain kingdoms were always separate from one another. It is therefore no surprise that building modern, nontyrannical states in Libya and Yemen is proving more difficult than in Tunisia and Egypt.

But it is in the Levant and Fertile Crescent where the next phase of conflict may unfold.

Iraq, because of the 2003 American invasion, is deep into a political evolution that cannot but affect the entire Arab world. This is because of Iraq's vast oil reserves (the second in the world behind Saudi Arabia); its large population of over 31 million; its geographical position at the juncture of the Sunni and Shiite worlds; its equidistance between Iran, Syria, and Saudi Arabia; and its historical and political significance as the former capital of the Abbasid Dynasty. Furthermore, Iraq is bedeviled by three legacies: almost half a century of brutal military dictatorship under various rulers, culminating in Saddam, that warped its political culture; a grim and violent history, ancient and modern, that extends far beyond the recent decades of dictatorship, and which has encouraged a harsh and suspicious national character (however essentialist this may sound); and severe ethnic and sectarian divisions.

Iraq has never been left alone. Once again, Freya Stark: "While Egypt lies parallel and peaceful to the routes of human traffic, Iraq is from earliest times a frontier province, right-angled and obnoxious to the predestined paths of man."[11] For Mesopotamia cut across one of history's bloodiest migration routes, pitting man against man and breeding pessimism as a consequence. Whether Iraq was being attacked from the Syrian desert in the west or the plateau of Elam in Iran to the east, it was a constant victim of occupation. From as early as the third millennium B.C., the ancient peoples of the Near East fought over control of Mesopotamia. Whether it was the Achaemenid Persian kings Darius and Xerxes who ruled Babylon, or the Mongol hordes that later swept down to overrun the land, or the long-running Ottoman rule that ended with the First World War, Iraq's has been a tragic history of occupation.[12]

Furthering this bloodshed, Mesopotamia has rarely been a demographically cohesive country. The Tigris and Euphrates, which run through Iraq, have long constituted a frontier zone where various groups, often the residue of these foreign invasions, clashed and overlapped. As the French orientalist Georges Roux painstakingly documents in *Ancient Iraq,* since antiquity, north, south, and center have usually been in pitched battle. Rulers of the first city-states, the southern Sumerians, fought the central-Mesopotamian Akkadians. They both fought the north-inhabiting Assyrians. The Assyrians, in turn, fought the Babylonians. And this was to say nothing of the many pockets of Persians who lived amid the native Mesopotamians, forming another source of strife.[13] Only the most suffocating of tyrannies could stave off the utter disintegration to which this frontier region was prone. As the scholar Adeed Dawisha notes, "The fragility of the social order was [throughout history] structural to the land of Mesopotamia."[14] And this fragile order, which pitted group against group in a densely populated river valley with no protective boundaries, led ultimately and seemingly inexorably to a twentieth-century tyranny straight out of antiquity: a tyranny which, the moment it was toppled, led to several years of bloodcurdling anarchy with atrocities that had an ancient aura.

For Iraq is burdened by modern as well as by ancient history. Mesopotamia was among the most weakly governed parts of the Ottoman Empire; another case of a vague geographical expression—a loose assemblage of tribes, sects, and ethnicities further divided by the Turks into the *vilayets* of Kurdish Mosul, Sunni Baghdad, and Shiite Basra, going from north to south. When the British tried to "sculpt" a polity between the Tigris and Euphrates following the Turkish collapse they created a witches' brew of Kurdish separatism, Shiite tribalism, and Sunni assertiveness.[15] To connect the oil fields of Kurdistan in the north with a port on the Persian Gulf in the south—as part of a land-and-sea strategy to defend India—the British brought together ethnic and sectarian forces that would be difficult to assuage by normal means.

The rise of Arab nationalism following World War II led to further divisions. Iraqi officers and politicians were pitted against each other: those who saw Iraq's problematic identity as best subsumed beneath the rubric of a single Arab nation stretching from the Maghreb to Mesopotamia, versus those who strove against heavy odds for a united Iraq that, despite its geographic illogic, would quell its own sectarian passions. In any case, almost four decades of fractious, unstable, and feeble democracy since 1921, interspersed with revolts and semi-authoritarianism in the name of the royal palace, came to an abrupt end on July 14, 1958, when a military coup deposed Iraq's pro-Western government. King Faisal II, who had ruled for the past nineteen years, and his family were lined up against a wall and shot. The prime minister, Nuri al-Said, was shot and buried; afterward his corpse was disinterred, then burned and mutilated by a mob. This was not a random act, but one indicative of the wanton and perverse violence that has often characterized Iraqi political life. In fact, the killing of the entire Hashemite royal family, like that of the killing of the family of Czar Nicholas II in Russia in 1918, was a deeply symbolic crime that presaged decades of state-inflicted murder and torture from which Iraq will take more years to recover. The line of East Bloc–style tyrannies began with Brigadier Abd al-Karim Qasim and ended with Saddam Hussein, each dictator more extreme than the next; only thus could a state of such disparate groups and political forces be held together.

Nevertheless, as Dawisha writes, "Historical recollection is neither linear nor cumulative. . . . So while undoubtedly much of Iraq's history was authoritarian, there also were rays of democratic hope."[16] As Iraq struggles to avoid slipping back into either tyranny or anarchy under the burden of primordial loyalties, it is worth keeping in mind that from 1921 through 1958 it did know a functioning democracy of sorts. Moreover, geography itself is subject to different interpretations. With all of Mesopotamia's proclivity for human division, as Marshall Hodgson makes us aware, such a state, in fact, is not wholly artificial, and does have a basis in antiquity. The very panel of cultivation generated by the Tigris and Euphrates makes for one of the Middle East's signal demographic and environmental facts.

Still, any Iraqi democracy that emerges in the second decade of the twenty-first century is going to be uncertain, corrupt, inefficient, and considerably unruly, with political assassinations possibly a regular part of life. In short, a democratic Iraq, despite prodigious petroleum wealth and an American-trained military, will be a weak state at least in the near term. And its feuding politicians will reach out for financial and political support to contiguous powers—principally Iran and Saudi Arabia—and, as a consequence, become to some extent playthings of them. Iraq could become again a larger version of civil war–wracked Lebanon in the 1970s and 1980s. Because the stakes are so large in Iraq—those in power will have corrupt access to the incredible oil wealth—the infighting, as we have seen, will be severe and persistent. A pro-Western outpost in the heart of the Arab world requires the state to be internally strong. There is little sign of that yet.

A weakened Mesopotamia would seem to represent an opportunity for another demographic or natural resource hub of the Arab world to assume prestige and leadership. But it is difficult to see in what direction that will come. The Saudis are by nature nervous, hesitant, and vulnerable, because of their own immense oil wealth coupled with a relatively small population that, nevertheless, is characterized by hordes of male youth prone to both radicalization and a yearning for democratization—the same cohort that we have seen spark revolutions in Tunisia and Egypt. The post-Mubarak era in Egypt, which has the Arab world's largest population, will feature governments whose energies, democratic or not, will be devoted to consolidating control internally, and attending to the demographic challenges that are associated with the headwaters of the White and Blue Niles being located in the two Sudans and Ethiopia. (Ethiopia, with 83 million people, has an even larger population than Egypt, while both northern and southern Sudan have over 40 million. Struggles over water use will increasingly burden all these governments in the twenty-first century.) It is the very weakness of the Arab world that Turkey and Iran, with their appeals to the larger Muslim *Umma*, will seek to take advantage of.

This weakness is not only expressed by post-invasion Iraq, but by Syria, too. Syria is another critical geographic pole of the Arab world—both in medieval and modern times. Indeed, it laid claim to being the Cold War era's *throbbing heart of Arabism.*

Leaving the Taurus Mountains in a southeastward direction in 1998, and descending steeply from Asia Minor into the Syrian plain—punctuated by pine and olive trees with the occasional limestone hill—I left behind a confident and industrialized society in Turkey, its nationalism bolstered by the geographical logic of the Black Sea to the north, the Mediterranean to the south and west, and mountain fastnesses to the east and southeast. In this natural fortress, Islam had been subsumed within the rubric of democracy. But now I entered an artificial piece of territory on a sprawling desert, held together only by Baathist ideology and an attendant personality cult. Photos of President Hafez al-Assad on every shop window and car windshield defaced the landscape. Geography did not determine Syria's destiny—or Turkey's—but it was a starting point.

Geography and history tell us that Syria, with a population of twenty million, will continue to be the epicenter of turbulence in the Arab world. Aleppo in northern Syria is a bazaar city with greater historical links to Mosul and Baghdad in Iraq than to Damascus, Syria's capital. Whenever Damascus's fortunes declined, Aleppo recovered its greatness. Wandering through the souks of Aleppo, it is striking how distant and irrelevant Damascus seems. Aleppo's souks are dominated by Kurds, Turks, Circassians, Arab Christians, Armenians, and others, unlike the Damascus souk, which is more a world of Sunni Arabs. As in Pakistan and the former Yugoslavia, in Syria each sect and religion is associated with a specific geographical region. Between Aleppo and Damascus is the increasingly Islamist Sunni heartland of Homs and Hama. Between Damascus and the Jordanian border are the Druze, and in the mountain stronghold contiguous to Lebanon are the Alawites, both remnants of a wave of Shiism from Persia and Mesopotamia that a thousand years ago swept over Syria. Free and fair elections in 1947, 1949, and 1954 exacerbated these divisions by dividing the vote along regional, sectarian, and ethnic lines. The late Hafez al-Assad came to power in 1970 after twenty-one changes of government in the previous twenty-four years. For three decades he was the Leonid Brezhnev of the Arab world, staving off the future by failing to build a civil society at home.

Whereas Yugoslavia still had an intellectual class at the time of its breakup, Syria did not, so stultifying was the elder Assad's regime.

During the Cold War and early Post Cold War years, Syria's fervent pan-Arabism was a substitute for its weak identity as a state. Greater Syria was an Ottoman-era geographical term that included present-day Lebanon, Jordan, and Israel-Palestine, to which the truncated borders of the current Syrian state do great violence. This historic Greater Syria was called by Princeton scholar Philip K. Hitti "the largest small country on the map, microscopic in size but cosmic in influence," encompassing in its geography, at the confluence of Europe, Asia, and Africa, "the history of the civilized world in miniature form."[17] Syria furnished the Greco-Roman world with some of its most brilliant thinkers, Stoics and Neoplatonists among them. Syria was the seat of the Umayyad Empire, the first Arab dynasty after Muhammad, which was larger than Rome at its zenith. And it was the scene of arguably the greatest drama in history between Islam and the West: the Crusades.

But the Syria of recent decades has been a ghost of this great geographical and historical legacy. And the Syrians are poignantly aware of it; for, as they know, the loss of Lebanon cut off much of Syria's outlet to the Mediterranean, from which its rich cultural depositories had breathed life. Ever since France sundered Lebanon from Syria in 1920, the Syrians have been desperate to get it back. That is why the total Syrian withdrawal from Lebanon that George W. Bush demanded in the wake of the February 2005 assassination of anti-Syrian Lebanese prime minister Rafik Hariri would have undermined the very political foundation of the minority Alawite regime in Damascus right then and there. The Alawites, a heterodox Shiite sect, demographically spill over into both Syria and Lebanon. An Alawite ministate in northwestern Syria is not an impossibility following the collapse of the Alawite regime in Damascus.

In fact, following Iraq and Afghanistan, the next target of Sunni jihadists could be Syria itself: in the Syrian regime, headed through early 2012 by Bashar al-Assad, the jihadists have had an enemy that is "at once tyrannical, secular, *and* heretical."[18] This Alawite regime was close to Shiite Iran, and stands guilty of murdering tens of thousands of Sunni Islamists in the 1970s and 1980s. Jihadists have deep logistical familiarity with Syria—sustaining the jihad in Iraq necessitated a whole network of safe houses inside Syria. Truly, no one has a feel for what a post-authoritarian, post-Assad Syria will eventually turn out to be. How deep is sectarianism? It may not be deep at all, but once the killing starts, people revert to long-repressed sectarian identities. It may also be that a post-Assad Syria will do better than a post-Saddam Iraq, precisely because the tyranny in the former was much less severe than in the latter, making Syria a less damaged society. Traveling from Saddam's Iraq to Assad's Syria, as I did on occasion, was like coming up for liberal humanist air. On the other hand, Yugoslavia was a more open society throughout the Cold War than its Balkan neighbors, and look at how ethnic and religious differences undid that society! The minority Alawites have kept the peace in Syria; it would seem unlikely that Sunni jihadists could do the same. They might be equally as brutal, but without the sophisticated knowledge of governance that the Alawites acquired during forty years in power.

Of course, it does not have to turn out that way at all. For there is a sturdy geographical basis for peace and political rebirth in Syria. Remember again Hodgson: these countries such as Syria and Iraq really do have roots in agricultural terrain; they are not entirely man-made. Syria, despite its present borders, still represents the heart of the Levantine world, which means a world of multiple ethnic and religious identities united by commerce.[19] The Syrian-born poet Ali Ahmad Said (known by his pen name "Adonis") constitutes the very expression of this other Syria, with its wealth of civilizational interaction, that, as we know from the work of William McNeill, forms the core drama of history. Adonis exhorts his fellow Syrians to renounce Arab nationalism and forge a new state identity based on Syria's very eclecticism and diversity: in effect, a twenty-first-century equivalent of early-twentieth-century Beirut, Alexandria, and Smyrna. Adonis, like the Assads, is an Alawite, but one who instead of embracing Arabism and the police state as shields for his minority status has embraced cosmopolitanism instead.[20] Rather than look toward the desert, Adonis looks toward the Mediterranean, on which modern Syria, despite the loss of Lebanon, still has considerable real estate. The Mediterranean stands for an ethnic and sectarian synthesis, which is the only ideational basis for a stable democracy in Syria. McNeill, Hodgson, and Adonis really do overlap in terms of Syria's promise.[21]

The implications of this for the rest of geographical Greater Syria—Lebanon, Jordan, and Israel—are immense. Whether or not there is a jihadist revolt in Syria to follow the democratic one—in the event that a democracy worthy of Adonis does not take root—Syria appears destined to become a less centralized, and, therefore, a weaker state. And it will be one with a significant youth bulge: 36 percent of the population is fourteen years old or younger. A weakened Syria could mean the emergence of Beirut as the cultural and economic capital of Greater Syria, with Damascus paying the price for its decades-long, Soviet-like removal from the modern world. Yet with the poor, Hezbollah-trending Shiites of south Beirut continuing to gain demographic sway over the rest of that city, and Sunni Islamists having more political influence in Damascus, Greater Syria could become a far more unstable geography than it is now.

Jordan might yet survive such an evolution, because the Hashemite dynasty (unlike the Alawite one) has spent decades building a state consciousness through the development of a unified elite. Jordan's capital of Amman is filled with former government ministers loyal to the Jordanian monarchy—men who were not imprisoned or killed as a result of cabinet reshuffles, but who were merely allowed to become rich. But, once more, the curse is in the demographics: 70 percent of Jordan's population of 6.3 million is urban, and almost a third are Palestinian refugees, who have a higher birth rate than the indigenous East Bankers. (As for the East Bankers themselves, the traditional relationship between the tribes and the monarchy has frayed as tribal culture has itself evolved, with pickup trucks and cellphones having long replaced camels.) Then there are the 750,000 Iraqi refugees in Jordan, making Jordan per capita the host of the largest refugee population on earth.

Again, we are back to the truth of a closed and claustrophobic geography, according to Paul Bracken, in which the poor and crowded
urban masses have had their emotions further whipped up by electronic media, according to Elias Canetti. Because of the violence in
Iraq and Afghanistan over the past decade, we became indifferent to
just how unstable are the so-called stable parts of the Middle East. We
did so at our peril—as the Arab uprisings have shown. The uprisings
began as expressions of yearning for civil society and individual dignity, which calcified national security regimes had robbed people of.
But in the future urbanization and electronic communications could
lead to less benign expressions of public rage. The crowd baying at
real and perceived injustices is the new postmodern tiger that the next
generation of Arab leaders will struggle to keep under control.

I crossed the border from Jordan to Israel several times. The Jordan
River valley is part of a deep rift in the earth's surface that stretches
from Syria for 3,700 miles south to Mozambique. Thus, the switch-
back, westering descent to the Jordan River from the biscuit-brown
tableland of the Jordanian town of Irbid was dizzyingly dramatic.
The road in the late 1990s was lined with dusty garages, rickety fruit
stands, and knots of young men hanging about, smoking. At the bottom lay a ribbon of green fields along the river, where, on the other
side, in Israel, the mountains rose just as steeply. The Jordanian border post and customs offices were a series of old cargo containers in
a vacant lot. The river is narrow. You cross it in a bus in literally
seconds. On the opposite side was a landscaped park separating the
traffic lanes: like a traffic island anywhere in the West, but a wonder
after the bleak, dust-strewn public spaces of Jordan and much of the
Arab world. The Israeli immigration hall was like any small air termi-
nal in the United States. The Israeli security men wore Timberland
shirts barely tucked into their jeans to make room for their handguns.
After weeks in the Arab world, these young men seemed so tradition-
less. Beyond the immigration hall lay new sidewalks, benches, and
tourist facilities; again, like any place in the West. And yet it was an

empty, unfriendly public space; nobody was simply hanging about, as in the Arab world, where unemployment was endemic. The Israelis manning the booths were impersonal, rude. Traditional Middle Eastern hospitality was absent. Even though I had lived in Israel in the 1970s and had served in its military, arriving here the way I had allowed me to see it anew. Israel seemed so unnatural to the Middle East, and yet it was such a blunt, sturdy fact.

To the entire Muslim world, at once united and enraged by mass media, the plight of the Palestinians represents a totemic injustice in the affairs of humankind. The Israeli occupation of the West Bank may not have been a visible factor in the first stages of the Arab Spring but we shouldn't kid ourselves. The facts have, to a certain extent, become meaningless; perceptions are everything. Undergirding it all is geography. While Zionism shows the power of ideas, the battle over land between Israelis and Palestinians—between Jews and Muslims, as both the Turks and the Iranians would have it—is a case of utter geographical determinism.

"Jews will very soon become a minority in the lands they occupy or rule from the Jordan River to the Mediterranean (by some calculations this has already happened), and some demographers forecast that in fifteen years they will make up as little as 42 percent of the population in this area." So wrote Benjamin Schwarz, the national editor of *The Atlantic,* in that magazine in 2005, in an article entitled "Will Israel Live to 100?" Since then little has changed to affect those calculations, or his dispassionate analysis. The birth rate in the occupied Arab territories is ludicrously higher than in Israel: in Gaza, population growth is double that of Israel, with the average woman having more than five children over her adult lifetime. Consequently, in the first decade of the twenty-first century, a consensus emerged within the Israeli political, military, and intelligence communities that Israel must withdraw from virtually all of the occupied territories or become an essentially Apartheid-like state—if not immediately, then over time. The result was "the fence": an Israeli-built barrier that effectively seals off Israel from the demographically expanding and impoverished Palestinian population in the West Bank. Arnon Soffer, an

Israeli geographer, calls the fence "a last desperate attempt to save the state of Israel." But Jewish settlements close to the Green Line in the occupied territories may, as Schwarz writes, "have roots too deep and may well be too integral to the daily life of too many Israelis to be forsaken."[22] And then there is the basic principle and premise of Palestinian ideology, the "right of return": which applies to the 700,000 Palestinians displaced from Israel upon its birth and their descendants, a population that may now number five million. In 2001, 98.7 percent of Palestinian refugees dismissed compensation in place of the right of return. Finally, there are the Israeli Arabs to consider: those living within Israel's pre-1967 borders. While the population growth among Israeli Jews is 1.4 percent, among Israeli Arabs it is 3.4 percent: the median age of Jews is thirty-five; that of Arabs is fourteen.

In a rational world, one might hope for a peace treaty between Israelis and Palestinians in which the Israelis would cede back the occupied territories and disband most settlements, and the Palestinians would give up the right of return. In such a circumstance, a Greater Israel, at least as an economic concept, would constitute a regional magnet on the Mediterranean toward which not only the West Bank and Gaza, but Jordan, southern Lebanon, and southern Syria including Damascus would orient themselves. But few peoples seem psychologically further apart as of this writing, and so divided amongst themselves—and, therefore, politically immobilized—as Israelis and Palestinians. One can only hope that the political earthquake in the Arab world in 2011 and early 2012 will prod Israel into making pivotal territorial concessions.

The Middle East hangs on a thread of fateful human interactions, the more so because of a closed and densely packed geography. Geography has not disappeared in the course of the revolutions in communications and weaponry; it has simply gotten more valuable, more precious, to more people.

In such a world, universal values must be contingent on circumstances. We pray for the survival of a Hashemite Jordan and a united post-Assad Syria, even as we pray for the end of the mullahs' dictatorship in Iran. In Iran, democracy is potentially our friend, making Greater Iran from Gaza to Afghanistan a force for good rather than for evil. Thus might the calculus in the entire Middle East be shifted; thus might Hezbollah and Hamas be tamed, and Israeli-Palestinian peace prospects improved. But in Jordan, it is hard to imagine a more moderate and pro-Western regime than the current undemocratic monarchy. Likewise, democracy in Saudi Arabia is potentially our enemy. In Syria, democracy should come incrementally; lest the political organization of Greater Syria be undone by Sunni jihadists, as happened in Mesopotamia between 2006 and 2007.

European leaders in the nineteenth century and the beginning of the twentieth were engrossed by the so-called Eastern Question: that is, the eruptions of instability and nationalist yearnings caused by the seemingly interminable rotting-away of the Ottoman Empire. The Eastern Question was settled by the cataclysm of World War I, from which the modern Arab state system emerged, helped forged as it was by age-old geographical features and population clusters that Marshall Hodgson writes about so eloquently. But a hundred years on, the durability of that post-Ottoman state system in the heart of the Oikoumene should not be taken for granted.

Part III

AMERICA'S DESTINY

Chapter XV

BRAUDEL, MEXICO, AND GRAND STRATEGY

The late Oxford historian Hugh Trevor-Roper wrote in 1972 that no group of scholars had a more "fertilizing effect" on the study of history than the so-called *Annales* group, founded in 1929 by Lucien Febvre and Marc Bloch, and named for the Paris periodical in which they frequently published: *Annales d'Histoire Economique et Sociale.* Foremost among these Frenchmen was Fernand Braudel. In 1949, Braudel published *The Mediterranean and the Mediterranean World in the Age of Philip II*, a work that broke new ground in historical writing by its emphasis on geography, demography, materialism, and the environment.[1] Braudel brought nature itself into a work of history, thereby immeasurably enriching the discipline, as well as helping to restore geography to its proper place in academia. His massive two-volume effort is particularly impressive because he wrote much of it while a prisoner of the Germans during World War II. In Braudel's vast tapestry of a narrative, permanent and unchanging environ-

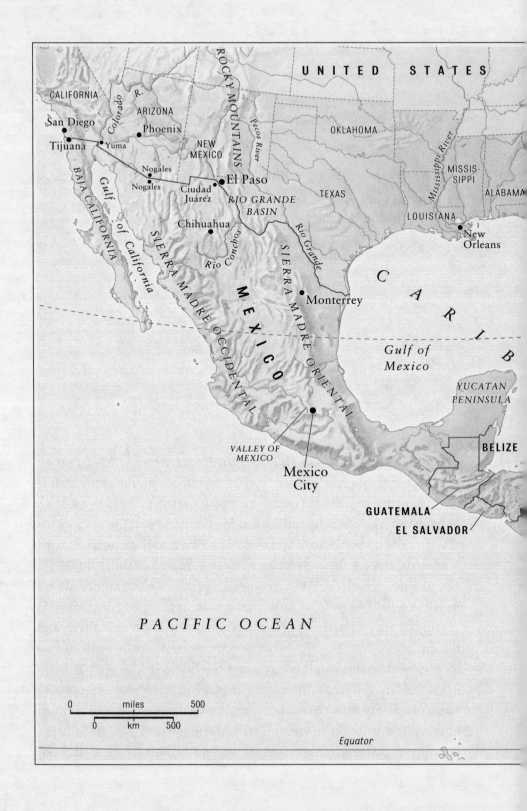

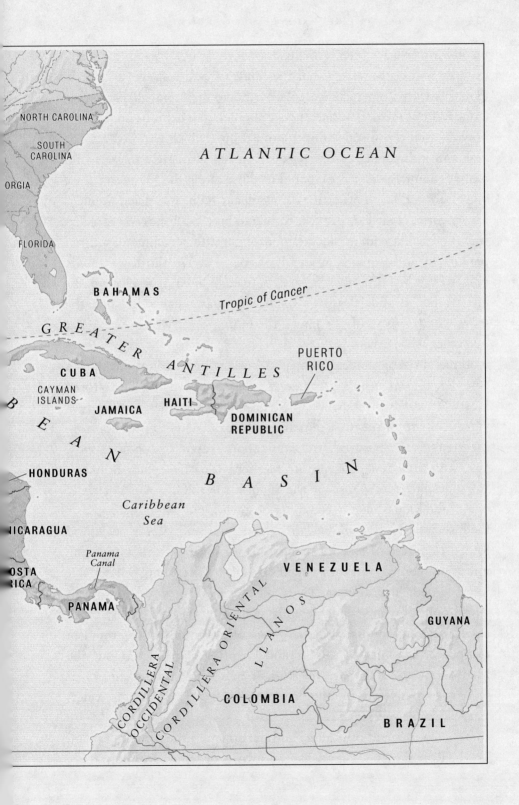

mental forces lead to enduring historical trends that go on for many decades and centuries, so that the kinds of political events and regional wars with which we concern ourselves seem almost preordained, if not mere minutiae. It was Braudel who helps us understand how the rich forest soils of northern Europe, which required little to make an individual peasant productive, led ultimately to freer and more dynamic societies compared to those along the Mediterranean, where poorer, more precarious soils meant there was a requirement for irrigation that led, in turn, to oligarchies. Such poverty-stricken soils, combined with an uncertain, drought-afflicted climate, spurred the Greeks and Romans in search of conquest.[2] In short, we delude ourselves in believing that we are completely in control of our destinies; rather, Braudel leads us to the attendant realization that the more we are aware of our limits, the more power we have to affect outcomes within them.

Braudel's geographical compass identifies the Mediterranean as a complex of seas near a great desert, the Sahara. Thus, he restored North Africa to prominence in Mediterranean studies, and so provided context for the mass migration of workers in our own era from the Mediterranean's southern Islamic shores (upon whose stony massifs Latin sank few roots) to its northern Christian ones. Braudel's story, despite its emphasis on the Spanish ruler Philip II, is not really one of individual men overcoming obstacles, but rather of men and their societies subtly molded by impersonal and deeply structural forces. In an era of climate change, of warming Arctic seas opening up to commercial traffic, of potential sea-level rises that spell disaster for crowded, littoral countries in the tropical Third World, and of world politics being fundamentally shaped by the availability of oil and other commodities, Braudel's epic of geographical determinism is ripe for reading. In fact, Braudel with his writings about the Mediterranean establishes the literary mood-context for an era of scarcity and environmentally driven events in an increasingly water-starved, congested planet.

The achievement of Braudel and the others of the *Annales* school, Trevor-Roper writes, "is to have drawn geography, sociology, law, ideas into the broad stream of history, and thereby to have refreshed, nourished, and strengthened that stream." After all, Trevor-Roper goes on: "Geography, climate, population determine communications, economy, political organization."[3] Braudel, who unlike Mackinder, Spykman, or Mahan lacks a specific theory of geopolitics for us to investigate, nevertheless achieves something greater. For he is more than a geographer or strategist. He is a historian whose narrative has a godlike quality in which every detail of human existence is painted against the canvas of natural forces. If geography ever approaches literature, it does so with Braudel. In a sense, he is a summation of all the strategic thinkers we have encountered thus far.

Oxford archaeologist Barry Cunliffe notes that perhaps Braudel's signal contribution to the way in which history is perceived is his concept of "varying wavelengths of time." At the base is the *longue durée:* slow, imperceptibly changing geographical time, "of landscapes that enable and constrain." Above this, at a faster wavelength, come the "medium-term cycles," what Braudel himself refers to as *conjonctures,* that is, systemic changes in demographics, economics, agriculture, society, and politics. Cunliffe explains that these are essentially "collective forces, impersonal and usually restricted in time to no more than a century." Together the *longue durée* and *conjonctures* provide the largely hidden "basic structures" against which human life is played out. My very highlighting of geography has been designed to put emphasis on these basic structures. Braudel calls the shortest-term cycle *l'histoire événmentielle*—the daily vicissitudes of politics and diplomacy that are the staple of media coverage. Braudel's analogy is the sea: in the deepest depths is the sluggish movement of water masses that bear everything; above that the tides and swells; and finally at the surface, in Cunliffe's words, "the transient flecks of surf, whipped up and gone in a minute."[4]

It is impossible to speculate on how geopolitics will play out over the inhuman timeframe of much of Braudel's analysis, especially given the controversy over climate change and its effects on specific regions. To talk about relations between, say, America and Europe a hundred or two hundred years hence is ridiculous, because of so many factors that have yet to even appear. Rather, think of Braudel as simply encouraging us to take a more distant and dispassionate view of our own foibles. For example, reading Braudel, with the events of the first decade of the twenty-first century uppermost in one's mind, it is impossible to avoid the question: Are the wars in Iraq and Afghanistan transient flecks of surf only; or are they part of something deeper, more profound, and structural in America's destiny? For that matter, might World War I and World War II even, which saw violence on a scale never before experienced in history, belong merely to *l'histoire événmentielle*? Braudel, precisely because he places the events of humankind against the pressure of natural forces, facilitates thinking in terms of the *longue durée*.

I offer up Braudel as prologue to a remarkable moment at a Washington conference in June 2009, where a question was raised that gives particular urgency to my inquiry on the relevance of geography for the United States in the twenty-first century. It was a question that Braudel would have liked, taking people away from the obsessions of the moment toward a grander and longer-term perspective. The event was sponsored by the Center for a New American Security, where I am a senior fellow. The circumstance was a panel discussion on what were the next steps that needed to be taken in Afghanistan and Pakistan, with a special emphasis on the fine-tuning of counterinsurgency. Panelists proceeded to engage the inside baseball of "Af-Pak," as the Afghanistan-Pakistan border region has come to be addressed by the Washington cognoscenti. Then another panelist, Boston University professor Andrew Bacevich, made an impolite observation, which I—sitting in the front row—will paraphrase:

A historian looking at this panel from the viewpoint of the distant future might conclude, Bacevich surmised, that while the United States was deeply focused on Afghanistan and other parts of the Greater Middle East, a massive state failure was developing right on America's southern border, with far more profound implications for the near and distant future of America, its society, and American power than anything occurring half a world away. What have we achieved in the Middle East with all of our interventions since the 1980s? Bacevich asked. Why not fix Mexico instead? How we might have prospered had we put all that money, expertise, and innovation that went into Iraq and Afghanistan into Mexico.

Therein, sheathed in a simple question, lies the most elemental critique of American foreign policy since the end of the Cold War: a critique that, as we shall see, goes far beyond Mexico, encompasses Eurasia, and yet is rooted in North American geography. I start with Bacevich only because his frustration is stark and his bona fides particularly impressive—and poignant: a West Point graduate and Vietnam veteran, his son was killed in Iraq. But whereas Bacevich in his books can be a polemicist with overwhelming disregard for East Coast elites and all manner of entanglements in which they embroil America overseas, there are others whose views substantially dovetail with his. Their analysis, along with Bacevich's, is above all rooted in a conscious attempt to get beyond *l'histoire événmentielle* to the longer term. When I think about what truly worries all of these analysts, Braudel's *longue durée* comes to mind.

Bacevich along with Stephen Walt, John Mearsheimer, Paul Pillar, Mark Helprin, Ted Galen Carpenter, and the late Samuel Huntington are not, in every case, the most well-known voices in foreign policy analysis, and putting them in the same category is itself a bit of a stretch. Yet in a composite sense they have questioned the fundamental direction of American foreign policy for the longer term. Walt is a professor at Harvard and Mearsheimer at the University of Chicago, but with all the prestige which those appointments carry, their book *The Israel Lobby and U.S. Foreign Policy,* published in 2007, came in for very rough treatment because of its allegation that Israel's supporters in America were essentially the culprits behind the Iraq War, a war which everyone in this group of analysts was against. Helprin, a novelist and former Israeli soldier, takes no prisoners in his belief that China will be America's primary military adversary, a belief that Mearsheimer also shares. They both, along with Pillar, a former CIA analyst, remain in high dudgeon about the diversion of American resources to useless wars in the Middle East while China acquires the latest defense technology. Indeed, even if we do stabilize Afghanistan and Pakistan, China will be the main beneficiary, able to build roads and pipelines throughout the region as part of its quest for energy and strategic minerals and metals. Meanwhile, Carpenter warns severely about the danger that a violence-plagued Mexico represents; as did Huntington in his last years. To merge their thoughts, as well as those of others I could name, all of whom dwell more or less in the realist camp of foreign policy circles, is to reach the conclusion that America faces three primary geopolitical dilemmas: a chaotic Eurasian heartland in the Middle East, a rising and assertive Chinese superpower, and a state in deep trouble in Mexico. And the challenges we face with China and Mexico are most efficiently dealt with by wariness of further military involvement in the Middle East. This is the only way that American power can sustain itself for the decades to come, and survive part of the *longue durée*.

Of course, there is safety, a certain smugness for that matter, in such long-term thinking. None of these men has adequately addressed what, for instance, would actually happen if we were to withdraw precipitously, say, from Afghanistan. Would the intelligence that has led to successful drone attacks on al Qaeda in Waziristan dry up? Would Ayman al-Zawahiri and other surviving luminaries of al Qaeda make triumphal entries in front of al Jazeera television cameras into Jalalabad? Would Afghanistan become a radicalized Taliban state under the tutelage of Pakistani intelligence? Would India, the global pivot state of the twenty-first century, lose respect for the United States as a consequence? Would Iran informally annex western Afghanistan? And what would have happened to Iraq had we withdrawn completely in 2006, at the height of the violence there, as some of these analysts would have no doubt wished? Would the Balkan-level sectarian atrocities have soared to the level of Rwanda, with a million killed rather than a hundred or two hundred thousand? For one would have to be particularly cold-blooded not to realize the monumental effect on individual lives in such different outcomes. Moreover, what would have happened in the region, and to America's reputation for power, had we so withdrawn? How would such quick withdrawals be carried out? Don't ever say that things cannot get much worse than they are, because they can.

Truly, withdrawing precipitously from Iraq or Afghanistan would be irresponsible because—like it or not—merely by invading these places and staying there so long, we have acquired substantial stakes in the outcomes. Nevertheless, it would be unfair to judge these analysts and others who agree with them solely on the minutiae of Iraq and Afghanistan. For the wellspring of emotion behind their beliefs is that we never should have gotten involved in these countries in the first place. No matter how Iraq eventually turns out, the body count, both American and Iraqi, will haunt American foreign policy debates for decades, just as Vietnam did. They constitute more than just *l'histoire événmentielle*.

To be sure, these analysts are not concerned about what to do next in Afghanistan and Iraq. Instead—again, merging their thoughts—they are asking themselves, what has been the cost of our blunders already? Can we as a great power be salvaged? And where do we put our best efforts, in terms of highly selective military deployments and civilian aid, so that America can help preserve the balance of power in Eurasia and not be inundated over the decades by Mexicans fleeing a troubled state? As Jakub Grygiel puts it: "Geographic isolation is a strategic blessing and should not be squandered by an expansionary strategy."[5]

So how much have we squandered already? Michael Lind, a scholar at the New America Foundation in Washington, agrees with Bacevich about the foolishness of both the Iraq War and the escalation of the war in Afghanistan. But he parts company with Bacevich on whether America can afford such conflicts. Lind argues that relatively little of the national debt is the result of military spending, let alone of two simultaneous wars, and that reducing health care costs is far more central to America's fiscal solvency than recent imperial-like adventurism, as much as he opposes it.[6] In fact, a look at some of the blunders of empires past may put the debacles of Iraq and Afghanistan in some perspective, both in terms of their effect on U.S.

foreign policy already, and their effect on our ability to deal with the future challenges in the Middle East, China, and Mexico throughout the course of the twenty-first century.

In 1449, returning from a failed campaign in Mongolia, the army of Ming China was surrounded by Mongol forces. Without water, the Chinese panicked. Trusting in Mongol mercy, Grygiel writes, "many shed their armor and ran toward the enemy lines." As many as half a million Chinese soldiers were slaughtered and the Ming emperor became a prisoner of the Mongols. The Ming army adventure in Mongolia marked the start of the long decline of the Ming Dynasty. The Ming army never again attempted to confront the Mongols in the northern steppe, even as tension with the Mongols would sap the energy of the Ming leadership. This led to China's retreat from maritime Asia, which would help encourage the entry of European powers into the Rimland.[7]

Nothing so disastrous has occurred following the America adventure in Iraq—our military and economic position around the world, and especially in East Asia, is sturdy and shows no signs of retrenchment, let alone retreat. We lost under 5,000 troops and 32,000 seriously wounded, a terrible price, but not an entire invasion force of half a million. The U.S. Army, which bore the brunt of the Iraq fighting, stands at almost half a million active-duty personnel, and precisely because of its experience in irregular warfare in Iraq is now better trained, doctrinally more flexible, and intellectually more subtle than ever. The same goes for the Marine Corps.

Not in Iraq, nor in Afghanistan, did the United States make the kind of pivotal blunder that late medieval Venice did. It wasn't only Venice's privileged geographical position between western and eastern Mediterranean trade routes that allowed it to create a seaborne empire; rather, it was the fact that Venice was protected from the Italian mainland by a few miles of water, and protected by invasion from the sea by long sandbars. One cause of Venice's decline starting in the fifteenth century was its decision to become a power on mainland

Italy. By going to war repeatedly against Verona, Padua, Florence, Milan, and the League of Cambrai, Venice was no longer detached from "deadly" balance-of-power politics on land, and this had an adverse effect on its ability to project sea power.[8] The Venetian example should cause alarm among American policymakers if—and only if—the United States were to make a habit of military interventions on land in the Greater Middle East. But if America can henceforth restrict itself to being an air and sea power, it can easily avoid Venice's fate. It is the permanence of small wars that can undo us, not the odd, once every third of a century miscalculation, however much tragedy and consternation that causes.

In this light, Iraq during the worst fighting in 2006 and 2007 might be compared to the Indian Mutiny against the British in 1857 and 1858, when the orientalists and other pragmatists in the British power structure, who wanted to leave traditional India as it was, lost some sway to evangelical and utilitarian reformers who wanted to modernize and Christianize India—to make it more like England. But the attempt to bring the fruits of Western civilization to the Indian Subcontinent were met with a revolt against imperial authority. Delhi, Luknow, and other cities were besieged and captured before being retaken by colonial forces. Yet the debacle did not signal the end of the British Empire, which expanded even for another century. Instead, it signaled the transition from an ad hoc imperium fired by an evangelical lust to impose its values to a calmer and more pragmatic empire built on international trade and technology.[9]

Ancient history, too, offers up examples that cast doubt on whether Afghanistan and Iraq, in and of themselves, have doomed us. Famously, there is the Sicilian Expedition recounted by Thucydides in the Sixth Book of *The Peloponnesian War*. Fourteen years elapsed from Athens's first foray into Sicily to its final disaster there in the naval battle of Syracuse in 413 B.C., the same number of years between the early forays of the John F. Kennedy administration in Vietnam and President Gerald Ford's final withdrawal after Saigon was overrun. The Sicilian War split the home front in Athens, as did the Vietnam and Iraq wars. Paralyzed by pessimism and recriminations, it was some time before Athenians were willing to resume in earnest the bipolar conflict with Sparta. Sicily, as it turned out, had not been altogether crucial to the survival of Athens's democracy and its maritime empire. For despite having lost and suffered so much, Athens still had the resources to lead an alliance, even as the adventure in Sicily would prove to be the turning point in the Peloponnesian War, which Athens lost.

There also is the larger example of the decline of Rome, detailed in 1976 by Edward N. Luttwak in his book *The Grand Strategy of the Roman Empire: From the First Century* A.D. *to the Third*. Luttwak's method is, rather than to talk about decline in general, to discuss it in terms of Rome's grand strategy. Luttwak identifies three chronological stages of Roman grand strategy. The first is the Julio-Claudian system, or that of the republican empire, in which the client states that surrounded the empire's Italianate core were sufficiently impressed with the "totality" of Roman power to carry out the empire's wishes, without the need of occupation armies. In this stage, diplomacy—not military force—was an active ingredient of Roman coercion, even as an overwhelming formation of Roman troops lay in a "vast circle" around Rome. Because these troops were not needed for the occupation of client states, or for territorial defense in any sense, they were, in Luttwak's words, "inherently mobile and freely redeployable." Here was power at its zenith, prudently exercised, run on an economy-of-force principle. A surge capacity was readily available for any military contingency, and all in the Mediterranean world knew it. Thus everyone feared Rome. One thinks of Ronald Reagan's America, with a massive buildup of the military that Defense Secretary Caspar Weinberger was, nevertheless, hell-bent not to use, so as to nurture the reputation of power without the need for risky adventures. The Antonine system, in place from the mid-first century to the mid-third, reflected what Luttwak calls the "territorialization" of the empire: for Rome now felt the need to deploy its military everywhere, in the client states themselves, in order to secure their fealty, and so the economy-of-force principle was lost. Nevertheless, the empire was prosperous, and there was widespread, voluntary Romanization of the barbarian tribes, "eliminating the last vestiges of nativist disaffection" for the time being. Yet this very Romanization of the empire would over time create unity among different tribes, allowing them to band together in common cause against Rome, for they were now joined in a culture that was still not their own. Think of how globalization, which in a sense constitutes an Americanization of the world, nevertheless serves as a vehicle to defy American hegemony. Hence came the third system to constitute Rome's grand strategy: Diocletian's "defense-in-depth," whereby the border peoples coalesced into formal confederations able to challenge Rome, and so the state was on the defensive everywhere, with emergency deployments constant. The surge capacity that even the second system retained was lost. With its legions at the breaking point, fewer and fewer feared Rome.[10]

Alas, we are in frighteningly familiar territory. Just as Roman power stabilized the Mediterranean littoral, the American Navy and Air Force patrol the global commons to the benefit of all, even as this very service—as with Rome's—is taken for granted, and what has lain exposed over the past decade was the overstretch of the U.S. Army and Marine Corps, busy trying to tamp down rebellions in far corners of the earth. America must, therefore, contemplate a grand strategy that seeks to restore its position from something akin to Rome's third system to its second; or to its first. While America does not have client states, it does have allies and like-minded others, whom it needs to impress in order to make them more effective on its behalf. America can do that best through an active diplomacy and the buildup of a reserve of troops, used sparingly, so as to restore its surge capacity, of the kind Rome enjoyed under the original Julio-Claudian system. Rome's very longevity proved its grand strategy a success, and yet its ultimate decline and tumultuous fall in Western Europe was due to a failure to adapt to the formation of new national groupings to its north that would provide the outlines of modern European states. Because of these formations, the Roman Empire was headed for extinction in any case. But it need not have happened as soon as it did, and in the way that it did.

Rome's real failure in its final phase of grand strategy was that it did not provide a mechanism for a graceful retreat, even as it rotted from within. But it is precisely—and counterintuitively—by planning for such a deft exit from a hegemony of sorts that a state or empire can actually prolong its position of strength. There is nothing healthier for America than to prepare the world for its own obsolescence. That way it labors for a purpose, and not merely to enjoy power for its own sake.

How does America prepare itself for a prolonged and graceful exit from history as a dominant power? Like Byzantium, it can avoid costly interventions, use diplomacy to sabotage enemies, employ intelligence assets to strategic use, and so on.[11] It can also—and this leads back to Bacevich—make sure it is not undermined from the south the way Rome was from the north. America is bordered by oceans to the east and west, and to the north by the Canadian Arctic, which provides for only a thin band of middle-class population on America's border. (The American-Canadian frontier is the most extraordinary of the world's frontiers because it is long, artificial, and yet has ceased to matter.[12]) But it is in the Southwest where America is vulnerable. Here is the one area where America's national and imperial boundaries are in some tension: where the coherence of America as a geographically cohesive unit can be questioned.[13] For the historical borderland between America and Mexico is broad and indistinct, much like that of the Indian Subcontinent in the northwest, even as it reveals civilizational stresses. Stanford historian David Kennedy notes, "The income gap between the United States and Mexico is the largest between any two contiguous countries in the world," with American GDP nine times that of Mexico.[14]

America's foreign policy emanates from the domestic condition of its society, and nothing will affect its society more than the dramatic movement of Latin history northward. Mexico and Central America constitute a growing demographic powerhouse with which the United States has an inextricable relationship. Mexico's population of 111 million plus Central America's of 40 million constitute half the population of the United States. Because of NAFTA (the North American Free Trade Agreement), 85 percent of all Mexico's exports go to the United States, even as half of all Central America's trade is with the U.S. While the median age of Americans is nearly thirty-seven, demonstrating the aging tendency of its population, the median age in Mexico is twenty-five and is much lower than that in Central America (twenty in Guatemala and Honduras, for example). The destiny of the United States will be north–south, rather than the east–west, *sea-to-shining-sea* of continental and patriotic myth. (This will be amplified by the scheduled 2014 widening of the Panama Canal, which will open the Caribbean Basin to megaships from East Asia, leading to the further development of Gulf of Mexico port cities in the United States, from Texas to Florida.)[15]

Half the length of America's southern frontier is an artificial boundary line in the desert established by treaties following the Mexican-American War of 1846–1848. Crossing this border once, having traveled by bus north from Mexico City, was as much of a shock for me as crossing the Jordan-Israel border and the Berlin Wall. Surrounded by beggars on the broken sidewalk of Nogales, Sonora, I stared at the American flag indicating the border. The pedestrian crossing point to Nogales, Arizona, was in a small building. Merely by touching the door handle, I entered a new physical world. The solidly constructed handle with its high-quality metal, the clean glass, and the precise manner in which the room's ceramic tiles were fitted seemed a revelation after weeks amid slipshod Mexican construction. There were only two people in the room: an immigration official and a customs official. Neither talked to the other. In government enclosures of that size in Mexico and other Third World countries there were always crowds of officials and hangers-on lost in animated conversation, sipping tea or coffee. Looking through the window at the car lanes, I saw how few people there were to garrison the border station, yet how efficiently it ran. Soon, as in Israel, I was inside a perfectly standardized yet cold and alienating environment, with empty streets and the store logos made of tony polymers rather than of rusted metal and cheap plastic. Because of the turbulence and semi-anarchy I had experienced amid over 100 million Mexicans for weeks just to the south, these quiet streets appeared vulnerable, unnatural even. Arnold Toynbee writes, in reference to the barbarians and Rome, that when a frontier between a highly and less highly developed society "ceases to advance, the balance does not settle down to a stable equilibrium but inclines, with the passage of time, in the more backward society's favor."[16]

Since 1940, Mexico's population has risen more than five-fold. Between 1970 and 1995 it nearly doubled. Between 1985 and 2000 it rose by over a third. Mexico's population of 111 million is now more than a third that of the United States, and growing at a faster rate. Nevertheless, East Coast elites display relatively little interest in Mexico. The actual daily challenges, incidents, and business and cultural interactions between Mexico and the border states of California, Arizona, New Mexico, and Texas are geographically distant from the concerns of East Coast elites: which, instead, focus on the wider world and on America's place in it. Truly, Mexico registers far less in the elite imagination than does Israel or China, or India even. Yet Mexico could affect America's destiny more than any of those countries. Mexico, together with the United States and Canada, comprises the most crucial of the continental satellites hovering around Mackinder's World-Island.

In the Valley of Mexico once stood the great lake holding the two Aztec Venices of Tenochtitlán and Tlatelolco: here now stands Mexico City. This is the Nile valley of the New World, "the matrix of civilization" for both North and South America, in the words of historian Henry Bamford Parkes, from where the cultivation of maize spread over the two continents. Lying midway between the Atlantic and Pacific, and joining along with Central America the two continental landmasses of the Western Hemisphere, the Valley of Mexico and the country that has grown out of it form one of the earth's great civilizational cores.[17]

Yet Mexico, unlike Egypt, exhibits no geographical unity. Two great mountain ranges, the Sierra Madre Occidental and the Sierra Madre Oriental, lie on either side of a rugged central plateau. Then there are other, cross-cutting mountain ranges, mainly in the south: the Sierra Madre del Sur, the Sierra Madre de Oaxaca, and so on. Mexico is so mountainous that if it were flattened it would be the size of Asia. The Yucatán Peninsula and Baja California are both essentially separate from the rest of Mexico, which is itself infernally divided. This is the context to understand northern Mexico's ongoing, undeclared, substantially unreported, and undeniable unification with the Southwestern United States, and consequent separation from the rest of Mexico.

Northern Mexico's population has more than doubled since the North American Free Trade Agreement was signed in 1994. The U.S. dollar is now a common unit of exchange as far south as Culiacán, halfway to Mexico City. Northern Mexico is responsible for 87 percent of all *maquiladora* (duty-free) manufacturing and 85 percent of all U.S.-Mexico trade. The northeastern Mexican city of Monterrey, one of the country's largest, is intimately connected with the Texas banking, manufacturing, and energy industries. David Danelo, a former U.S. Marine now working for U.S. Customs, who has studied northern Mexico extensively, and has traveled throughout all six Mexican border states, told me he has yet to meet a person there with more than one degree of separation from the United States. As he told me, "Northern Mexico retains a sense of cultural polarity; frontier *norteños* see themselves as the antithesis of Mexico City's [city slicker] *chilangos.*" Still, northern Mexico contains its own geographical divisions. The lowlands and desert in Sonora in the west are generally stable; the Rio Grande basin in the east is the most developed and interconnected with the United States—culturally, economically, and hydrologically—and has benefited the most from NAFTA.[18] In the center are the mountains and steppes, which are virtually lawless: witness the border city of Ciudad Juárez, across from El Paso, Texas, wracked by running gun battles and serial killers. Ciudad Juárez is the murder capital of Mexico, where 700 people were murdered in the early months of 2010 alone. In 2009, more than 2,600 died violently in a city of 1.2 million; some 200,000 more may have fled.[19] In Chihuahua, the state in which Ciudad Juárez is located, the homicide rate was 143 per 100,000—one of the worst in the Western Hemisphere. The northern mountains and steppe have always been the bastion of Mexico's tribes: the drug cartels, Mennonites, Yaqui Indians, and so forth. This harsh frontier was difficult for the Spanish to tame. Later on, in the 1880s, it was a lair for Geronimo and his Apaches. Think of other remote highlands that provided refuge for insurgents: the Chinese communists in Shaanxi, the Cuban revolutionaries in the Sierra Maestra, and al Qaeda and the Taliban in Waziristan.[20] The drug cartels come out of this geographical tradition.

The fact that most of the drug-related homicides have occurred in only six of Mexico's thirty-two states, mostly in the north, is another indicator of how northern Mexico is separating out from the rest of the country (though the violence in Veracruz and the regions of Michoacán and Guerrero is also notable). If the military-led offensive to crush the drug cartels launched in 2006 by conservative president Felipe Calderón completely falters, and Mexico City goes back to cutting deals with the cartels, then the capital may in a functional sense lose control of the north, with grave implications for the United States. Mexico's very federalism—a direct product of its disjointed and mountainous geography—with 2 federal, 32 state, and over 1,500 municipal police agencies, makes reform that much harder. Robert C. Bonner, former administrator of the U.S. Drug Enforcement Administration, writes that if the gangs succeed, "the United States will share a 2,000-mile border with a narcostate controlled by powerful transnational drug cartels that threaten the stability of Central and South America."[21]

The late Harvard professor Samuel Huntington, who made a career out of clairvoyance, devoted his last book to the challenge that Mexico posed to the United States.[22] In *Who Are We? The Challenges to America's National Identity,* published in 2004, Huntington posited that Latin history was demographically moving north into the U.S., and would consequently change the American character.[23]

Huntington argues that it is a partial truth, not a total truth, that America is a nation of immigrants; America is a nation of Anglo-Protestant settlers and immigrants both, with the former providing the philosophical and cultural backbone of the society. For only by adopting Anglo-Protestant culture do immigrants become American. America is what it is, Huntington goes on, because it was settled by British Protestants, not by French, Spanish, or Portuguese Catholics. Because America was born Protestant, it did not have to become so, and America's classical liberalism emerges from this very fact. Dissent, individualism, republicanism ultimately all devolve from Protestantism. "While the American Creed is Protestantism without God, the American civil religion is Christianity without Christ." But this Creed, Huntington reasons, might be subtly undone by an advancing Hispanic, Catholic, pre-Enlightenment society.[24]

Huntington writes:

Mexican immigration is leading toward the demographic *reconquista* of areas Americans took from Mexico by force in the 1830s and 1840s, Mexicanizing them in a manner comparable to, although different from, the Cubanization that has occurred in southern Florida. It is also blurring the border between Mexico and America, introducing a very different culture.[25]

Boston College professor Peter Skerry writes that one of Huntington's "more startlingly original and controversial insights" is that while Americans champion diversity, "today's immigrant wave is actually the *least* diverse in our history. To be sure," Skerry continues, paraphrasing Huntington, "non-Hispanic immigrants are more diverse than ever. But overall, the 50 percent of immigrants who are Hispanic make for a much less diverse cohort than ever. For Huntington, this diminished diversity makes assimilation less likely."[26] And as David Kennedy observes, "the variety and dispersal of the immigrant stream" smoothed the progress of assimilation. "Today, however, one large immigrant stream is flowing into a defined region from a single cultural, linguistic, religious, and national source: Mexico . . . the sobering fact is that the United States has had no experience compa-rable to what is now taking place in the Southwest."[27] By 2050, one-third the population of the United States could be Spanish-speaking.[28]

Geography is at the forefront of all these arguments. Here is Hun-tington: "No other immigrant group in American history has asserted or has been able to assert a historical claim to American territory. Mexicans and Mexican-Americans can and do make that claim." Most of Texas, New Mexico, Arizona, California, Nevada, and Utah were part of Mexico until the 1835–1836 Texan War of Indepen-dence and the 1846–1848 Mexican-American War. Mexico is the only country that the United States has invaded, occupied its capital, and annexed a good deal of its territory. Consequently, as Skerry points out, Mexicans arrive in the United States, settle in areas of the country that were once part of their homeland, and so "enjoy a sense of being on their own turf" that other immigrants do not share. Mex-ican Americans into the third generation and beyond maintain their competence in their native language to a far greater degree than do other immigrants, largely because of the geographical concentration of Hispanic communities that manifests the demographic negation of the Texan and Mexican-American wars. What's more, Mexican natu-ralization rates are among the lowest of all immigrant groups. Hun-tington points out that a nation is a "remembered community," that is, one with a historical memory of itself. Mexican Americans, who account for 12.5 percent of the U.S. population, not counting other Hispanics, and are, more or less, concentrated in the Southwest, con-tiguous to Mexico, are for the first time in America's history amend-ing our historical memory.[29]

University of New Mexico professor Charles Truxillo predicts that by 2080 the Southwestern states of the U.S. and the northern states of Mexico will band together to form a new country, "La República del Norte." By 2000, six of twelve important cities on the U.S. side of the border were over 90 percent Hispanic, and only two (San Diego, California, and Yuma, Arizona) were less than 50 percent Hispanic.[30]

The blurring of America's Southwestern frontier is becoming a geographical fact that all the security devices on the actual border itself cannot invalidate. Nevertheless, while I admire Huntington's ability to isolate and expose a fundamental dilemma that others in academia and the media are too polite to address, I do not completely agree with his conclusions. Huntington believes in a firm reliance on American nationalism in order to preserve its Anglo-Protestant culture and values in the face of the partial Latinoization of our society. I believe that while geography does not necessarily determine the future, it does set contours on what is achievable and what isn't. And the organic connection between Mexico and America—geographical, historical, and demographic—is simply too overwhelming to suppose that, as Huntington hopes, American nationalism can stay as pure as it is. Huntington correctly derides cosmopolitanism (and imperialism, too) as elite visions. But a certain measure of cosmopolitanism, Huntington to the contrary, is inevitable and not to be disparaged.

America, I believe, will actually emerge in the course of the twenty-first century as a Polynesian-cum-mestizo civilization, oriented from north to south, from Canada to Mexico, rather than as an east to west, racially lighter-skinned island in the temperate zone stretching from the Atlantic to the Pacific. This multiracial assemblage will be one of sprawling suburban city-states, each in a visual sense progressively similar to the next, whether Cascadia in the Pacific Northwest or Omaha-Lincoln in Nebraska, each nurturing its own economic relationships with cities and trading networks throughout the world, as technology continues to collapse distances. America, in my vision, would become the globe's preeminent duty-free hot zone for business transactions, a favorite place of residence for the global elite. In the tradition of Rome, it will continue to use its immigration laws to asset-strip the world of its best and brightest, and to further diversify an immigrant population that, as Huntington fears, is defined too much by Mexicans. In this vision, nationalism will be, perforce, diluted a bit, but not so much as to deprive America of its unique identity, or to undermine its military. In short, America is no longer an island, protected by the Atlantic and Pacific. It is brought closer to the rest of the world not only by technology, but by the pressures of Mexican and Central American demography.

But this vision requires a successful Mexico, not a failed state. If President Calderón and his successors can succeed in the mission to break the back of the drug cartels once and for all (a very difficult prospect, to say the least) then the United States will have achieved a strategic victory greater than any possible in the Middle East. A stable and prosperous Mexico, working in organic concert with the United States, would be an unbeatable combination in geopolitics. A post-cartel Mexico, combined with a stabilized and pro-American Colombia (now almost a fact), would fuse together the Western Hemisphere's largest, third largest, and fourth largest countries in terms of population, easing America's continued sway over Latin America and the Greater Caribbean. In a word, Bacevich is correct in his inference: fixing Mexico is more important than fixing Afghanistan.

Unfortunately, as Bacevich claims, Mexico is a possible disaster that our concentration on the Greater Middle East has diverted us from; and if it stays that way, it will lead to more immigration, legal and especially illegal, that will create the scenario that Huntington fears. Calderón's offensive against the drug lords has claimed 47,000 lives since 2006, with close to 4,000 victims in the first half of 2010 alone. Moreover, the cartels have graduated to military-style assaults, with complex traps set and escape routes closed off. "These are warfighting tactics they're using," concludes Javier Cruz Angulo, a Mexican security expert. "It's gone way beyond the normal strategies of organized crime." Ted Galen Carpenter, vice president for defense and foreign policy studies at the Cato Institute in Washington, writes: "If that trend persists, it is an extremely worrisome development for the health, perhaps even the viability, of the Mexican state." The weaponry used by the cartels is generally superior to that of the Mexican police and comparable to that of the Mexican military. Coupled with military-style tactics, the cartels can move, in Carpenter's words, "from being mere criminal organizations to being a serious insurgency." United Nations peacekeepers have deployed in places with less violence than Ciudad Juárez and Tijuana. Already, police officers and local politicians are resigning their posts for fear of assassination, and Mexican business and political elites are sending their families out of the country, even as there is sustained middle- and upper-middle-class flight to the United States.[31]

Mexico is now at a crossroads: it is either in the early phase of finally taking on the cartels, or it is sinking into further disorder; or both. Because its future hangs in the balance, what the United States does could be pivotal. But while this is happening, the U.S. security establishment has been engaged in other notoriously corrupt and unstable societies half a world away, Iraq until 2011 and Afghanistan at least until 2014.

Unlike those places, the record of U.S. military involvement in the Mexican border area is one of reasonable success. Even as proximity to Mexico threatens the United States demographically, it helps in a logistical sense when trying to control the border. As Danelo points out, during the nineteenth and twentieth centuries, the United States and Mexico reduced banditry on the border through binational cooperation. From 1881 to 1910, Mexican president Porfirio Díaz joined with American presidents to jointly patrol the border. Mexican *rurales* rode with Texas Rangers in pursuing the Comanche. In Arizona, Mexican and American soldiers mounted joint campaigns against Apaches. Today, the job of thwarting drug cartels in rugged and remote terrain in the mountains and steppe reaching back from Ciudad Juárez is a job for the military, quietly assisting Mexican authorities, but the legal framework for such cooperation does not exist, partly because of strict interpretation of nineteenth-century posse comitatus laws on the U.S. side.[32] While we have spent hundreds of billions of dollars to affect historical outcomes in Eurasia, we are curiously passive about what is happening to a country with which we share a long land border, that verges on disorder, and whose population is close to double that of Iraq and Afghanistan combined.

Surely, one can argue that, with Herculean border controls, a functional and nationalist America can coexist alongside a dysfunctional and partially chaotic Mexico. But that is mainly true in the short run.

In the long run, looking deep into the twenty-first century and beyond, again, as Toynbee notes, a border between a highly developed society and a less highly developed society will not attain an equilibrium, but will advance in the more backward society's favor. In other words, the preservation of American nationalism to the degree that would satisfy Huntington is unachievable unless Mexico reaches First World status. And if Mexico does reach First World status, then it might become less of a threat, and the melding of the two societies only quickens. Either way, because of the facts that the map imposes, we are headed for a conjoining of Mexico and America in some form; though, of course, the actions of policymakers on both sides of the border can determine on what terms and under what circumstances that occurs. Here is Toynbee:

> The erection of a [Roman] *limes* sets in motion a play of social forces which is bound to end disastrously for the builders. A policy of non-intercourse with the barbarians beyond is quite impracticable. Whatever the imperial government may decide, the interests of traders, pioneers, adventurers, and so forth will inevitably draw them beyond the frontier.[33]

Toynbee also writes that "a universal state is imposed by its founders, and accepted by its subjects, as a panacea for the ills of a Time of Troubles." He mentions "Middle Empire" Egypt, the Neo-Babylonian Empire, Achaemenid Persia, the Seleucid Monarchy, the Roman Peace, and the *Pax Hanica* in the Sinic world as all examples of essentially universal states in which different peoples and confessions coexisted for mutual benefit. Rome, in particular, mastered the vexing issue of dual loyalty, with citizenship of the world-city of Rome and of the particular local territory not in contradiction.[34] It may be, therefore, that a universal state will on some future morrow prove the panacea for the Time of Troubles now afflicting northern Mexico and the American Southwest in the border region.

It would be hard to exaggerate the significance of such a monumental shift in the conception of national myth and sovereignty, even as it occurs as we speak in what, by the standards of the media, is geological time. When I hitchhiked across the United States in 1970, I palpably experienced how no other continent has been as well suited to nation building as the temperate zone of North America. The Appalachians had provided a western boundary for a nascent community of states through the end of the eighteenth century, but river valleys cutting through these mountains, such as the Mohawk and the Ohio, allowed for penetration of the West by settlers. Beyond the Appalachians the settlers found a flat panel of rich farmland without geographical impediments where, in the nineteenth century, wealth could be created and human differences ground down to form a distinctive American culture. The Greater Mississippi basin together with the Intercoastal Waterway has more miles of navigable rivers than the rest of the world combined, and it overlays the world's largest contiguous piece of arable earth. By the time westering pioneers reached a truly daunting barrier—the Great American Desert, both east and west of the Rocky Mountains—the transcontinental railroad was at hand.[35] "The U.S. Atlantic Coast possesses more major ports than the rest of the Western Hemisphere combined . . . the Americans are not important because of who they are, but because of where they live," notes a Stratfor document.[36] When the geographer Arnold Guyot examined the continental United States in 1849, before the Civil War and the triumph of the Industrial Revolution, he regarded it along with Europe and Asia as one of the "continental cores" that were destined to control the world. But he believed back then that America would lead the way over the other two cores. The reasons: America was protected behind a "screen of ocean" on two sides that, nevertheless, allowed it to interact with Eurasia; and its development was assured by the "interconnectibility of the well-watered interior" of the continent.[37] "Here, then, is the United States," writes James Fairgrieve in 1917,

> taking its place in the circle of lands, a new *orbis terrarium;* and yet outside the [Eurasian] system which has hitherto mattered, compact and coherent, with enormous stores of energy, facing

Atlantic and Pacific, having relations with east and west of Euro-Asia, preparing by a fortified Panama Canal to fling her one fleet into either ocean.[38]

That continental majesty, framed by two oceans, is still there. But another conceptual geography is beginning to overlap with it, that of Coronado's 1540–1542 journey of exploration from central-western Mexico north through Arizona, New Mexico, Texas, Oklahoma, and Kansas. Whereas Lewis and Clark's 1804–1806 exploration of the Louisiana and Oregon territories brought America from the Atlantic to the Pacific, and thus laid the ideational foundation of a modern, continental nation-state, Coronado's exploration—south-to-north rather than east-to-west—while earlier in time, was in its own way postmodern: for it was not bounded by any national consciousness, and provided an orientation for a future universal state stretching from semitropical Mexico to temperate North America. Francisco Vázquez de Coronado was in search of gold, plunder, and easy wealth. His was a medieval mentality. But the new Hispanic migrants heading north are not medieval. They are in search of jobs—which often entail backbreaking manual labor—and thus they are willing to work hard for material gain. They are being transformed by the Anglo-Protestant work ethic just as they transform America's Anglo-Protestant culture.

The quality and fluidity of this cultural and binational interaction will, arguably, more than any other individual dynamic, determine how well America interacts with Mackinder's World-Island (Eurasia and Africa). American foreign policy will likely be both wise and un-wise by turns in the course of the decades. But American economic power, cultural power, moral power, and even political and military power will be substantially affected by whether we can develop into a cohesive, bilingual supra-state-of-sorts with Mexico and Canada or, instead, become trapped by a dysfunctional, vast, and increasingly unruly border region that engenders civilizational tension between

America's still dominant Anglo-Protestant culture and its Hispanic counterpart. Huntington's fears are justified; it is his solution that is partly wrong.

Keep in mind that, as we know from Paul Bracken and others, the earth's political geography increasingly constitutes a closed, claustrophobic system. Cultural and political interchanges across the seas will become more and more organic. Thus, if the United States and Mexico do not eventually come together to the degree that the U.S. and Canada already have—if we do not have Mexico as an intimate and dependable ally in world forums—it will adversely affect America's other relationships, especially as Mexico's (and Central America's) population grows at a much higher rate than ours, and thus Mexico will assume more importance as time goes on. Braudel's exploration of the sixteenth-century Mediterranean makes clear the role that natural forces like geography play over time: that is why Mexico must play a central function in any grand strategy we decide upon.

Think of the future world as roughly resembling the millet system of the old Ottoman Empire: a "network of geographically intermingled communities," in Toynbee's words, rather than a "patchwork of . . . segregated parochial states."[39] Each relationship will affect the others as never before. As we have seen, future decades will see rail, road, and pipelines connecting all of Eurasia through a Central Asian and particularly an Afghan hub. An organic and united Eurasia will demand as a balancer an organic and united North America, from the Canadian Arctic to the Central American jungles. Not to continue to deepen links with Mexico and Central America, whose combined populations account for half the population of that of the United States, would be to see Mexico and perhaps some of its southern neighbors slip into a hostile diplomatic and political orbit in a world where Eurasia will be closer than ever before. The way to guard against a pro-Iranian Venezuela and other radical states that may emerge from time to time in the Western Hemisphere is to wrap the Greater Caribbean into a zone of free trade and human migration that, perforce, would be American dominated, as Mexico's and Central America's younger populations supply the labor force for America's aging one. Of course, this is happening already, but the intensity of the human exchange will, and should, increase.

"Global war, as well as global peace," writes Nicholas Spykman, "means that all fronts and all areas are interrelated. No matter how remote they are from each other, success or failure in one will have an immediate and determining effect on the others."[40] That is far truer today than it was in 1944 when that statement was published posthumously. It will be far truer in the future. Robert Strausz-Hupé notes, "The history of Greece is the struggle for survival against the cyclic irruptions of Asia."[41] Think of how close ancient Greece was to Persia, and one may get a sense of how close we are to Eurasia now, given the revolution in transportation and communications. Making sure that one power in the Eastern Hemisphere does not become unduly dominant, so as to threaten the United States in the Western Hemisphere, will be a much easier task if we advance unity in the Western Hemisphere in the first place.

We must be a balancing power in Eurasia and a unifying power in North America—doing both will be easier than doing just one. Preserving the balance of power, of course, must be done for a specific purpose that goes beyond the physical and economic protection of the United States. And that purpose is to use the stability guaranteed by a balance of power in the Eastern Hemisphere to advance nothing less than the liberal intellectual cause of a *Mitteleuropa* writ large across the globe. Just as Stephen Dedalus affirms "his significance as a conscious rational animal," in effect resisting fate, we must never give in to geography, but must fundamentally be aware of it in our quest for a better world. For the yearning after the Post Cold War ideal of a cosmopolitan Central Europe which informed the beginning of this study is where we are at the end of it. Whether or not that goal is achievable, it is something always worth striving for, hopefully with Mexico by our side. Mackinder intuited this in his call for vibrant and independent buffer states between Maritime Europe and the Heartland, noting that a world balanced is a world free.

Acknowledgments

The idea for this book originated in a magazine article, the impetus for which came from the editors at *Foreign Policy*, notably Christian Brose and Susan Glasser. As the book developed, a shortened version of the China chapter ran as a cover story in *Foreign Affairs*, for which I thank James F. Hoge Jr., Gideon Rose, and Stephanie Giry. The Center for a New American Security (CNAS) in Washington published a paper that was a shortened version of the India chapter, for which I thank Kristen Lord, vice president and director of studies there. In fact, the book could not have been completed without the institutional support I received from CNAS, for which I thank CEO Nathaniel Fick, President John Nagl, and Director of Development Venilde Jeronimo. Sections of the Preface are adapted from several previous books of mine, as noted on the copyright page. Throughout this editorial process, help and inspiration came from Jakub Grygiel at the Paul Nitze School of Advanced International Studies of the

Johns Hopkins University. Other help came from Army Lieutenant General (Retired) Dave Barno, CNAS senior advisor Richard Fontaine, former CNAS researcher Seth Myers, *Atlantic* editors James Gibney and Yvonne Rolzhausen, Naval Academy professor Stephen Wrage, and Professor Brian W. Blouet of the College of William and Mary.

At Random House, my editor, Jonathan Jao, provided seasoned advice on all fronts. Kate Medina also provided encouragement. Once more, I thank my literary agents, Carl D. Brandt and Marianne Merola, for their assistance in helping to guide me from one project to another.

Elizabeth Lockyer, my assistant, worked on the maps. My wife, Maria Cabral, once again provided emotional support.

Notes

Preface: Frontiers

1. Jeremy Black, *Maps and History: Constructing Images of the Past* (New Haven: Yale University Press, 1997), p. 85.
2. James C. Scott, *The Art of Not Being Governed: An Anarchist History of Upland Southeast Asia* (New Haven: Yale University Press, 2009), p. ix.
3. The province was later renamed Khyber Pakhtunkhwa.
4. Sugata Bose, *A Hundred Horizons: The Indian Ocean in the Age of Global Empire* (Cambridge: Harvard University Press, 2006), p. 56.
5. Golo Mann, *The History of Germany Since 1789,* translated by Marian Jackson (London: Chatto & Windus, 1968), pp. 525 and 880, 1987 Peregrine edition.
6. Ernest Gellner, *Muslim Society* (New York: Cambridge University Press, 1981), pp. 38, 41, 180, 187.

PART I: VISIONARIES

Chapter I: From Bosnia to Baghdad

1. Francis Fukuyama, "The End of History," *The National Interest,* Washington, Summer 1989. Book version: *The End of History and the Last Man* (New York: The Free Press, 1992).

2. Jonathan C. Randal, "In Africa, Unrest in One-Party States," *International Herald Tribune,* Paris, March 27, 1990.

3. Timothy Garton Ash, "Bosnia in Our Future," *New York Review of Books,* December 21, 1995.

4. Carl E. Schorske, *Fin-de-Siècle Vienna: Politics and Culture* (New York: Knopf, 1980); Claudio Magris, *Danube* (New York: Farrar, Straus and Giroux, 1986, 1989), p. 268.

5. Timothy Garton Ash, *The File: A Personal History* (New York: Random House, 1997), p. 51.

6. Michael Ignatieff, *Isaiah Berlin: A Life* (New York: Holt, 1998), p. 24.

7. Timothy Garton Ash, "Does Central Europe Exist?," *New York Review of Books,* October 9, 1986.

8. W. H. Parker, *Mackinder: Geography as an Aid to Statecraft* (Oxford: Clarendon Press, 1982), p. 201; K. A. Sinnhuber, "Central Europe–Mitteleuropa–Europe Centrale: An Analysis of a Geographical Term," *Transactions of the Institute of British Geographers,* vol. 20, 1954; Arthur Butler Dugan, "Mackinder and His Critics Reconsidered," *The Journal of Politics,* May 1962, p. 250.

9. Saul B. Cohen, *Geography and Politics in a World Divided* (New York: Random House, 1963), pp. 79–83.

10. Halford J. Mackinder, *Democratic Ideals and Reality: A Study in the Politics of Reconstruction* (Washington: National Defense University, 1919, 1942), p. 90.

11. Cohen, *Geography and Politics in a World Divided,* p. 222.

12. Colin S. Gray, *Another Bloody Century: Future Warfare* (London: Weidenfeld & Nicolson, 2005), pp. 37, 95, 176–77.

13. Michael Ignatieff, "Homage to Bosnia," *New York Review of Books,* April 21, 1994.

14. James Joyce, *Ulysses* (New York: Modern Library, 1922, 1934), p. 697, 1990 Vintage edition.

15. Timothy Garton Ash, "Kosovo and Beyond," *New York Review of Books,* June 24, 1999. He was referring to a line in Auden's poem "September 1, 1939," published in 1940.

16. Timothy Garton Ash, "Cry, the Dismembered Country," *New York Review of Books,* January 14, 1999.

17. I have my own history regarding the story of these delayed interventions. My book *Balkan Ghosts: A Journey Through History* (New York: St. Martin's) was reportedly a factor in President Bill Clinton's decision not to militarily intervene in 1993, thus putting off the dispatch of NATO forces into the Balkans for two years. *Balkan Ghosts,* a record of my experiences in the Balkans in the 1980s, appeared first as works in progress in *The Atlantic Monthly* before the Berlin Wall fell. Then, in June 1991, Chapter 3 of *Balkan Ghosts* (about Macedonia) appeared in *The Atlantic.* According to a former State Department official, quoted in *The Washington Post* (February 21, 2002), that article was instrumental in getting "the first and only preventive deployment of U.N. peacekeepers in the former Yugoslavia." Though a 1990 CIA report warned of Yugoslavia disintegrating, the State Department "was in a state of denial . . . until Kaplan's article came along." As it happens, the deployment of 1,500 peacekeepers in Macedonia prevented violence that later broke out in Bosnia and Kosovo. *Balkan Ghosts* was published in book form in March 1993. That same month I published an article about Yugoslavia in *Reader's Digest,* in which I wrote: "Unless we can break the cycle of hatred and revenge—by standing forcefully for self-determination and minority rights—the gains from the end of the Cold War will be lost. All aid, all diplomatic efforts, all force if force is used, must be linked to the simple idea that all the people of Yugoslavia deserve freedom from violence." Soon after, I appeared on television to publicly urge intervention in the Balkans. I also urged intervention on the front page of *The Washington Post*'s Outlook section on April 17, 1994, more than a year before we finally intervened. *Balkan Ghosts* paints a grim picture of ethnic relations in southeastern Europe, but it is only the grimmest human landscapes where intervention has usually been required in the first place: one need never idealize a human landscape in order to take action on its behalf. And as we would learn later in Iraq, when you do intervene, you should do so without illusions. Though my

books and articles were read by the president and others, at no
point did anyone in the Clinton administration contact me in
any way concerning my work, and how it might be applied to
specific events and policy choices that arose after the book was
completed.

18. Leon Wieseltier, "Force Without Force: Saving NATO, Losing
    Kosovo," *New Republic,* Washington, April 26 and May 3, 1999.

19. Leon Wieseltier, "Winning Ugly: The War Ends, Sort Of. The Peace
    Begins, Sort Of," *New Republic,* Washington, June 28, 1999.

20. Ibid.

21. Leon Wieseltier, "Useless," *New Republic,* Washington, April 17,
    2006.

22. Bob Woodward, *State of Denial: Bush at War, Part III* (New York:
    Simon & Schuster, 2006), pp. 84–85.

23. Stephen Walt and John Mearsheimer, *The Israel Lobby and U.S. For-
    eign Policy* (New York: Farrar, Straus and Giroux, 2007).

24. Israel at the time of 9/11 was undergoing frequent terrorist attacks
    and so naturally was at the receiving end of American sympathy. De-
    mands for it to freeze settlement activity in the occupied territories
    would resume later on, though. During the buildup to the Iraq War, I
    wrote that if Bush was successful in Iraq and achieved a second term,
    he should end "the domination by Israeli overlords of three million
    Palestinians in the West Bank and Gaza," a situation which I called
    "particularly untenable." "A Post-Saddam Scenario," *Atlantic
    Monthly,* Boston, November 2002.

25. Robert D. Kaplan, *Warrior Politics: Why Leadership Demands a
    Pagan Ethos* (New York: Random House, 2002), p. 84.

26. Hobbes and Berlin are great precisely because of their nuance.
    Hobbes's philosophy may represent a grim view of humanity, but he
    was also a liberal modernizer, because at the time of his writings
    modernization meant the breakdown of the medieval order through
    the establishment of a central authority, which his Leviathan repre-
    sented. Likewise Berlin, while the embodiment of liberal humanism,
    was also a realist who recognized, for example, that the search for
    sufficient food and shelter came before the search for freedom.

27. Actually, advance columns of American forces in the First Gulf War
    had come within 150 kilometers of Baghdad. But the bulk of the
    troops were based in Kuwait and the Saudi desert.

Chapter II: The Revenge of Geography

1. Robert D. Kaplan, "Munich Versus Vietnam," The Atlantic Online, May 4, 2007.

2. Hans J. Morgenthau, *Politics Among Nations: The Struggle for Power and Peace,* revised by Kenneth W. Thompson and W. David Clinton (New York: McGraw Hill, 1948, 2006), pp. 3, 6, 7, 12; Thucydides, *The Peloponnesian War,* translated by Thomas Hobbes (1629) (Chicago: University of Chicago Press, 1989); Anastasia Bakolas, "Human Nature in Thucydides," Wellesley College, unpublished; Robert D. Kaplan, *Warrior Politics: Why Leadership Demands a Pagan Ethos* (New York: Random House, 2001).

3. Morgenthau, *Politics Among Nations,* pp. xviii–xix, 37, 181, 218–20, 246, 248; William Cabell Bruce, *John Randolph of Roanoke* (New York: G. P. Putnam's Sons, 1922), vol. 2, p. 211; John J. Mearsheimer, "The False Promise of International Institutions," *International Security,* Cambridge, Massachusetts, Winter 1994–1995.

4. Thomas Hobbes, *Leviathan,* 1651, Chapter 15.

5. Fareed Zakaria, "Is Realism Finished?," *The National Interest,* Winter 1992–1993.

6. Raymond Aron, *Peace and War: A Theory of International Relations* (Garden City: Doubleday, 1966), p. 321; José Ortega y Gasset, *The Revolt of the Masses* (Notre Dame, IN: University of Notre Dame Press, 1985), p. 129.

7. Black, *Maps and History: Constructing Images of the Past* (New Haven: Yale University Press, 1997), pp. 58, 173, 216.

8. Halford J. Mackinder, *Democratic Ideas and Reality: A Study in the Politics of Reconstruction* (New York: Henry Holt and Company, 1919), pp. 15–16, 1996 National Defense University edition.

9. Morgenthau, *Politics Among Nations,* p. 165.

10. Alfred Thayer Mahan, *The Problem of Asia and Its Effect Upon International Policies* (London: Sampson Low, Marston, 1900), p. 56, 2005 Elibron edition.

11. W. H. Parker, *Mackinder: Geography as an Aid to Statecraft* (Oxford: Clarendon Press, 1988), pp. 93, 130–31.

12. W. Gordon East, *The Geography Behind History* (New York: Norton, 1965, 1967), p. 120.

13. Nicholas J. Spykman, *America's Strategy in World Politics: The*

United States and the Balance of Power, with a new introduction by
Francis P. Sempa (New York: Harcourt, Brace, 1942), pp. xv, 41.
2007 Transaction edition.

14. East, *The Geography Behind History,* p. 38.
15. *Federalist* No. 8.
16. Williamson Murray, "Some Thoughts on War and Geography," *Journal of Strategic Studies,* Routledge, London, 1999, pp. 212, 214;
    Colin S. Gray, "The Continued Primacy of Geography," *Orbis,* Philadelphia, Spring 1996, p. 2.
17. Mackubin Thomas Owens, "In Defense of Classical Geopolitics,"
    Naval War College Review, Newport, Rhode Island, Autumn 1999,
    p. 72.
18. Spykman, *America's Strategy in World Politics,* p. 92.
19. James Fairgrieve, *Geography and World Power* (New York: E. P.
    Dutton, 1917), pp. 273–74.
20. John Western, Department of Geography, Syracuse University.
21. John Gallup and Jeffrey Sachs, "Location, Location: Geography and
    Economic Development," *Harvard International Review,* Cambridge,
    Winter 1998–1999. In part, they are extrapolating from the work of
    Jared Diamond.
22. M. C. Ricklefs, Bruce Lockhart, Albert Lau, Portia Reyes, and
    Maitrii Aung-Thwin, *A New History of Southeast Asia* (New York:
    Palgrave Macmillan, 2010), p. 21.
23. John Adams, *Works* (Boston: Little, Brown, 1850–1856), vol. 4,
    p. 401.
24. Robert D. Kaplan, *Warrior Politics: Why Leadership Demands a
    Pagan Ethos* (New York: Random House, 2001), pp. 101–2.
25. Spykman, *America's Strategy in World Politics,* p. 43.
26. Murray, "Some Thoughts on War and Geography," p. 213.
27. Jakub J. Grygiel, *Great Powers and Geopolitical Change* (Baltimore:
    Johns Hopkins University Press, 2006), p. 15.
28. Gray, "The Continued Primacy of Geography"; Murray, "Some
    Thoughts on War and Geography," p. 216.
29. Morgenthau, *Politics Among Nations,* p. 124.
30. Isaiah Berlin, *Four Essays on Liberty* (Oxford: Oxford University
    Press, 1969).
31. See Daniel J. Mahoney's "Three Decent Frenchmen," a review of
    Tony Judt's *The Burden of Responsibility, The National Interest,*

Summer 1999; see, too, *History, Truth and Liberty: Selected Writings of Raymond Aron,* edited by Franciszek Draus (Chicago: University of Chicago Press, 1985).

32. Norman Davies, *God's Playground: A History of Poland,* vol. 1, *The Origins to 1795* (New York: Columbia University Press, 2005 [1981]), p. viii.

Chapter III: Herodotus and His Successors

1. William H. McNeill, *The Rise of the West: A History of the Human Community* (Chicago: University of Chicago Press, 1963), pp. 22, 27.

2. Freya Stark, "Iraq," in *Islam To-day,* edited by A. J. Arberry and Rom Landau (London: Faber & Faber, 1943).

3. Ibn Khaldun, *The Muqaddimah: An Introduction to History* (1377), translated by Franz Rosenthal, 1967 Princeton University Press edition, pp. 133, 136, 140, 252; Robert D. Kaplan, *Mediterranean Winter* (New York: Random House, 2004), p. 27.

4. Georges Roux, *Ancient Iraq* (London: Allen & Unwin, 1964), pp. 267, 284, 297, 299.

5. McNeill, *The Rise of the West,* pp. 32, 41–42, 46, 50, 64.

6. James Fairgrieve, *Geography and World Power* (New York: E. P. Dutton, 1917), pp. 26–27, 30, 32.

7. McNeill, *The Rise of the West,* pp. 69, 71; Roux, *Ancient Iraq,* pp. 24–25.

8. McNeill, *The Rise of the West,* pp. 167, 217, 243.

9. Ibid., pp. 250, 484, 618.

10. Ibid., p. 535.

11. Arthur Helps, preface to 1991 abridged English-language edition of Oswald Spengler, *The Decline of the West* (Oxford, UK: Oxford University Press).

12. Ibid., p. 249.

13. Oswald Spengler, *The Decline of the West,* translated by Charles Francis Atkinson (New York: Knopf, 1962 [1918, 1922]), pp. 324, 345, 352.

14. Ibid., pp. 177–78, 193–94, 353–54; Arnold J. Toynbee, *A Study of History,* abridgement of vols. 7–10 by D. C. Somervell (New York: Oxford University Press, 1957), pp. 144–45.

15. Ibid., pp. 451, 539.

16. W. Gordon East, *The Geography Behind History* (New York: Norton, 1967), p. 128.

17. Arnold J. Toynbee, *A Study of History,* abridgement of vols. 1–6 by D. C. Somervell (New York: Oxford University Press, 1946), pp. 123, 237.

18. Toynbee, *A Study of History,* vols. 1–6, pp. 146, 164–66; Jared Diamond, *Collapse: How Societies Choose to Fail or Succeed* (New York: Viking, 2005), pp. 79, 81, 106–7, 109, 119–20, 136–37, 157, 159, 172, 247, 276.

19. By no means was Europe alone in this regard. For example, Toynbee notes how the inhabitants of the Andean plateau were challenged by a bleak climate and poor soil, even as the inhabitants of the Pacific coast of South America were challenged by heat and drought that necessitated irrigation works. The difference, though, between Europe and South America, which Toynbee does not indicate, is that Europe, with its natural deepwater ports, lay athwart many trade and migration routes. Toynbee, *A Study of History,* vol. 1, p. 75.

20. McNeill, *The Rise of the West,* pp. 565, 724.

21. Ibid., p. 253.

22. Ibid., pp. 722, 724.

23. Ibid., p. 728.

24. Robert Gilpin, *War and Change in World Politics* (New York: Cambridge University Press, 1981).

25. Morgenthau, *Politics Among Nations: The Struggle for Power and Peace,* revised by Kenneth W. Thompson and W. David Clinton (New York: McGraw Hill, 2006), pp. 354–57.

26. Ibid., p. 357.

27. McNeill, *The Rise of the West,* p. 807.

28. Ibid, p. 352.

29. Toynbee, *A Study of History,* vols. 1–6, p. 284.

30. Toynbee, *A Study of History,* vols. 7–10, p. 121.

31. For examples of Eurocentric mapping conventions, see Jeremy Black, *Maps and History,* pp. 60, 62.

32. Marshall G. S. Hodgson, *The Venture of Islam: Conscience and History in a World Civilization,* vol. 1: *The Classical Age of Islam* (Chicago: University of Chicago Press, 1974), pp. 50, 56, 60–61, 109–11.

33. Ibid., pp. 114, 120–24, 133; Marshall G. S. Hodgson, *The Venture*

of Islam: Conscience and History in a World Civilization, vol. 2: *The Expansion of Islam in the Middle Periods* (Chicago: University of Chicago Press, 1974), pp. 65, 71.

34. Hodgson, *The Classical Age of Islam,* pp. 154, 156, 158.

35. Ibid., pp. 151, 204–6, 229.

36. Toynbee, *A Study of History,* vols. 1–6, p. 271.

37. Ibid., p. 268. The Abyssinian highlands were more inaccessible still, and would remain under heavy Christian influence.

38. Hodgson, *The Expansion of Islam in the Middle Periods,* pp. 54, 396, 400–401.

39. Marshall G. S. Hodgson, *The Venture of Islam: Conscience and History in a World Civilization,* vol. 3: *The Gunpowder Empires and Modern Times* (Chicago: University of Chicago Press, 1974), pp. 114, 116.

40. All direct quotes are from David Grene's 1987 University of Chicago Press translation. I have also drawn on material from the introductions to other translations by A. R. Burn and Tom Griffith.

41. Boris Pasternak, *Doctor Zhivago,* translated by Max Hayward and Manya Harari (New York: Pantheon, 1958), p. 43.

42. Hodgson, *The Classical Age of Islam,* p. 25.

Chapter IV: The Eurasian Map

1. Jakub J. Grygiel, *Great Powers and Geopolitical Change* (Baltimore: Johns Hopkins University Press, 2006), pp. 2, 24; Mackubin Thomas Owens, "In Defense of Classical Geopolitics," *Naval War College Review,* Newport, Rhode Island, Autumn 1999, pp. 60, 73; Saul B. Cohen, *Geography and Politics in a World Divided* (New York: Random House, 1963), p. 29.

2. Paul Kennedy, "The Pivot of History: The U.S. Needs to Blend Democratic Ideals with Geopolitical Wisdom," *The Guardian,* London, June 19, 2004; Cohen, *Geography and Politics in a World Divided,* p. xiii.

3. Zbigniew Brzezinski, *The Grand Chessboard: American Primacy and Its Geostrategic Imperatives* (New York: Basic Books, 1997), p. 37.

4. Hans J. Morgenthau, *Politics Among Nations: The Struggle for Power and Peace,* revised by Kenneth W. Thompson and W. David Clinton (New York: McGraw Hill, 1948), pp. 170–71.

5.   Halford J. Mackinder, *Democratic Ideals and Reality: A Study in Politics of Reconstruction* (Washington, DC: National Defense University, 1919, 1942), p. 205; W. H. Parker, *Mackinder: Geography as an Aid to Statecraft* (Oxford: Clarendon Press, 1982), pp. 211–12.

6.   Mackinder, *Democratic Ideals and Reality,* p. 155.

7.   H. J. Mackinder, "On the Necessity of Thorough Teaching in General Geography as a Preliminary to the Teaching of Commercial Geography," *Journal of the Manchester Geographical Society,* 1890, vol. 6; Parker, *Mackinder,* pp. 95–96.

8.   H. J. Mackinder, "The Geographical Pivot of History," *The Geographical Journal,* London, April 1904, p. 422.

9.   Ibid., p. 421.

10. Ibid., p. 422.

11. Mackinder, *Democratic Ideals and Reality,* p. 72; James Fairgrieve, *Geography and World Power,* p. 103.

12. The United States would know a similar fate, as World War II left it virtually unscathed, even as the infrastructures of Europe, the Soviet Union, China, and Japan were laid waste, granting America decades of economic and political preeminence.

13. Toynbee, *A Study of History,* abridgement of vols. 7–10 by D. C. Somervell (New York: Oxford University Press, 1946), pp. 151, 168.

14. Geoffrey Sloan, "Sir Halford J. Mackinder: The Heartland Theory Then and Now," in *Geopolitics, Geography and Strategy,* edited by Colin S. Gray and Geoffrey Sloan (London: Frank Cass, 1999), p. 19.

15. Kennedy, "The Pivot of History: The U.S. Needs to Blend Democratic Ideals with Geopolitical Wisdom."

16. Parker, *Mackinder,* p. 154.

17. Gerry Kearns, *Geopolitics and Empire: The Legacy of Halford Mackinder* (New York: Oxford University Press, 2009), p. 38.

18. Parker, *Mackinder,* p. 121.

19. Daniel J. Mahoney, "Three Decent Frenchmen," *The National Interest,* Washington, Summer 1999; Franciszek Draus, *History, Truth and Liberty: Selected Writings of Raymond Aron* (Chicago: University of Chicago Press, 1985).

20. Grygiel, *Great Powers and Geopolitical Change,* p. 181; Raymond Aron, *Peace and War: A Theory of International Relations* (Garden City: Doubleday, 1966), pp. 197–98.

21. Mackinder, *Democratic Ideals and Reality,* p. 2.

22. Ibid., p. 1.

23. Parker, *Mackinder,* p. 160.

24. Ibid., p. 163.

25. Mackinder, *Democratic Ideals and Reality,* pp. 24–25, 28, 32; Parker, *Mackinder,* 122–23; Fairgrieve, *Geography and World Power,* pp. 60–62.

26. Mackinder, *Democratic Ideals and Reality,* pp. 22, 38, 41, 46.

27. Ibid., pp. 46, 48.

28. Brzezinski, *The Grand Chessboard,* p. 31.

29. Mackinder, *Democratic Ideals and Reality,* pp. 41–42, 47.

30. Ibid., p. xviii, from introduction by Stephen V. Mladineo.

31. Mackinder, *Democratic Ideals and Reality,* pp. 95–99, 111–12, 115; Cohen, *Geography and Politics in a World Divided,* pp. 85–86; James Fairgrieve, *Geography and World Power* (London: University of London Press, 1915).

32. Sloan, "Sir Halford J. Mackinder: The Heartland Theory Then and Now," p. 31.

33. Arthur Butler Dugan, "Mackinder and His Critics Reconsidered," *The Journal of Politics,* May 1962.

34. Brian W. Blouet, *Halford Mackinder: A Biography* (College Station: Texas A & M Press, 1987), pp. 150–51.

35. Mackinder, *Democratic Ideals and Reality,* pp. 55, 78; Cohen, *Geography and Politics in a World Divided,* pp. 42–44.

36. Mackinder, *Democratic Ideals and Reality,* pp. 64–65.

37. Ibid., p. 116.

38. Ibid., pp. 74, 205.

39. Ibid., p. 201.

Chapter V: The Nazi Distortion

1. Robert Strausz-Hupé, *Geopolitics: The Struggle for Space and Power* (New York: G. P. Putnam's Sons, 1942), pp. 48–53; Parker, *Mackinder: Geography as an Aid to Statecraft* (Oxford: Clarendon Press, 1982), pp. 178–80.

2. Strausz-Hupé, *Geopolitics,* pp. 59–60.

3. Ibid., pp. 60–61, 68–69.

4. Ibid., pp. 142, 154–55.

5. Ibid., pp. 85, 101, 140, 197, 220.

6. Holger H. Herwig, "*Geopolitik:* Haushofer, Hitler and Leben-sraum," in *Geopolitics: Geography and Strategy,* edited by Colin S. Gray and Geoffrey Sloan (London: Frank Cass, 1999), p. 233.

7. Brian W. Blouet, *Halford Mackinder: A Biography* (College Station: Texas A & M Press, 1987), pp. 190–91.

8. Strausz-Hupé, *Geopolitics,* p. 264.

9. Ibid., p. 191.

10. Ibid., pp. 196, 218.

11. Paul Bracken, *Fire in the East: The Rise of Asian Military Power and the Second Nuclear Age* (New York: HarperCollins, 1999), p. 30.

Chapter VI: The Rimland Thesis

1. Brian W. Blouet, *Halford Mackinder: A Biography* (College Station: Texas A & M Press, 1987), p. 192.

2. Nicholas J. Spykman, "Geography and Foreign Policy I," *The American Political Science Review,* Los Angeles, February 1938; Francis P. Sempa, "The Geopolitical Realism of Nicholas Spykman," introduction to Nicholas J. Spykman, *America's Strategy in World Politics* (New Brunswick: Transaction Publishers, 2007).

3. Nicholas J. Spykman, *America's Strategy in World Politics: The United States and the Balance of Power* (New York: Harcourt, Brace, 1942), pp. xvii, xviii, 7, 18, 20–21, 2008 Transaction edition.

4. Ibid., pp. 42, 91; Robert Strausz-Hupé, *Geopolitics: The Struggle for Space and Power* (New York: G. P. Putnam's Sons, 1942), p. 169; Halford J. Mackinder, *Democratic Ideals and Reality: A Study in the Politics of Reconstruction* (Washington, DC: National Defense University, 1919, 1942), p. 202; Daniel J. Boorstin, *Hidden History: Exploring Our Secret Past* (New York: Vintage, 1987, 1989), p. 246; James Fairgrieve, *Geography and World Power,* pp. 18–19, 326–27.

5. Spykman, *America's Strategy in World Politics,* p. 89.

6. Ibid., pp. 49–50, 60.

7. Ibid., p. 50.

8. Ibid., pp. 197, 407.

9. Ibid., p. 182.

10. Nicholas John Spykman, *The Geography of the Peace,* edited by Helen R. Nicholl (New York: Harcourt, Brace, 1944), p. 43.

11. Mackinder, *Democratic Ideals and Reality,* p. 51.

12. W. H. Parker, *Mackinder: Geography as an Aid to Statecraft* (Oxford: Clarendon Press, 1982), p. 195.

13. Henry A. Kissinger, *Nuclear Weapons and Foreign Policy* (New York: Doubleday, 1957), pp. 125, 127.

14. Spykman, *America's Strategy in World Politics,* pp. 135–37, 460, 469.

15. Ibid., p. 466.

16. Michael P. Gerace, "Between Mackinder and Spykman: Geopolitics, Containment, and After," *Comparative Strategy,* University of Reading, UK, 1991.

17. Spykman, *America's Strategy in World Politics,* p. 165.

18. Ibid., p. 166.

19. Ibid., p. 178; Albert Wohlstetter, "Illusions of Distance," *Foreign Affairs,* New York, January 1968.

20. Parker, *Mackinder,* p. 186.

21. Geoffrey Kemp and Robert E. Harkavy, *Strategic Geography and the Changing Middle East* (Washington, DC: Brookings Institution Press, 1997), p. 5.

Chapter VII: The Allure of Sea Power

1. A. T. Mahan, *The Problem of Asia: And Its Effect Upon International Policies* (London: Sampson Low, Marston, 1900), pp. 27–28, 42–44, 97, 161; Cohen, *Geography and Politics in a World Divided* (New York: Random House, 1963), pp. 48–49.

2. Robert Strausz-Hupé, *Geopolitics: The Struggle for Space and Power* (New York: G. P. Putnam's Sons, 1942), pp. 253–54.

3. A. T. Mahan, *The Influence of Sea Power Upon History, 1660–1783* (Boston: Little, Brown, 1890), pp. 225–26, 1987 Dover edition.

4. Strausz-Hupé, *Geopolitics,* pp. 244–45.

5. Jon Sumida, "Alfred Thayer Mahan, Geopolitician," in *Geopolitics, Geography and Strategy,* edited by Colin S. Gray and Geoffrey Sloan (London: Frank Cass, 1999), pp. 53, 55, 59; Jon Sumida, *Inventing Grand Strategy and Teaching Command: The Classic Works of Alfred Thayer Mahan* (Baltimore: Johns Hopkins University Press, 1997), pp. 41, 84.

6. Mahan, *The Influence of Sea Power Upon History,* p. 25.

7. Ibid., pp. iii, 8, 26–27, 50–52, 67.

8. Ibid., pp. iv–vi, 15, 20–21, 329.

9. Ibid., pp. 29, 138.

10. Ibid., pp. 29, 31, 33–34, 138; Eric Grove, *The Future of Sea Power* (Annapolis: Naval Institute Press, 1990), pp. 224–25.

11. Norman Angell, *The Great Illusion* (New York: Cosimo Classics, 1909, 2007), pp. 310–11.

12. James R. Holmes and Toshi Yoshihara, *Chinese Naval Strategy in the 21st Century: The Turn to Mahan* (New York: Routledge, 2008), p. 39.

13. Julian S. Corbett, *Principles of Maritime Strategy* (London: Longmans, Green and Co., 1911), pp. 87, 152–53, 213–14, 2004 Dover edition.

14. U.S. Navy, U.S. Marine Corps, U.S. Coast Guard, "A Cooperative Strategy for 21st Century Seapower," Washington, DC, and Newport, Rhode Island, October 2007.

15. John J. Mearsheimer, *The Tragedy of Great Power Politics* (New York: W. W. Norton, 2001), pp. 210, 213, 365.

Chapter VIII: The "Crisis of Room"

1. Paul Bracken, *Fire in the East: The Rise of Asian Military Power and the Second Nuclear Age* (New York: HarperCollins, 1999), pp. 33–34.

2. Ibid., pp. xxv–xxvii, 73.

3. Ibid., pp. 2, 10, 22, 24–25.

4. Ibid., pp. 26–31.

5. Ibid., pp. 37–38.

6. Ibid., pp. 42, 45, 47–49, 63, 97, 113.

7. Ibid., p. 156.

8. Ibid., p. 110.

9. Ibn Khaldun, *The Muqaddimah: An Introduction to History* (1377), translated by Franz Rosenthal, pp. 93, 109, 133, 136, 140, 1967 Princeton University Press edition.

10. R. W. Southern, *The Making of the Middle Ages* (New Haven: Yale University Press, 1953), pp. 12–13.

11. George Orwell, *1984* (New York: Harcourt, Brace, 1949), p. 124.

12. Thomas Pynchon, foreword to George Orwell, *1984* (New York: Penguin, 2003).

13. Oswald Spengler, *The Decline of the West,* translated by Charles Francis Atkinson (New York: Vintage, 1922, 2006), p. 395.
14. Bracken, *Fire in the East,* pp. 123–24.
15. Ibid., pp. 89, 91.
16. Jakub Grygiel, "The Power of Statelessness: The Withering Appeal of Governing," *Policy Review,* Washington, April–May 2009.
17. Randall L. Schweller, "Ennui Becomes Us," *The National Interest,* Washington, DC, December 16, 2009.

PART II: THE EARLY-TWENTY-FIRST-CENTURY MAP

Chapter IX: The Geography of European Divisions

1. Saul B. Cohen, *Geography and Politics in a World Divided* (New York: Random House, 1963), p. 157.
2. William Anthony Hay, "Geopolitics of Europe," *Orbis,* Philadelphia, Spring 2003.
3. Claudio Magris, *Danube* (New York: Farrar, Straus and Giroux, 1988, 1989), p. 18.
4. Barry Cunliffe, *Europe Between the Oceans: Themes and Variations: 9000 BC–AD 1000* (New Haven: Yale University Press, 2008), pp. vii, 31, 38, 40, 60, 318, 477.
5. Tony Judt, "Europe: The Grand Illusion," *New York Review of Books,* July 11, 1996.
6. Cunliffe, *Europe Between the Oceans,* p. 372.
7. Hay, "Geopolitics of Europe."
8. Peter Brown, *The World of Late Antiquity: AD 150–750* (London: Thames & Hudson, 1971), pp. 11, 13, 20.
9. Henri Pirenne, *Mohammed and Charlemagne* (ACLS Humanities e-book 1939, 2008).
10. Fernand Braudel, *The Mediterranean: And the Mediterranean World in the Age of Philip II,* translated by Sian Reynolds (New York: Harper & Row, 1949), p. 75.
11. Cunliffe, *Europe Between the Oceans,* pp. 42–43.
12. Robert D. Kaplan, *Eastward to Tartary: Travels in the Balkans, the Middle East, and the Caucasus* (New York: Random House, 2000), p. 5.

13. Philomila Tsoukala, "A Family Portrait of a Greek Tragedy," *New York Times,* April 24, 2010.

14. Judt, "Europe: The Grand Illusion."

15. Jack A. Goldstone, "The New Population Bomb: The Four Megatrends That Will Change the World," *Foreign Affairs,* New York, January–February 2010.

16. Hay, "Geopolitics of Europe."

17. Judt, "Europe: The Grand Illusion."

18. Zbigniew Brzezinski, *The Grand Chessboard: American Primacy and Its Geostrategic Imperatives* (New York: Basic Books, 1997), pp. 69–71.

19. Colin S. Gray, *Another Bloody Century: Future Warfare* (London: Weidenfeld & Nicolson, 2005), p. 37.

20. Josef Joffe in conversation, Madrid, May 5, 2011, Conference of the Fundación para el Análisis y los Estudios Sociales.

21. Geoffrey Sloan, "Sir Halford Mackinder: The Heartland Theory Then and Now," in *Geopolitics: Geography and Strategy,* edited by Colin S. Gray and Geoffrey Sloan (London: Frank Cass, 1999), p. 20.

22. Steve LeVine, "Pipeline Politics Redux," *Foreign Policy,* Washington, DC, June 10, 2010; "BP Global Statistical Review of World Energy," June 2010.

23. Hay, "Geopolitics of Europe."

24. Halford J. Mackinder, *Democratic Ideals and Reality: A Study in the Politics of Reconstruction* (Washington, DC: National Defense University, 1919, 1942), p. 116.

Chapter X: Russia and the Independent Heartland

1. Alexander Solzhenitsyn, *August 1914,* translated by Michael Glenny (New York: Farrar, Straus and Giroux, 1971, 1972), p. 3.

2. Saul B. Cohen, *Geography and Politics in a World Divided* (New York: Random House, 1963), p. 211.

3. G. Patrick March, *Eastern Destiny: Russia in Asia and the North Pacific* (Westport, CT: Praeger, 1996), p. 1.

4. Philip Longworth, *Russia: The Once and Future Empire from Pre-History to Putin* (New York: St. Martin's Press, 2005), pp. 16–17.

5. March, *Eastern Destiny,* pp. 4–5; W. Bruce Lincoln, *The Conquest of*

a Continent: Siberia and the Russians (New York: Random House, 1994), p. xx, 2007 Cornell University Press edition.

6. A Tatar is a Turkic-speaking Sunni Muslim of which there were many in the Mongol armies, leading to the name being used interchangeably with Mongol.

7. March, *Eastern Destiny*, p. 18.

8. James H. Billington, *The Icon and the Axe: An Interpretive History of Russian Culture* (New York: Knopf, 1966), p. 11.

9. Ibid., pp. 18–19, 26.

10. Longworth, *Russia*, p. 1.

11. Lincoln, *The Conquest of a Continent*, p. 19.

12. Longworth, *Russia*, pp. 48, 52–53.

13. Robert Strausz-Hupé, *The Zone of Indifference* (New York: G. P. Putnam's Sons, 1952), p. 88.

14. Longworth, *Russia*, pp. 94–95; March, *Eastern Destiny*, p. 28.

15. Robert D. Kaplan, introduction to *Taras Bulba*, translated by Peter Constantine (New York: Modern Library, 2003).

16. Alexander Herzen, *My Past and Thoughts*, translated by Constance Garnett (Berkeley: University of California Press, 1968, 1982), p. 97.

17. Longworth, *Russia*, p. 200.

18. Denis J. B. Shaw, *Russia in the Modern World: A New Geography* (Oxford: Blackwell, 1999), pp. 230–32.

19. Ibid., pp. 5, 7; D. W. Meinig, "The Macrogeography of Western Imperialism," in *Settlement and Encounter*, edited by F. H. Gale and G. H. Lawson (Oxford: Oxford University Press, 1968), pp. 213–40.

20. Lincoln, *The Conquest of a Continent*, p. xix.

21. Longworth, *Russia*, p. 322.

22. Colin Thubron, *In Siberia* (New York: HarperCollins, 1999), pp. 99, 122.

23. Lincoln, *The Conquest of a Continent*, p. 57.

24. Ibid., pp. 89, 395.

25. There is, too, the question of a warming Arctic, which would unblock the ice-bound White, Barents, Kara, Laptev, and East Siberian seas, to which all of Siberia's mighty rivers flow, unleashing the region's economic potential.

26. March, *Eastern Destiny*, pp. 51, 130.

27. Simon Saradzhyan, "Russia's Red Herring," ISN Security Watch, Zurich, May 25, 2010.

28. March, *Eastern Destiny*, p. 194.

29. Shaw, *Russia in the Modern World*, p. 31.

30. Soviet maps of Europe henceforth included all of European Russia, a cartographic device which ensured that Moscow was not viewed as an outsider. It also made Eastern European states appear more central, with Soviet republics like Ukraine and Moldova becoming, in effect, the new Eastern Europe. Jeremy Black, *Maps and History: Constructing Images of the Past* (New Haven: Yale University Press, 2009), p. 151.

31. Shaw, *Russia in the Modern World*, pp. 22–23.

32. March, *Eastern Destiny*, pp. 237–38.

33. Saradzhyan, "Russia's Red Herring."

34. Zbigniew Brzezinski, *The Grand Chessboard: American Primacy and Its Geostrategic Imperative* (New York: Basic Books, 1997), p. 98.

35. John Erickson, " 'Russia Will Not Be Trifled With': Geopolitical Facts and Fantasies," in *Geopolitics, Geography and Strategy*, edited by Colin S. Gray and Geoffrey Sloan (London: Frank Cass, 1999), pp. 242–43, 262.

36. Brzezinski, *The Grand Chessboard*, p. 110.

37. Dmitri Trenin, "Russia Reborn: Reimagining Moscow's Foreign Policy," *Foreign Affairs*, New York, November–December 2009.

38. Shaw, *Russia in the Modern World*, p. 248.

39. Trenin, "Russia Reborn."

40. Paul Bracken, *Fire in the East: The Rise of Asian Military Power and the Second Nuclear Age* (New York: HarperCollins, 1999), p. 17.

41. W. H. Parker, *Mackinder: Geography as an Aid to Statecraft* (Oxford: Clarendon Press, 1982), p. 157.

42. Philip Stephens, "Putin's Russia: Frozen in Decline," *Financial Times*, London, October 14, 2011.

43. Paul Dibb, "The Bear Is Back," *The American Interest*, Washington, DC, November–December 2006.

44. Brzezinski, *The Grand Chessboard*, p. 46.

45. Richard B. Andres and Michael Kofman, "European Energy Security: Reducing Volatility of Ukraine-Russia Natural Gas Pricing Disputes," National Defense University, Washington, DC, February 2011.

46. Dibb, "The Bear Is Back."

47. Martha Brill Olcott, *The Kazakhs* (Stanford: Hoover Institution Press, 1987, 1995), pp. 57–58.

48. Olivier Roy, *The New Central Asia: The Creation of Nations* (New York: New York University Press, 1997, 2000), pp. xiv–xvi, 8–9, 66–69, 178.

49. Andres and Kofman, "European Energy Security."

50. Olcott, *The Kazakhs*, p. 271.

51. Dilip Hiro, *Inside Central Asia: A Political and Cultural History of Uzbekistan, Turkmenistan, Kazakhstan, Kyrgyzstan, Tajikistan, Turkey, and Iran* (New York: Overlook Duckworth, 2009), pp. 205, 281, 293.

52. Martin C. Spechler and Dina R. Spechler, "Is Russia Succeeding in Central Asia?," *Orbis*, Philadelphia, Fall 2010.

53. James Brooke, "China Displaces Russia in Central Asia," *Voice of America*, November 16, 2010.

54. Olcott, *The Kazakhs*, p. 273.

55. Hiro, *Inside Central Asia*, p. 262.

56. Parker, *Mackinder*, p. 83.

Chapter XI: The Geography of Chinese Power

1. H. J. Mackinder, "The Geographical Pivot of History," *The Geographical Journal*, London, April 1904.

2. Halford J. Mackinder, *Democratic Ideals and Reality: A Study in the Politics of Reconstruction* (Washington, DC: National Defense University, 1919, 1942), pp. 46–48, 203.

3. China, located in the temperate zone, has a population of 1.32 billion and its GDP totaled $4,326 billion in 2008, whereas Russia, located between the Arctic and the temperate zone, has a population of 141 million and its GDP totaled $1,601 billion in 2008. Simon Saradzhyan, "Russia's Red Herring," ISN Security Watch, Zurich, May 25, 2010.

4. John Keay, *China: A History* (London: HarperCollins, 2008), p. 13.

5. Ibid., p. 231.

6. Patricia Buckley Ebrey, *China: The Cambridge Illustrated History* (New York: Cambridge University Press, 1996), p. 108.

7. John King Fairbank and Merle Goldman, *China: A New History* (Cambridge: Harvard University Press, 1992, 2006), p. 23.

8. M. Taylor Fravel, *Strong Borders, Secure Nation: Cooperation and Conflict in China's Territorial Disputes* (Princeton: Princeton University Press, 2008), pp. 41–42.

9. Jakub J. Grygiel, *Great Powers and Geopolitical Change* (Baltimore: Johns Hopkins University Press, 2006), p. 133. Additionally, Owen Lattimore writes: "Obviously a line of cleavage existed somewhere between the territories and peoples that could advantageously be included in the Chinese Empire and those that could not. This was the line that the Great Wall was intended to define." Owen Lattimore, "Origins of the Great Wall," *Geographical Review,* vol. 27, 1937.

10. Fairbank and Goldman, *China: A New History,* pp. 23, 25, 45.

11. Ebrey, *China,* p. 57.

12. Saul B. Cohen, *Geography and Politics in a World Divided* (New York: Random House, 1963), pp. 238–39.

13. Keay, *China,* maps pp. 8–9, 53.

14. Ebrey, *China,* p. 164.

15. Fairbank and Goldman, *China: A New History,* pp. 41–42.

16. Beijing's position, writes geographer T. R. Tregear, served the needs of the Yuan, Ming, and Qing dynasties into the modern era by its sufficiently central location enabling it to govern China, even as it was close enough to guard the steppe-lands to the north and west. T. R. Tregear, *A Geography of China* (London: Transaction, 1965, 2008), pp. 94–95.

17. The threat of "barbarian" invasions is a theme in the work of the late China hand Owen Lattimore. Owen Lattimore, "China and the Barbarians," in *Empire in the East,* edited by Joseph Barnes (New York: Doubleday, 1934).

18. Keay, *China,* p. 259.

19. Fairbank and Goldman, *China: A New History,* p. 109.

20. Ebrey, *China,* p. 227.

21. "Map of Nineteenth Century China and Conflicts," www.fordham .edu/halsall, reprinted in *Reshaping Economic Geography* (Washington, DC: The World Bank, 2009), p. 195.

22. G. Patrick March, *Eastern Destiny: Russia in Asia and the North Pacific* (Westport, CT: Praeger, 1996), pp. 234–35.

23. The theory of hydraulic societies was promulgated by twentieth-century German American historian and Sinologist Karl Wittfogel,

who explained that they originally developed in ancient river valley civilizations, where vast pools of corviable labor existed to build great irrigation works.

24. Fairbank and Goldman, *China: A New History,* p. 5.

25. Yale professor Jonathan D. Spence writes of Galdan, the Zunghar warrior loyal to the Dalai Lama in Tibet, whose forces were finally defeated in northern Outer Mongolia by a Qing (Manchu) invading army numbering some eighty thousand in 1696. Jonathan D. Spence, *The Search for Modern China* (New York: Norton, 1990), p. 67.

26. David Blair, "Why the Restless Chinese Are Warming to Russia's Frozen East," *Daily Telegraph,* London, July 16, 2009.

27. Spence, *The Search for Modern China,* p. 97.

28. Fitzroy Maclean, *Eastern Approaches* (New York: Little, Brown, 1949), p. 120.

29. Spence, *The Search for Modern China,* p. 13.

30. Owen Lattimore, "Inner Asian Frontiers: Chinese and Russian Margins of Expansion," *The Journal of Economic History,* Cambridge, England, May 1947.

31. Uttam Kumar Sinha, "Tibet's Watershed Challenge," *Washington Post,* June 14, 2010.

32. Edward Wong, "China Quietly Extends Footprints into Central Asia," *New York Times,* January 2, 2011.

33. S. Frederick Starr and Andrew C. Kuchins, with Stephen Benson, Elie Krakowski, Johannes Linn, and Thomas Sanderson, "The Key to Success in Afghanistan: A Modern Silk Road Strategy," Central Asia-Caucasus Institute and the Center for Strategic and International Studies, Washington, DC, 2010.

34. Zbigniew Brzezinski, *The Grand Chessboard: American Primacy and Its Geostrategic Imperatives* (New York: Basic Books, 1997), p. 167.

35. Dan Twining, "Could China and India Go to War over Tibet?," ForeignPolicy.com, Washington, DC, March 10, 2009.

36. Owen Lattimore, "Chinese Colonization in Manchuria," *Geographical Review,* London, 1932; Tregear, *A Geography of China,* p. 270.

37. Hillary Clinton, "America's Pacific Century," *Foreign Policy,* Washington, DC, November 2011.

38. Dana Dillon and John J. Tkacik Jr., "China's Quest for Asia," *Policy Review,* Washington, DC, December 2005–January 2006.

39. Robert S. Ross, "The Rise of Chinese Power and the Implications for the Regional Security Order," *Orbis,* Philadelphia, Fall 2010.

40. John J. Mearsheimer, *The Tragedy of Great Power Politics* (New York: W. W. Norton, 2001), p. 135.

41. M. Taylor Fravel, "Regime Insecurity and International Co-operation: Explaining China's Compromises in Territorial Disputes," *International Security,* Fall 2005.

42. Grygiel, *Great Powers and Geopolitical Change,* p. 170.

43. Spence, *The Search for Modern China,* p. 136.

44. James Fairgrieve, *Geography and World Power,* pp. 242–43.

45. James Holmes and Toshi Yoshihara, "Command of the Sea with Chinese Characteristics," *Orbis,* Philadelphia, Fall 2005.

46. Ross, "The Rise of Chinese Power and the Implications for the Regional Security Order" (see Ross's footnotes which accompany his quote); Andrew F. Krepinevich, "China's 'Finlandization' Strategy in the Pacific," *Wall Street Journal,* September 11, 2010.

47. Seth Cropsey, "Alternative Maritime Strategies," grant proposal; Robert S. Ross, "China's Naval Nationalism: Sources, Prospects, and the U.S. Response," *International Security,* Cambridge, Massachusetts, Fall 2009; Robert D. Kaplan, "How We Would Fight China," *Atlantic Monthly,* Boston, June 2005; Mark Helprin, "Why the Air Force Needs the F-22," *Wall Street Journal,* February 22, 2010.

48. Holmes and Yoshihara, "Command of the Sea with Chinese Characteristics."

49. Ross, "The Rise of Chinese Power and the Implications for the Regional Security Order."

50. Andrew Erickson and Lyle Goldstein, "Gunboats for China's New 'Grand Canals'? Probing the Intersection of Beijing's Naval and Oil Security Policies," *Naval War College Review,* Newport, Rhode Island, Spring 2009.

51. Nicholas J. Spykman, *America's Strategy in World Politics: The United States and the Balance of Power* (New York: Harcourt, Brace, 1948), p. xvi. The phrase first appeared in Nicholas J. Spykman and Abbie A. Rollins, "Geographic Objectives in Foreign Policy II," *The American Political Science Review,* August 1939.

52. This will be especially true if the canal and land bridge proposed for linking the Indian and Pacific oceans come to fruition.

53. Spykman, *America's Strategy in World Politics,* p. 60.

54. Andrew S. Erickson and David D. Yang, "On the Verge of a Game-Changer: A Chinese Antiship Ballistic Missile Could Alter the Rules in the Pacific and Place U.S. Navy Carrier Strike Groups in Jeopardy," *Proceedings,* Annapolis, Maryland, May 2009.

55. Jacqueline Newmyer, "Oil, Arms, and Influence: The Indirect Strategy Behind Chinese Military Modernization," *Orbis,* Philadelphia, Spring 2009.

56. Howard W. French, "The Next Empire," *The Atlantic,* Washington, May 2010.

57. Pat Garrett, "Indian Ocean 21," November 2009.

58. Julian S. Corbett, *Principles of Maritime Strategy* (London: Longmans, Green, 1911), pp. 213–214, 2004 Dover edition.

59. Robert S. Ross, "The Geography of the Peace: East Asia in the Twenty-First Century," *International Security,* Cambridge, Massachusetts, Spring 1999.

60. Mearsheimer, *The Tragedy of Great Power Politics,* pp. 386, 401–2.

Chapter XII: India's Geographical Dilemma

1. James Fairgrieve, *Geography and World Power,* p. 253.

2. K. M. Panikkar, *Geographical Factors in Indian History* (Bombay: Bharatiya Vidya Bhavan, 1954), p. 41. A limiting factor in the importance of these rivers is that, as Panikkar writes, they "flow through uplands and not valleys, and do not therefore spread their fertilizing waters on the countryside" (p. 37).

3. Fairgrieve, *Geography and World Power,* pp. 253–54.

4. H. J. Mackinder, *Eight Lectures on India* (London: Visual Instruction Committee of the Colonial Office, 1910), p. 114.

5. Burton Stein, *A History of India* (Oxford: Blackwell, 1998), pp. 6–7.

6. Persian traveled to India as a literary language in the twelfth century, with its formal role consolidated in the sixteenth.

7. Panikkar, *Geographical Factors in Indian History,* p. 21.

8. Nicholas Ostler, *Empires of the Word: A Language History of the World* (New York: HarperCollins, 2005), p. 223.

9. André Wink, *Al-Hind: The Making of the Indo-Islamic World,*

vol. 1: *Early Medieval India and the Expansion of Islam 7th–11th Centuries* (Boston: Brill Academic Publishers, 1996), Chapter 4.

10. Stein, *A History of India*, pp. 75–76.

11. Adam Watson, *The Evolution of International Society: A Comparative Historical Analysis* (London: Routledge, 1992), pp. 78–82.

12. Stein, *A History of India*, p. 121.

13. Fairgrieve, *Geography and World Power*, p. 261.

14. Panikkar, *Geographical Factors in Indian History*, p. 43.

15. Fairgrieve, *Geography and World Power*, p. 262.

16. Robert D. Kaplan, *Monsoon: The Indian Ocean and the Future of American Power* (New York: Random House, 2010), pp. 119, 121.

17. Panikkar, *Geographical Factors in Indian History*, pp. 40, 44.

18. Kaplan, *Monsoon*, pp. 122–23; John F. Richards, *The New Cambridge History of India: The Mughal Empire* (New York: Cambridge University Press, 1993), pp. 239, 242.

19. Richard M. Eaton, *The Rise of Islam and the Bengal Frontier, 1204–1760* (Berkeley: University of California Press, 1993), pp. xxii–xxiii, 313.

20. George Friedman, "The Geopolitics of India: A Shifting, Self-Contained World," Stratfor, December 16, 2008.

21. The geographical and cultural relationship between India and Iran is almost equally close.

22. The Punjab means "five rivers," all tributaries of the Indus: the Beas, Chenab, Jhelum, Ravi, and Sutlej.

23. André Wink, *Al-Hind: The Making of the Indo-Islamic World*, vol. 2: *The Slave Kings and the Islamic Conquest, 11th–13th Centuries* (Leiden: Brill, 1997), pp. 1, 162; Muzaffar Alam, *The Crisis of Empire in Mughal North India: Awadh and the Punjab, 1707–1748* (New Delhi: Oxford University Press, 1986), pp. 11, 141, 143.

24. Aitzaz Ahsan, *The Indus Saga and the Making of Pakistan* (Karachi: Oxford University Press, 1996), p. 18.

25. S. Frederick Starr and Andrew C. Kuchins, with Stephen Benson, Elie Krakowski, Johannes Linn, and Thomas Sanderson, "The Key to Success in Afghanistan: A Modern Silk Road Strategy," Central Asia–Caucasus Institute and the Center for Strategic and International Studies, Washington, DC, 2010.

26. Friedman, "The Geopolitics of India."

27. Fairgrieve, *Geography and World Power*, p. 253.

Chapter XIII: The Iranian Pivot

1. William H. McNeill, *The Rise of the West: A History of the Human Community* (Chicago: University of Chicago Press, 1963), p. 167.

2. Marshall G. S. Hodgson, *The Venture of Islam: Conscience and History in a World Civilization,* vol. 1: *The Classical Age of Islam* (Chicago: University of Chicago Press, 1974), pp. 50, 60, 109.

3. John King Fairbank and Merle Goldman, *China: A New History* (Cambridge: Harvard University Press, 1992, 2006), pp. 40–41.

4. Geoffrey Kemp and Robert E. Harkavy, *Strategic Geography and the Changing Middle East* (Washington, DC: Brookings Institution Press, 1997), pp. 15–17.

5. Ibid., p. xiii. Recent discoveries and developments concerning tar sands and shale deposits, particularly in North America, call these statistics into question.

6. Charles M. Doughty, *Travels in Arabia Deserta* (Cambridge: Cambridge University Press, 1888), vol. 1, p. 336, 1979 Dover edition.

7. Bruce Riedel, "Brezhnev in the Hejaz," *The National Interest,* Washington, DC, September–October 2011.

8. Alexei Vassiliev, *The History of Saudi Arabia* (New York: New York University Press, 2000), pp. 29, 79–80, 88, 136, 174, 177, 182; Robert Lacey, *The Kingdom* (London: Hutchinson, 1981), p. 221.

9. Peter Mansfield, *The Arabs* (New York: Penguin, 1976), pp. 371–72.

10. Kemp and Harkavy, *Strategic Geography and the Changing Middle East,* map, p. 113.

11. Freya Stark, *The Valleys of the Assassins: And Other Persian Travels* (London: John Murray, 1934).

12. Peter Brown, *The World of Late Antiquity,* AD 150–750 (London: Thames & Hudson, 1971), p. 160.

13. Ibid., p. 163.

14. W. Barthold, *An Historical Geography of Iran* (Princeton: Princeton University Press, 1903, 1971, 1984), pp. x–xi, 4.

15. Nicholas Ostler, *Empires of the Word: A Language History of the World* (New York: HarperCollins, 2005), p. 31.

16. Michael Axworthy, *A History of Iran: Empire of the Mind* (New York: Basic Books, 2008), p. 3.

17. Hodgson, *The Classical Age of Islam,* p. 125.

18. Axworthy, *A History of Iran,* p. 34.

19. Ibid., p. 78.

20. Philip K. Hitti, *The Arabs: A Short History* (Princeton: Princeton University Press, 1943), p. 109.

21. Brown, *The World of Lat Antiquity,* pp. 202–3.

22. Axworthy, *A History of Iran,* p. 120.

23. Arnold J. Toynbee, *A Study of History,* abridgement of vols. 1–6 by D. C. Somervell (New York: Oxford University Press, 1946), p. 346.

24. Dilip Hiro, *Inside Central Asia: A Political and Cultural History of Uzbekistan, Turkmenistan, Kazakhstan, Kyrgyzstan, Tajikistan, Turkey, and Iran* (New York: Overlook Duckworth, 2009), p. 359.

25. Olivier Roy, *The Failure of Political Islam,* translated by Carol Volk (Cambridge: Harvard University Press, 1992, 1994), pp. 168–70.

26. Marshall G. S. Hodgson, *The Venture of Islam: Conscience and History in a World Civilization,* vol. 3: *The Gunpowder Empires and Modern Times* (Chicago: University of Chicago Press, 1974), pp. 22–23.

27. Roy, *The Failure of Political Islam,* p. 168.

28. James J. Morier, *The Adventures of Hajji Baba of Ispahan* (London: John Murray, 1824), p. 5, 1949 Cresset Press edition.

29. Roy, *The Failure of Political Islam,* p. 172.

30. Ibid., 174–75.

31. Vali Nasr, *Forces of Fortune: The Rise of the New Muslim Middle Class and What It Will Mean for Our World* (New York: Free Press, 2009).

32. Roy, *The Future of Political Islam,* p. 193.

33. M. K. Bhadrakumar, "Russia, China, Iran Energy Map," *Asia Times,* 2010.

34. Axworthy, *A History of Iran,* p. 162.

35. Robert Baer, "Iranian Resurrection," *The National Interest,* Washington, DC, November–December 2008.

36. Robert D. Kaplan, *The Ends of the Earth: A Journey at the Dawn of the 21st Century* (New York: Random House, 1996), p. 242.

Chapter XIV: The Former Ottoman Empire

1. George Friedman, *The Next 100 Years: A Forecast for the 21st Century* (New York: Doubleday, 2009), p. 7.

2. William Langer and Robert Blake, "The Rise of the Ottoman Turks

and Its Historical Background," *American Historical Review,* 1932; Jakub J. Grygiel, *Great Powers and Geopolitical Change* (Baltimore: Johns Hopkins University Press, 2006), p. 96.

3. Herbert Adams Gibbons, *The Foundation of the Ottoman Empire* (New York: Century, 1916); Grygiel, *Great Powers and Geopolitical Change,* pp. 96–97, 101.

4. Dilip Hiro, *Inside Central Asia: A Political and Cultural History of Uzbekistan, Turkmenistan, Kazakhstan, Kyrgyzstan, Tajikistan, Turkey, and Iran* (New York: Overlook Duckworth, 2009), p. 89; Dilip Hiro, "The Islamic Wave Hits Turkey," *The Nation,* June 28, 1986.

5. Hiro, *Inside Central Asia,* pp. 85–86.

6. Robert D. Kaplan, *Eastward to Tartary: Travels in the Balkans, the Middle East, and the Caucasus* (New York: Random House, 2000), p. 118.

7. Samuel P. Huntington, *The Clash of Civilizations and the Remaking of World Order* (New York: Simon & Schuster, 1996), pp. 85, 125, 177.

8. Erkan Turkmen, *The Essence of Rumi's Masnevi* (Konya, Turkey: Misket, 1992), p. 73.

9. Marc Champion, "In Risky Deal, Ankara Seeks Security, Trade," *Wall Street Journal,* May 18, 2010.

10. Geoffrey Kemp and Robert E. Harkavy, *Strategic Geography and the Changing Middle East* (Washington, DC: Brookings Institution Press, 1997), p. 105.

11. Freya Stark, *Islam To-day,* edited by A. J. Arberry and Rom Landau (London: Faber & Faber, 1943).

12. Robert D. Kaplan, "Heirs of Sargons," *The National Interest,* Washington, DC, July–August 2009.

13. Georges Roux, *Ancient Iraq* (London: Allen & Unwin, 1964).

14. Adeed Dawisha, *Iraq: A Political History from Independence to Occupation* (Princeton: Princeton University Press, 2009), p. 4.

15. Ibid., p. 5.

16. Ibid., pp. 286–87.

17. Philip K. Hitti, *History of Syria: Including Lebanon and Palestine* (New York: Macmillan, 1951), pp. 3–5.

18. Nibraz Kazimi, "Move Assad: Could Jihadists Overthrow the Syrian Government?," *New Republic,* June 25, 2010.

19. Michael Young, "On the Eastern Shore," *Wall Street Journal*, April 29, 2011.

20. Franck Salameh, "Assad Dynasty Crumbles," *The National Interest*, Washington, DC, April 27, 2011; see, too, Philip Mansel, *Levant* (New Haven: Yale University Press, 2011).

21. Unfortunately, despite the promise that Adonis's poetry exudes, he turned out to be a disappointment to demonstrators in the early days of the Arab Spring, refusing to side completely with the opposition to Bashar al-Assad. Nevertheless, his poetry still suggests an eclectic Syria built on a confection of cultures. Robert F. Worth, "The Arab Intellectuals Who Didn't Roar," *New York Times*, October 30, 2011.

22. Benjamin Schwarz, "Will Israel Live to 100?," *The Atlantic*, May 2005.

PART III: AMERICA'S DESTINY

Chapter XV: Braudel, Mexico, and Grand Strategy

1. Fernand Braudel, *The Mediterranean: And the Mediterranean World in the Age of Philip II*, vols. 1 and 2, translated by Sian Reynolds (New York: Harper & Row, 1949, 1972, 1973).

2. Ibid., vol. 1, pp. 243, 245–46.

3. H. R. Trevor-Roper, "Fernand Braudel, the Annales, and the Mediterranean," *The Journal of Modern History*, University of Chicago Press, December 1972.

4. Barry Cunliffe, *Europe Between the Oceans: Themes and Variations: 9000 BC–AD 1000* (New Haven: Yale University Press, 2008), pp. 17–18.

5. Jakub J. Grygiel, *Great Powers and Geopolitical Change* (Baltimore: Johns Hopkins University Press, 2006), p. 17.

6. Michael Lind, "America Under the Caesars," *The National Interest*, Washington, July–August 2010.

7. Grygiel, *Great Powers and Geopolitical Change*, p. 123.

8. Ibid., pp. 63, 79–83.

9. Francis G. Hutchins, *The Illusion of Permanence: British Imperialism in India* (Princeton: Princeton University Press, 1967), pp. 196–97; Niall Ferguson, *Empire: The Rise and Demise of the British World*

Order and the Lessons for Global Power (New York: Basic Books, 2003), pp. 137–38, 151–53; Robert D. Kaplan, *Imperial Grunts: The American Military on the Ground* (New York: Random House, 2005), p. 368.

10. Edward N. Luttwak, *The Grand Strategy of the Roman Empire: From the First Century* A.D. *to the Third* (Baltimore: Johns Hopkins University Press, 1976), pp. 192–94.

11. Edward N. Luttwak, *The Grand Strategy of the Byzantine Empire* (Cambridge: Harvard University Press, 2009).

12. W. H. Parker, *Mackinder: Geography as an Aid to Statecraft* (Oxford: Clarendon Press, 1982), p. 127; Robert Strausz-Hupé, *Geopolitics: The Struggle for Space and Power* (New York: G. P. Putnam's Sons, 1942), p. 240.

13. Bernard DeVoto, *The Course of Empire* (Boston: Houghton Mifflin, 1952), p. xxxii, 1989 American Heritage Library edition.

14. David M. Kennedy, "Can We Still Afford to Be a Nation of Immigrants?," *Atlantic Monthly,* November 1996.

15. Joel Kotkin, "The Rise of the Third Coast: The Gulf's Ascendancy in U.S.," *Forbes.com,* June 23, 2011.

16. Arnold J. Toynbee, *A Study of History,* abridgement of vols. 1–6 by D. C. Somervell (New York: Oxford University Press, 1934, 1946), p. 10.

17. Henry Bamford Parkes, *A History of Mexico* (Boston: Houghton Mifflin, 1960), pp. 3–4, 11.

18. David J. Danelo, "The Many Faces of Mexico," *Orbis,* Philadelphia, Winter 2011.

19. Jackson Diehl, "The Crisis Next Door: U.S. Falls Short in Helping Mexico End Its Drug War," *Washington Post,* July 26, 2010.

20. Mackubin T. Owens, "Editor's Corner," *Orbis,* Philadelphia, Winter 2011.

21. Robert C. Bonner, "The New Cocaine Cowboys: How to Defeat Mexico's Drug Cartels," *Foreign Affairs,* New York, July–August 2010.

22. Robert D. Kaplan, "Looking the World in the Eye: Profile of Samuel Huntington," *Atlantic Monthly,* December 2001.

23. Samuel P. Huntington, *Who Are We? The Challenges to America's National Identity* (New York: Simon & Schuster, 2004). Huntington's book drew in a small way on my own, which had put forward

a similar thesis. Robert D. Kaplan, *An Empire Wilderness: Travels into America's Future* (New York: Random House, 1998), Chapters 10–13.

24.   Huntington, *Who Are We?*, pp. 39, 59, 61, 63, 69, 106.

25.   Ibid., p. 221.

26.   Peter Skerry, "What Are We to Make of Samuel Huntington?," *Society*, New York, November–December 2005.

27.   Kennedy, "Can We Still Afford to Be a Nation of Immigrants?"

28.   Carlos Fuentes, *The Buried Mirror: Reflections on Spain and the New World* (Boston: Houghton Mifflin, 1992), p. 343.

29.   Huntington, *Who Are We?*, pp. 115–16, 229–30, 232, 238; Peter Skerry, *Mexican Americans: The Ambivalent Minority* (Cambridge: Harvard University Press, 1993), pp. 21–22, 289.

30.   Huntington, *Who Are We?*, pp. 246–47; *The Economist*, London, July 7, 2001.

31.   Ted Galen Carpenter, "Escape from Mexico," *The National Interest Online*, Washington, June 30, 2010.

32.   David Danelo, "How the U.S. and Mexico Can Take Back the Border—Together," Foreign Policy Research Institute, Philadelphia, April 2010.

33.   Arnold J. Toynbee, *A Study of History*, abridgement of vols. 7–10 by D. C. Somervell (New York: Oxford University Press, 1957), p. 124.

34.   Ibid., pp. 15–16, 75.

35.   Kaplan, *An Empire Wilderness*, p. 14. See the bibliography in that book.

36.   Stratfor.com, "The Geopolitics of the United States, Part 1: The Inevitable Empire," Austin, Texas, August 25, 2011.

37.   Saul B. Cohen, *Geography and Politics in a World Divided* (New York: Random House, 1963), p. 95.

38.   James Fairgrieve, *Geography and World Power*, p. 329.

39.   Toynbee, *A Study of History*, vols. 7–10, p. 173.

40.   Nicholas John Spykman, *The Geography of the Peace*, edited by Helen R. Nicholl (New York: Harcourt, Brace, 1944), p. 45.

41.   Robert Strausz-Hupé, *The Zone of Indifference* (New York: G. P. Putnam's Sons, 1952), p. 64.

Index

Page numbers in *italics* refer to maps.

ABOUT THE AUTHOR

ROBERT D. KAPLAN is the author of fourteen books on foreign affairs and travel translated into many languages, including *Monsoon: The Indian Ocean and the Future of American Power*; *Balkan Ghosts: A Journey Through History*; and *Warrior Politics: Why Leadership Demands a Pagan Ethos*. He has been a foreign correspondent for *The Atlantic* for more than a quarter-century. In 2011, *Foreign Policy* magazine named Kaplan among the world's "Top 100 Global Thinkers." In 2012, he joined Stratfor as chief geopolitical analyst.

From 2009 to 2011, he served under Secretary of Defense Robert Gates as a member of the Defense Policy Board. Since 2008, he has been a senior fellow at the Center for a New American Security in Washington. From 2006 to 2008, he was the Class of 1960 Distinguished Visiting Professor in National Security at the U.S. Naval Academy, Annapolis. Visit him on the Web at www.RobertDKaplan.com and at www.stratfor.com.

ABOUT THE TYPE

This book was set in Sabon, a typeface designed by the well-known German typographer Jan Tschichold (1902–74). Sabon's design is based upon the original letter forms of Claude Garamond and was created specifically to be used for three sources: foundry type for hand composition, Linotype, and Monotype. Tschichold named his typeface for the famous Frankfurt typefounder Jacques Sabon, who died in 1580.